THE FLASH
FINISH LINE

writer
JOSHUA WILLIAMSON

pencillers
CHRISTIAN DUCE
RAFA SANDOVAL
SCOTT KOLINS
HOWARD PORTER

inkers
CHRISTIAN DUCE
JORDI TARRAGONA
SCOTT KOLINS
HOWARD PORTER

colorists
LUIS GUERRERO
ARIF PRIANTO
HI-FI

letterer
STEVE WANDS

collection cover artists
HOWARD PORTER & HI-FI

VOL.
15

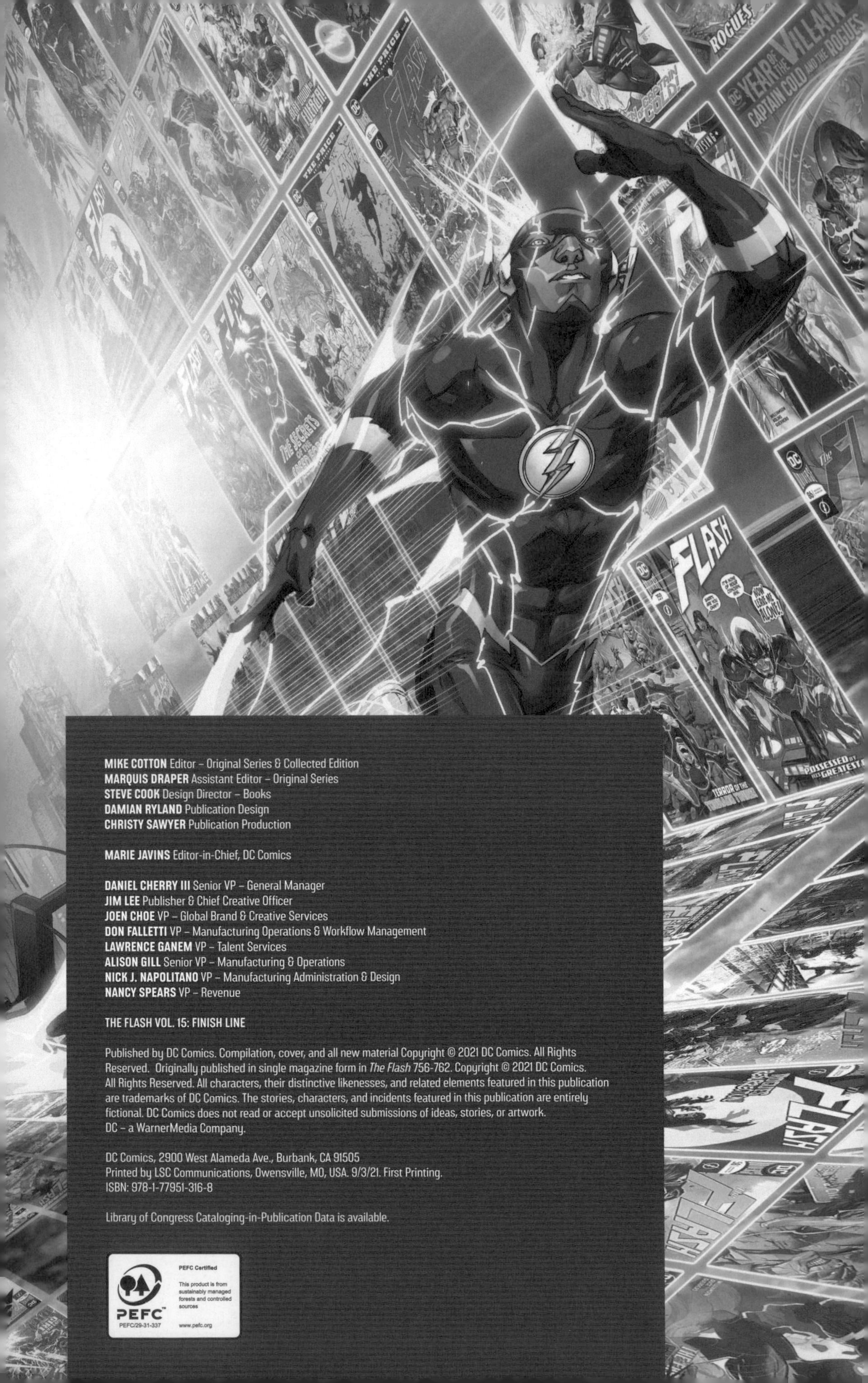
ROGUES
YEAR OF THE VILLAIN
CAPTAIN COLD AND THE ROGUES
THE PRICE
FLASH

MIKE COTTON Editor – Original Series & Collected Edition
MARQUIS DRAPER Assistant Editor – Original Series
STEVE COOK Design Director – Books
DAMIAN RYLAND Publication Design
CHRISTY SAWYER Publication Production

MARIE JAVINS Editor-in-Chief, DC Comics

DANIEL CHERRY III Senior VP – General Manager
JIM LEE Publisher & Chief Creative Officer
JOEN CHOE VP – Global Brand & Creative Services
DON FALLETTI VP – Manufacturing Operations & Workflow Management
LAWRENCE GANEM VP – Talent Services
ALISON GILL Senior VP – Manufacturing & Operations
NICK J. NAPOLITANO VP – Manufacturing Administration & Design
NANCY SPEARS VP – Revenue

THE FLASH VOL. 15: FINISH LINE

DC Comics, 2900 West Alameda Ave., Burbank, CA 91505
Printed by LSC Communications, Owensville, MO, USA. 9/3/21. First Printing.
ISBN: 978-1-77951-316-8

Library of Congress Cataloging-in-Publication Data is available.

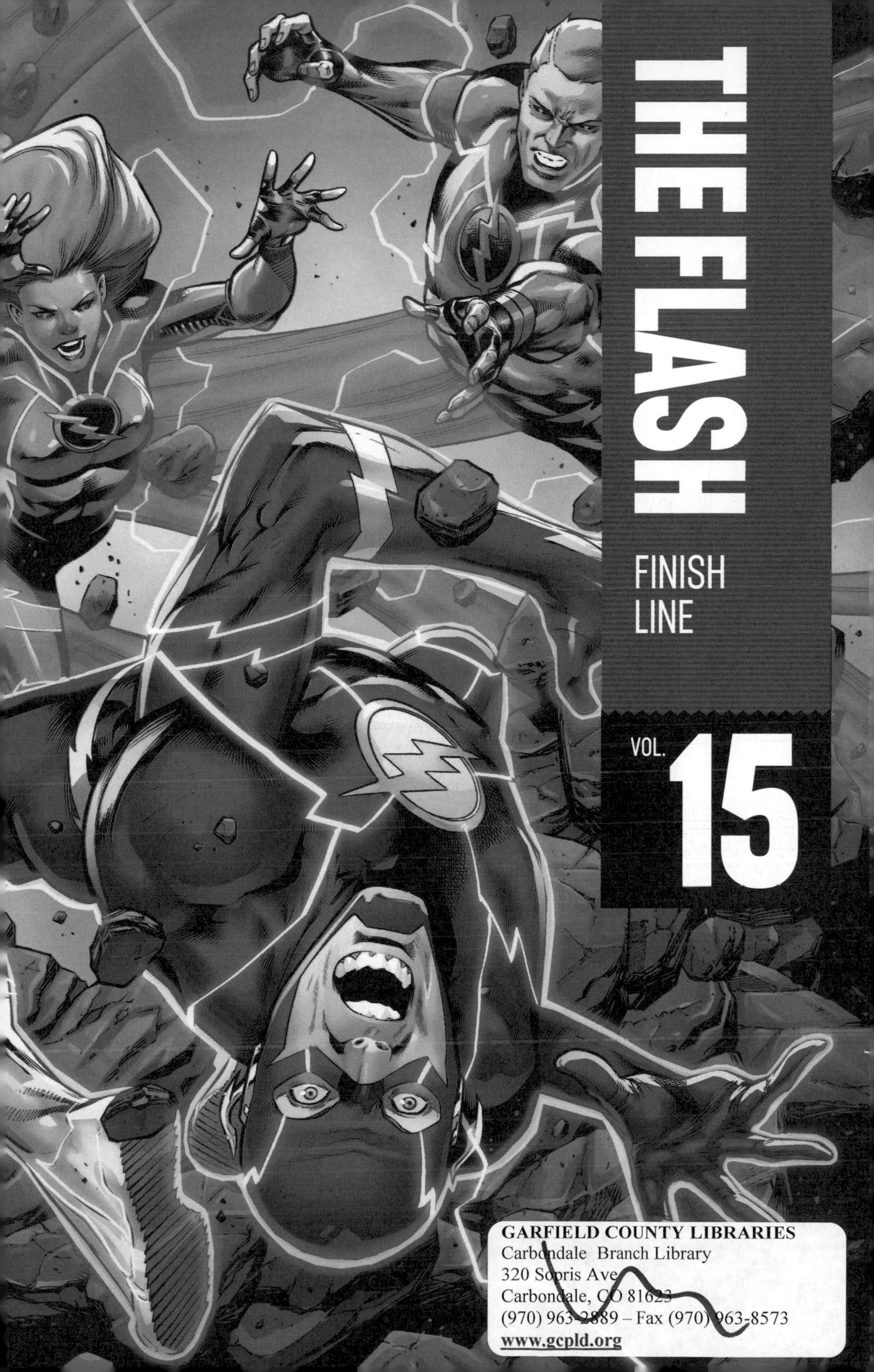

THE FLASH

FINISH LINE

VOL. 15

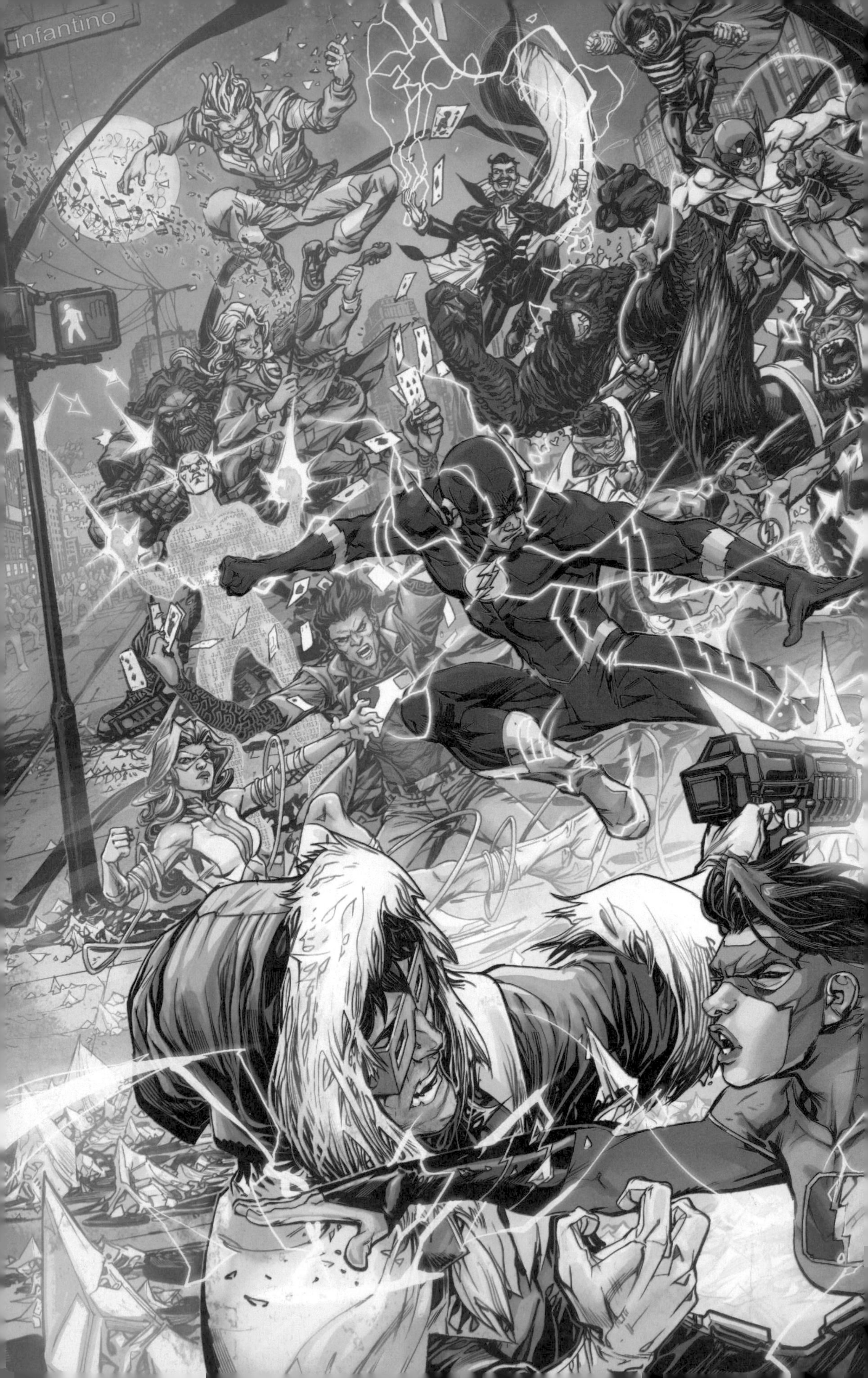
Infantino

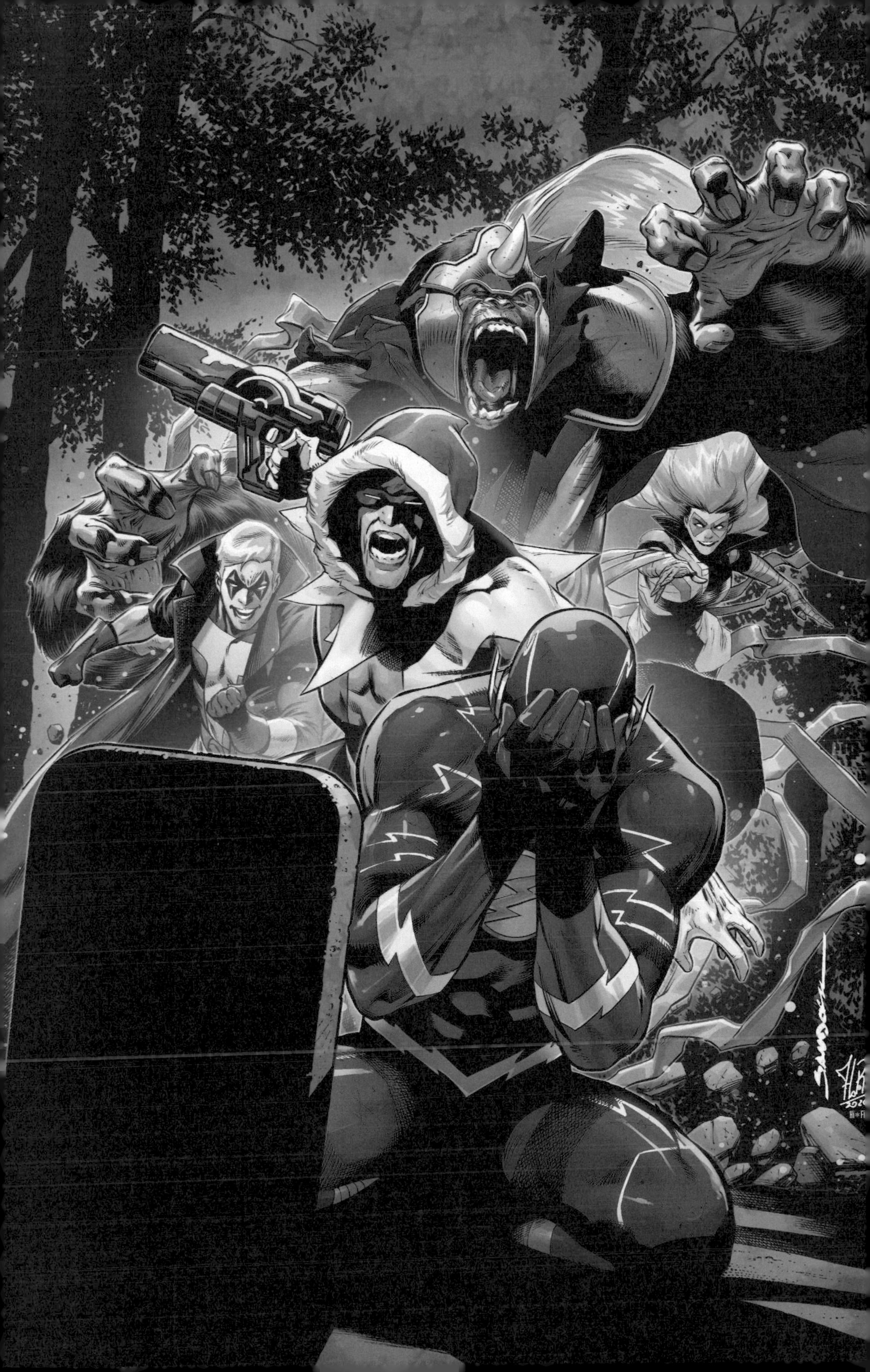

The Flash **#756** variant cover by
DANIEL WARREN JOHNSON and MIKE SPICER

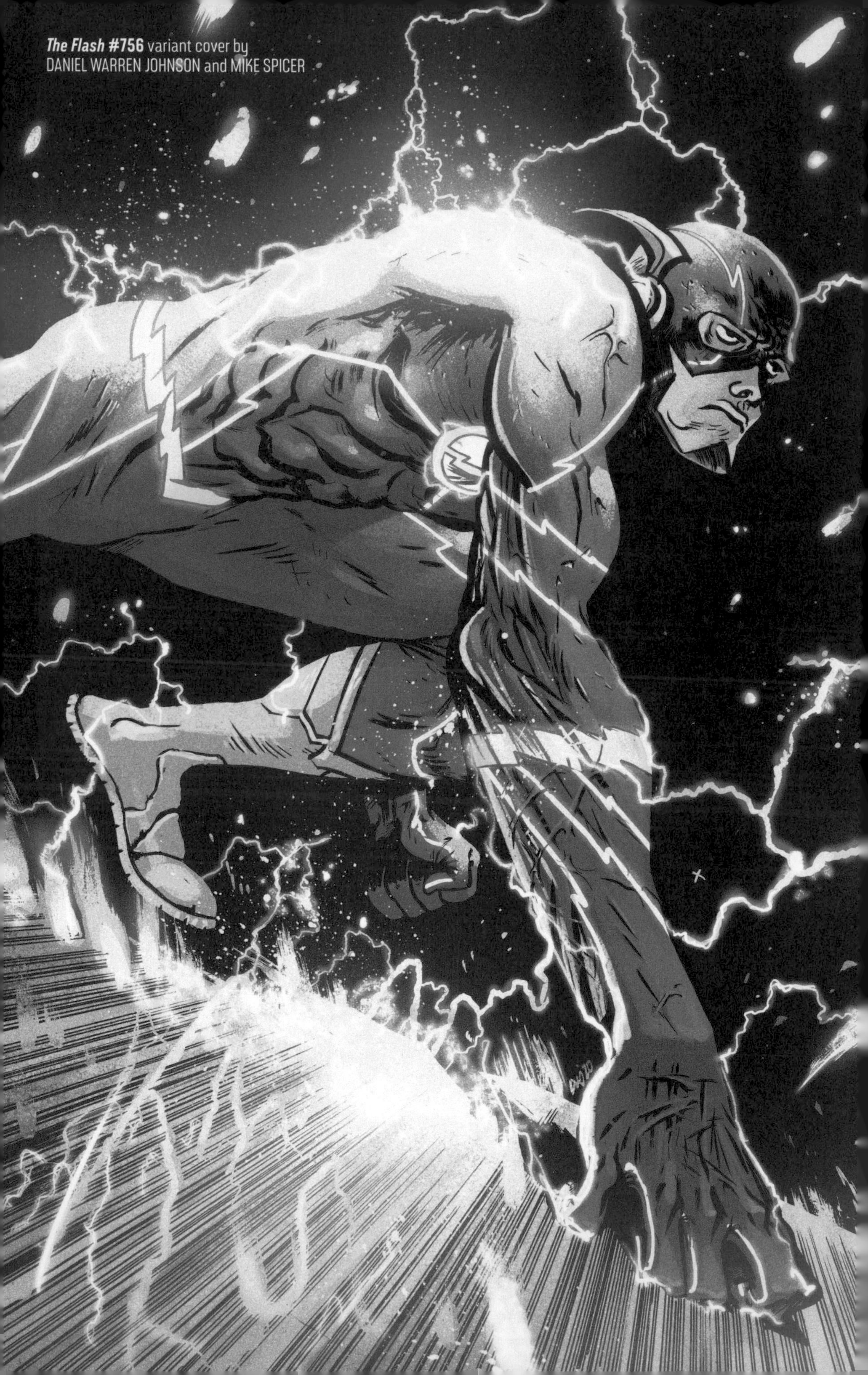

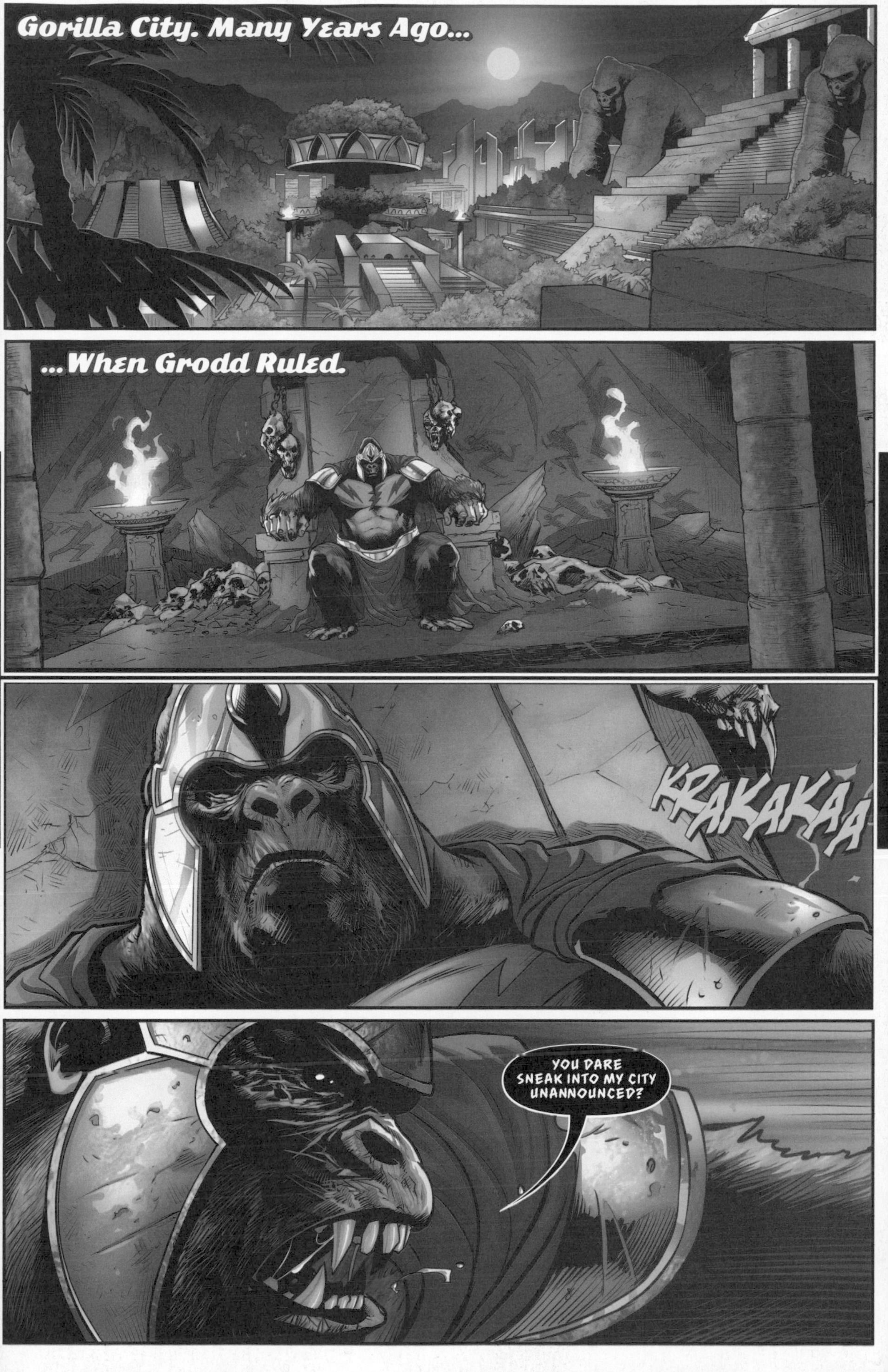
Gorilla City. Many Years Ago...
...When Grodd Ruled.
KRAKAKAA
YOU DARE SNEAK INTO MY CITY UNANNOUNCED?

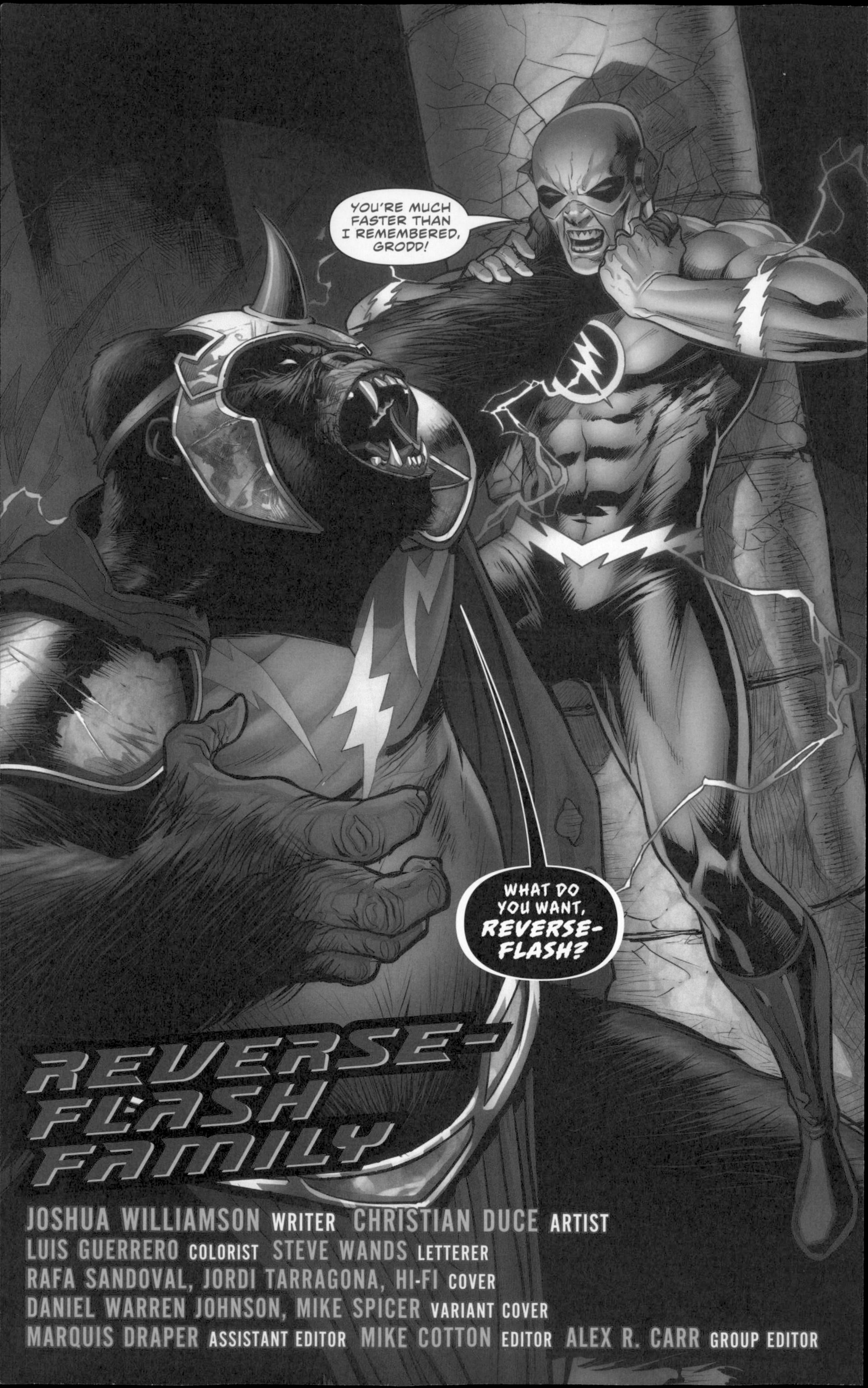

YOU'RE MUCH FASTER THAN I REMEMBERED, GRODD!
WHAT DO YOU WANT, REVERSE-FLASH?
REVERSE-FLASH FAMILY
JOSHUA WILLIAMSON WRITER CHRISTIAN DUCE ARTIST
LUIS GUERRERO COLORIST STEVE WANDS LETTERER
RAFA SANDOVAL, JORDI TARRAGONA, HI-FI COVER
DANIEL WARREN JOHNSON, MIKE SPICER VARIANT COVER
MARQUIS DRAPER ASSISTANT EDITOR MIKE COTTON EDITOR ALEX R. CARR GROUP EDITOR

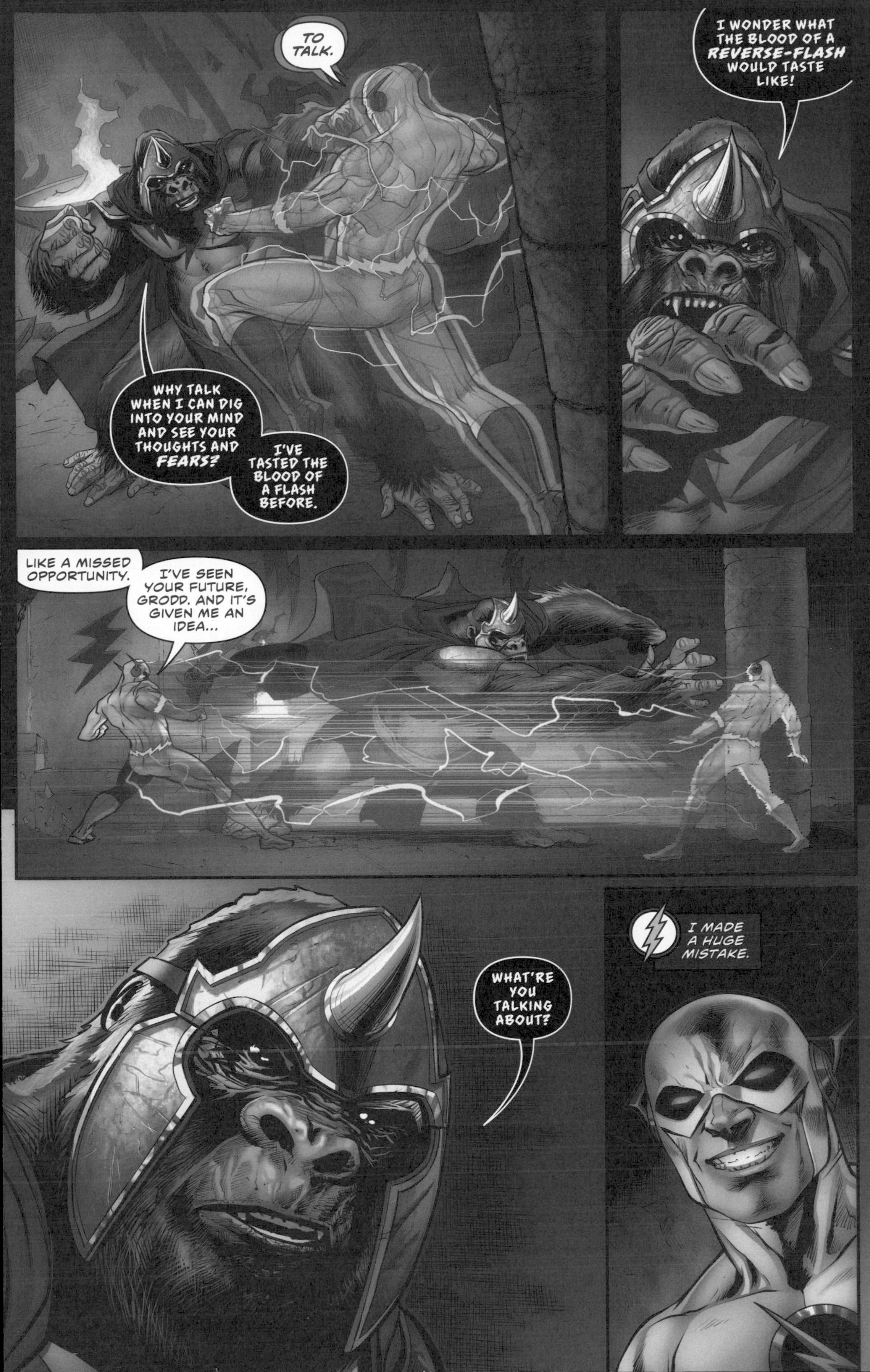
TO TALK.
WHY TALK WHEN I CAN DIG INTO YOUR MIND AND SEE YOUR THOUGHTS AND FEARS?
I'VE TASTED THE BLOOD OF A FLASH BEFORE.
I WONDER WHAT THE BLOOD OF A REVERSE-FLASH WOULD TASTE LIKE!
LIKE A MISSED OPPORTUNITY.
I'VE SEEN YOUR FUTURE, GRODD. AND IT'S GIVEN ME AN IDEA...
WHAT'RE YOU TALKING ABOUT?
I MADE A HUGE MISTAKE.

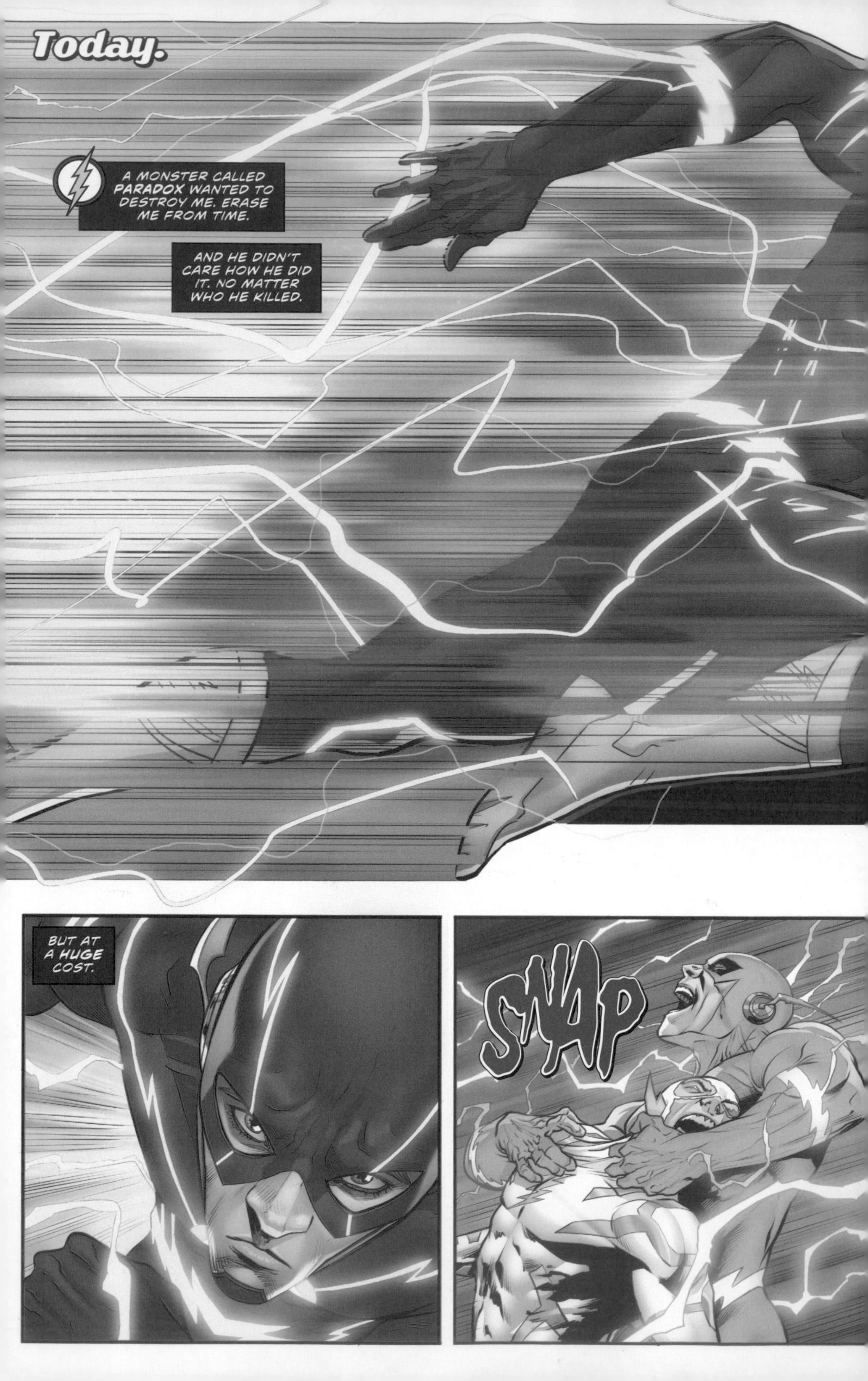
Today.
A MONSTER CALLED PARADOX WANTED TO DESTROY ME. ERASE ME FROM TIME.
AND HE DIDN'T CARE HOW HE DID IT. NO MATTER WHO HE KILLED.
BUT AT A HUGE COST.
SNAP

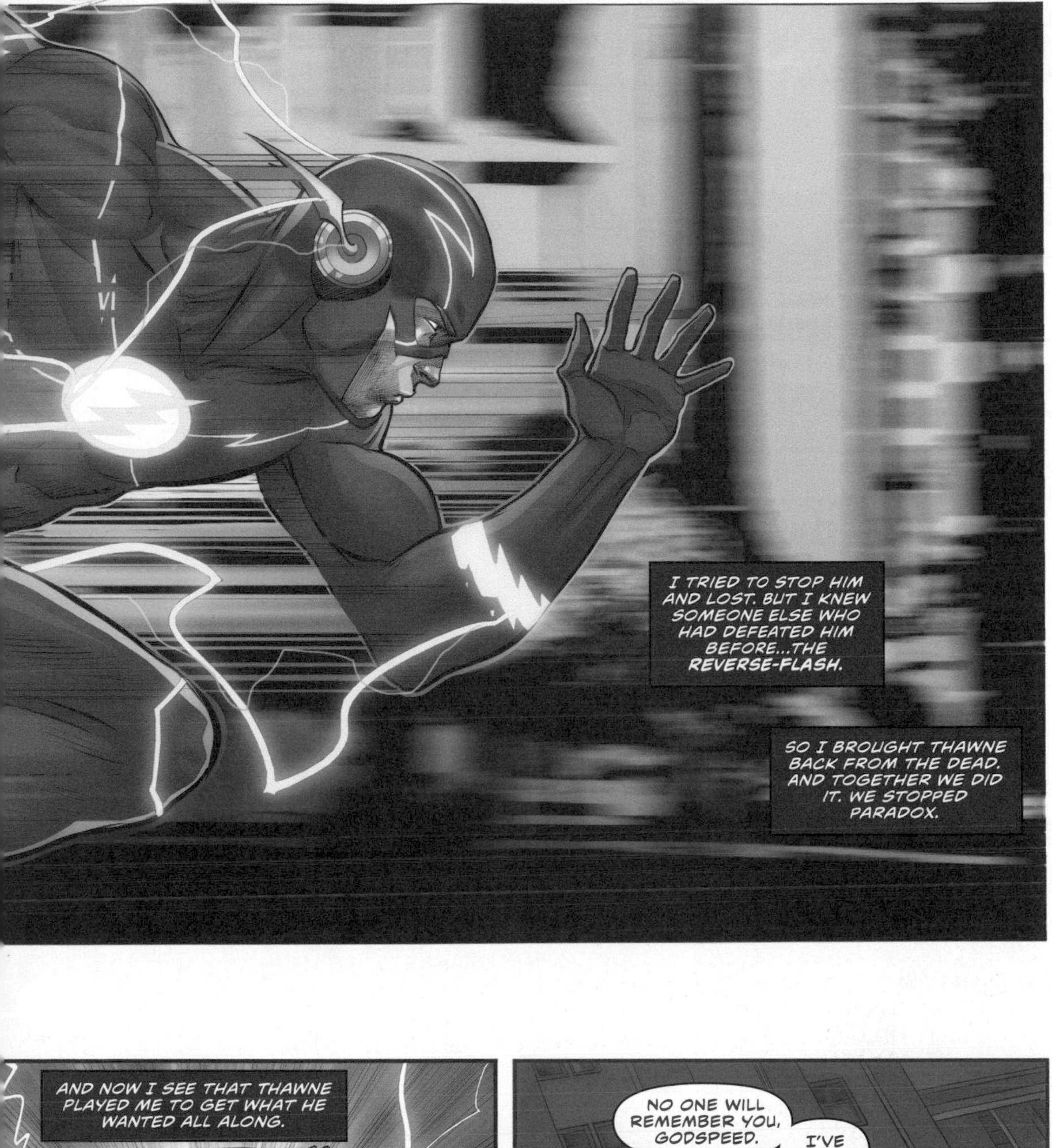
I TRIED TO STOP HIM AND LOST. BUT I KNEW SOMEONE ELSE WHO HAD DEFEATED HIM BEFORE...THE REVERSE-FLASH.
SO I BROUGHT THAWNE BACK FROM THE DEAD. AND TOGETHER WE DID IT. WE STOPPED PARADOX.

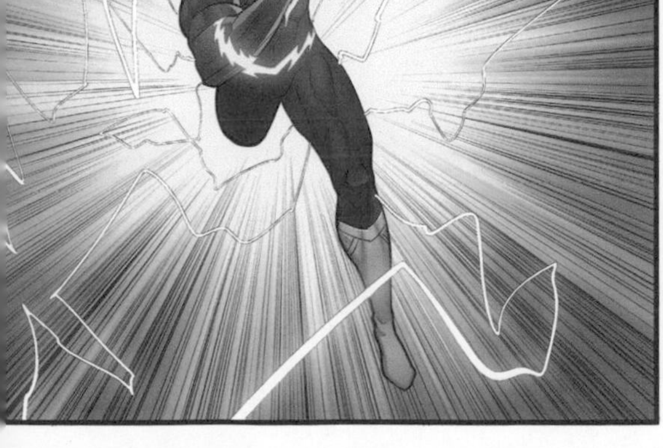
AND NOW I SEE THAT THAWNE PLAYED ME TO GET WHAT HE WANTED ALL ALONG.

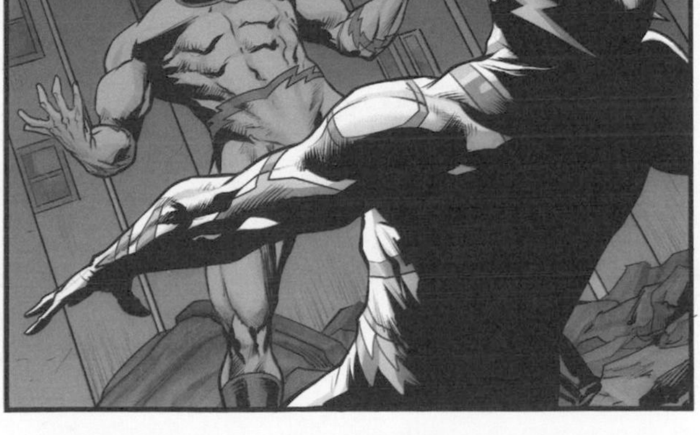
NO ONE WILL REMEMBER YOU, GODSPEED.
I'VE SEEN...

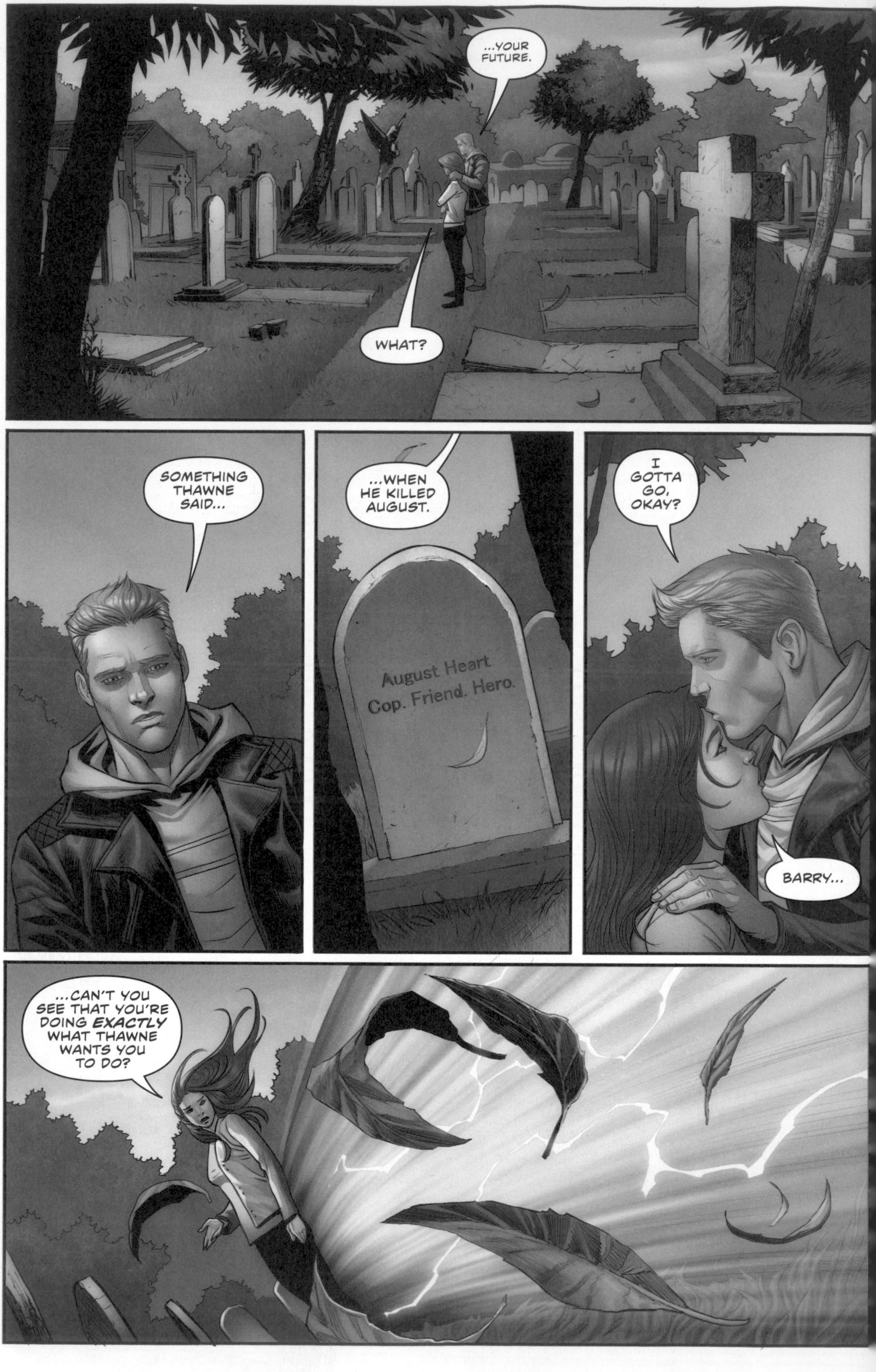
...YOUR FUTURE.
WHAT?
SOMETHING THAWNE SAID...
...WHEN HE KILLED AUGUST.
August Heart
Cop. Friend. Hero.
I GOTTA GO, OKAY?
BARRY...
...CAN'T YOU SEE THAT YOU'RE DOING EXACTLY WHAT THAWNE WANTS YOU TO DO?

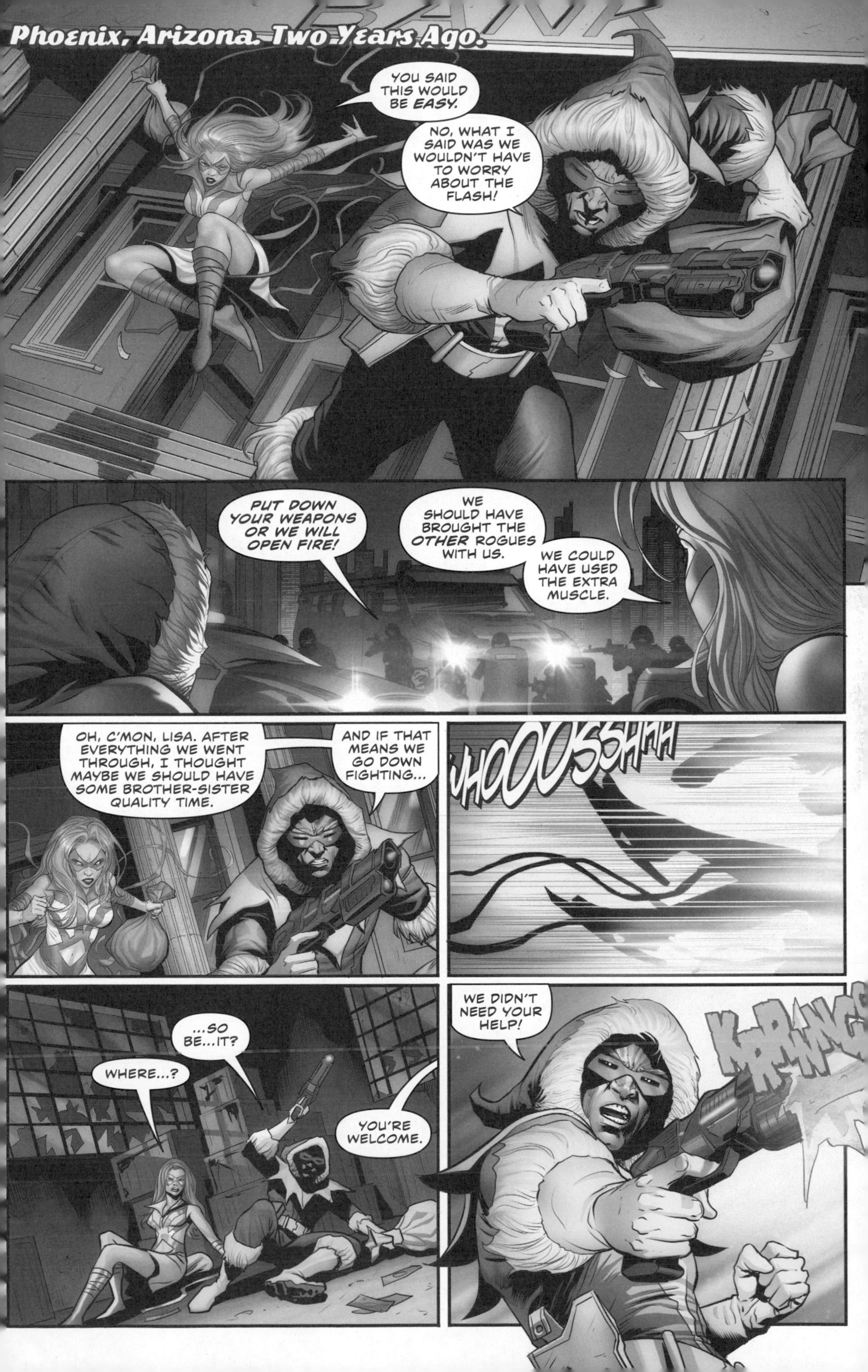

Phoenix, Arizona. Two Years Ago.
BANK
YOU SAID THIS WOULD BE EASY.
NO, WHAT I SAID WAS WE WOULDN'T HAVE TO WORRY ABOUT THE FLASH!
PUT DOWN YOUR WEAPONS OR WE WILL OPEN FIRE!
WE SHOULD HAVE BROUGHT THE OTHER ROGUES WITH US.
WE COULD HAVE USED THE EXTRA MUSCLE.
OH, C'MON, LISA. AFTER EVERYTHING WE WENT THROUGH, I THOUGHT MAYBE WE SHOULD HAVE SOME BROTHER-SISTER QUALITY TIME.
AND IF THAT MEANS WE GO DOWN FIGHTING...
WHOOOOSSHHH
...SO BE...IT?
WHERE...?
YOU'RE WELCOME.
WE DIDN'T NEED YOUR HELP!
KRANG

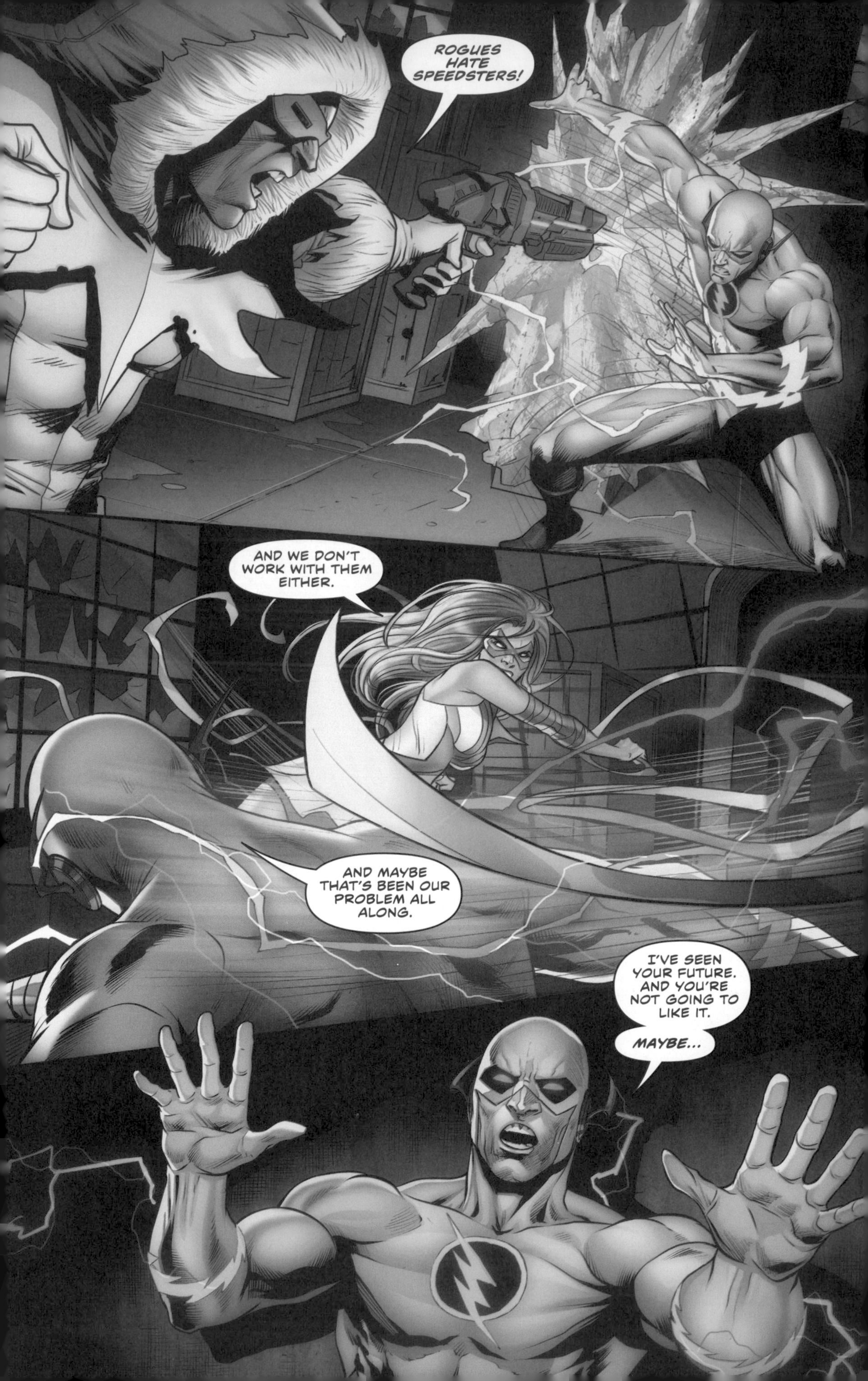
ROGUES HATE SPEEDSTERS!
AND WE DON'T WORK WITH THEM EITHER.
AND MAYBE THAT'S BEEN OUR PROBLEM ALL ALONG.
I'VE SEEN YOUR FUTURE. AND YOU'RE NOT GOING TO LIKE IT.
MAYBE...

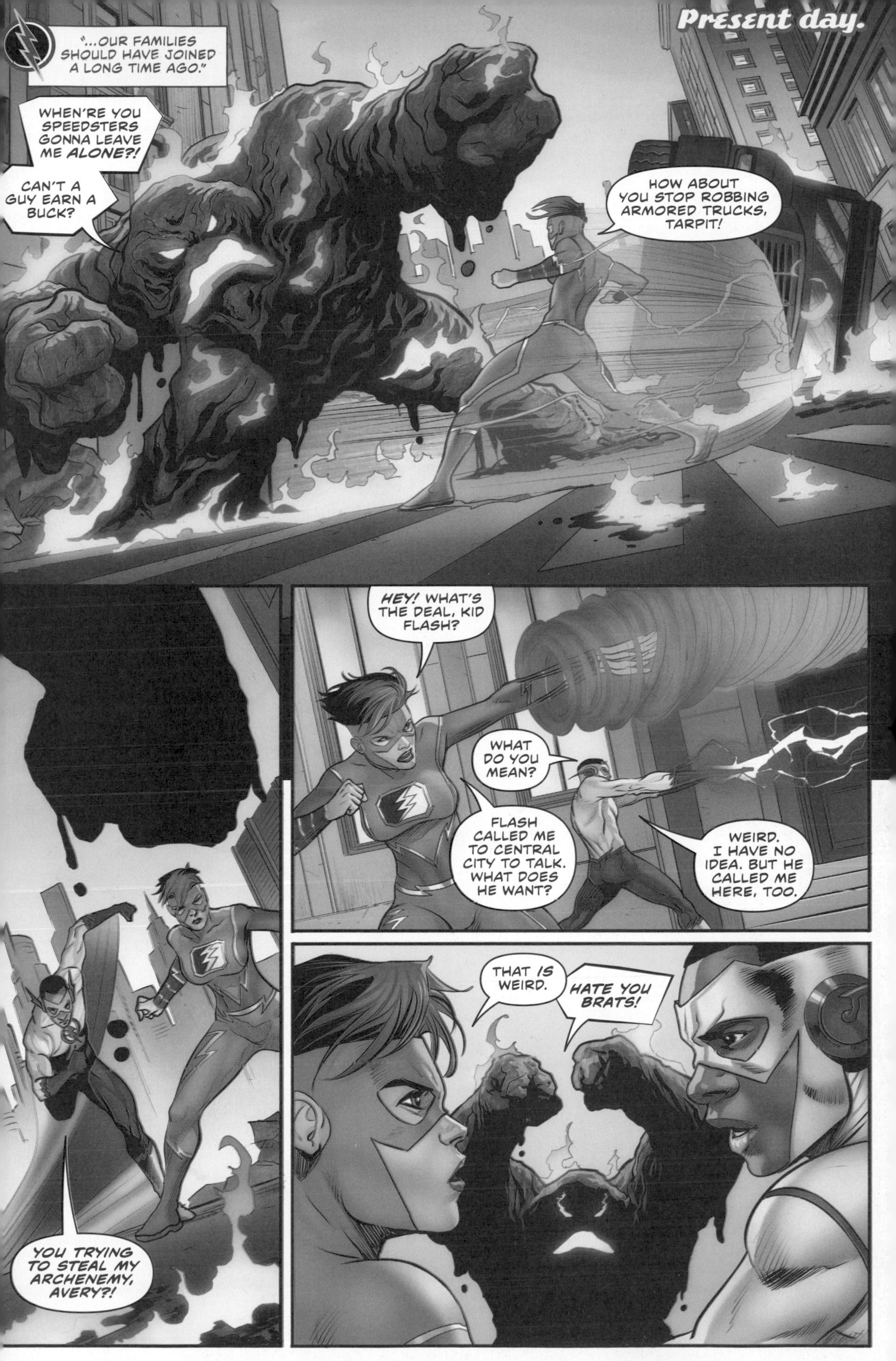
Present day.
"...OUR FAMILIES SHOULD HAVE JOINED A LONG TIME AGO."
WHEN'RE YOU SPEEDSTERS GONNA LEAVE ME ALONE?!
CAN'T A GUY EARN A BUCK?
HOW ABOUT YOU STOP ROBBING ARMORED TRUCKS, TARPIT!
HEY! WHAT'S THE DEAL, KID FLASH?
WHAT DO YOU MEAN?
FLASH CALLED ME TO CENTRAL CITY TO TALK. WHAT DOES HE WANT?
WEIRD. I HAVE NO IDEA. BUT HE CALLED ME HERE, TOO.
YOU TRYING TO STEAL MY ARCHENEMY, AVERY?!
THAT IS WEIRD.
HATE YOU BRATS!

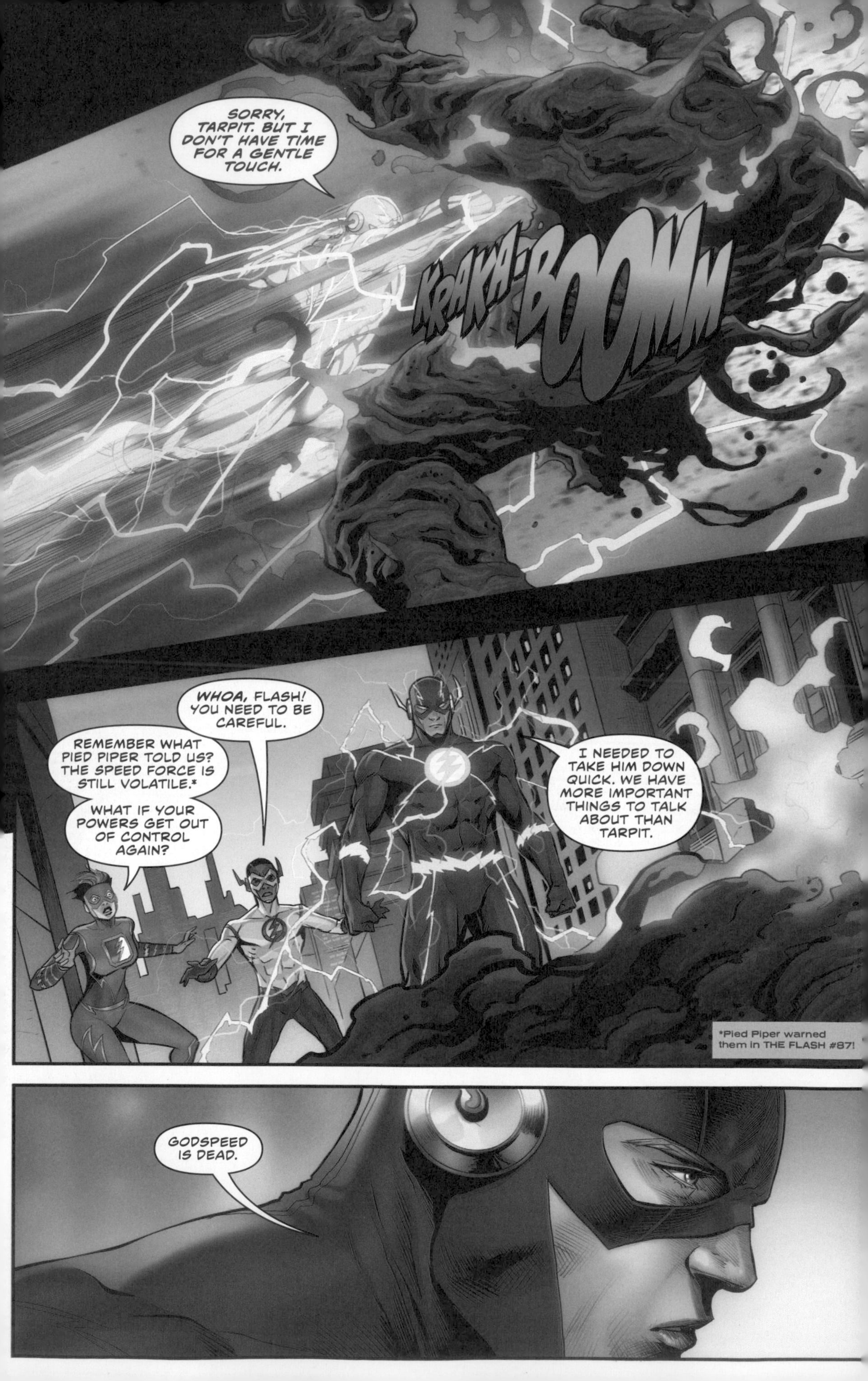
SORRY, TARPIT. BUT I DON'T HAVE TIME FOR A GENTLE TOUCH.
KRAKA-BOOMM
WHOA, FLASH! YOU NEED TO BE CAREFUL.
REMEMBER WHAT PIED PIPER TOLD US? THE SPEED FORCE IS STILL VOLATILE.*
WHAT IF YOUR POWERS GET OUT OF CONTROL AGAIN?
I NEEDED TO TAKE HIM DOWN QUICK. WE HAVE MORE IMPORTANT THINGS TO TALK ABOUT THAN TARPIT.
*Pied Piper warned them in THE FLASH #87!
GODSPEED IS DEAD.

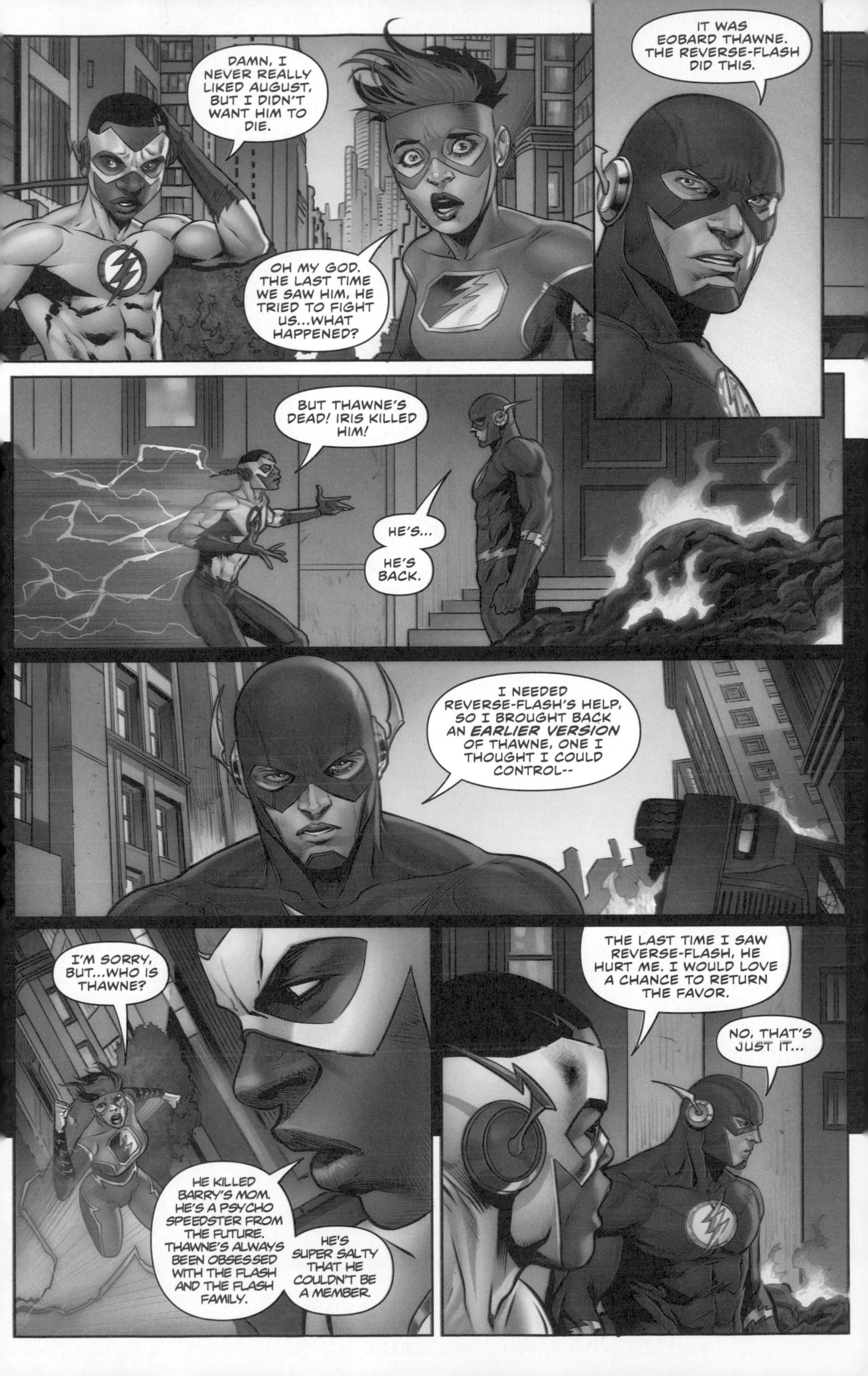
DAMN, I NEVER REALLY LIKED AUGUST, BUT I DIDN'T WANT HIM TO DIE.
OH MY GOD. THE LAST TIME WE SAW HIM, HE TRIED TO FIGHT US...WHAT HAPPENED?
IT WAS EOBARD THAWNE. THE REVERSE-FLASH DID THIS.
BUT THAWNE'S DEAD! IRIS KILLED HIM!
HE'S...
HE'S BACK.
I NEEDED REVERSE-FLASH'S HELP, SO I BROUGHT BACK AN *EARLIER VERSION* OF THAWNE, ONE I THOUGHT I COULD CONTROL--
I'M SORRY, BUT...WHO IS THAWNE?
HE KILLED BARRY'S MOM. HE'S A PSYCHO SPEEDSTER FROM THE FUTURE. THAWNE'S ALWAYS BEEN OBSESSED WITH THE FLASH AND THE FLASH FAMILY.
HE'S SUPER SALTY THAT HE COULDN'T BE A MEMBER.
THE LAST TIME I SAW REVERSE-FLASH, HE HURT ME. I WOULD LOVE A CHANCE TO RETURN THE FAVOR.
NO, THAT'S JUST IT...

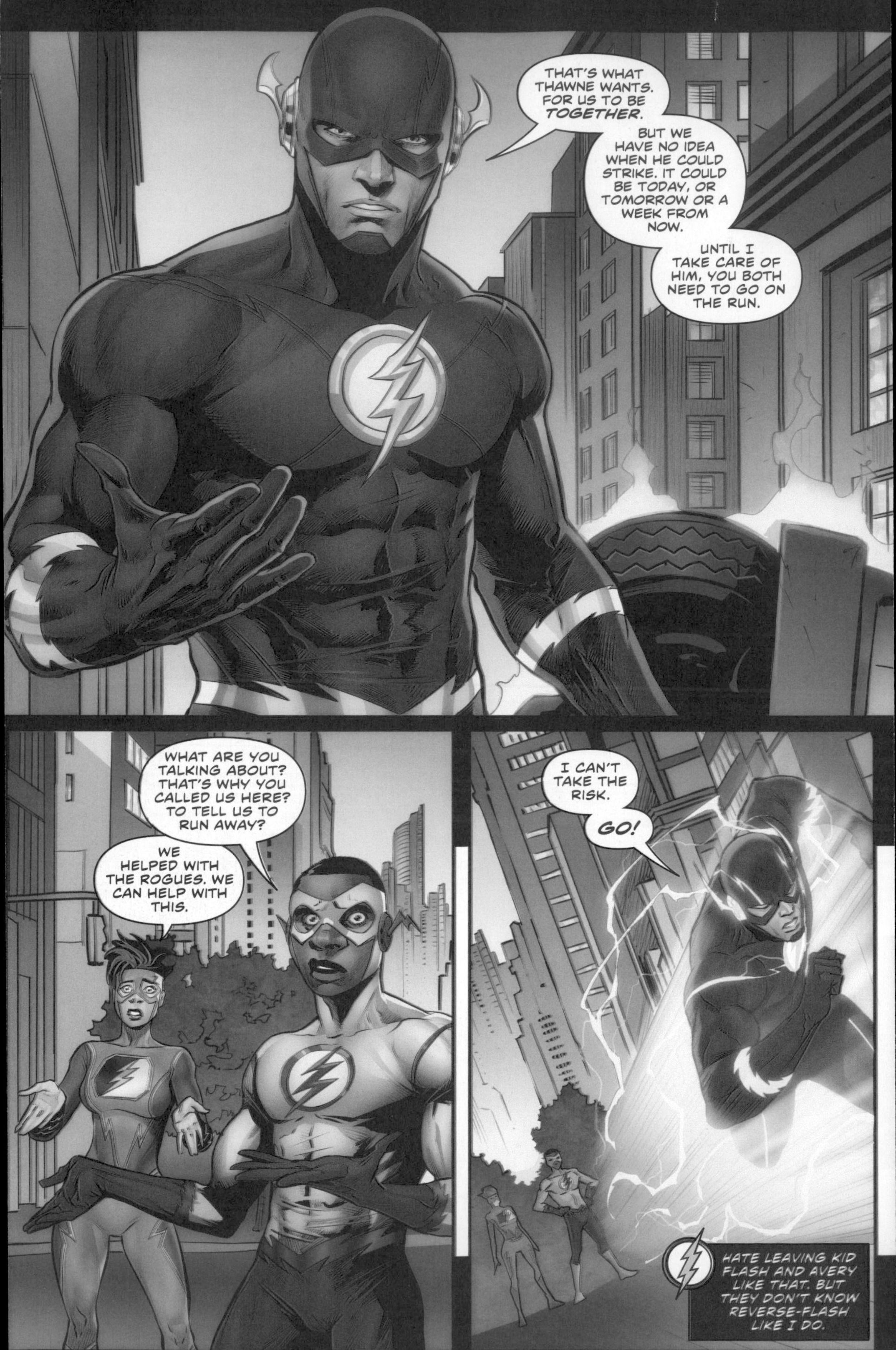
THAT'S WHAT THAWNE WANTS. FOR US TO BE *TOGETHER*.
BUT WE HAVE NO IDEA WHEN HE COULD STRIKE. IT COULD BE TODAY, OR TOMORROW OR A WEEK FROM NOW.
UNTIL I TAKE CARE OF HIM, YOU BOTH NEED TO GO ON THE RUN.
WHAT ARE YOU TALKING ABOUT? THAT'S WHY YOU CALLED US HERE? TO TELL US TO RUN AWAY?
WE HELPED WITH THE ROGUES. WE CAN HELP WITH THIS.
I CAN'T TAKE THE RISK.
GO!
HATE LEAVING KID FLASH AND AVERY LIKE THAT. BUT THEY DON'T KNOW REVERSE-FLASH LIKE I DO.

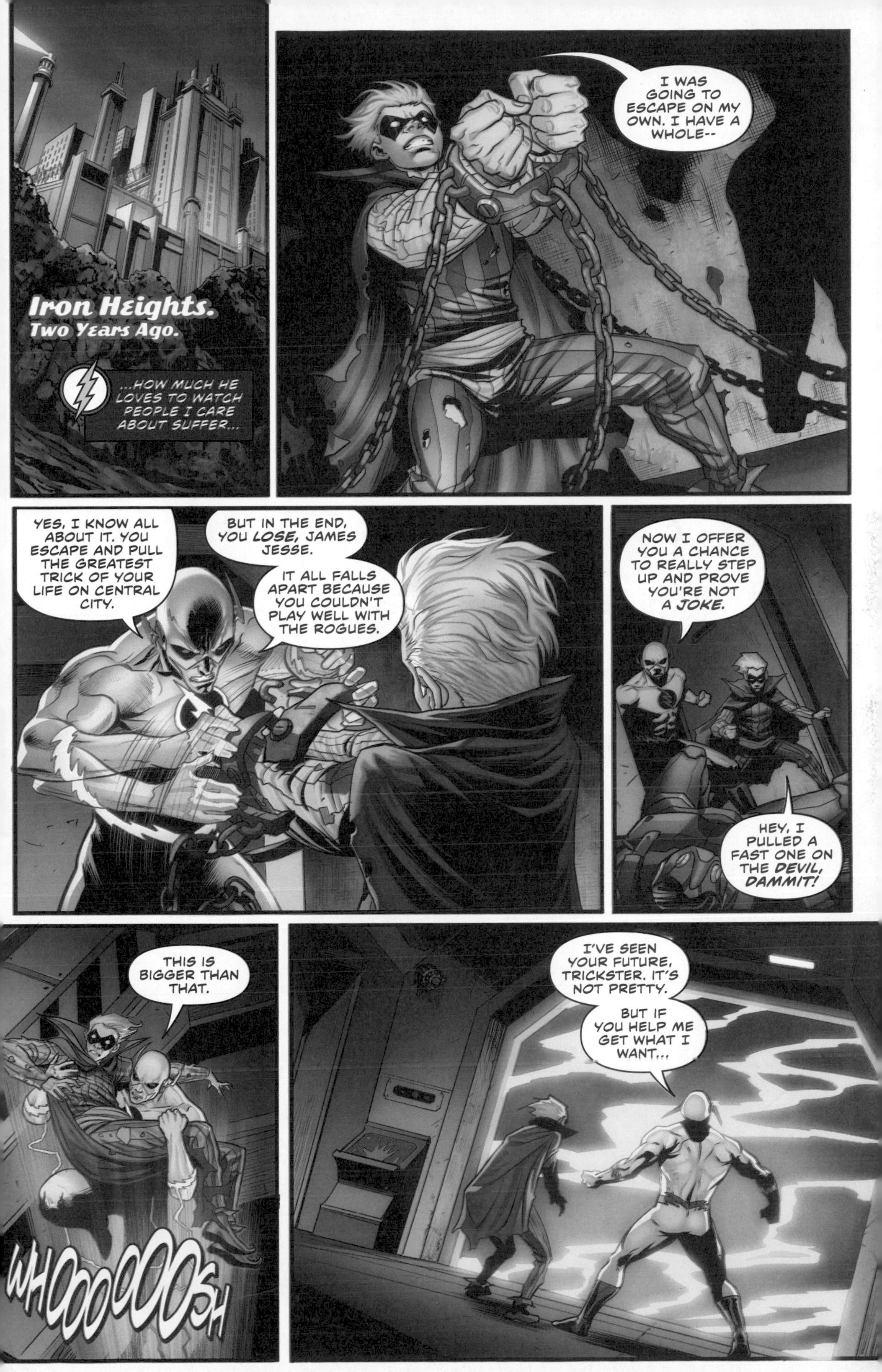
Iron Heights.
Two Years Ago.
...HOW MUCH HE LOVES TO WATCH PEOPLE I CARE ABOUT SUFFER...
I WAS GOING TO ESCAPE ON MY OWN. I HAVE A WHOLE--
YES, I KNOW ALL ABOUT IT. YOU ESCAPE AND PULL THE GREATEST TRICK OF YOUR LIFE ON CENTRAL CITY.
BUT IN THE END, YOU LOSE, JAMES JESSE.
IT ALL FALLS APART BECAUSE YOU COULDN'T PLAY WELL WITH THE ROGUES.
NOW I OFFER YOU A CHANCE TO REALLY STEP UP AND PROVE YOU'RE NOT A JOKE.
HEY, I PULLED A FAST ONE ON THE DEVIL, DAMMIT!
THIS IS BIGGER THAN THAT.
WHOOOOOOSH
I'VE SEEN YOUR FUTURE, TRICKSTER. IT'S NOT PRETTY.
BUT IF YOU HELP ME GET WHAT I WANT...

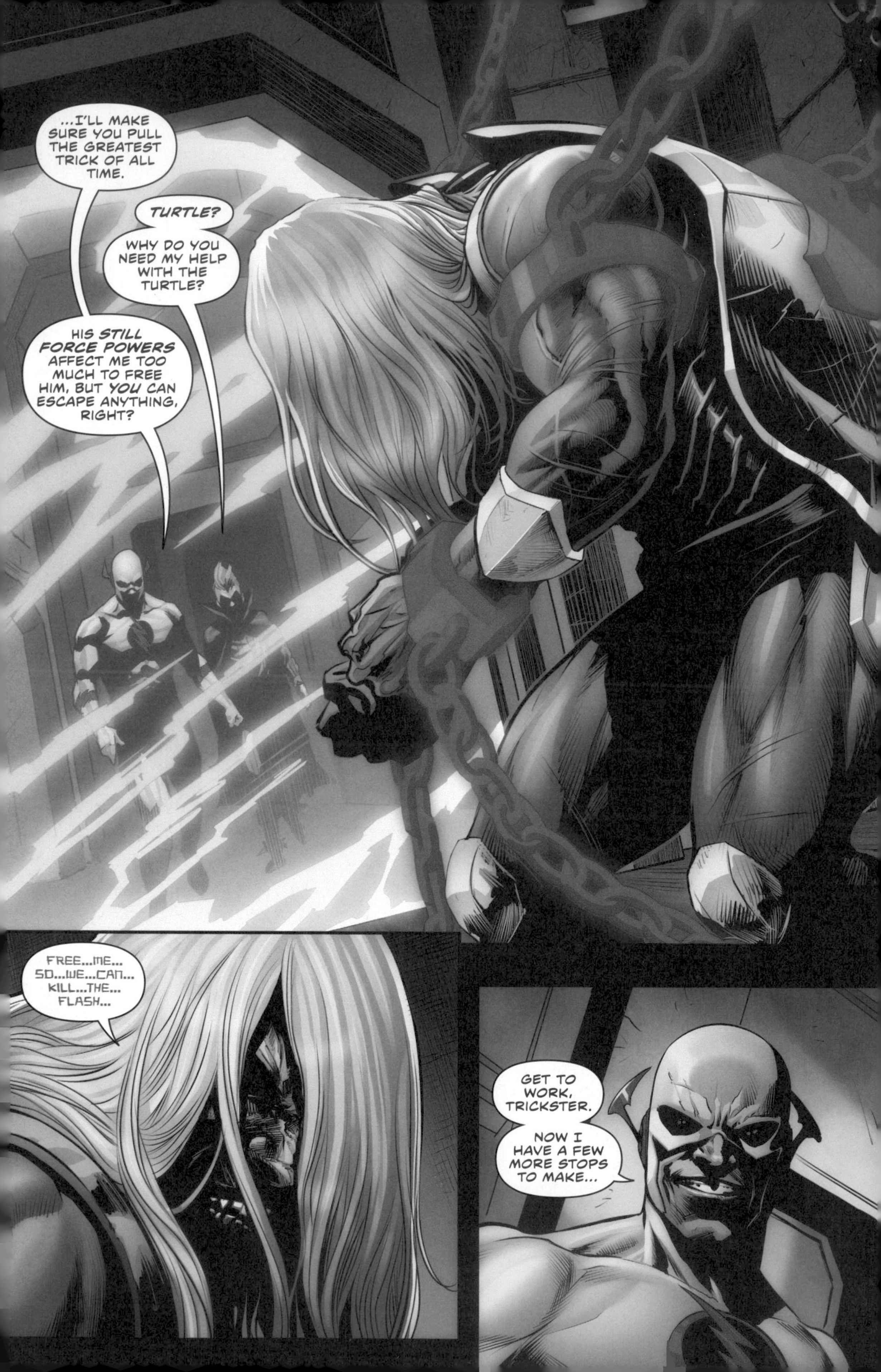
...I'LL MAKE SURE YOU PULL THE GREATEST TRICK OF ALL TIME.
TURTLE?
WHY DO YOU NEED MY HELP WITH THE TURTLE?
HIS STILL FORCE POWERS AFFECT ME TOO MUCH TO FREE HIM, BUT YOU CAN ESCAPE ANYTHING, RIGHT?
FREE...ME... SO...WE...CAN... KILL...THE... FLASH...
GET TO WORK, TRICKSTER.
NOW I HAVE A FEW MORE STOPS TO MAKE...

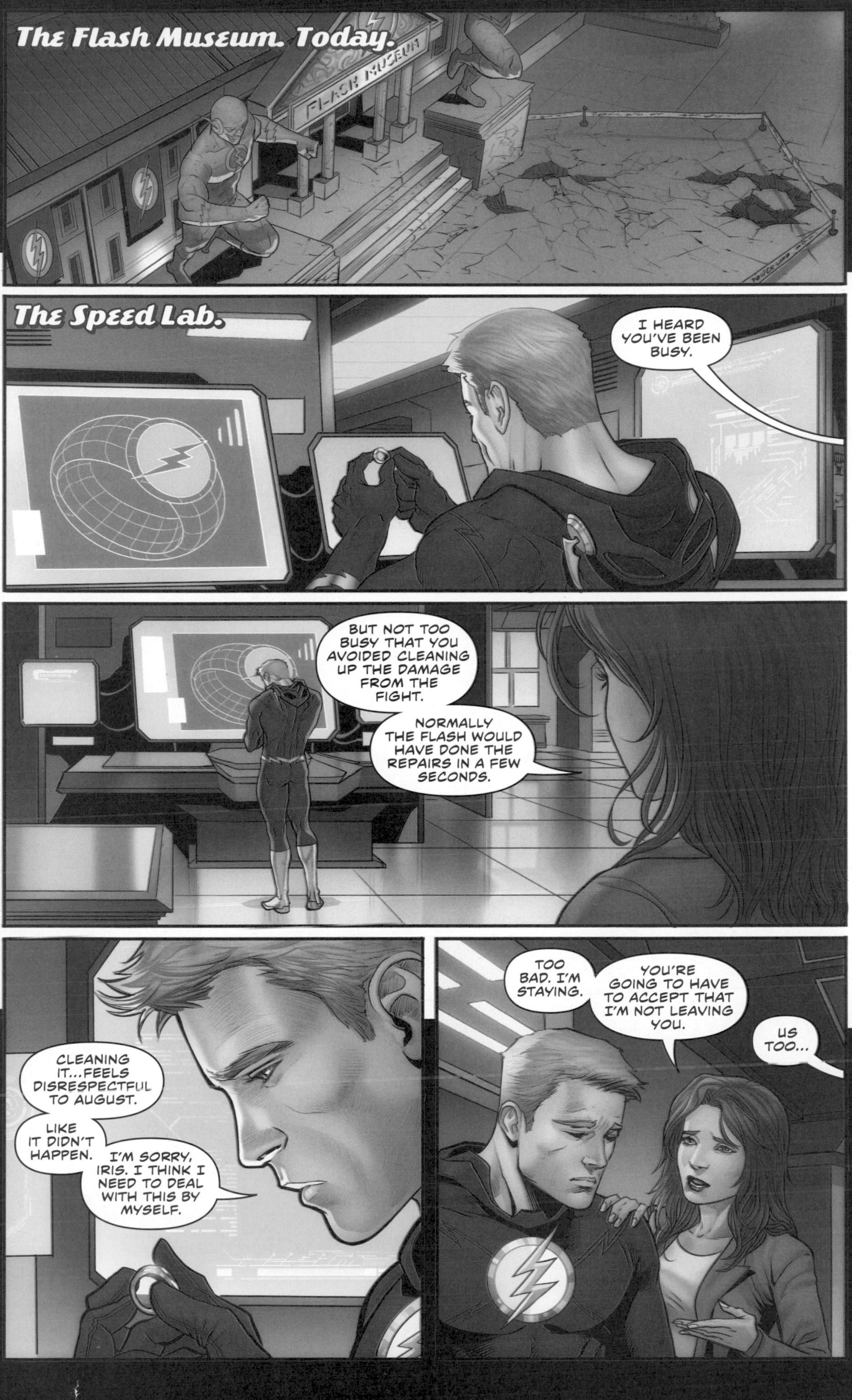
The Flash Museum. Today.
FLASH MUSEUM
The Speed Lab.
I HEARD YOU'VE BEEN BUSY.
BUT NOT TOO BUSY THAT YOU AVOIDED CLEANING UP THE DAMAGE FROM THE FIGHT.
NORMALLY THE FLASH WOULD HAVE DONE THE REPAIRS IN A FEW SECONDS.
CLEANING IT...FEELS DISRESPECTFUL TO AUGUST.
LIKE IT DIDN'T HAPPEN.
I'M SORRY, IRIS. I THINK I NEED TO DEAL WITH THIS BY MYSELF.
TOO BAD. I'M STAYING.
YOU'RE GOING TO HAVE TO ACCEPT THAT I'M NOT LEAVING YOU.
US TOO...

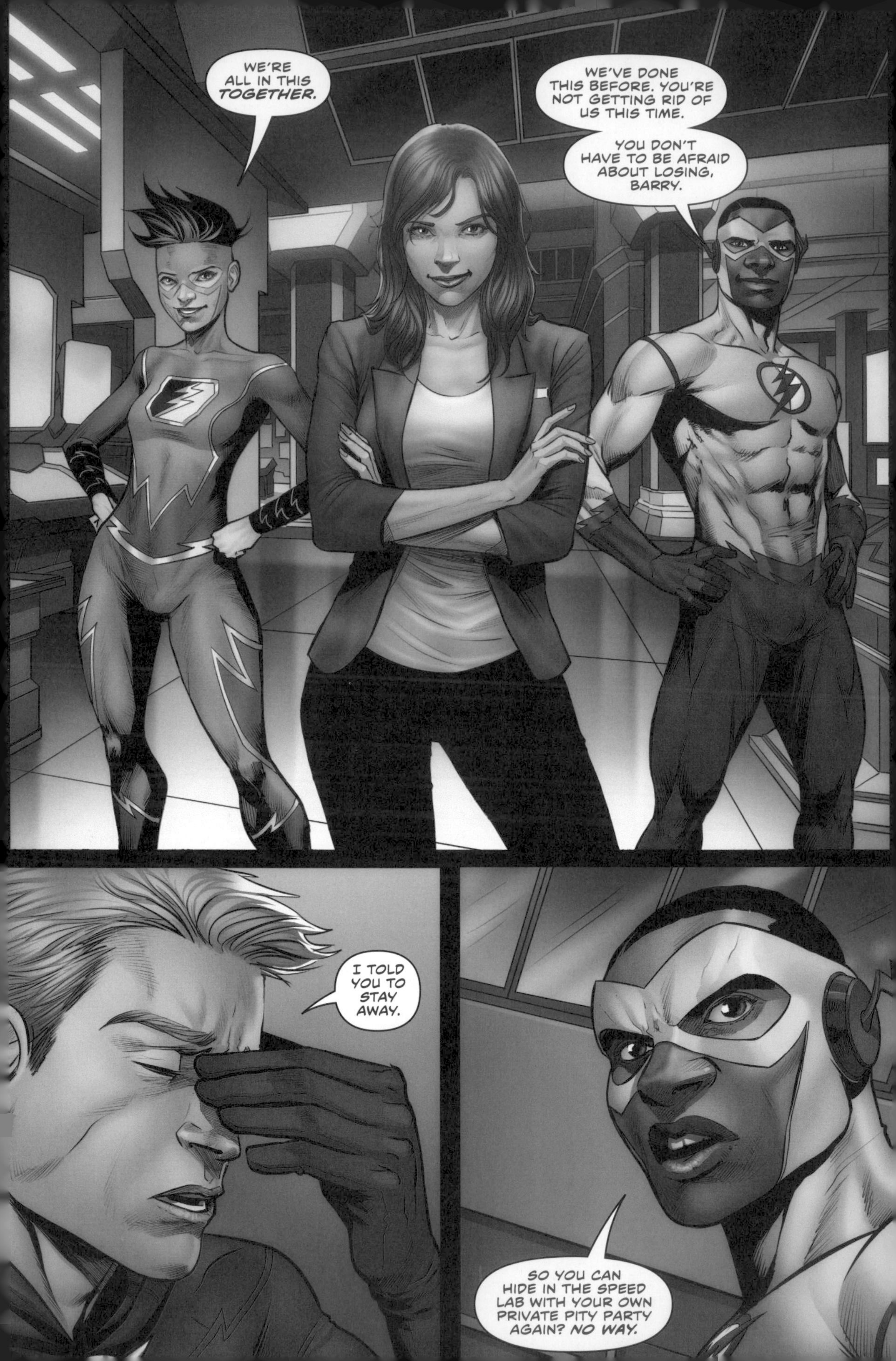
WE'RE ALL IN THIS *TOGETHER.*
WE'VE DONE THIS BEFORE. YOU'RE NOT GETTING RID OF US THIS TIME.
YOU DON'T HAVE TO BE AFRAID ABOUT LOSING, BARRY.
I TOLD YOU TO STAY AWAY.
SO YOU CAN HIDE IN THE SPEED LAB WITH YOUR OWN PRIVATE PITY PARTY AGAIN? *NO WAY.*

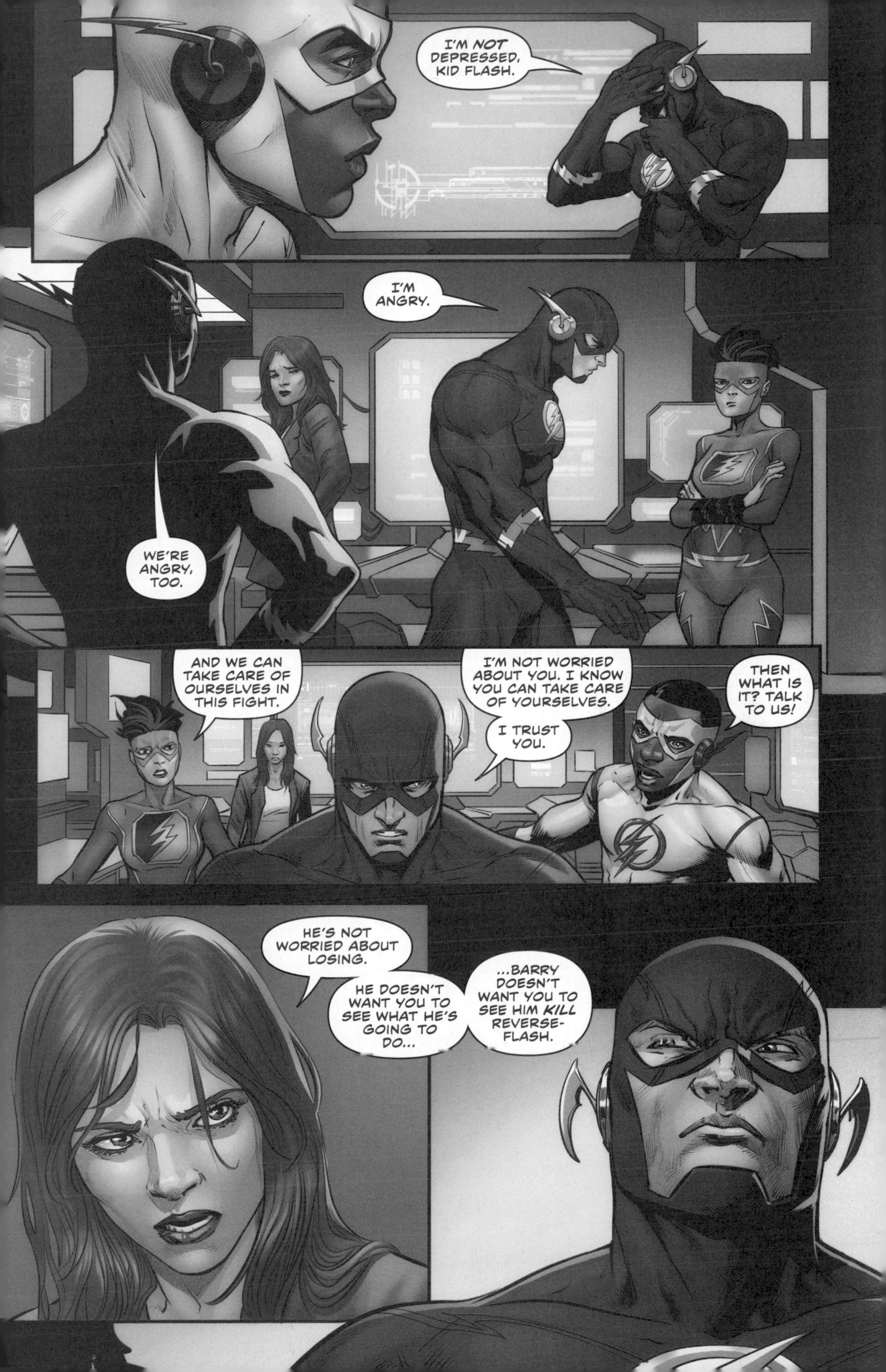
I'M *NOT* DEPRESSED, KID FLASH.
I'M ANGRY.
WE'RE ANGRY, TOO.
AND WE CAN TAKE CARE OF OURSELVES IN THIS FIGHT.
I'M NOT WORRIED ABOUT YOU. I KNOW YOU CAN TAKE CARE OF YOURSELVES.
I TRUST YOU.
THEN WHAT IS IT? TALK TO US!
HE'S NOT WORRIED ABOUT LOSING.
HE DOESN'T WANT YOU TO SEE WHAT HE'S GOING TO DO...
...BARRY DOESN'T WANT YOU TO SEE HIM *KILL* REVERSE-FLASH.

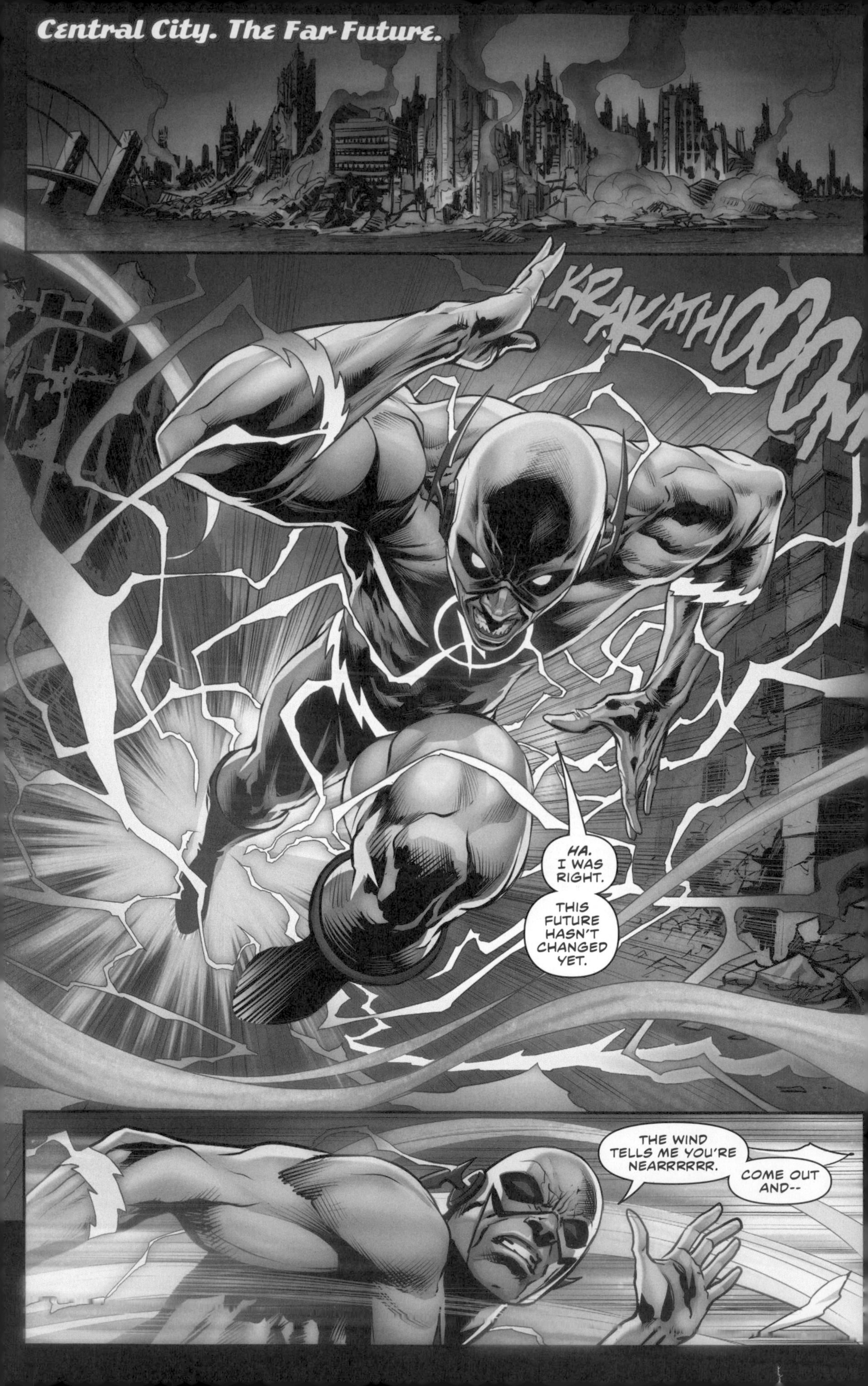
Central City. The Far Future.
KRAKATHOOOOM
HA. I WAS RIGHT.
THIS FUTURE HASN'T CHANGED YET.
THE WIND TELLS ME YOU'RE NEARRRRRR.
COME OUT AND--

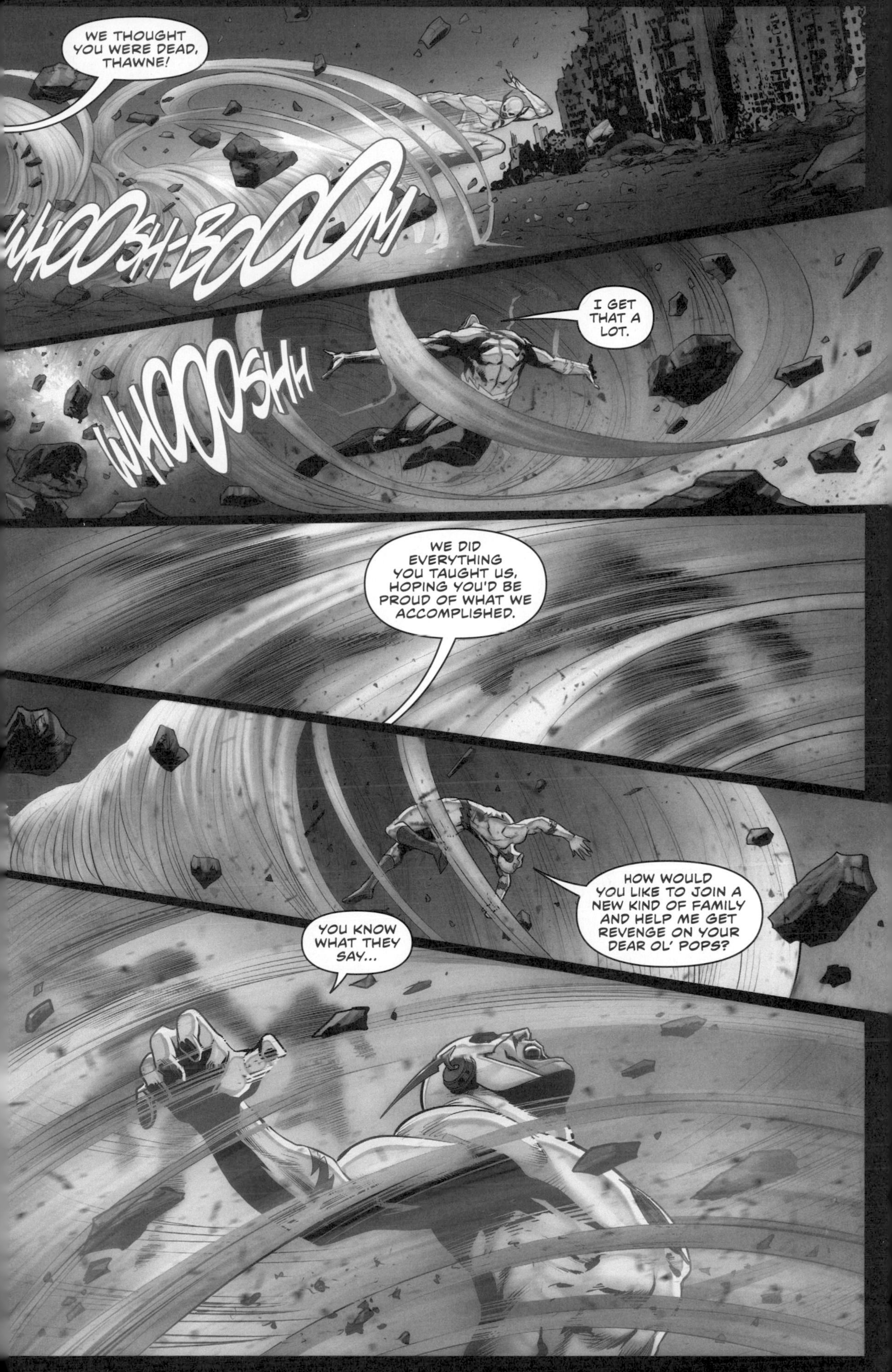
WE THOUGHT YOU WERE DEAD, THAWNE!
WHOOSH-BOOOM
I GET THAT A LOT.
WHOOOSHH
WE DID EVERYTHING YOU TAUGHT US, HOPING YOU'D BE PROUD OF WHAT WE ACCOMPLISHED.
HOW WOULD YOU LIKE TO JOIN A NEW KIND OF FAMILY AND HELP ME GET REVENGE ON YOUR DEAR OL' POPS?
YOU KNOW WHAT THEY SAY...

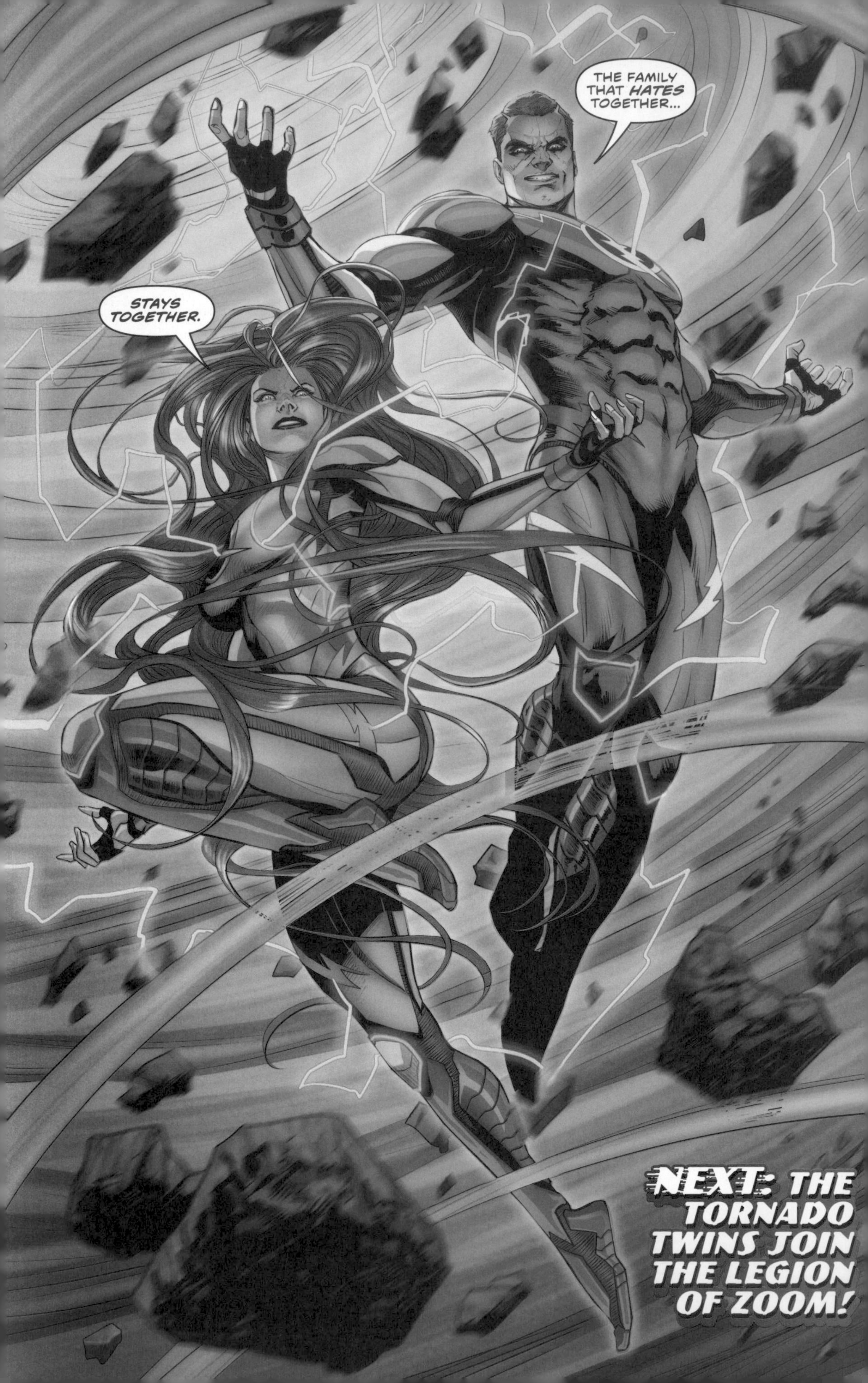
THE FAMILY THAT *HATES* TOGETHER...
STAYS TOGETHER.
NEXT: THE TORNADO TWINS JOIN THE LEGION OF ZOOM!

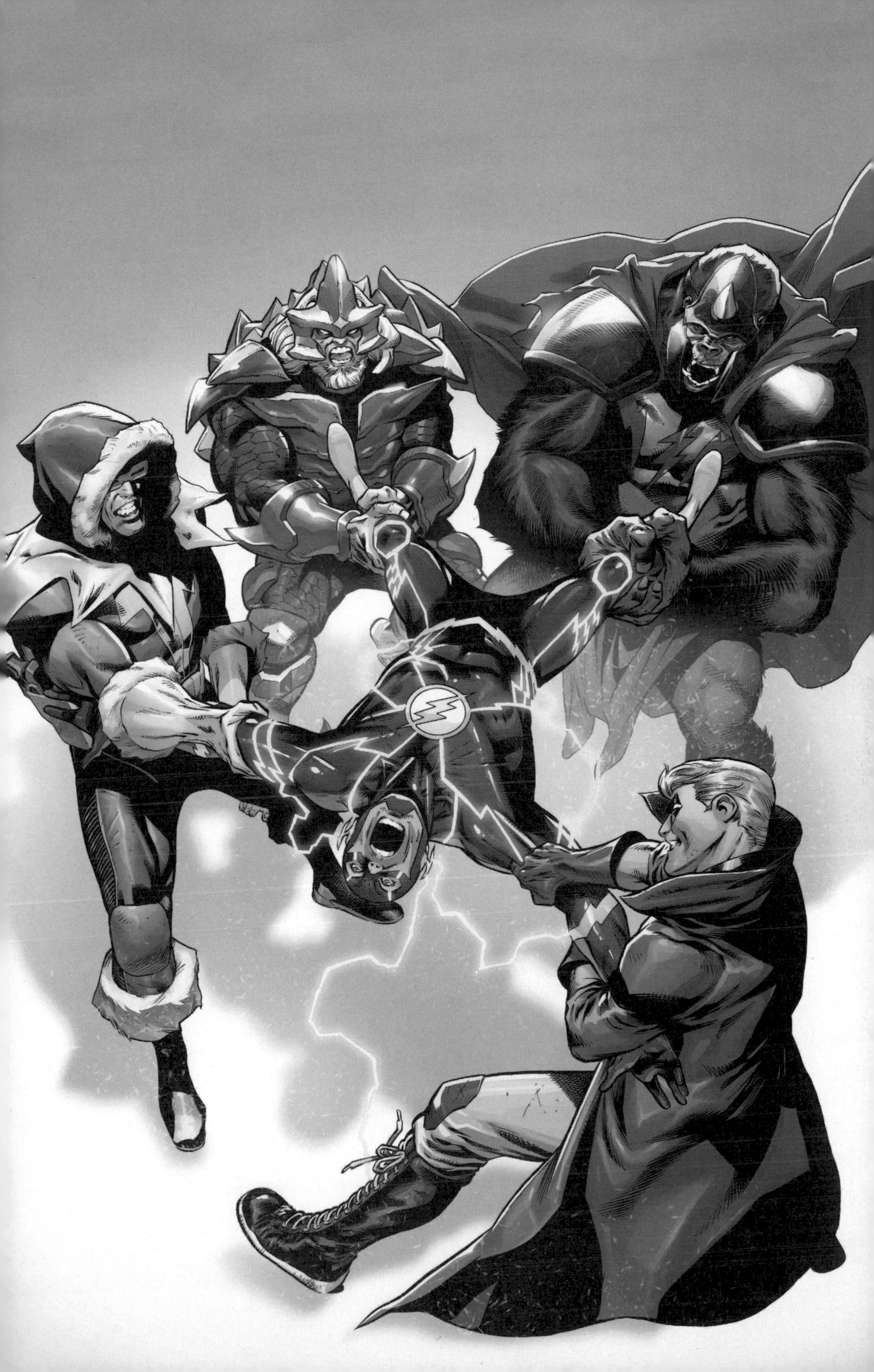

The Flash **#757** variant cover by INHYUK LEE

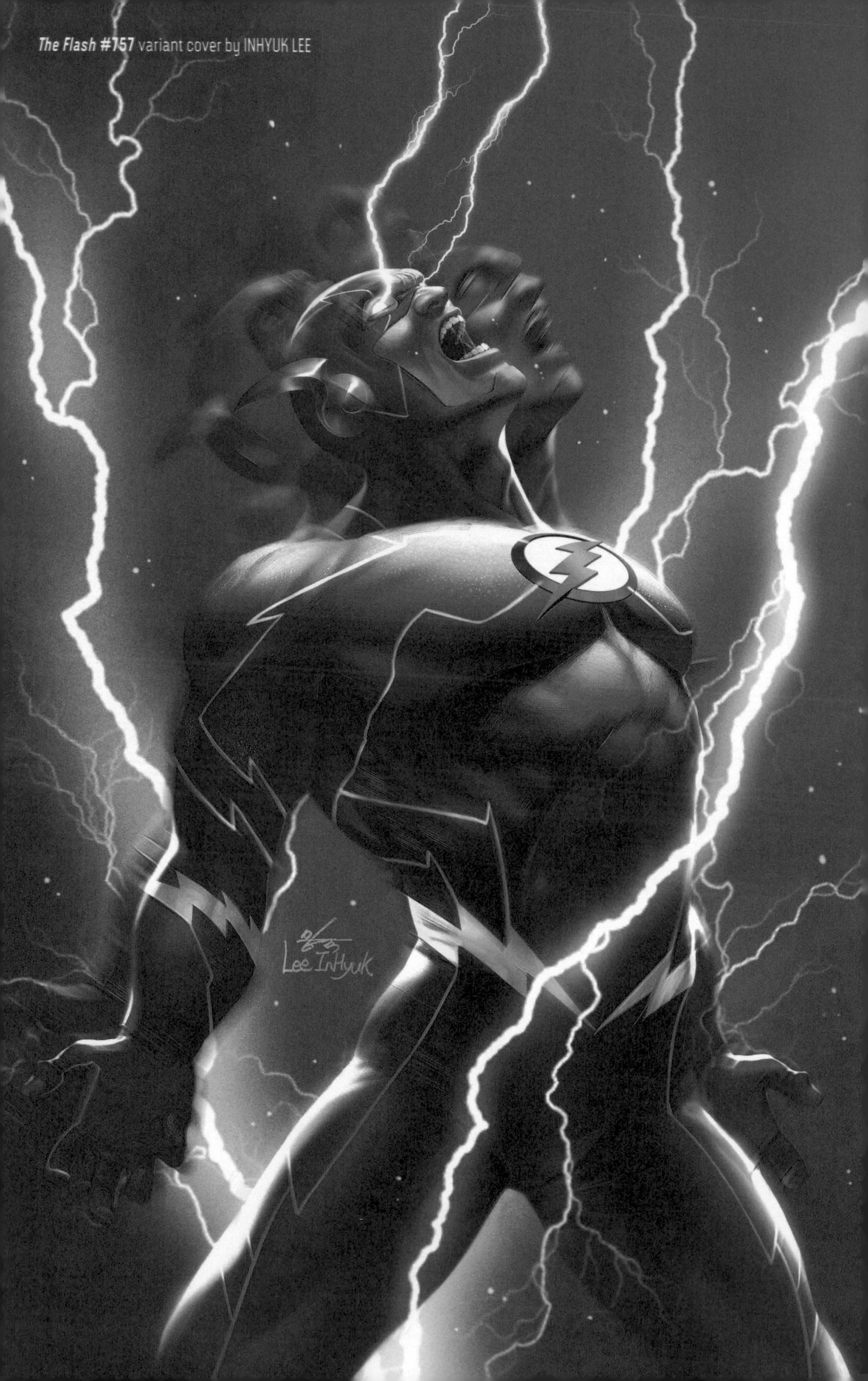
Lee InHyuk

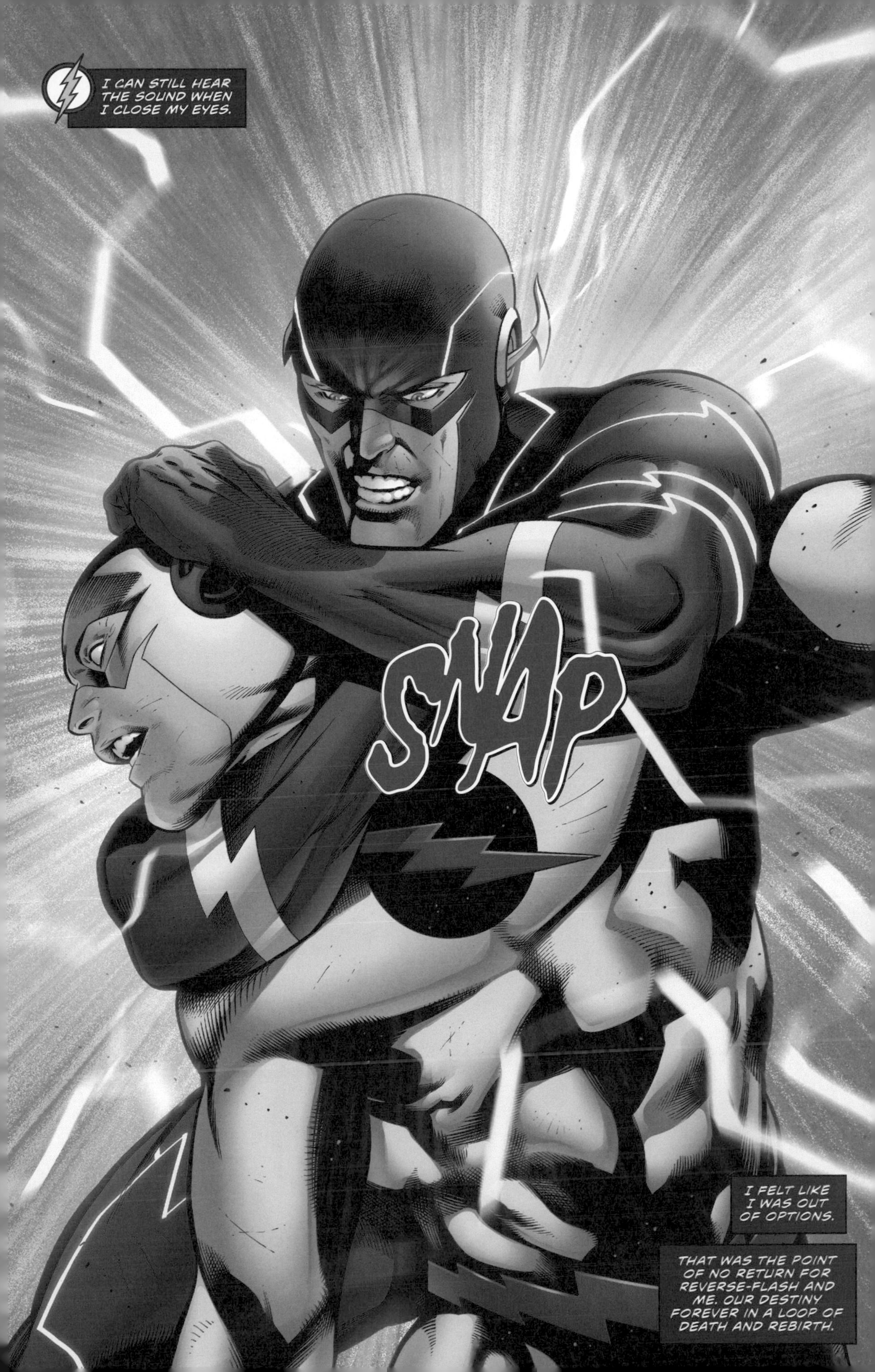
I CAN STILL HEAR THE SOUND WHEN I CLOSE MY EYES.
SNAP
I FELT LIKE I WAS OUT OF OPTIONS.
THAT WAS THE POINT OF NO RETURN FOR REVERSE-FLASH AND ME. OUR DESTINY FOREVER IN A LOOP OF DEATH AND REBIRTH.

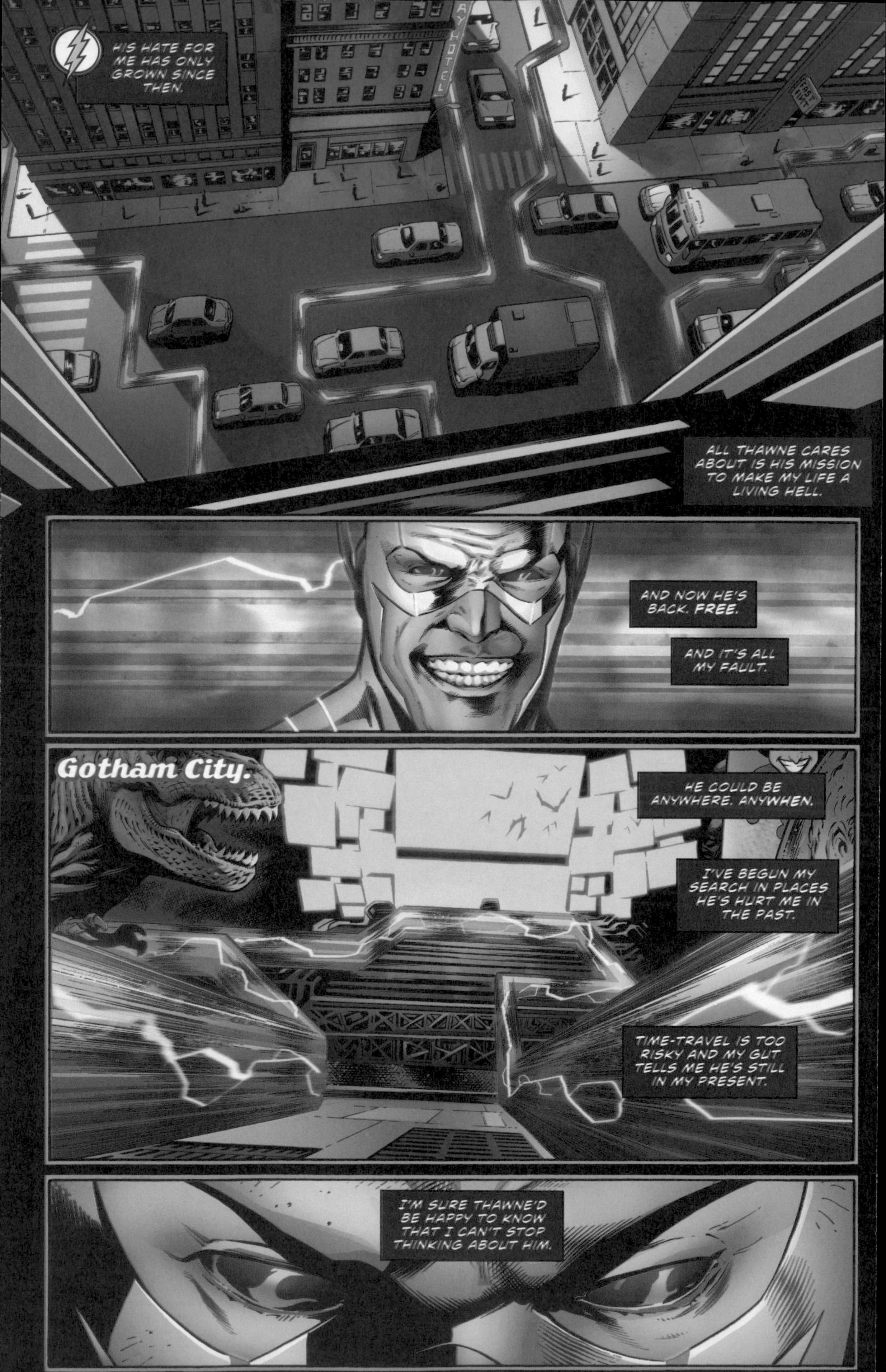

HIS HATE FOR ME HAS ONLY GROWN SINCE THEN.
HOTEL
FAST
ALL THAWNE CARES ABOUT IS HIS MISSION TO MAKE MY LIFE A LIVING HELL.
AND NOW HE'S BACK. FREE.
AND IT'S ALL MY FAULT.
Gotham City.
HE COULD BE ANYWHERE. ANYWHEN.
I'VE BEGUN MY SEARCH IN PLACES HE'S HURT ME IN THE PAST.
TIME-TRAVEL IS TOO RISKY AND MY GUT TELLS ME HE'S STILL IN MY PRESENT.
I'M SURE THAWNE'D BE HAPPY TO KNOW THAT I CAN'T STOP THINKING ABOUT HIM.

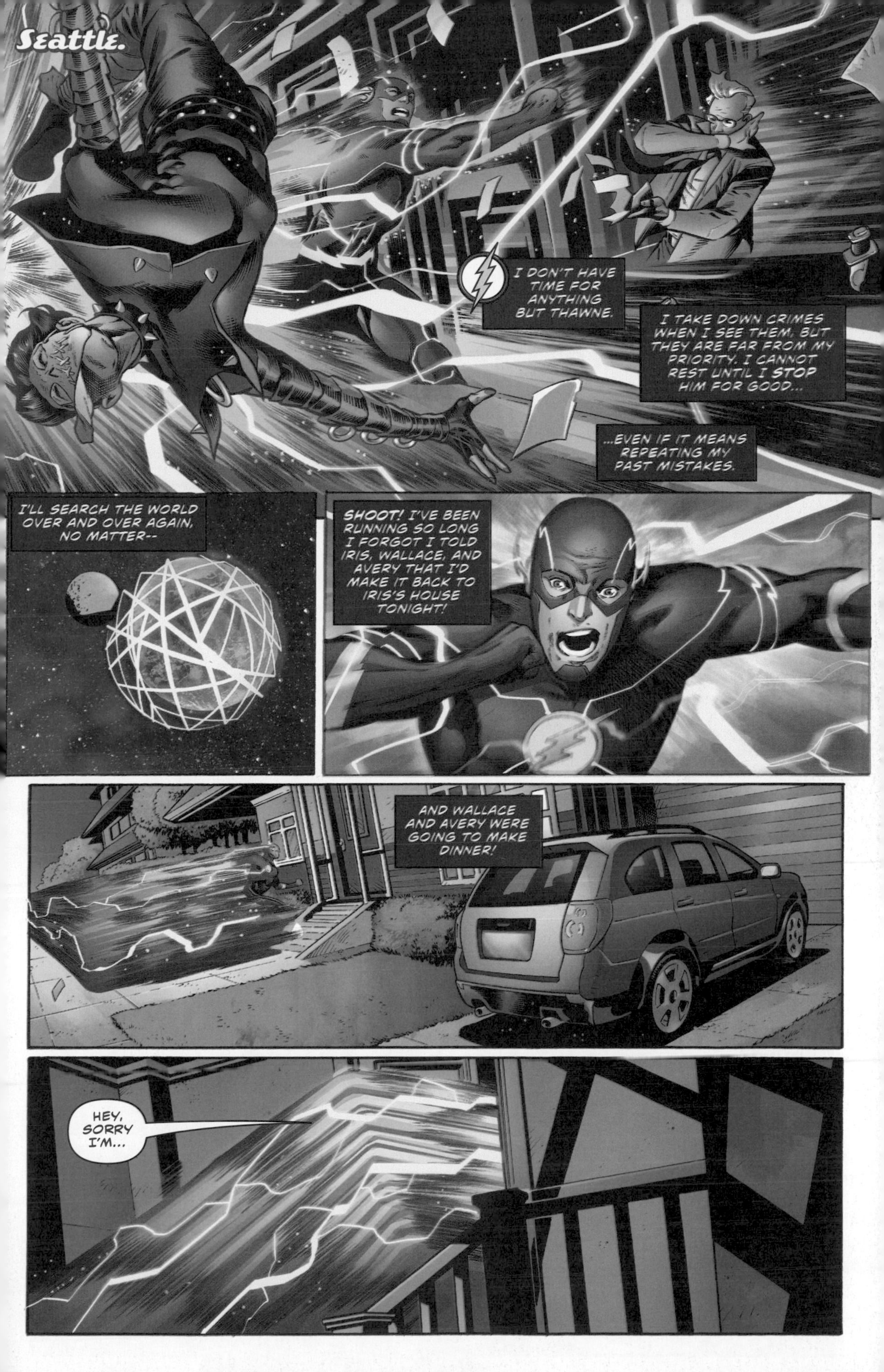
Seattle.
I DON'T HAVE TIME FOR ANYTHING BUT THAWNE.
I TAKE DOWN CRIMES WHEN I SEE THEM, BUT THEY ARE FAR FROM MY PRIORITY. I CANNOT REST UNTIL I STOP HIM FOR GOOD...
...EVEN IF IT MEANS REPEATING MY PAST MISTAKES.
I'LL SEARCH THE WORLD OVER AND OVER AGAIN, NO MATTER--
SHOOT! I'VE BEEN RUNNING SO LONG I FORGOT I TOLD IRIS, WALLACE, AND AVERY THAT I'D MAKE IT BACK TO IRIS'S HOUSE TONIGHT!
AND WALLACE AND AVERY WERE GOING TO MAKE DINNER!
HEY, SORRY I'M...

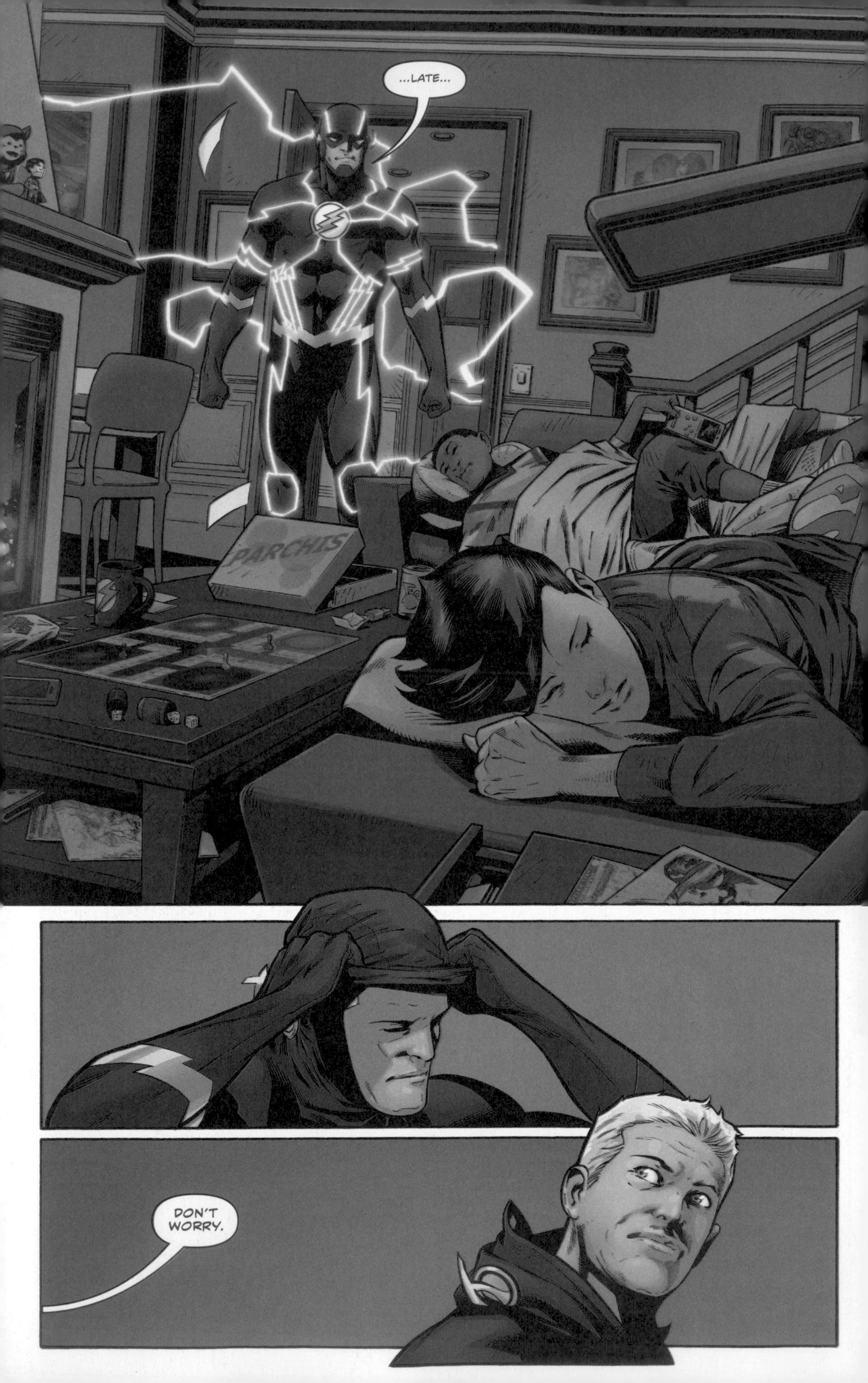
...LATE...
PARCHIS
DON'T WORRY.

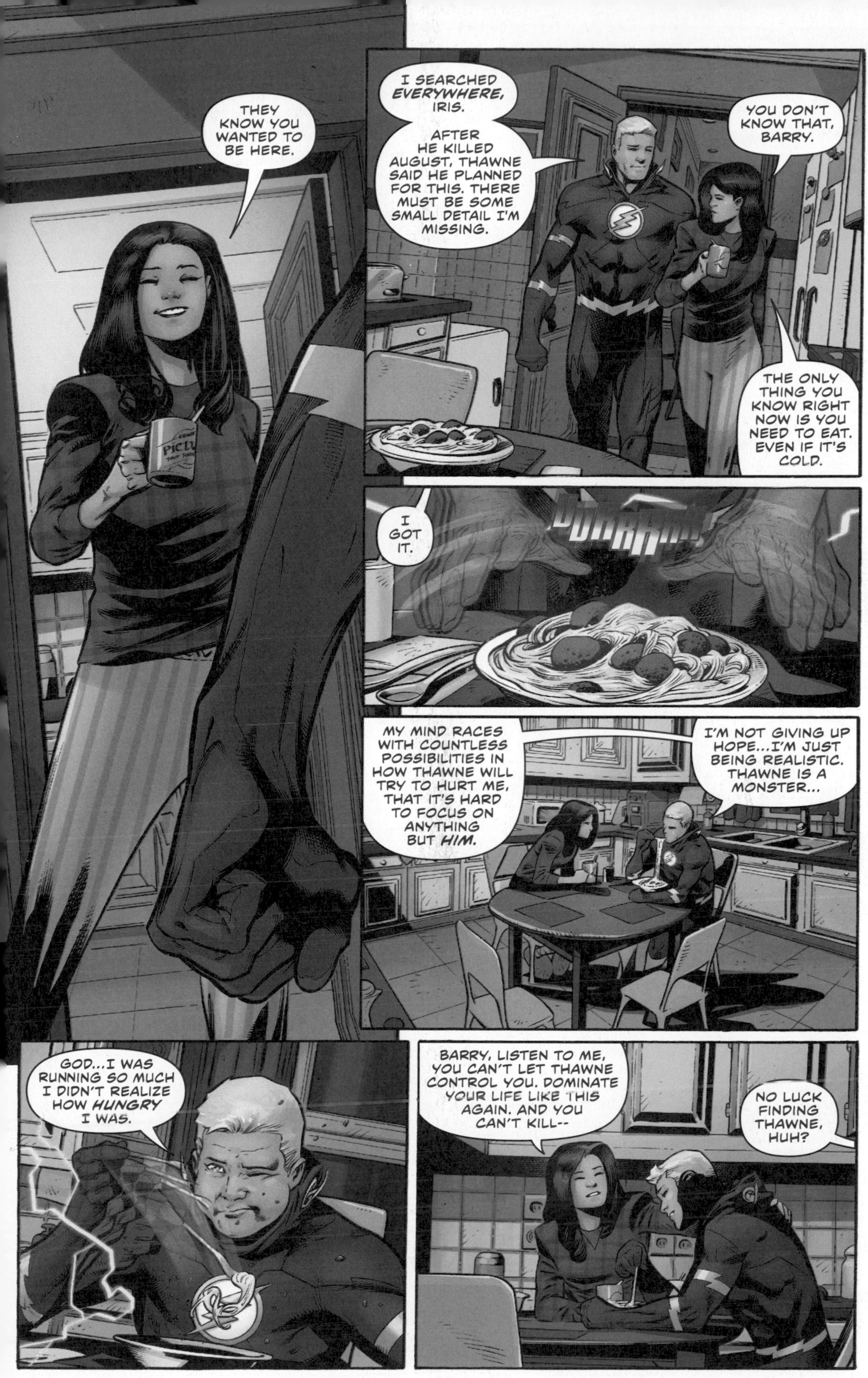
THEY KNOW YOU WANTED TO BE HERE.
I SEARCHED EVERYWHERE, IRIS.
AFTER HE KILLED AUGUST, THAWNE SAID HE PLANNED FOR THIS. THERE MUST BE SOME SMALL DETAIL I'M MISSING.
YOU DON'T KNOW THAT, BARRY.
THE ONLY THING YOU KNOW RIGHT NOW IS YOU NEED TO EAT. EVEN IF IT'S COLD.
I GOT IT.
MY MIND RACES WITH COUNTLESS POSSIBILITIES IN HOW THAWNE WILL TRY TO HURT ME, THAT IT'S HARD TO FOCUS ON ANYTHING BUT HIM.
I'M NOT GIVING UP HOPE...I'M JUST BEING REALISTIC. THAWNE IS A MONSTER...
GOD...I WAS RUNNING SO MUCH I DIDN'T REALIZE HOW HUNGRY I WAS.
NO LUCK FINDING THAWNE, HUH?
BARRY, LISTEN TO ME, YOU CAN'T LET THAWNE CONTROL YOU. DOMINATE YOUR LIFE LIKE THIS AGAIN. AND YOU CAN'T KILL--

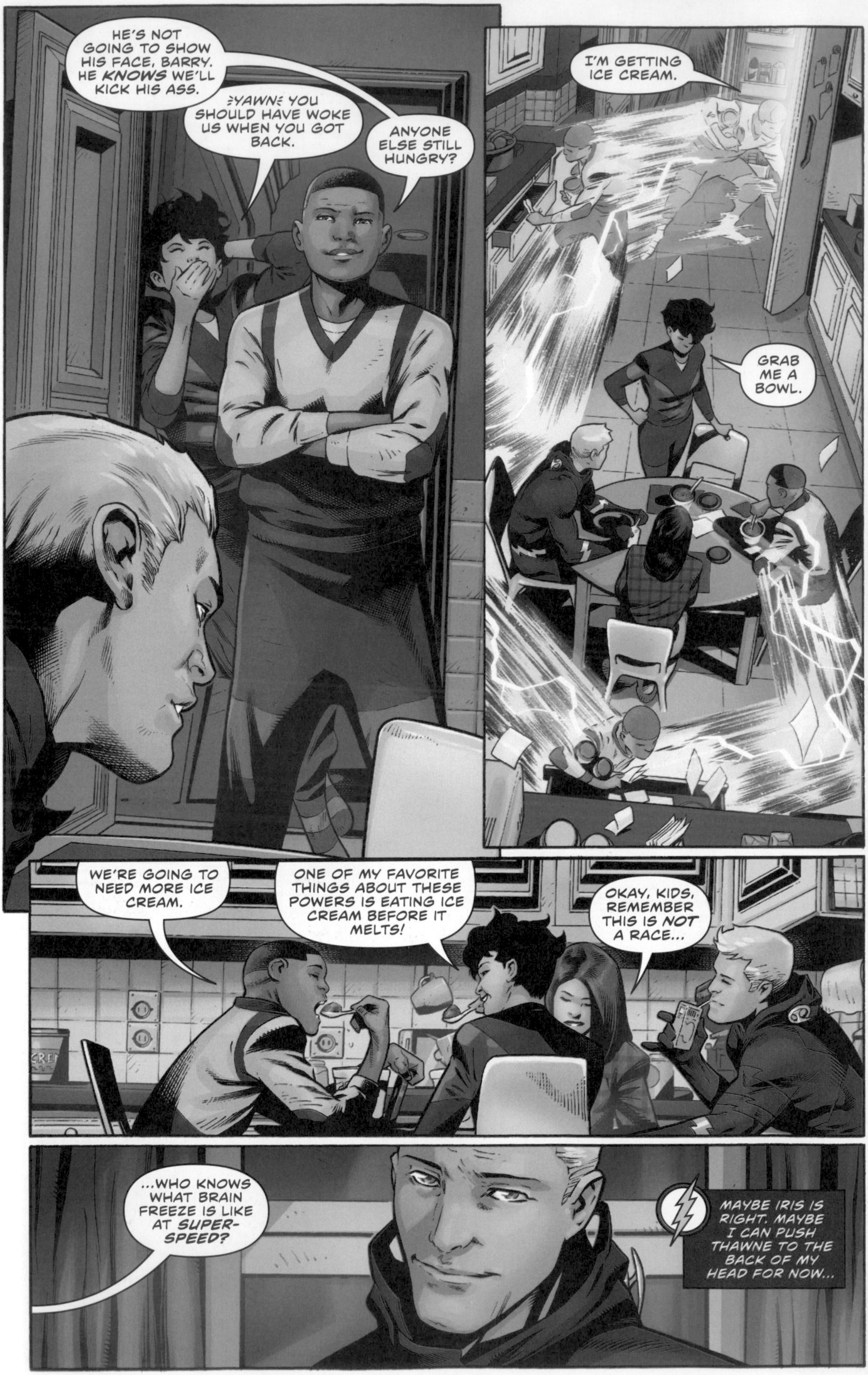
HE'S NOT GOING TO SHOW HIS FACE, BARRY. HE KNOWS WE'LL KICK HIS ASS.
=YAWN= YOU SHOULD HAVE WOKE US WHEN YOU GOT BACK.
ANYONE ELSE STILL HUNGRY?
I'M GETTING ICE CREAM.
GRAB ME A BOWL.
WE'RE GOING TO NEED MORE ICE CREAM.
ONE OF MY FAVORITE THINGS ABOUT THESE POWERS IS EATING ICE CREAM BEFORE IT MELTS!
OKAY, KIDS, REMEMBER THIS IS NOT A RACE...
...WHO KNOWS WHAT BRAIN FREEZE IS LIKE AT SUPER-SPEED?
MAYBE IRIS IS RIGHT. MAYBE I CAN PUSH THAWNE TO THE BACK OF MY HEAD FOR NOW...

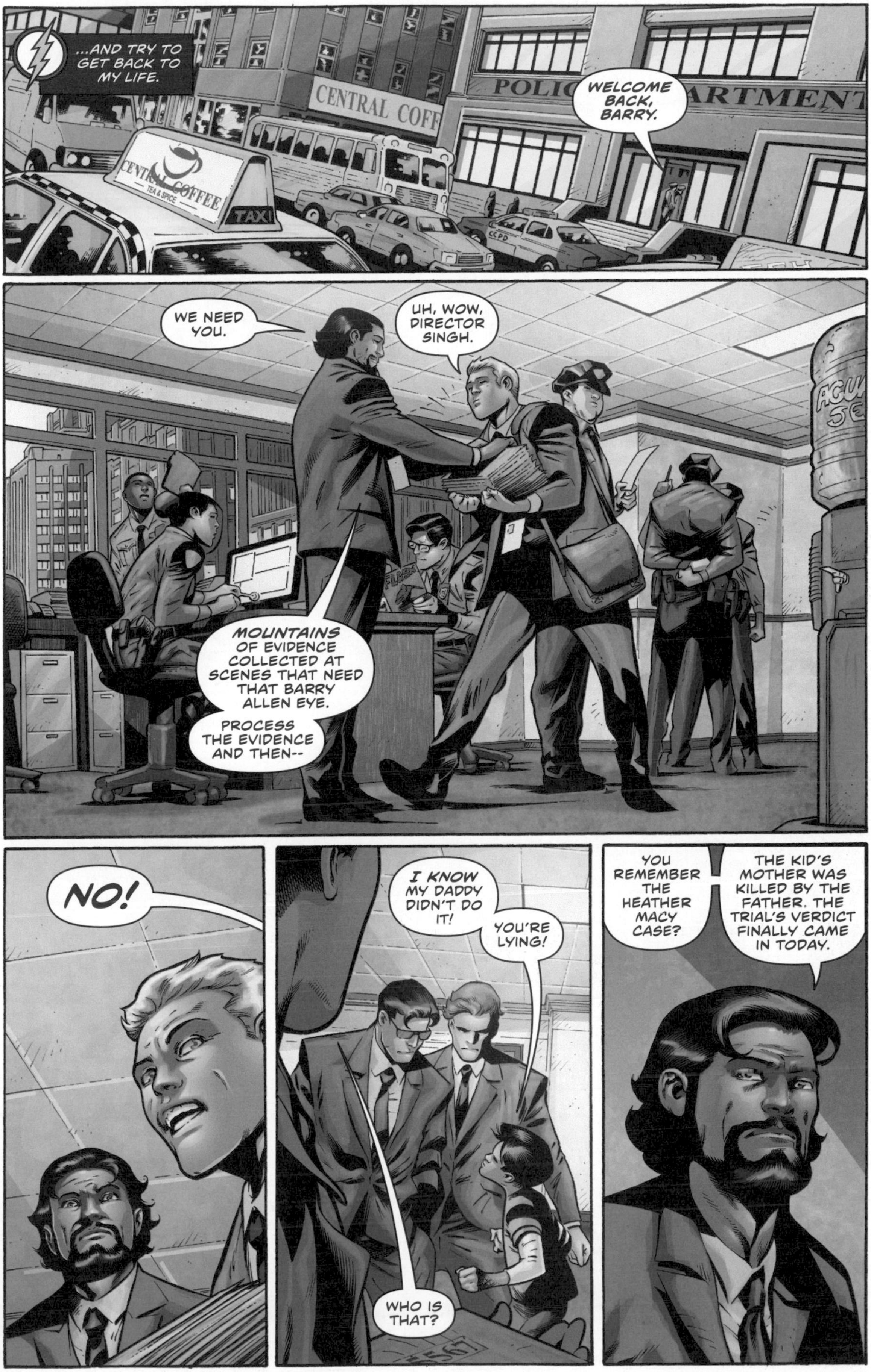
...AND TRY TO GET BACK TO MY LIFE.
CENTRAL COFFEE
TEA & SPICE
TAXI
CENTRAL COFF
WELCOME BACK, BARRY.
WE NEED YOU.
UH, WOW, DIRECTOR SINGH.
MOUNTAINS OF EVIDENCE COLLECTED AT SCENES THAT NEED THAT BARRY ALLEN EYE.
PROCESS THE EVIDENCE AND THEN--
NO!
I KNOW MY DADDY DIDN'T DO IT!
YOU'RE LYING!
WHO IS THAT?
YOU REMEMBER THE HEATHER MACY CASE?
THE KID'S MOTHER WAS KILLED BY THE FATHER. THE TRIAL'S VERDICT FINALLY CAME IN TODAY.

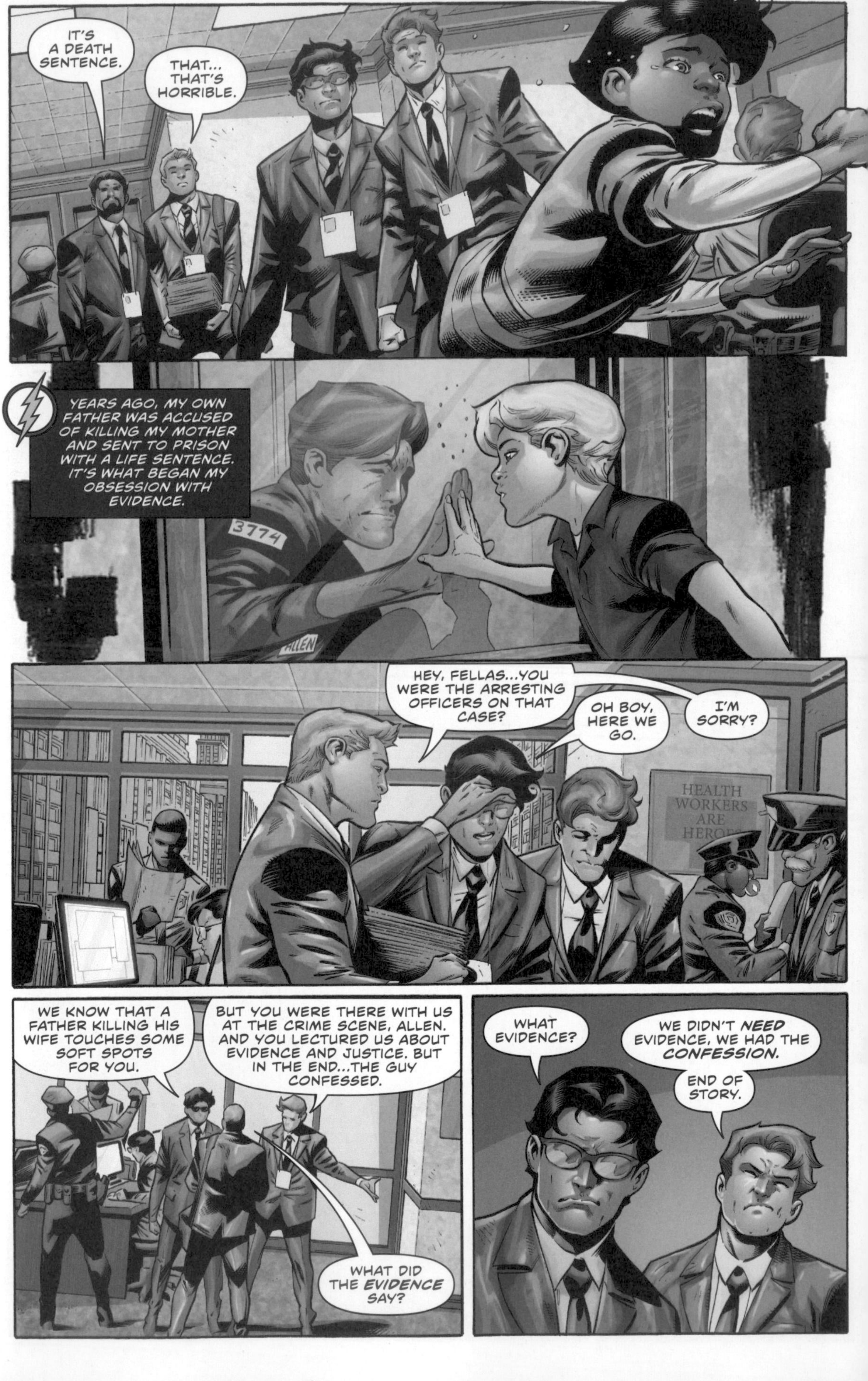
IT'S A DEATH SENTENCE.
THAT... THAT'S HORRIBLE.
YEARS AGO, MY OWN FATHER WAS ACCUSED OF KILLING MY MOTHER AND SENT TO PRISON WITH A LIFE SENTENCE. IT'S WHAT BEGAN MY OBSESSION WITH EVIDENCE.
3774
ALLEN
HEY, FELLAS...YOU WERE THE ARRESTING OFFICERS ON THAT CASE?
OH BOY, HERE WE GO.
I'M SORRY?
HEALTH WORKERS ARE HEROES
WE KNOW THAT A FATHER KILLING HIS WIFE TOUCHES SOME SOFT SPOTS FOR YOU.
BUT YOU WERE THERE WITH US AT THE CRIME SCENE, ALLEN. AND YOU LECTURED US ABOUT EVIDENCE AND JUSTICE. BUT IN THE END...THE GUY CONFESSED.
WHAT DID THE *EVIDENCE* SAY?
WHAT EVIDENCE?
WE DIDN'T *NEED* EVIDENCE, WE HAD THE ***CONFESSION.***
END OF STORY.

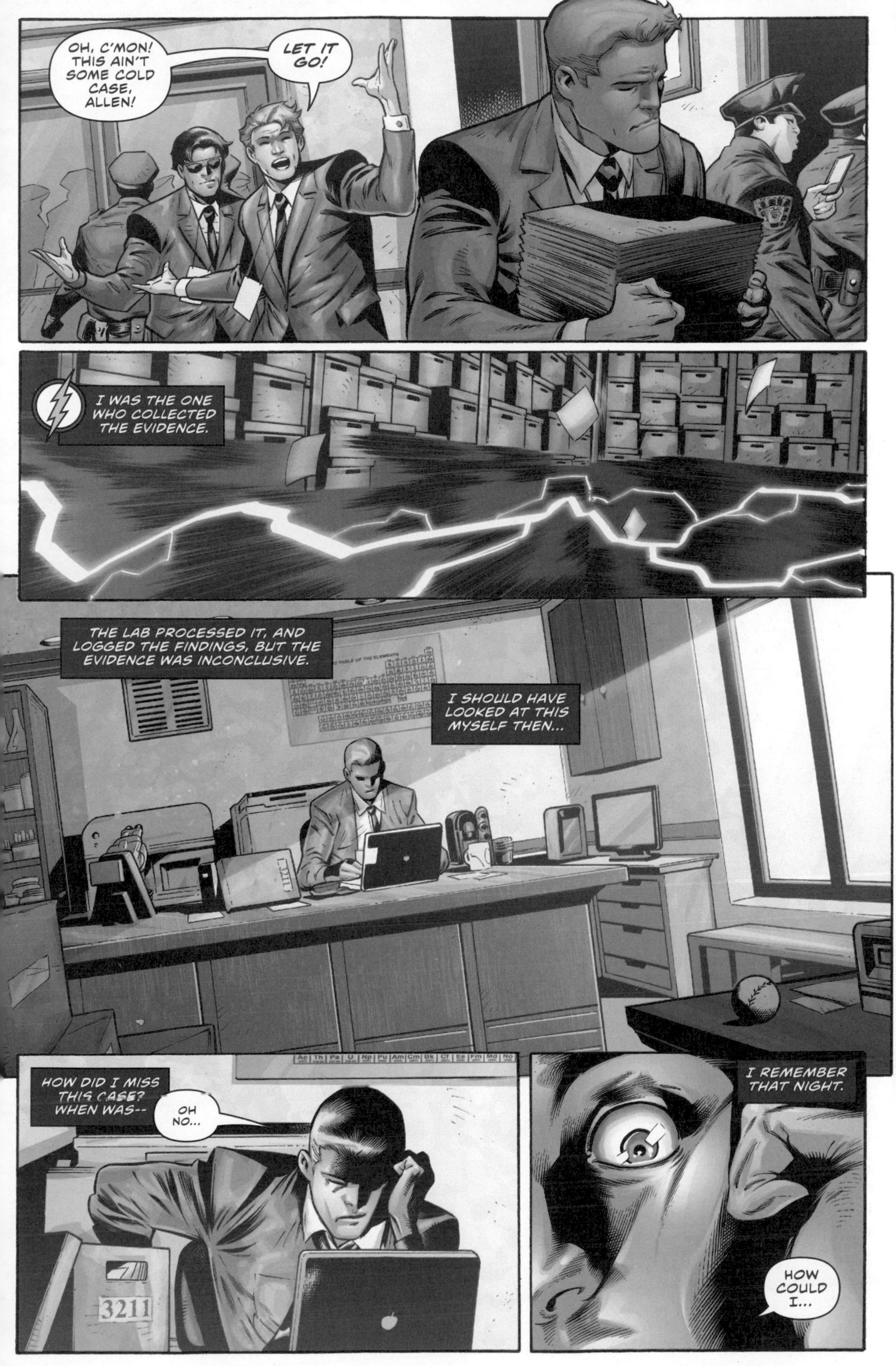
OH, C'MON! THIS AIN'T SOME COLD CASE, ALLEN!
LET IT GO!
I WAS THE ONE WHO COLLECTED THE EVIDENCE.
THE LAB PROCESSED IT, AND LOGGED THE FINDINGS, BUT THE EVIDENCE WAS INCONCLUSIVE.
I SHOULD HAVE LOOKED AT THIS MYSELF THEN...
HOW DID I MISS THIS CASE? WHEN WAS--
OH NO...
3211
I REMEMBER THAT NIGHT.
HOW COULD I...

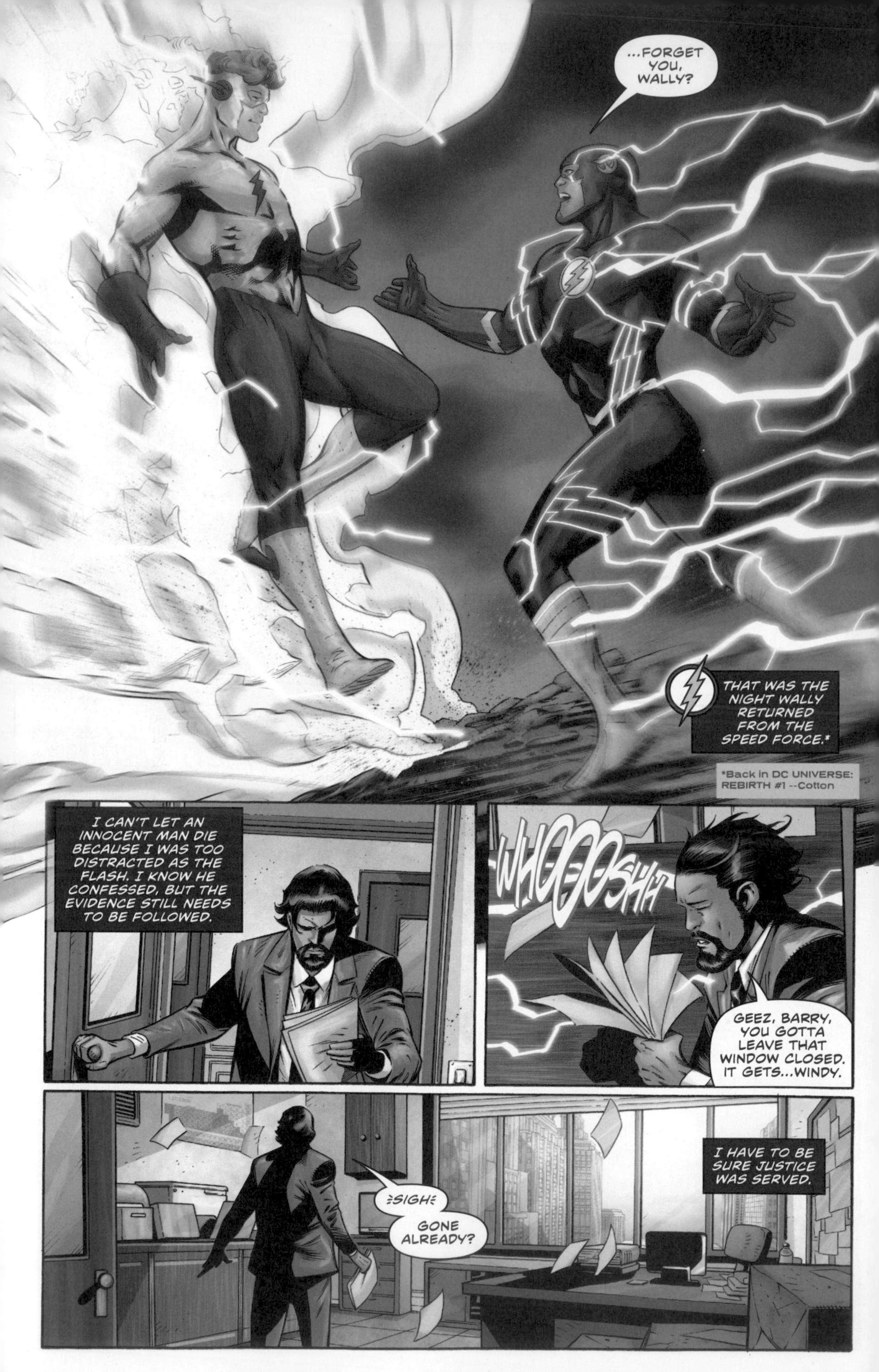
...FORGET YOU, WALLY?
THAT WAS THE NIGHT WALLY RETURNED FROM THE SPEED FORCE.*
*Back in DC UNIVERSE: REBIRTH #1 --Cotton
I CAN'T LET AN INNOCENT MAN DIE BECAUSE I WAS TOO DISTRACTED AS THE FLASH. I KNOW HE CONFESSED, BUT THE EVIDENCE STILL NEEDS TO BE FOLLOWED.
WHOOOOSHH
GEEZ, BARRY, YOU GOTTA LEAVE THAT WINDOW CLOSED. IT GETS...WINDY.
SIGH
GONE ALREADY?
I HAVE TO BE SURE JUSTICE WAS SERVED.

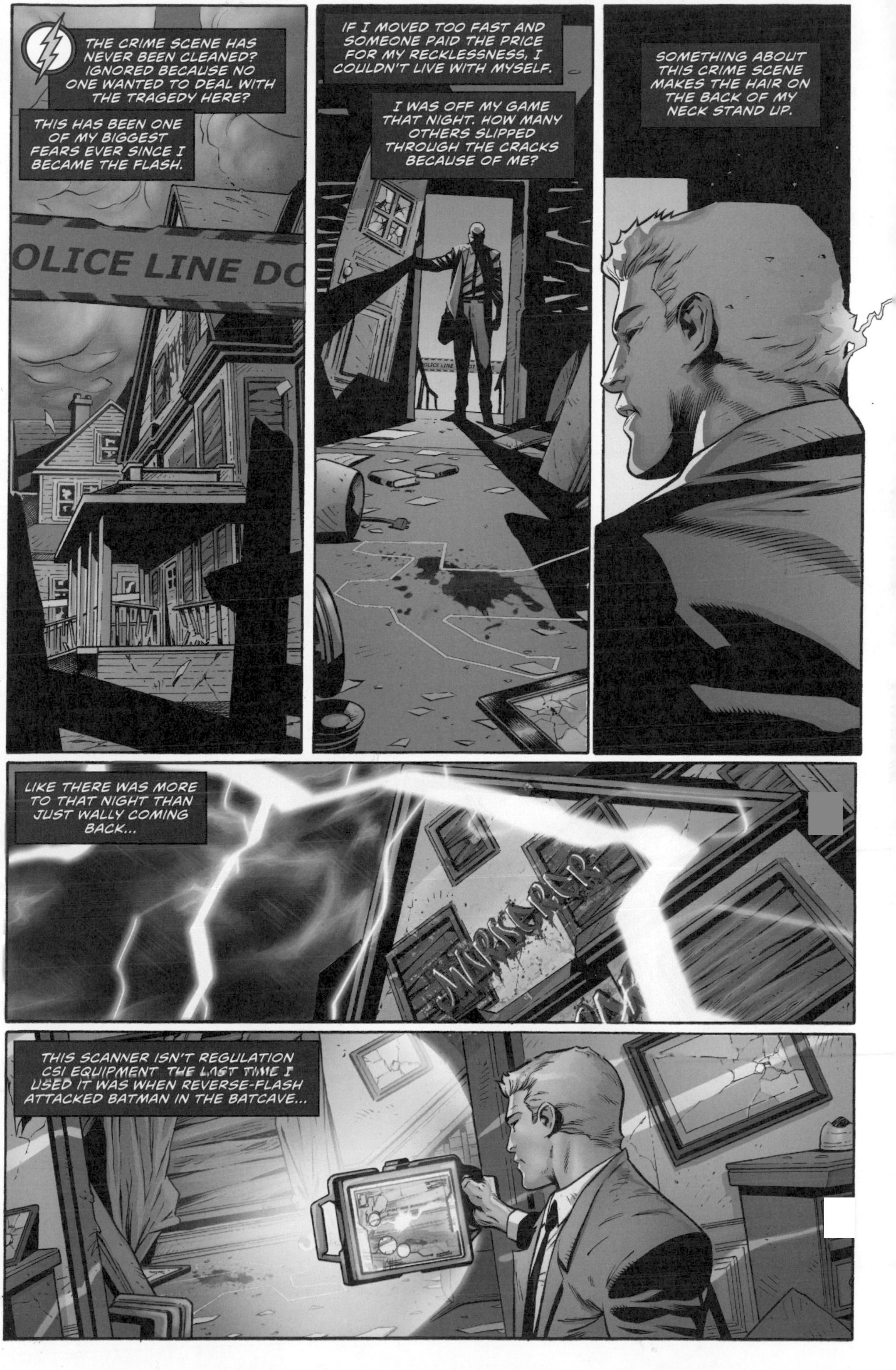
THE CRIME SCENE HAS NEVER BEEN CLEANED? IGNORED BECAUSE NO ONE WANTED TO DEAL WITH THE TRAGEDY HERE?
THIS HAS BEEN ONE OF MY BIGGEST FEARS EVER SINCE I BECAME THE FLASH.
OLICE LINE DO
IF I MOVED TOO FAST AND SOMEONE PAID THE PRICE FOR MY RECKLESSNESS, I COULDN'T LIVE WITH MYSELF.
I WAS OFF MY GAME THAT NIGHT. HOW MANY OTHERS SLIPPED THROUGH THE CRACKS BECAUSE OF ME?
SOMETHING ABOUT THIS CRIME SCENE MAKES THE HAIR ON THE BACK OF MY NECK STAND UP.
LIKE THERE WAS MORE TO THAT NIGHT THAN JUST WALLY COMING BACK...
THIS SCANNER ISN'T REGULATION CSI EQUIPMENT. THE LAST TIME I USED IT WAS WHEN REVERSE-FLASH ATTACKED BATMAN IN THE BATCAVE...

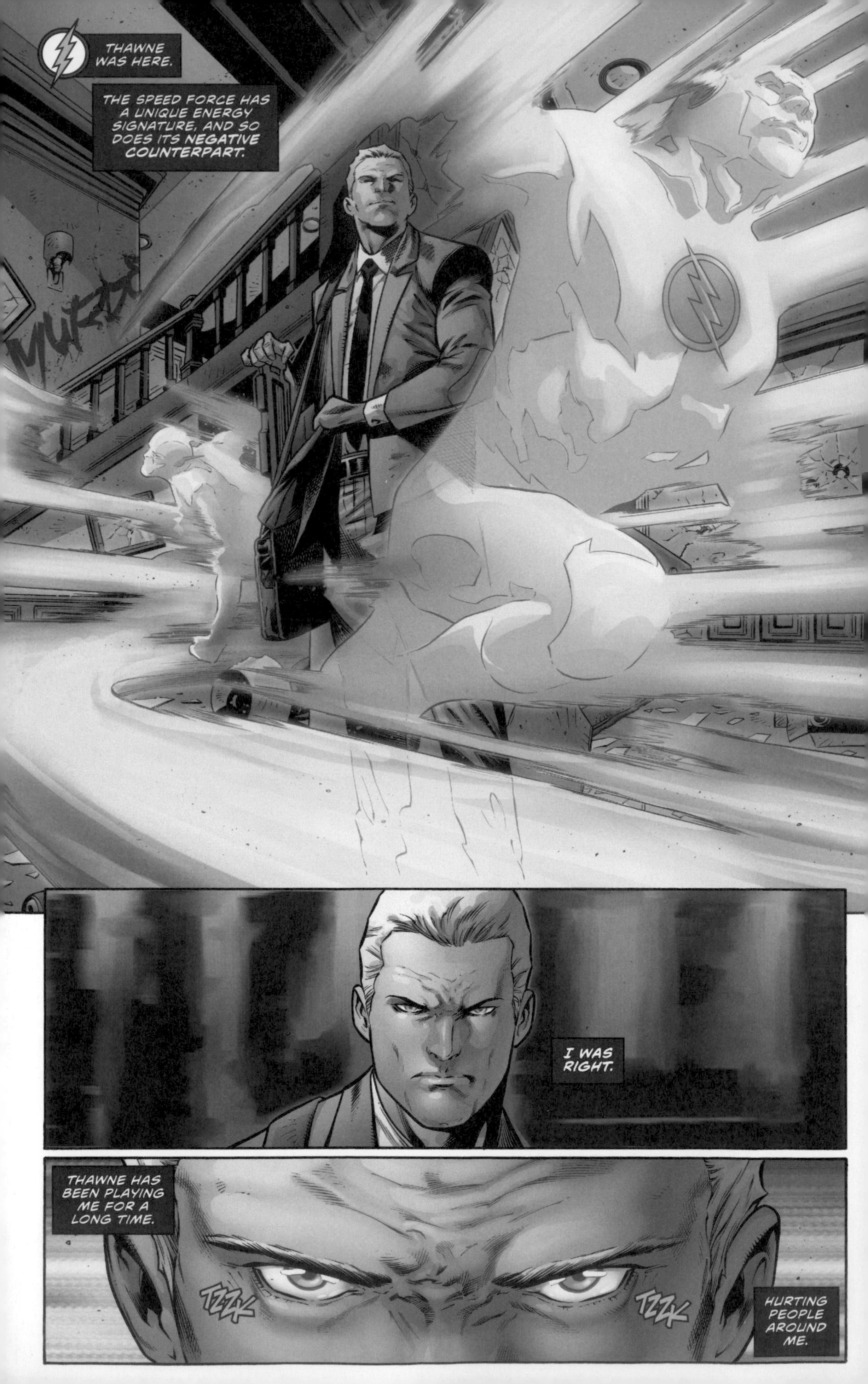
THAWNE WAS HERE.
THE SPEED FORCE HAS A UNIQUE ENERGY SIGNATURE, AND SO DOES ITS NEGATIVE COUNTERPART.
I WAS RIGHT.
THAWNE HAS BEEN PLAYING ME FOR A LONG TIME.
TZZK
TZZK
HURTING PEOPLE AROUND ME.

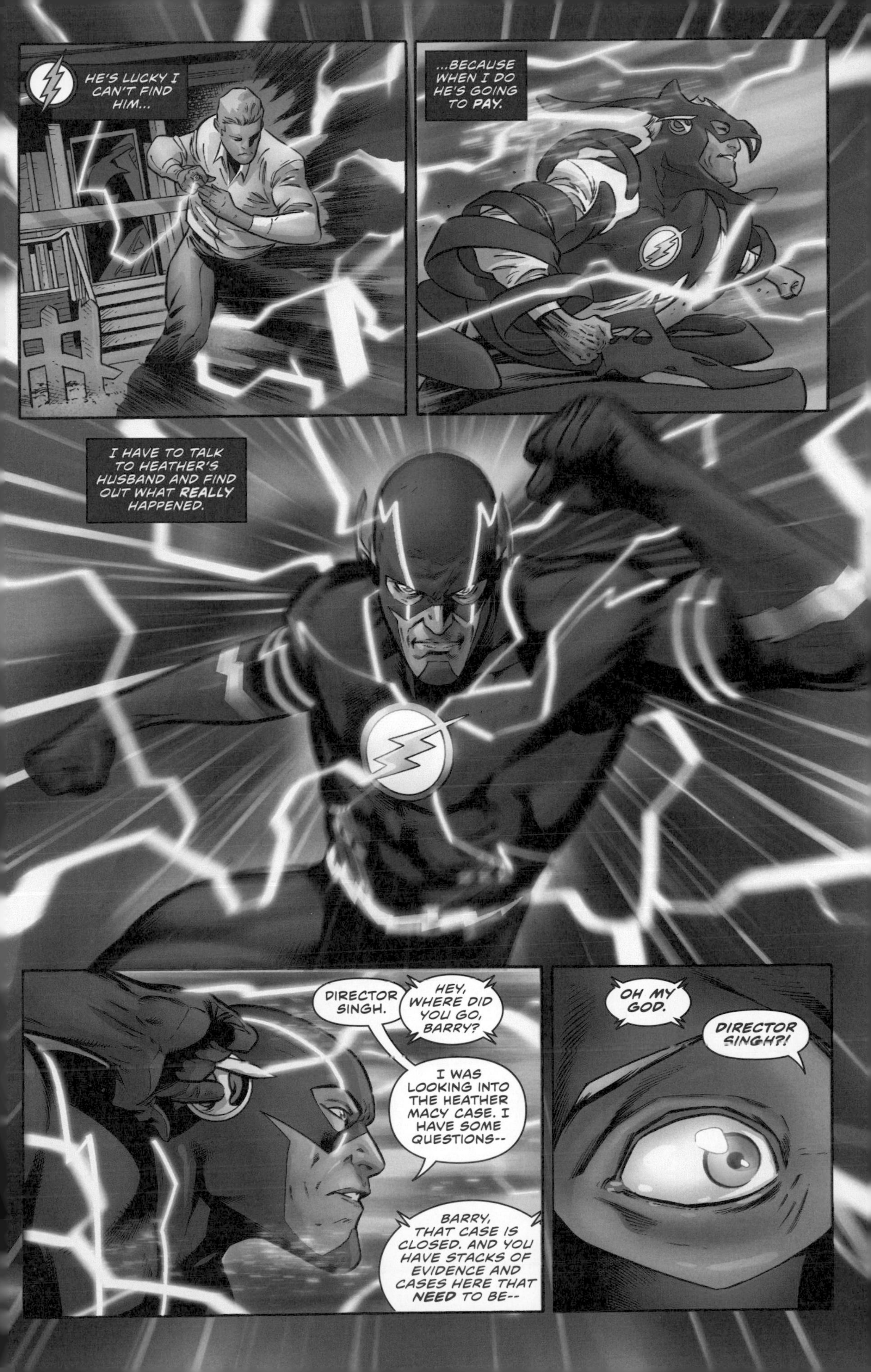
HE'S LUCKY I CAN'T FIND HIM...
...BECAUSE WHEN I DO HE'S GOING TO PAY.
I HAVE TO TALK TO HEATHER'S HUSBAND AND FIND OUT WHAT REALLY HAPPENED.
HEY, WHERE DID YOU GO, BARRY?
DIRECTOR SINGH.
I WAS LOOKING INTO THE HEATHER MACY CASE. I HAVE SOME QUESTIONS--
BARRY, THAT CASE IS CLOSED. AND YOU HAVE STACKS OF EVIDENCE AND CASES HERE THAT NEED TO BE--
OH MY GOD.
DIRECTOR SINGH?!

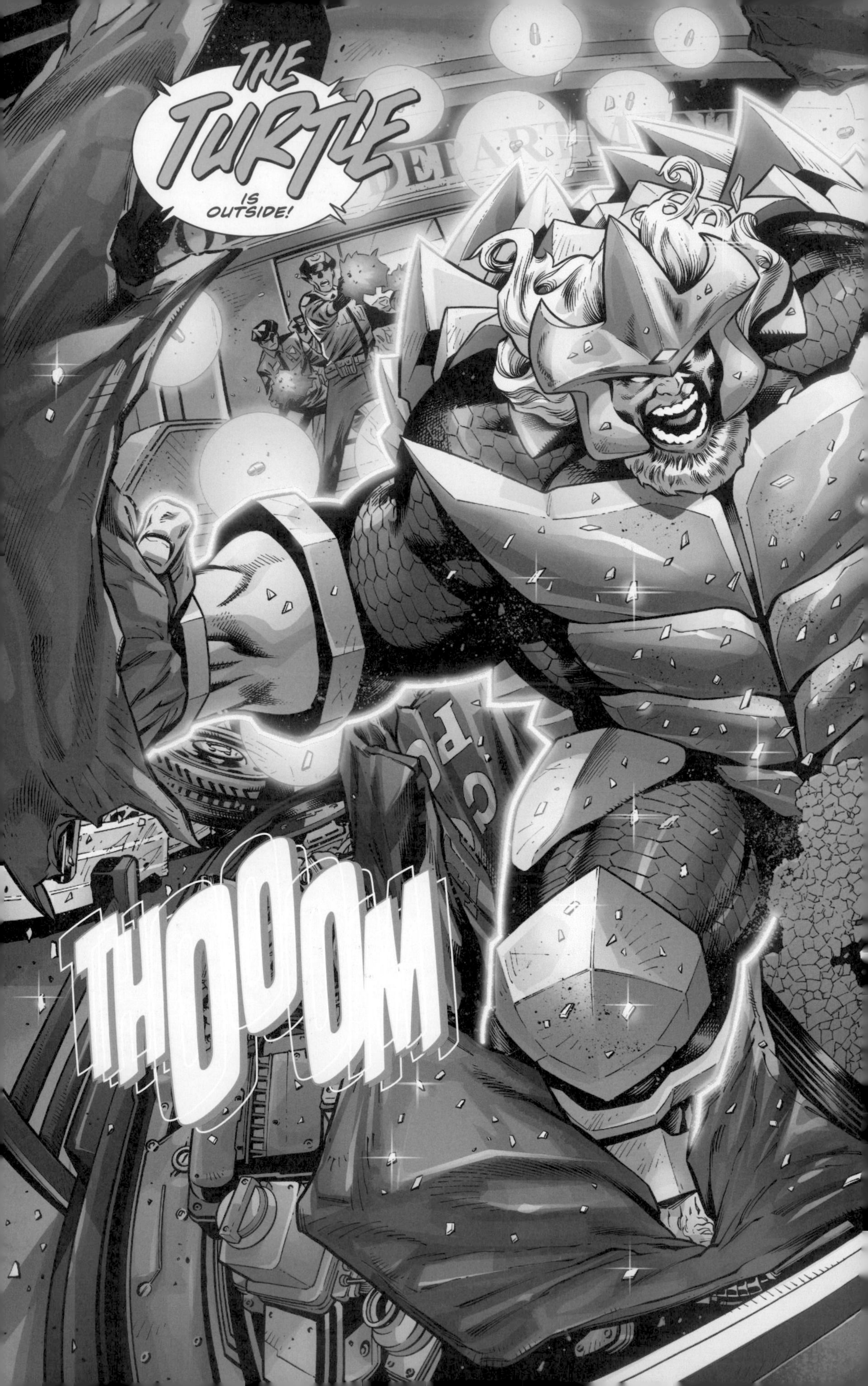
THE TURTLE IS OUTSIDE!
THOOOM

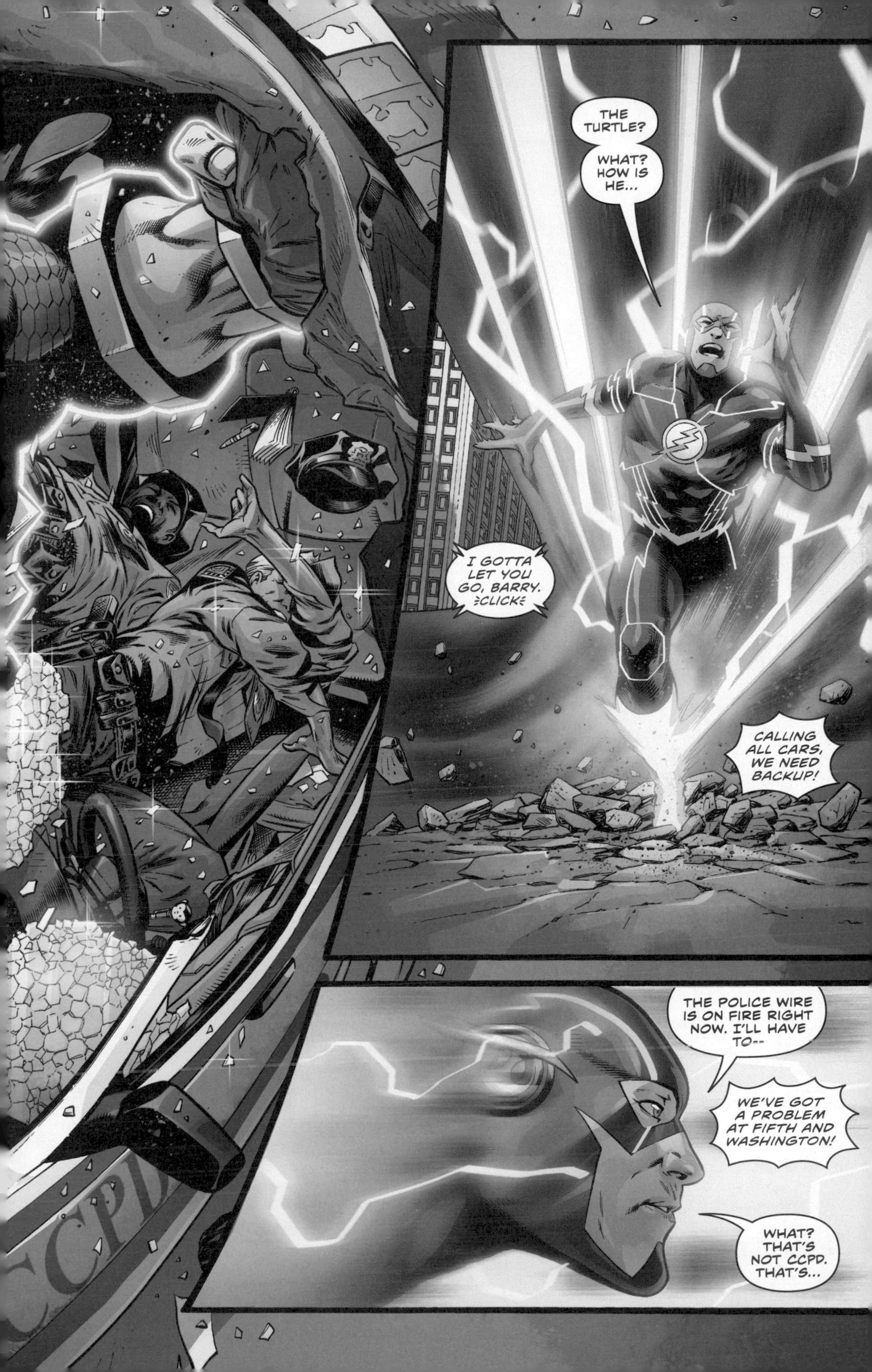
THE TURTLE?
WHAT? HOW IS HE...
I GOTTA LET YOU GO, BARRY. CLICK
CALLING ALL CARS, WE NEED BACKUP!
THE POLICE WIRE IS ON FIRE RIGHT NOW. I'LL HAVE TO--
WE'VE GOT A PROBLEM AT FIFTH AND WASHINGTON!
WHAT? THAT'S NOT CCPD. THAT'S...
CCPD

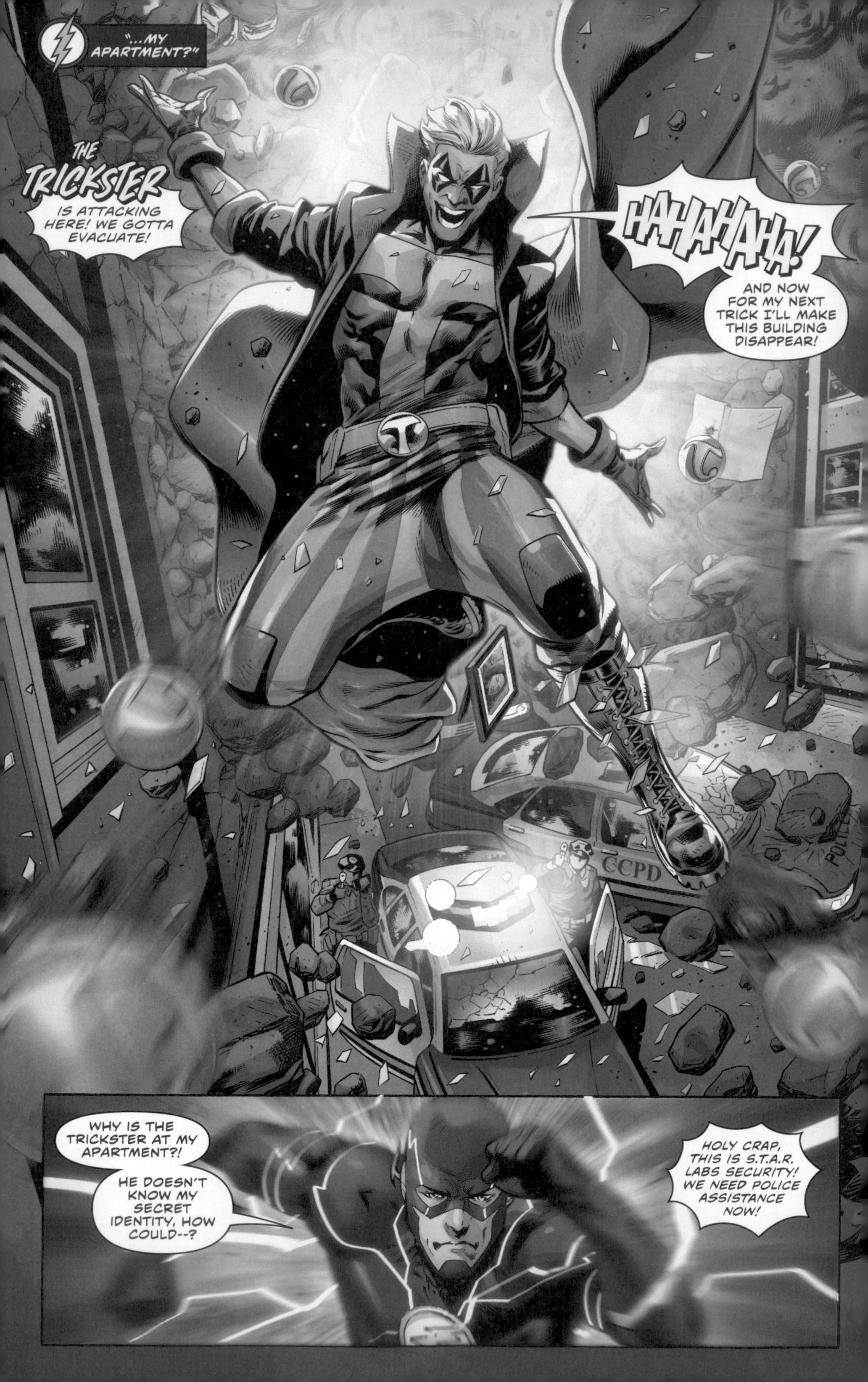

"...MY APARTMENT?"
THE TRICKSTER IS ATTACKING HERE! WE GOTTA EVACUATE!
HAHAHAHAHA!
AND NOW FOR MY NEXT TRICK I'LL MAKE THIS BUILDING DISAPPEAR!
CCPD
WHY IS THE TRICKSTER AT MY APARTMENT?!
HE DOESN'T KNOW MY SECRET IDENTITY, HOW COULD--?
HOLY CRAP, THIS IS S.T.A.R. LABS SECURITY! WE NEED POLICE ASSISTANCE NOW!

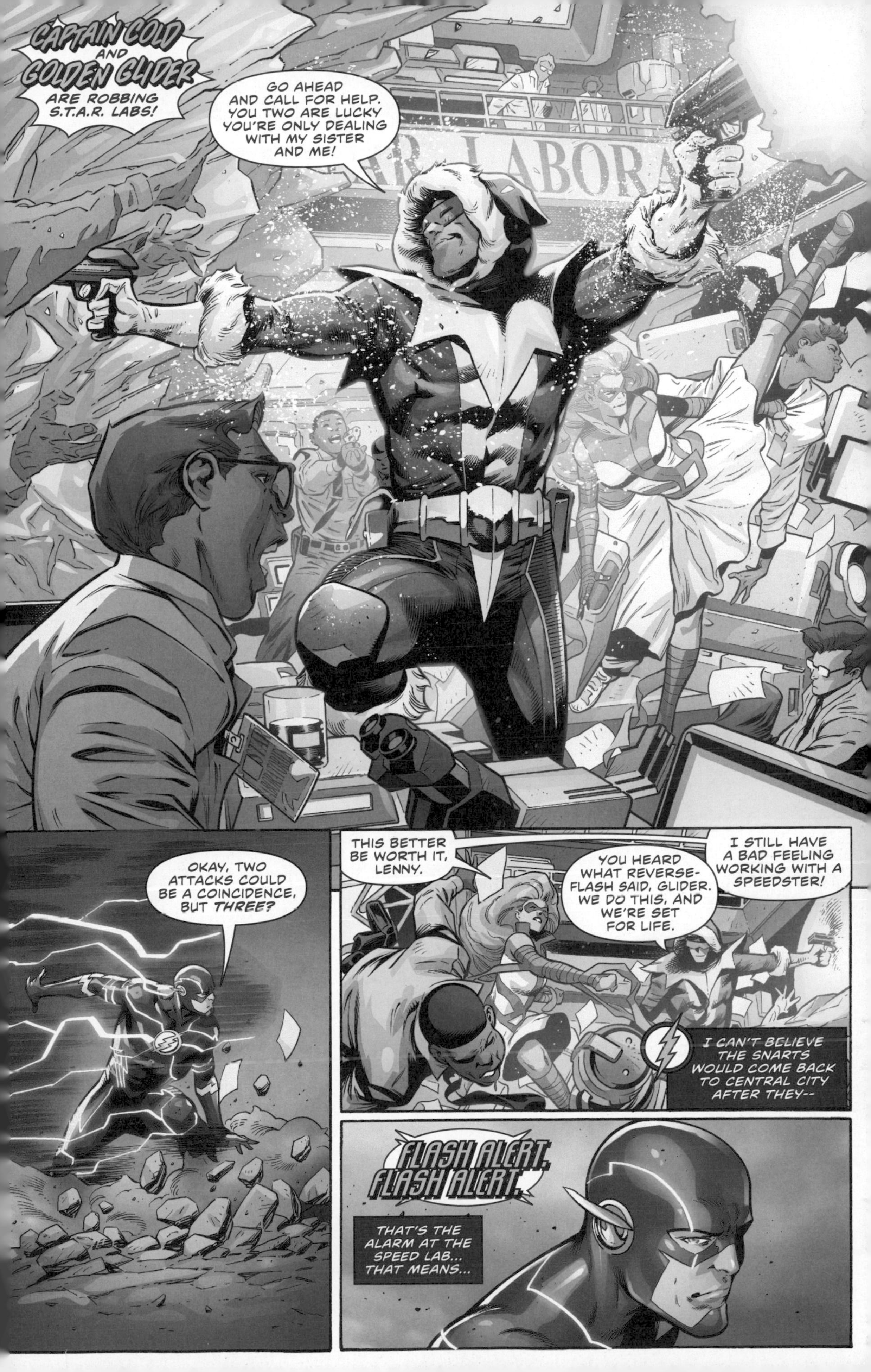
CAPTAIN COLD AND GOLDEN GLIDER ARE ROBBING S.T.A.R. LABS!
GO AHEAD AND CALL FOR HELP. YOU TWO ARE LUCKY YOU'RE ONLY DEALING WITH MY SISTER AND ME!
OKAY, TWO ATTACKS COULD BE A COINCIDENCE, BUT THREE?
THIS BETTER BE WORTH IT, LENNY.
YOU HEARD WHAT REVERSE-FLASH SAID, GLIDER. WE DO THIS, AND WE'RE SET FOR LIFE.
I STILL HAVE A BAD FEELING WORKING WITH A SPEEDSTER!
I CAN'T BELIEVE THE SNARTS WOULD COME BACK TO CENTRAL CITY AFTER THEY--
FLASH ALERT. FLASH ALERT.
THAT'S THE ALARM AT THE SPEED LAB... THAT MEANS...

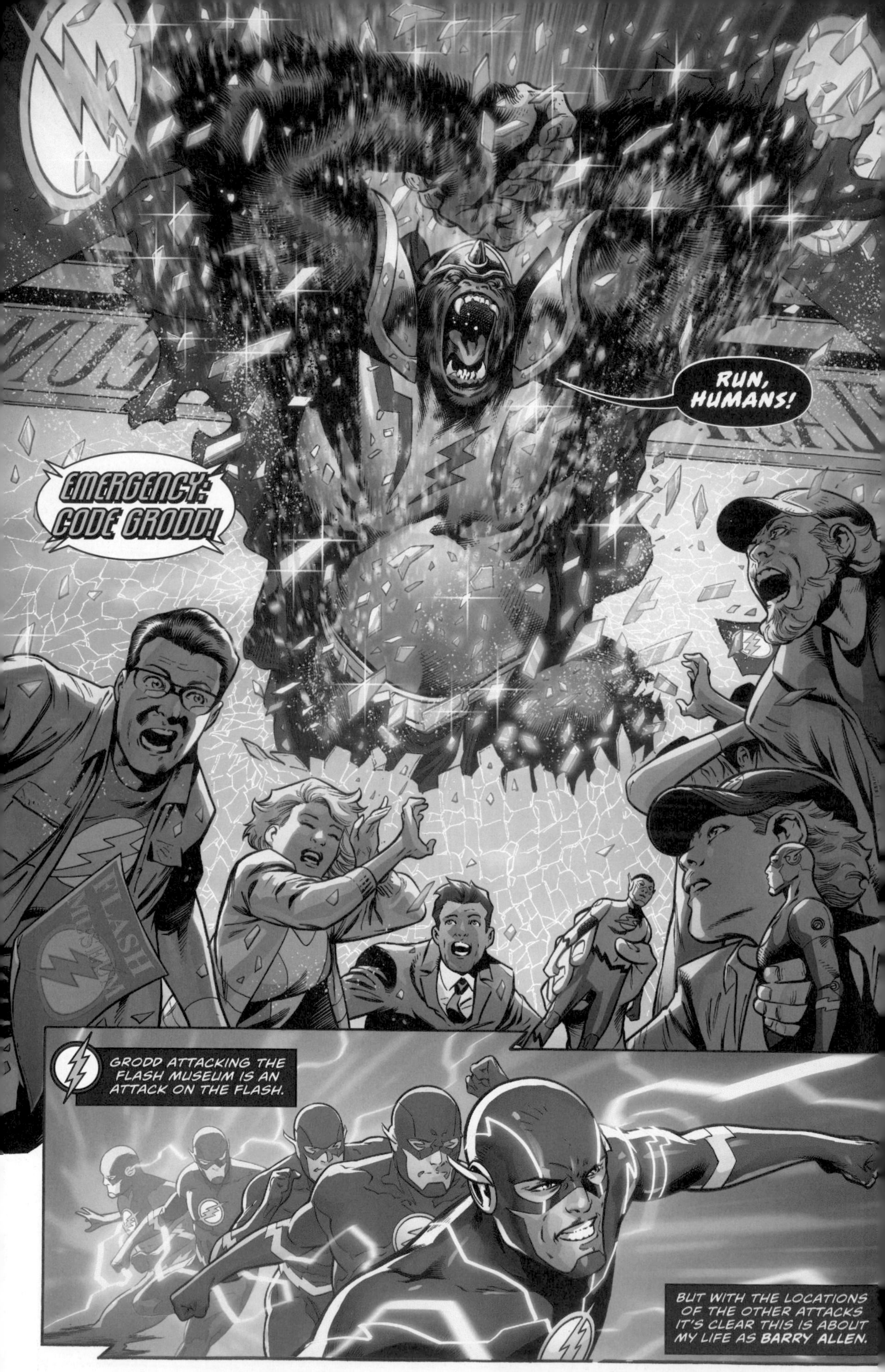

RUN, HUMANS!
EMERGENCY: CODE GRODD!
FLASH MUSEUM
GRODD ATTACKING THE FLASH MUSEUM IS AN ATTACK ON THE FLASH.
BUT WITH THE LOCATIONS OF THE OTHER ATTACKS IT'S CLEAR THIS IS ABOUT MY LIFE AS BARRY ALLEN.

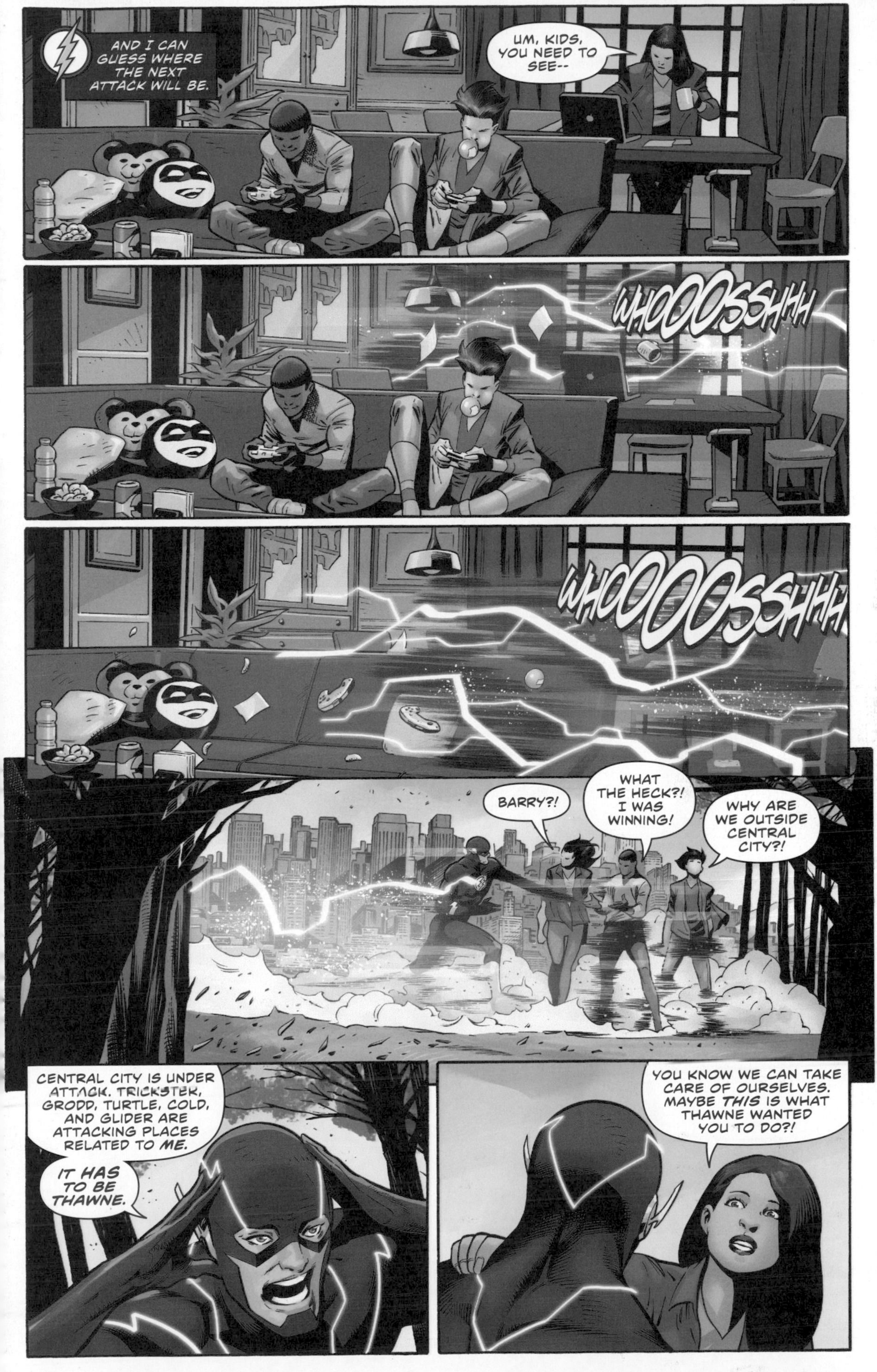
AND I CAN GUESS WHERE THE NEXT ATTACK WILL BE.
UM, KIDS, YOU NEED TO SEE--
WHOOOOSSHHH
WHOOOOOSSHHH
BARRY?!
WHAT THE HECK?! I WAS WINNING!
WHY ARE WE OUTSIDE CENTRAL CITY?!
CENTRAL CITY IS UNDER ATTACK. TRICKSTER, GRODD, TURTLE, COLD, AND GLIDER ARE ATTACKING PLACES RELATED TO ME.
IT HAS TO BE THAWNE.
YOU KNOW WE CAN TAKE CARE OF OURSELVES. MAYBE THIS IS WHAT THAWNE WANTED YOU TO DO?!

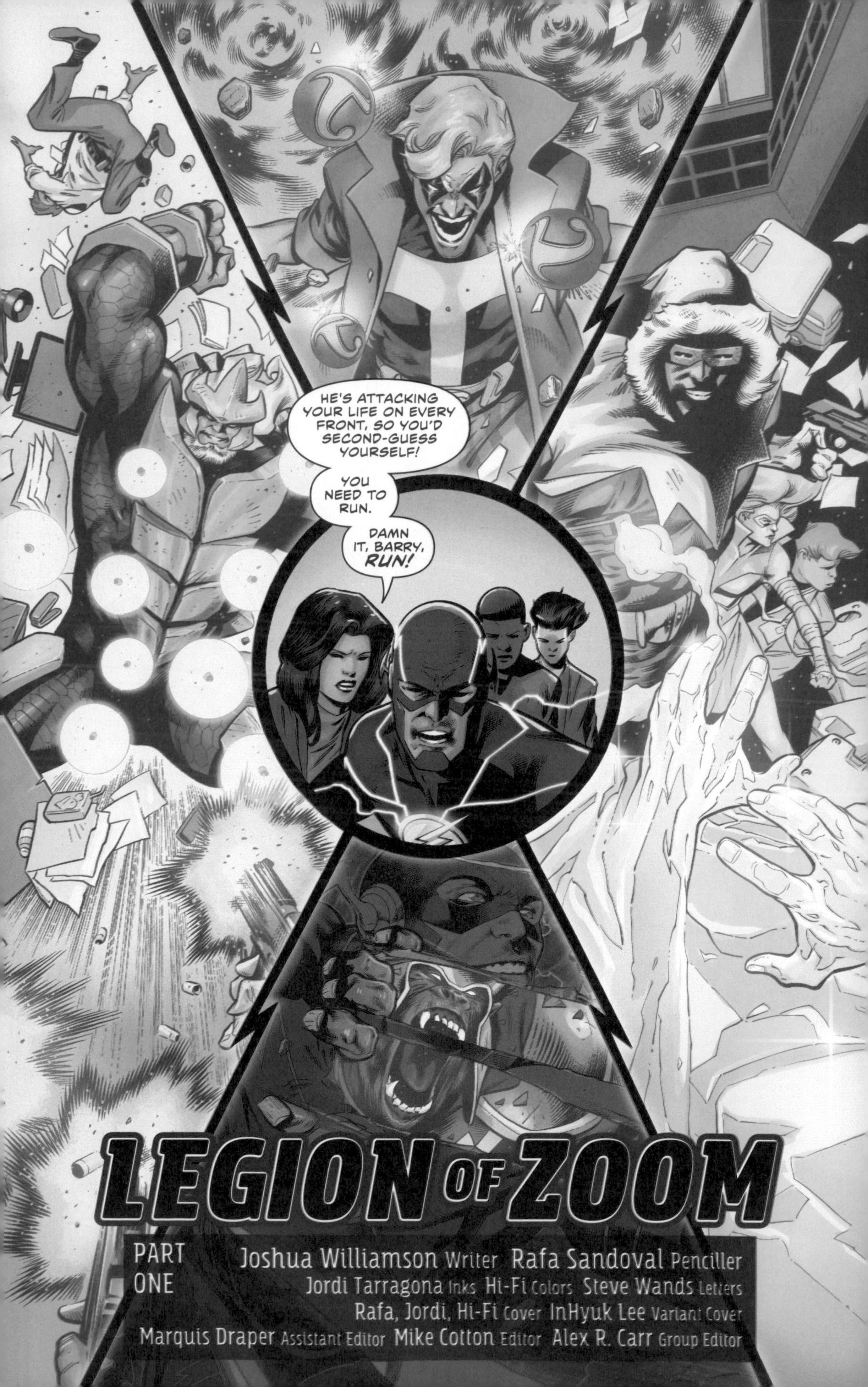

HE'S ATTACKING YOUR LIFE ON EVERY FRONT, SO YOU'D SECOND-GUESS YOURSELF!
YOU NEED TO RUN.
DAMN IT, BARRY, RUN!
LEGION OF ZOOM
PART ONE
Joshua Williamson Writer Rafa Sandoval Penciller
Jordi Tarragona Inks Hi-Fi Colors Steve Wands Letters
Rafa, Jordi, Hi-Fi Cover InHyuk Lee Variant Cover
Marquis Draper Assistant Editor Mike Cotton Editor Alex R. Carr Group Editor

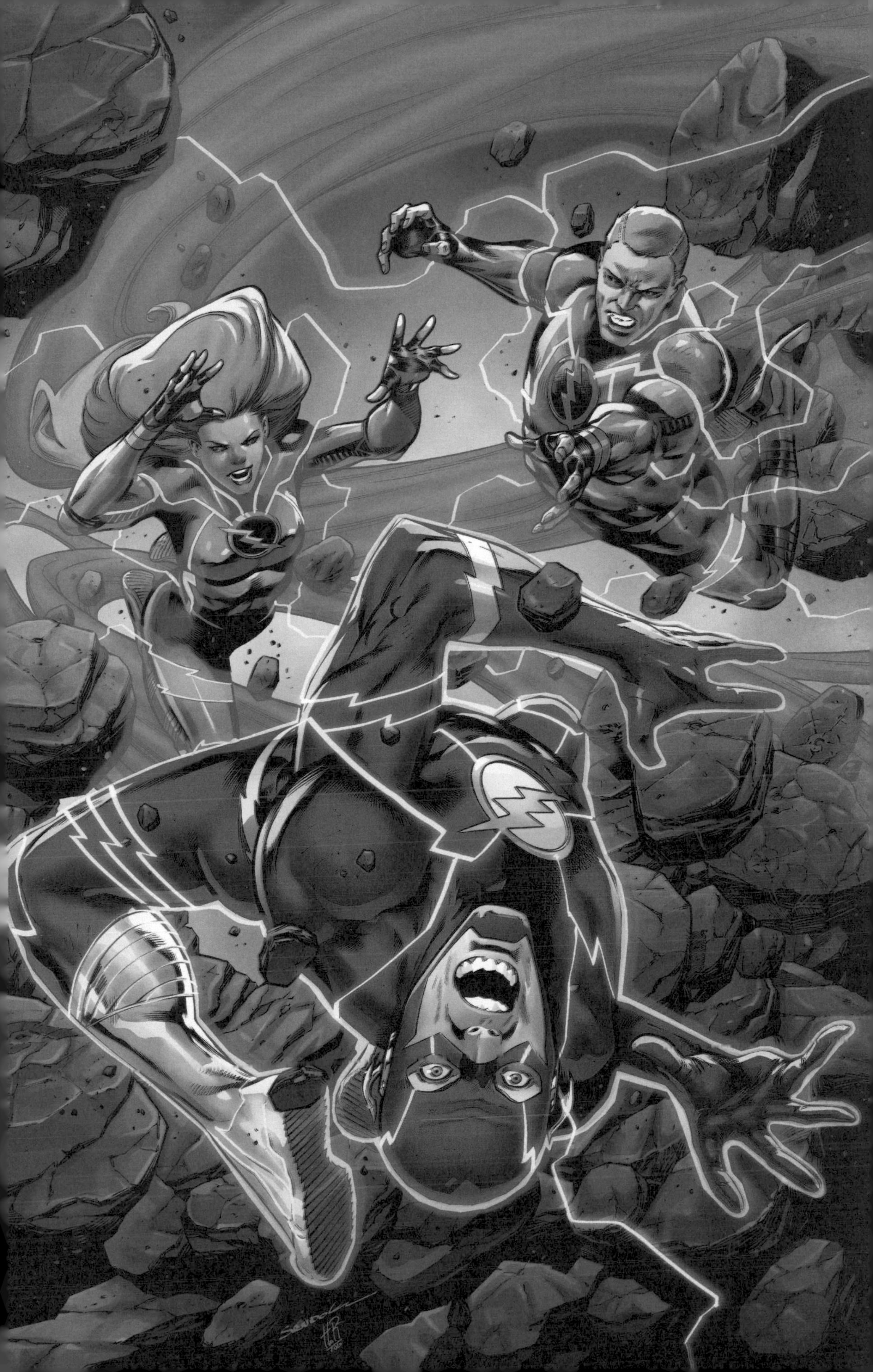

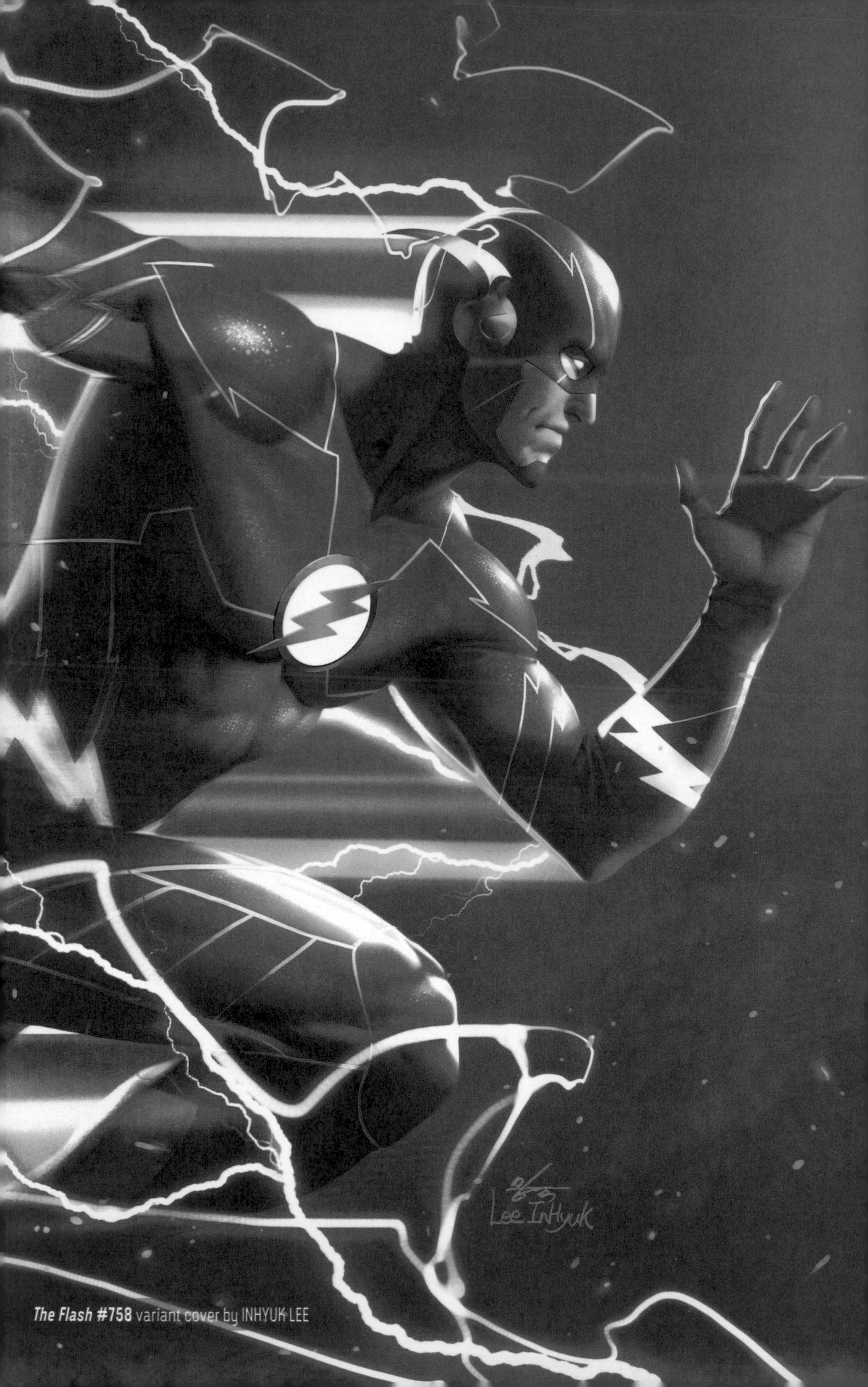
Lee InHyuk

***The Flash* #758** variant cover by INHYUK LEE

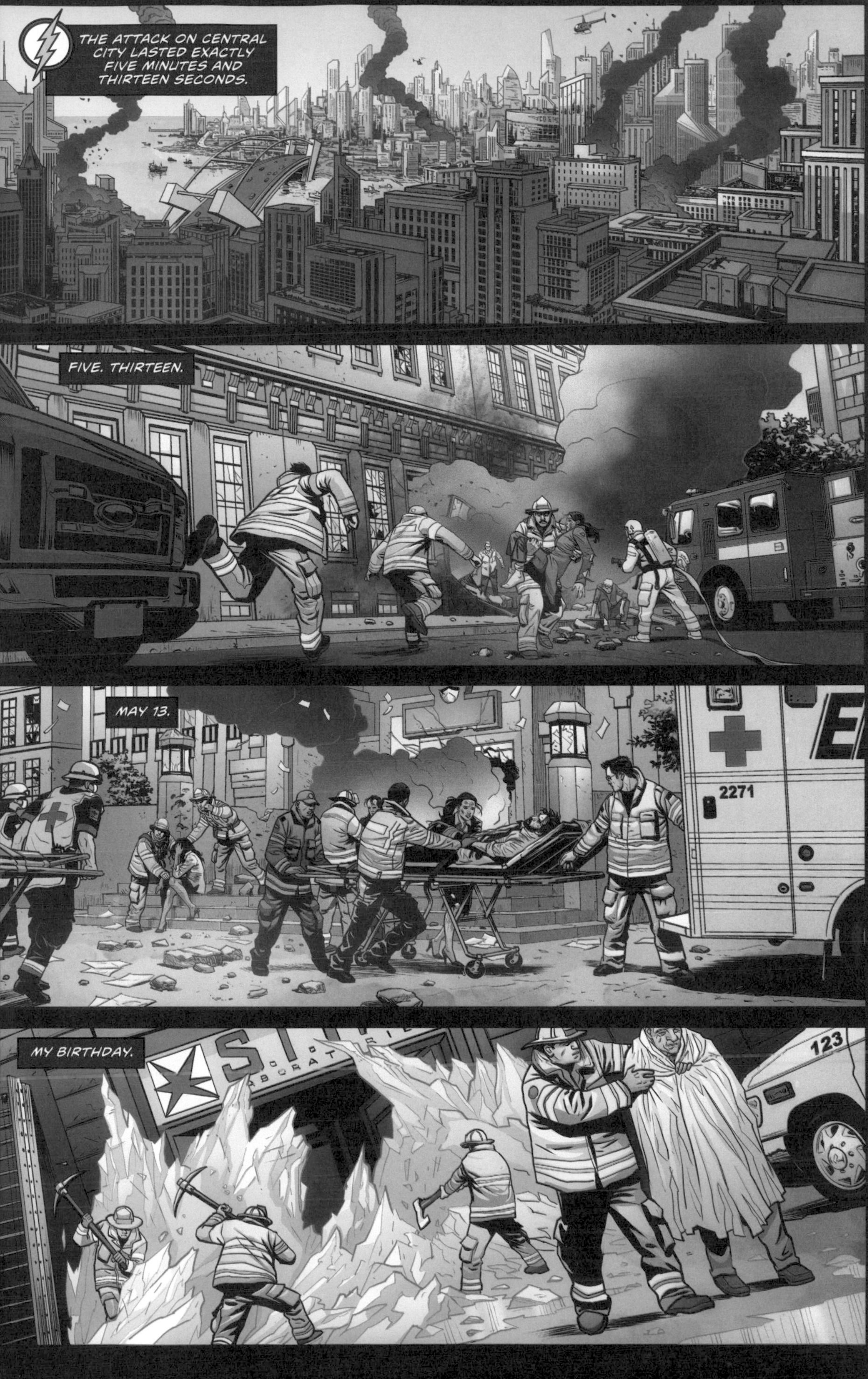
THE ATTACK ON CENTRAL CITY LASTED EXACTLY FIVE MINUTES AND THIRTEEN SECONDS.
FIVE. THIRTEEN.
MAY 13.
2271
MY BIRTHDAY.
123

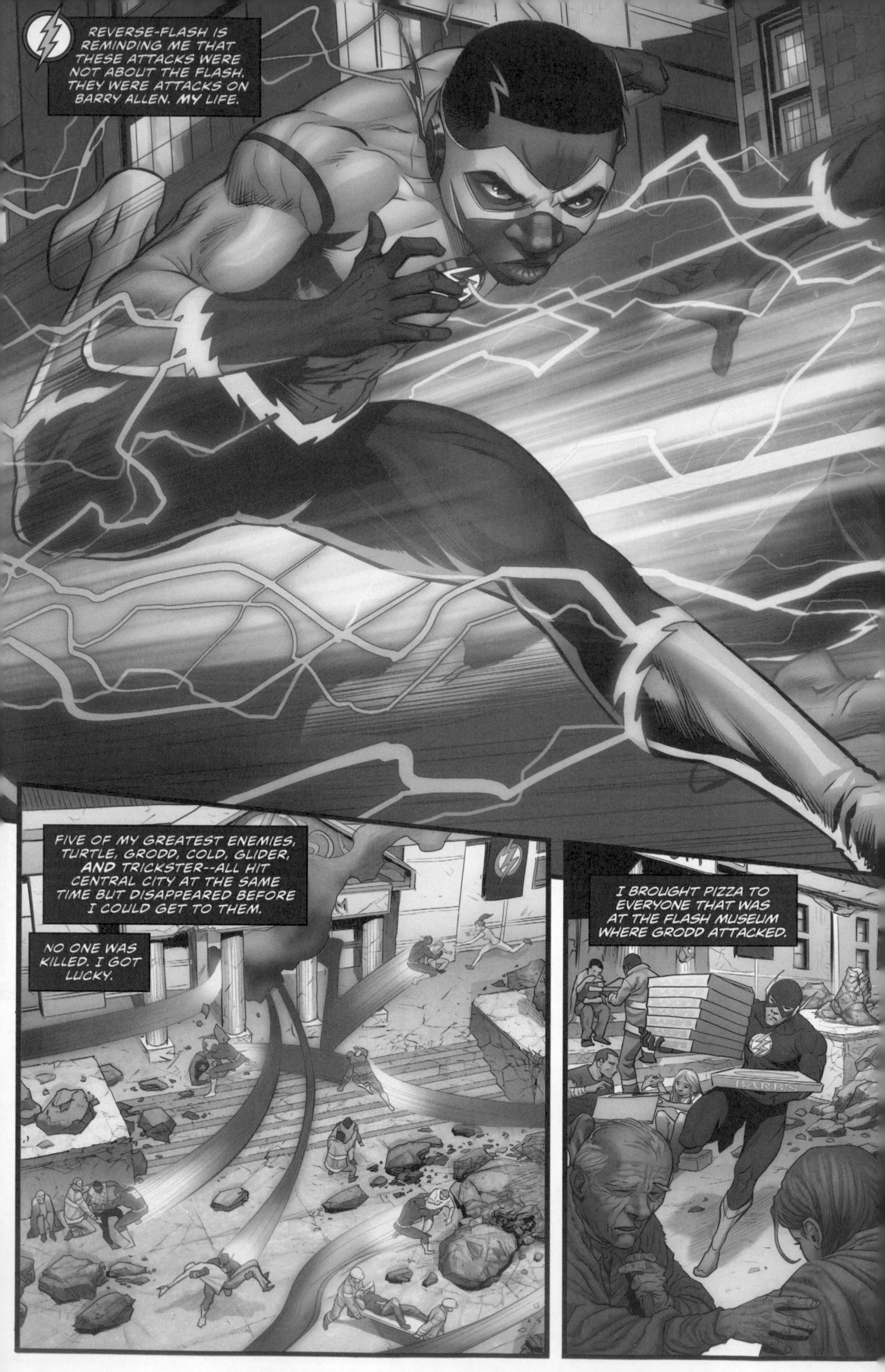
REVERSE-FLASH IS REMINDING ME THAT THESE ATTACKS WERE NOT ABOUT THE FLASH. THEY WERE ATTACKS ON BARRY ALLEN. MY LIFE.
FIVE OF MY GREATEST ENEMIES, TURTLE, GRODD, COLD, GLIDER, AND TRICKSTER--ALL HIT CENTRAL CITY AT THE SAME TIME BUT DISAPPEARED BEFORE I COULD GET TO THEM.
NO ONE WAS KILLED. I GOT LUCKY.
I BROUGHT PIZZA TO EVERYONE THAT WAS AT THE FLASH MUSEUM WHERE GRODD ATTACKED.
BARB'S

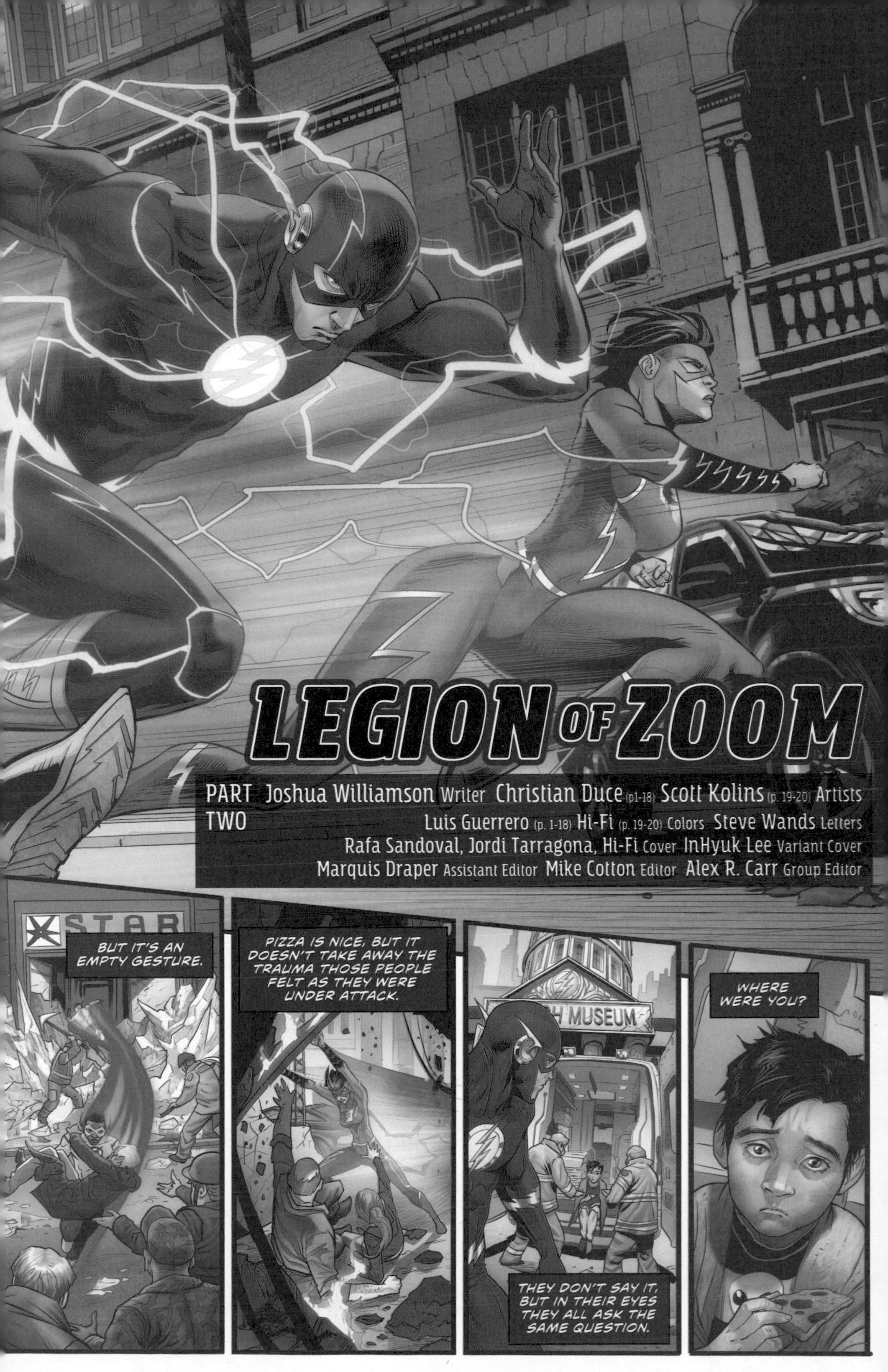
LEGION OF ZOOM
PART TWO
Joshua Williamson Writer Christian Duce (p1-18) Scott Kolins (p. 19-20) Artists
Luis Guerrero (p. 1-18) Hi-Fi (p. 19-20) Colors Steve Wands Letters
Rafa Sandoval, Jordi Tarragona, Hi-Fi Cover InHyuk Lee Variant Cover
Marquis Draper Assistant Editor Mike Cotton Editor Alex R. Carr Group Editor
STAR
BUT IT'S AN EMPTY GESTURE.
PIZZA IS NICE, BUT IT DOESN'T TAKE AWAY THE TRAUMA THOSE PEOPLE FELT AS THEY WERE UNDER ATTACK.
THEY DON'T SAY IT, BUT IN THEIR EYES THEY ALL ASK THE SAME QUESTION.
WHERE WERE YOU?

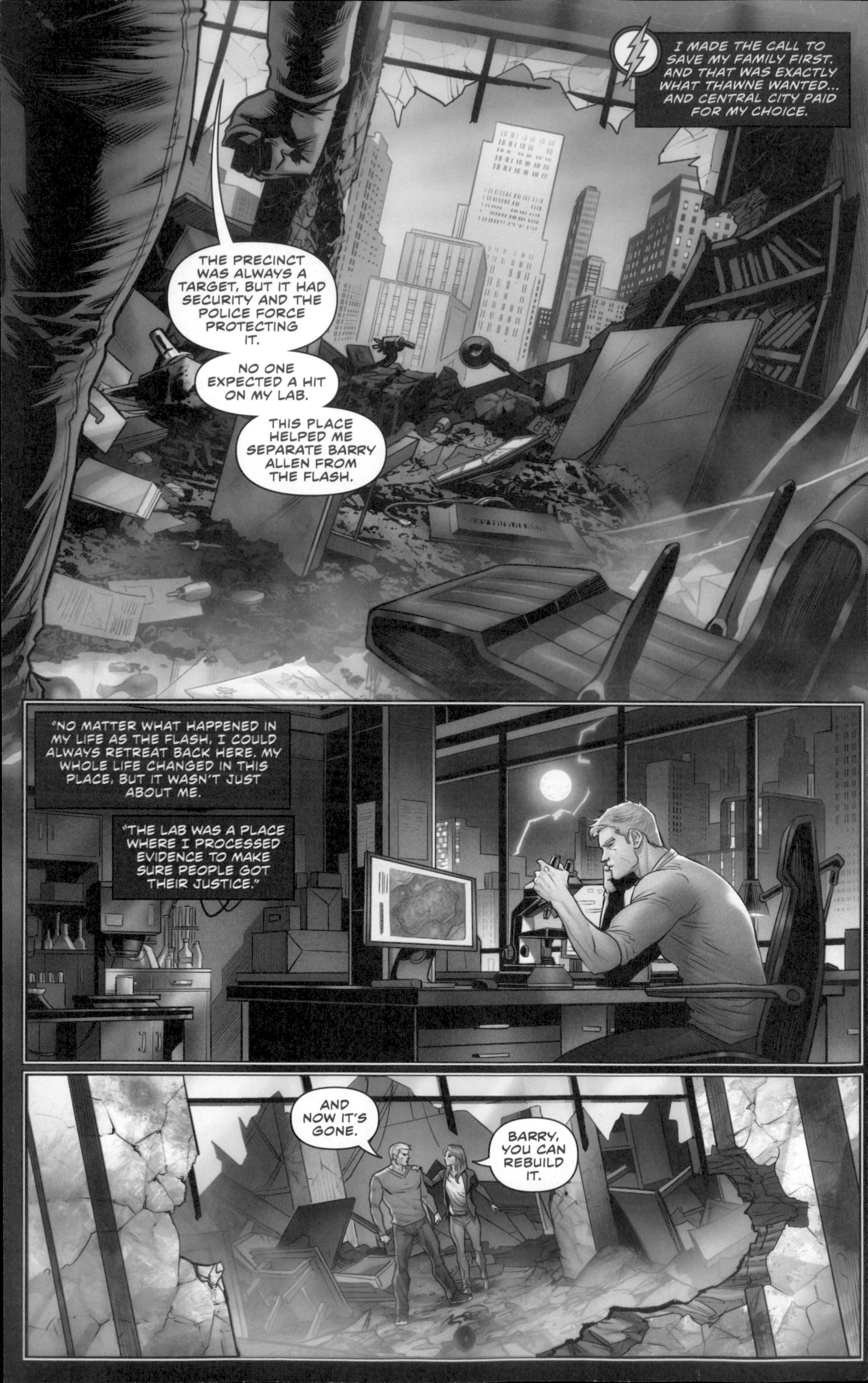
I MADE THE CALL TO SAVE MY FAMILY FIRST. AND THAT WAS EXACTLY WHAT THAWNE WANTED... AND CENTRAL CITY PAID FOR MY CHOICE.
THE PRECINCT WAS ALWAYS A TARGET, BUT IT HAD SECURITY AND THE POLICE FORCE PROTECTING IT.
NO ONE EXPECTED A HIT ON MY LAB.
THIS PLACE HELPED ME SEPARATE BARRY ALLEN FROM THE FLASH.
"NO MATTER WHAT HAPPENED IN MY LIFE AS THE FLASH, I COULD ALWAYS RETREAT BACK HERE. MY WHOLE LIFE CHANGED IN THIS PLACE, BUT IT WASN'T JUST ABOUT ME.
"THE LAB WAS A PLACE WHERE I PROCESSED EVIDENCE TO MAKE SURE PEOPLE GOT THEIR JUSTICE."
AND NOW IT'S GONE.
BARRY, YOU CAN REBUILD IT.

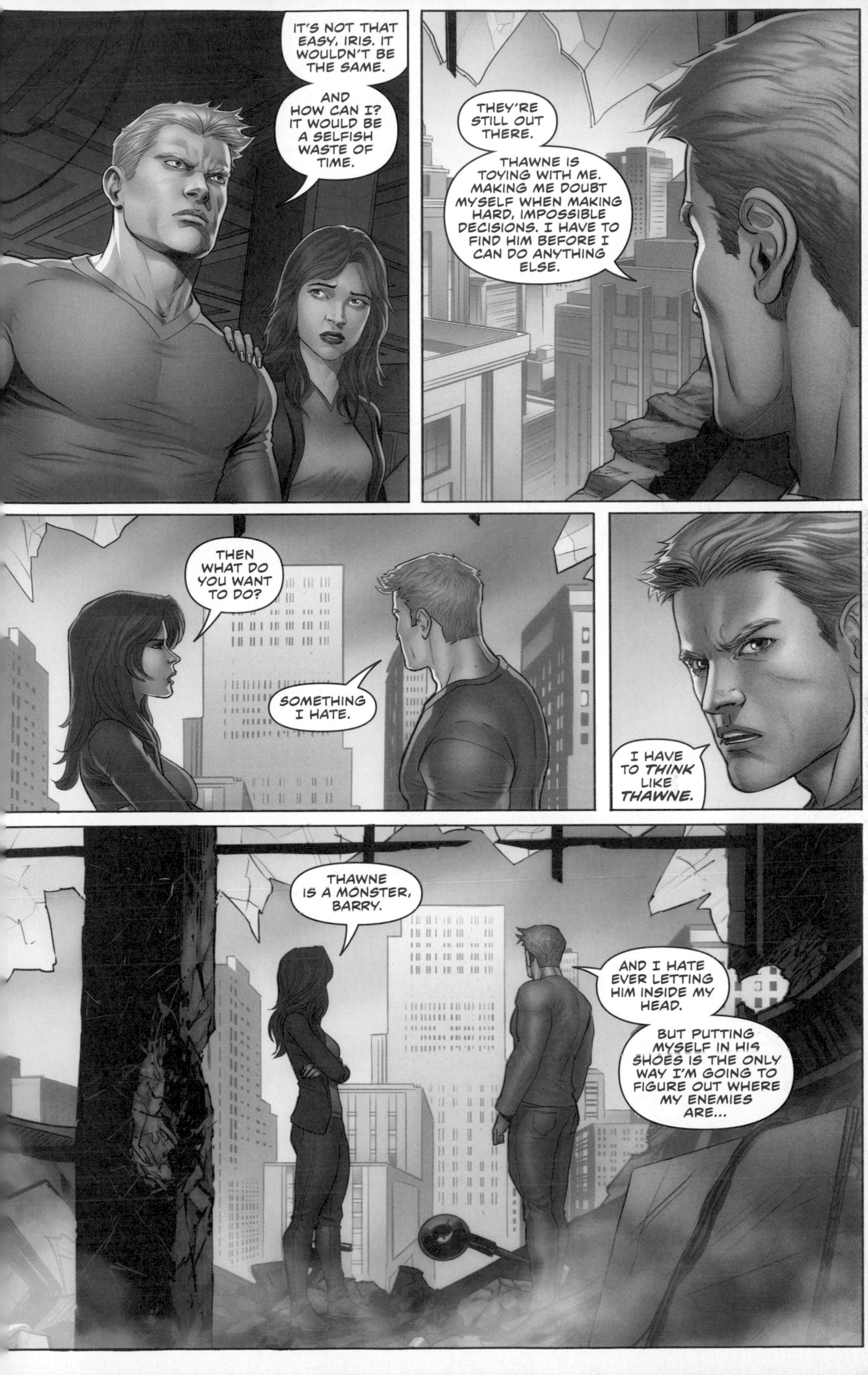
IT'S NOT THAT EASY, IRIS. IT WOULDN'T BE THE SAME.
AND HOW CAN I? IT WOULD BE A SELFISH WASTE OF TIME.
THEY'RE STILL OUT THERE.
THAWNE IS TOYING WITH ME. MAKING ME DOUBT MYSELF WHEN MAKING HARD, IMPOSSIBLE DECISIONS. I HAVE TO FIND HIM BEFORE I CAN DO ANYTHING ELSE.
THEN WHAT DO YOU WANT TO DO?
SOMETHING I HATE.
I HAVE TO THINK LIKE THAWNE.
THAWNE IS A MONSTER, BARRY.
AND I HATE EVER LETTING HIM INSIDE MY HEAD.
BUT PUTTING MYSELF IN HIS SHOES IS THE ONLY WAY I'M GOING TO FIGURE OUT WHERE MY ENEMIES ARE...

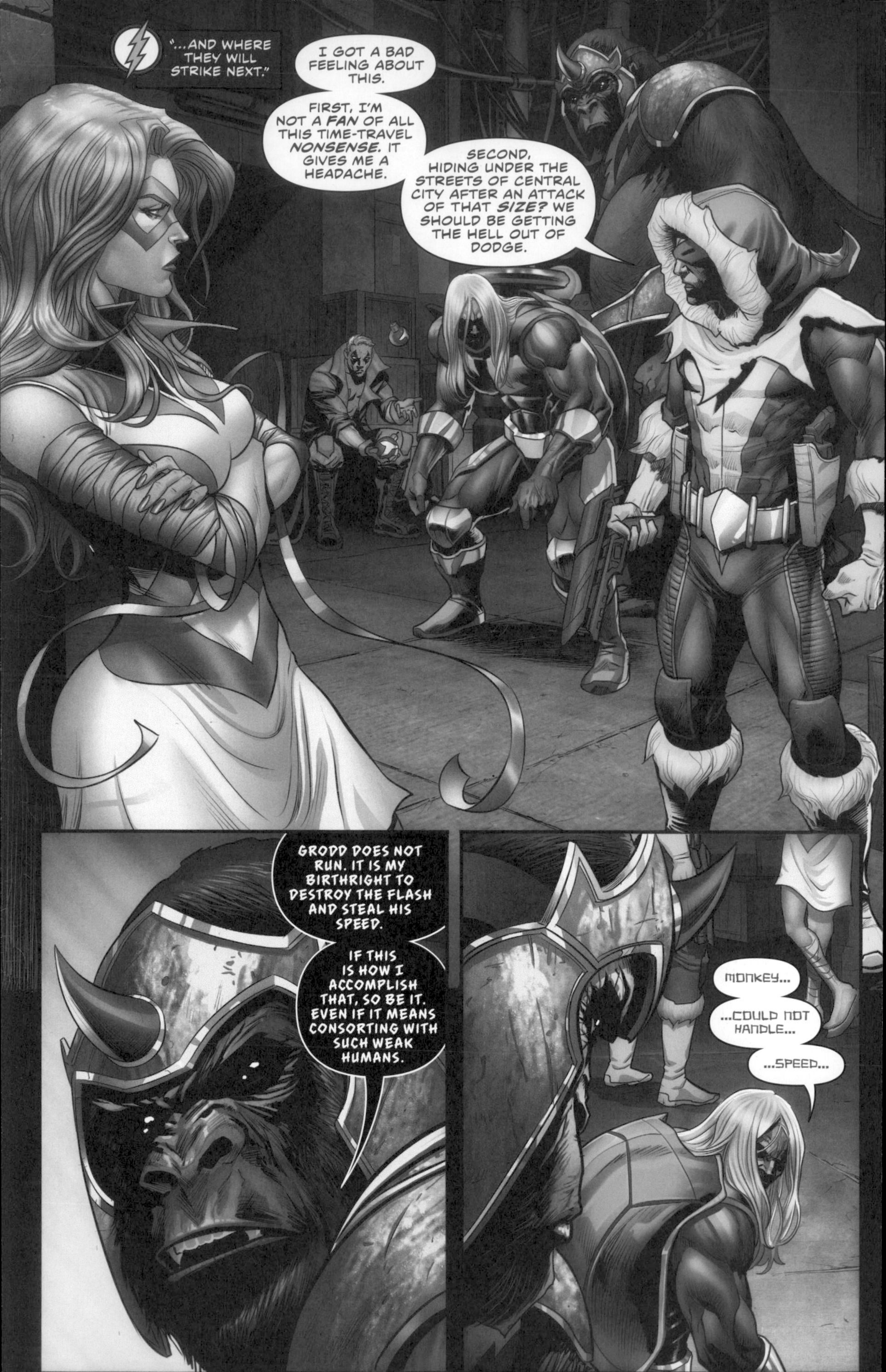
"...AND WHERE THEY WILL STRIKE NEXT."
I GOT A BAD FEELING ABOUT THIS.
FIRST, I'M NOT A FAN OF ALL THIS TIME-TRAVEL NONSENSE. IT GIVES ME A HEADACHE.
SECOND, HIDING UNDER THE STREETS OF CENTRAL CITY AFTER AN ATTACK OF THAT SIZE? WE SHOULD BE GETTING THE HELL OUT OF DODGE.
GRODD DOES NOT RUN. IT IS MY BIRTHRIGHT TO DESTROY THE FLASH AND STEAL HIS SPEED.
IF THIS IS HOW I ACCOMPLISH THAT, SO BE IT. EVEN IF IT MEANS CONSORTING WITH SUCH WEAK HUMANS.
MONKEY...
...COULD NOT HANDLE...
...SPEED...

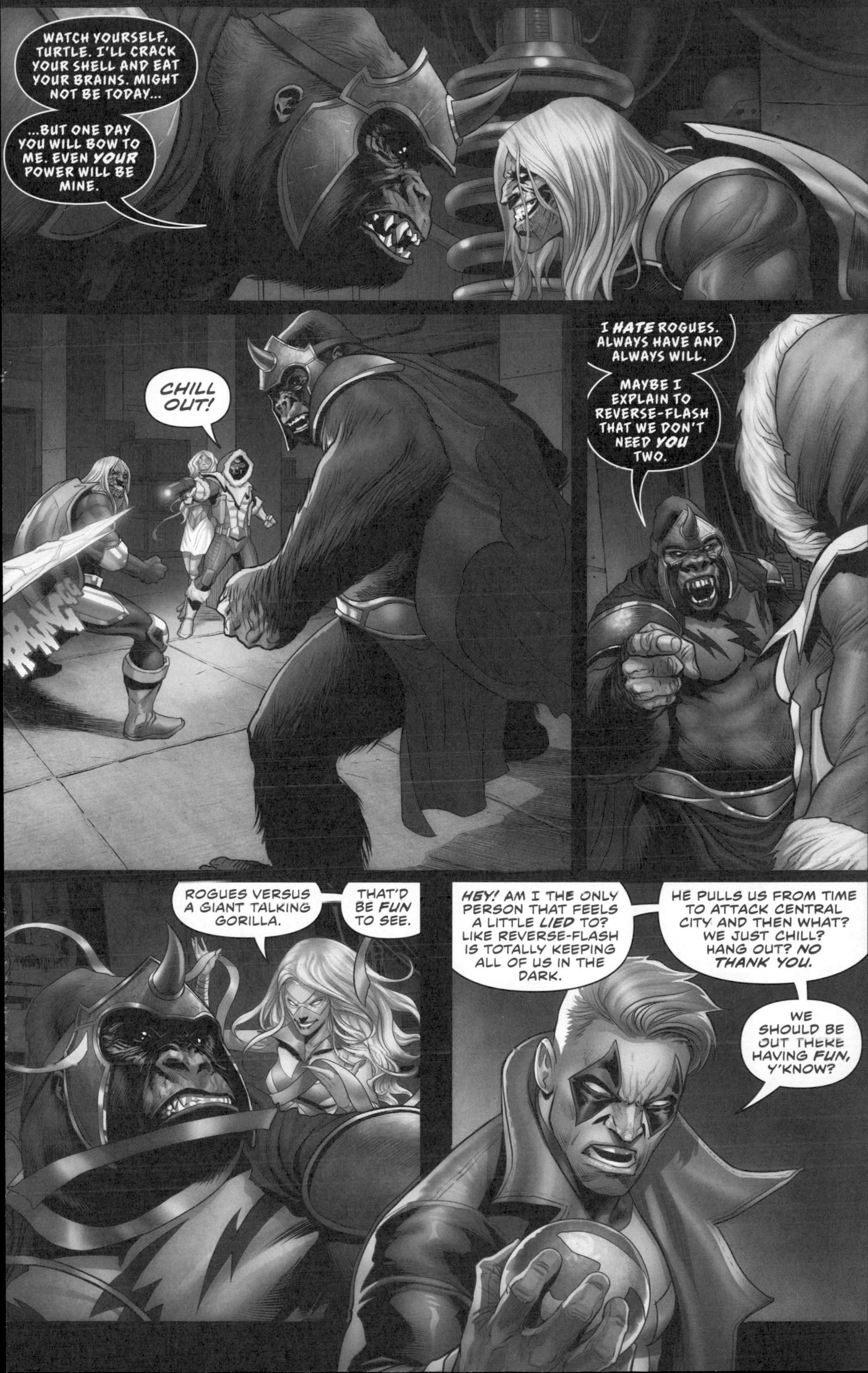
WATCH YOURSELF, TURTLE. I'LL CRACK YOUR SHELL AND EAT YOUR BRAINS. MIGHT NOT BE TODAY...
...BUT ONE DAY YOU WILL BOW TO ME. EVEN *YOUR* POWER WILL BE MINE.
CHILL OUT!
I *HATE* ROGUES. ALWAYS HAVE AND ALWAYS WILL.
MAYBE I EXPLAIN TO REVERSE-FLASH THAT WE DON'T NEED *YOU* TWO.
ROGUES VERSUS A GIANT TALKING GORILLA.
THAT'D BE *FUN* TO SEE.
HEY! AM I THE ONLY PERSON THAT FEELS A LITTLE *LIED* TO? LIKE REVERSE-FLASH IS TOTALLY KEEPING ALL OF US IN THE DARK.
HE PULLS US FROM TIME TO ATTACK CENTRAL CITY AND THEN WHAT? WE JUST CHILL? HANG OUT? *NO THANK YOU.*
WE SHOULD BE OUT THERE HAVING *FUN*, Y'KNOW?

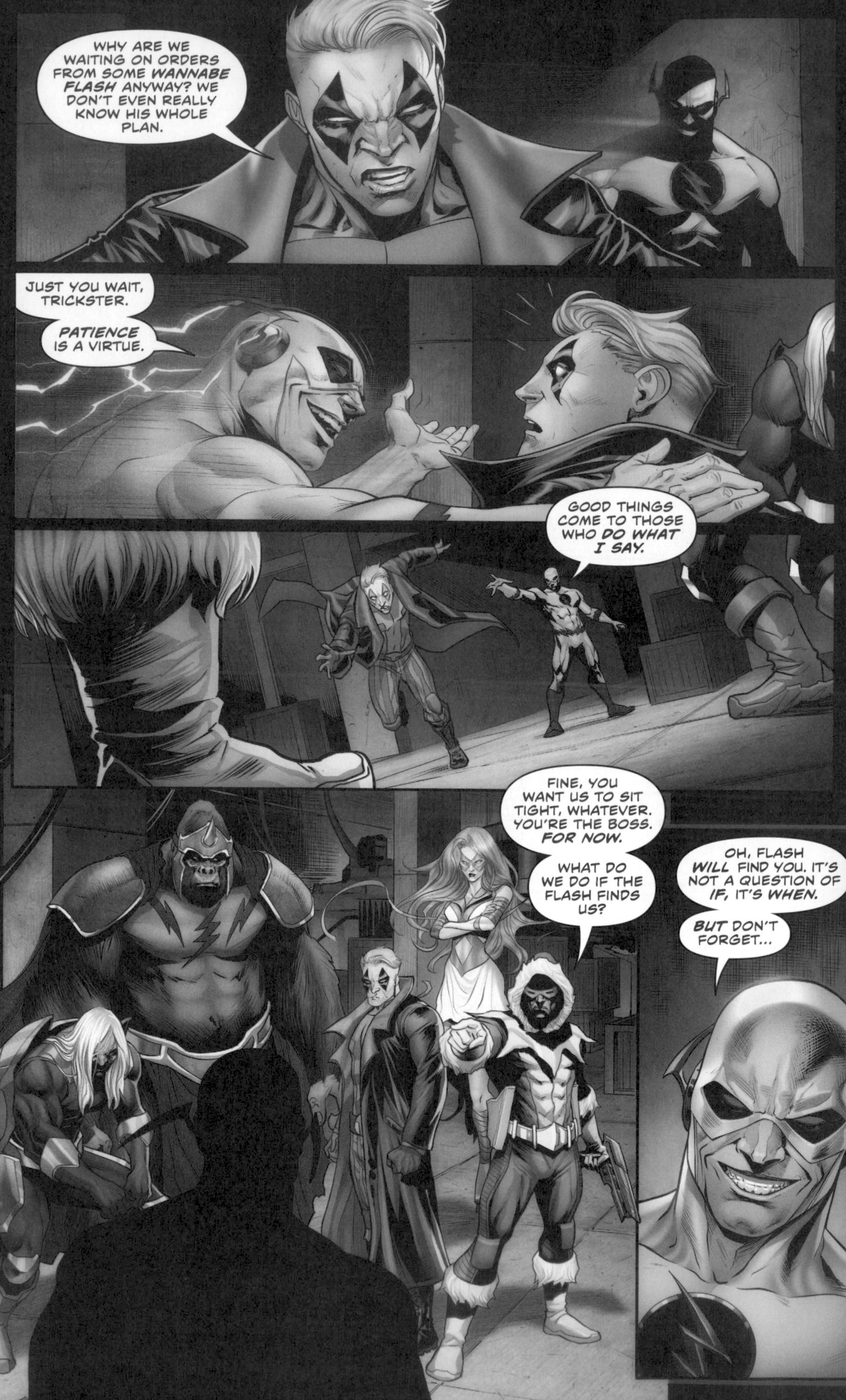
WHY ARE WE WAITING ON ORDERS FROM SOME *WANNABE FLASH* ANYWAY? WE DON'T EVEN REALLY KNOW HIS WHOLE PLAN.
JUST YOU WAIT, TRICKSTER.
PATIENCE IS A VIRTUE.
GOOD THINGS COME TO THOSE WHO *DO WHAT I SAY.*
FINE, YOU WANT US TO SIT TIGHT, WHATEVER. YOU'RE THE BOSS. *FOR NOW.*
WHAT DO WE DO IF THE FLASH FINDS US?
OH, FLASH *WILL* FIND YOU. IT'S NOT A QUESTION OF *IF*, IT'S *WHEN.*
BUT DON'T FORGET...

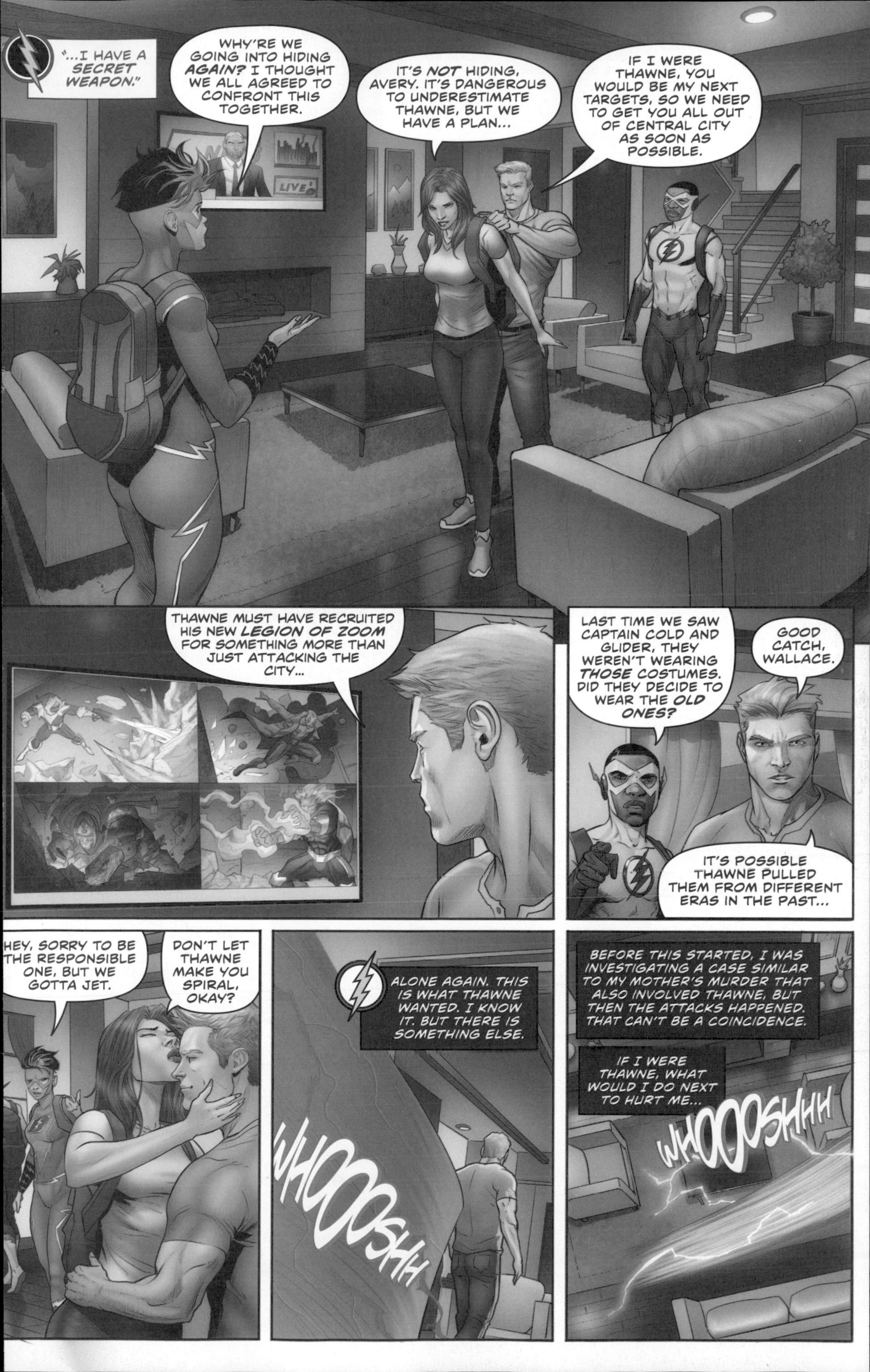
"...I HAVE A SECRET WEAPON."
WHY'RE WE GOING INTO HIDING AGAIN? I THOUGHT WE ALL AGREED TO CONFRONT THIS TOGETHER.
IT'S NOT HIDING, AVERY. IT'S DANGEROUS TO UNDERESTIMATE THAWNE, BUT WE HAVE A PLAN...
IF I WERE THAWNE, YOU WOULD BE MY NEXT TARGETS, SO WE NEED TO GET YOU ALL OUT OF CENTRAL CITY AS SOON AS POSSIBLE.
LIVE!
THAWNE MUST HAVE RECRUITED HIS NEW LEGION OF ZOOM FOR SOMETHING MORE THAN JUST ATTACKING THE CITY...
LAST TIME WE SAW CAPTAIN COLD AND GLIDER, THEY WEREN'T WEARING THOSE COSTUMES. DID THEY DECIDE TO WEAR THE OLD ONES?
GOOD CATCH, WALLACE.
IT'S POSSIBLE THAWNE PULLED THEM FROM DIFFERENT ERAS IN THE PAST...
HEY, SORRY TO BE THE RESPONSIBLE ONE, BUT WE GOTTA JET.
DON'T LET THAWNE MAKE YOU SPIRAL, OKAY?
WHOOOSHH
ALONE AGAIN. THIS IS WHAT THAWNE WANTED. I KNOW IT. BUT THERE IS SOMETHING ELSE.
BEFORE THIS STARTED, I WAS INVESTIGATING A CASE SIMILAR TO MY MOTHER'S MURDER THAT ALSO INVOLVED THAWNE, BUT THEN THE ATTACKS HAPPENED. THAT CAN'T BE A COINCIDENCE.
IF I WERE THAWNE, WHAT WOULD I DO NEXT TO HURT ME...
WHOOOSHHH

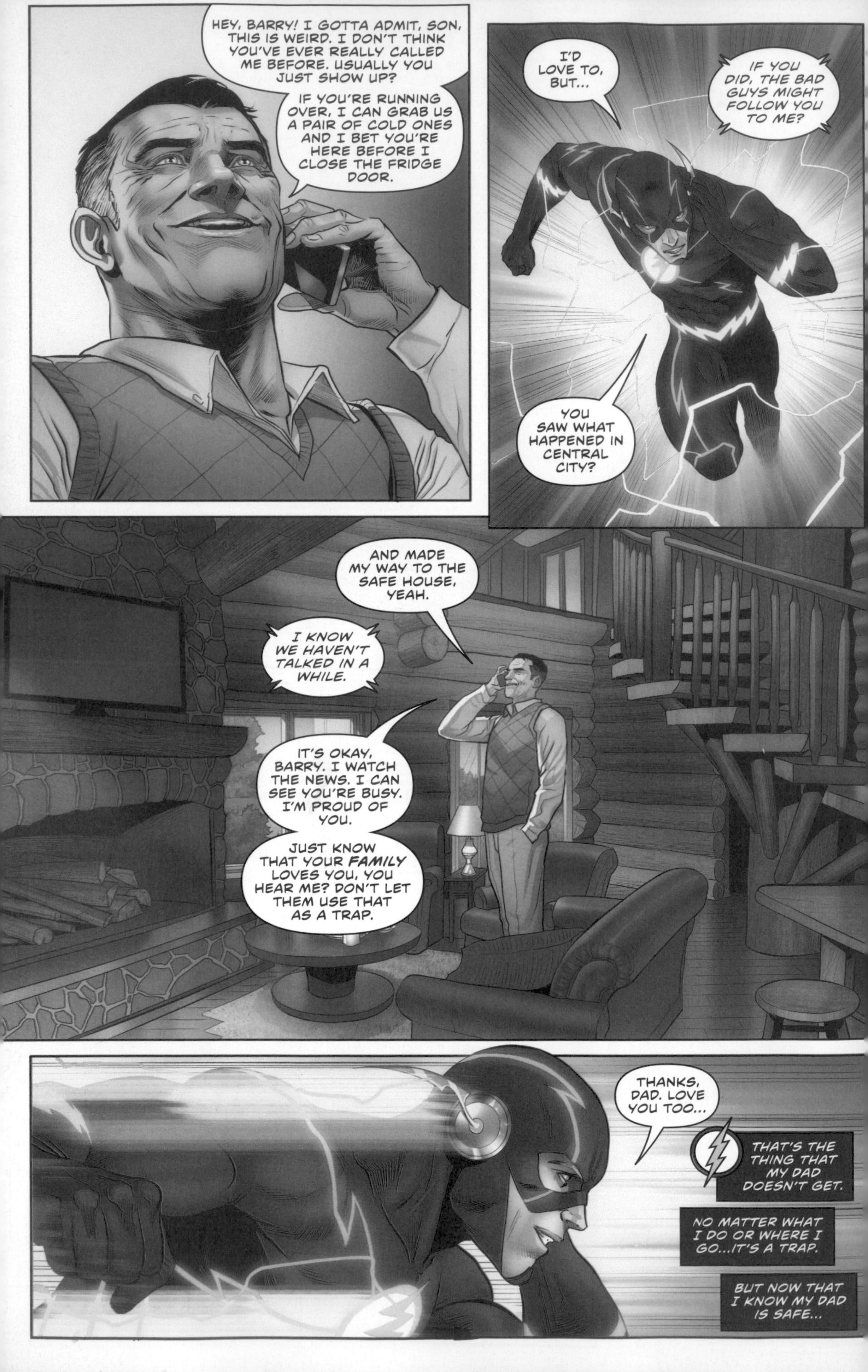
HEY, BARRY! I GOTTA ADMIT, SON, THIS IS WEIRD. I DON'T THINK YOU'VE EVER REALLY CALLED ME BEFORE. USUALLY YOU JUST SHOW UP?
IF YOU'RE RUNNING OVER, I CAN GRAB US A PAIR OF COLD ONES AND I BET YOU'RE HERE BEFORE I CLOSE THE FRIDGE DOOR.
I'D LOVE TO, BUT...
IF YOU DID, THE BAD GUYS MIGHT FOLLOW YOU TO ME?
YOU SAW WHAT HAPPENED IN CENTRAL CITY?
AND MADE MY WAY TO THE SAFE HOUSE, YEAH.
I KNOW WE HAVEN'T TALKED IN A WHILE.
IT'S OKAY, BARRY. I WATCH THE NEWS. I CAN SEE YOU'RE BUSY. I'M PROUD OF YOU.
JUST KNOW THAT YOUR FAMILY LOVES YOU, YOU HEAR ME? DON'T LET THEM USE THAT AS A TRAP.
THANKS, DAD. LOVE YOU TOO...
THAT'S THE THING THAT MY DAD DOESN'T GET.
NO MATTER WHAT I DO OR WHERE I GO...IT'S A TRAP.
BUT NOW THAT I KNOW MY DAD IS SAFE...

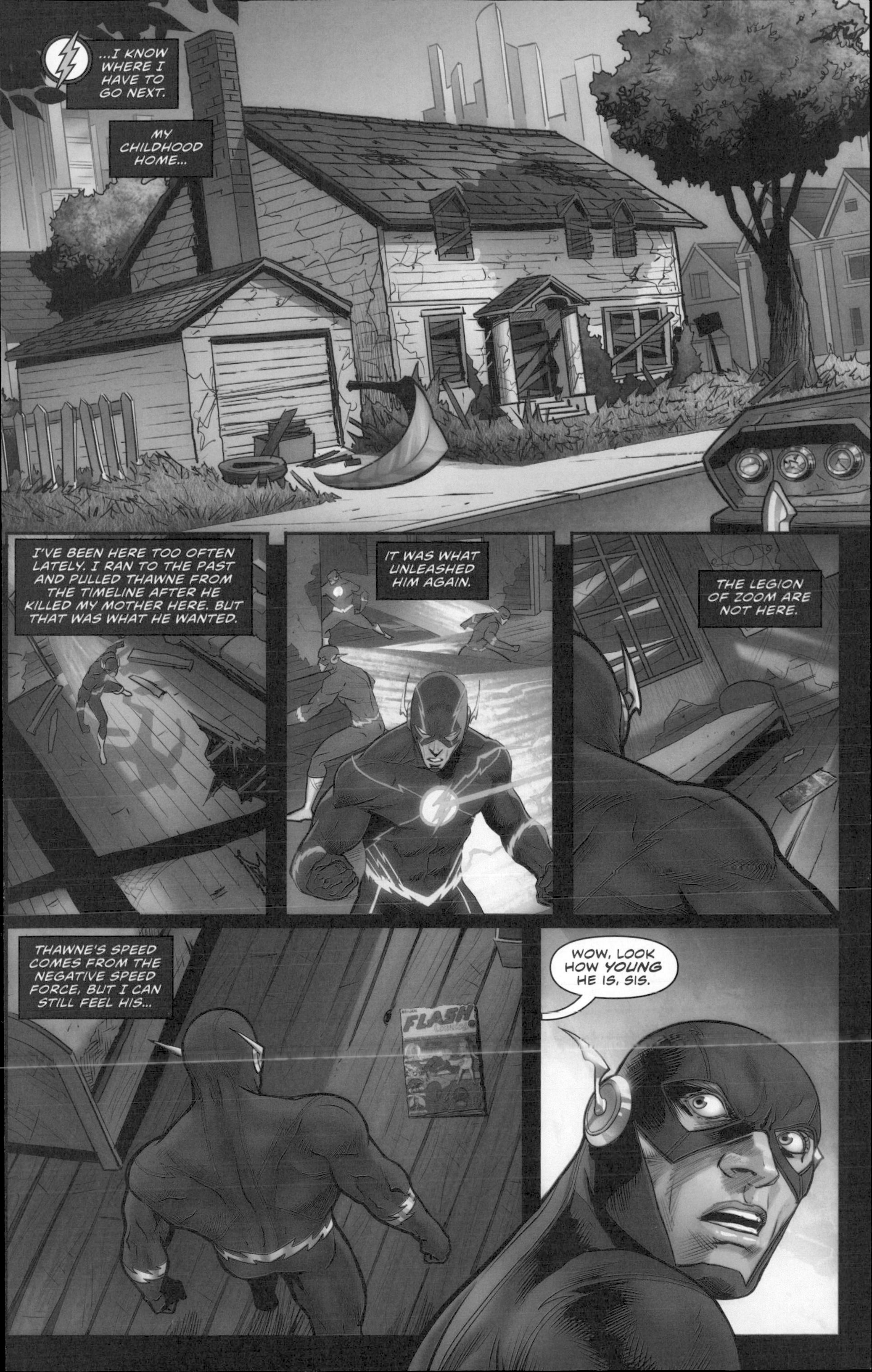
...I KNOW WHERE I HAVE TO GO NEXT.
MY CHILDHOOD HOME...
I'VE BEEN HERE TOO OFTEN LATELY. I RAN TO THE PAST AND PULLED THAWNE FROM THE TIMELINE AFTER HE KILLED MY MOTHER HERE. BUT THAT WAS WHAT HE WANTED.
IT WAS WHAT UNLEASHED HIM AGAIN.
THE LEGION OF ZOOM ARE NOT HERE.
THAWNE'S SPEED COMES FROM THE NEGATIVE SPEED FORCE, BUT I CAN STILL FEEL HIS...
FLASH
WOW, LOOK HOW YOUNG HE IS, SIS.

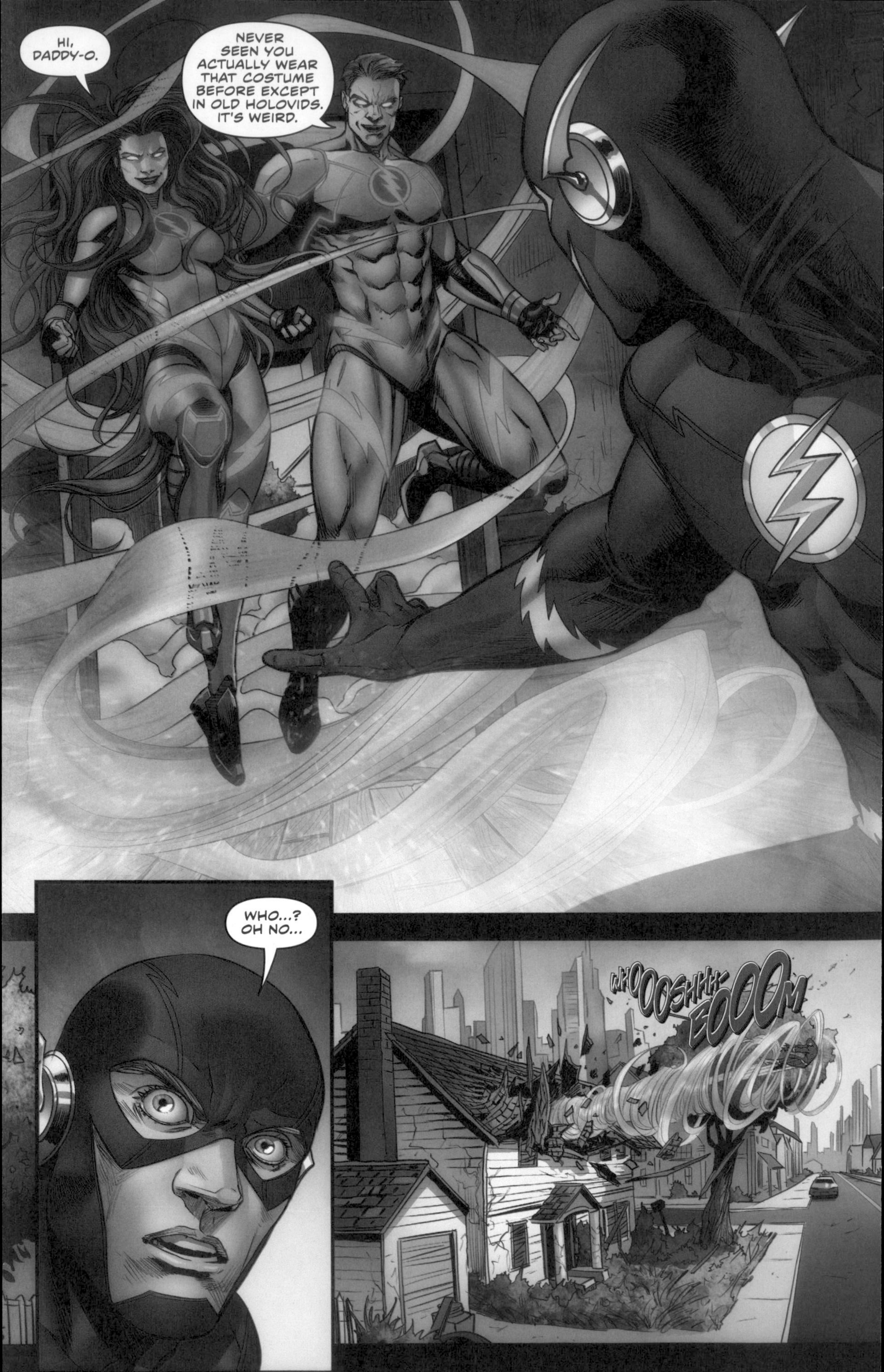
HI, DADDY-O.
NEVER SEEN YOU ACTUALLY WEAR THAT COSTUME BEFORE EXCEPT IN OLD HOLOVIDS. IT'S WEIRD.
WHO...? OH NO...
WHOOOSHHH-BOOOM

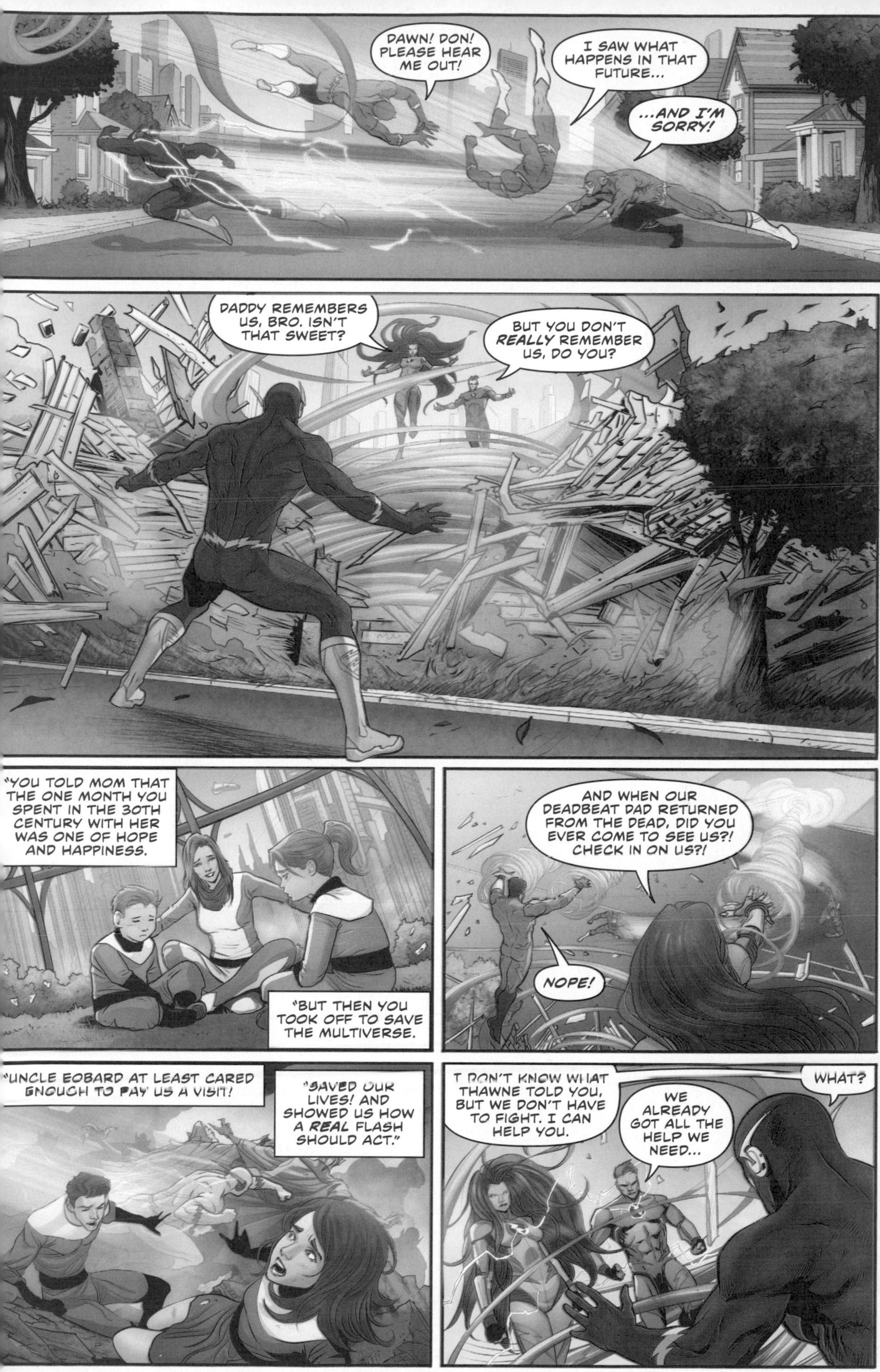
DAWN! DON! PLEASE HEAR ME OUT!
I SAW WHAT HAPPENS IN THAT FUTURE...
...AND I'M SORRY!
DADDY REMEMBERS US, BRO. ISN'T THAT SWEET?
BUT YOU DON'T REALLY REMEMBER US, DO YOU?
"YOU TOLD MOM THAT THE ONE MONTH YOU SPENT IN THE 30TH CENTURY WITH HER WAS ONE OF HOPE AND HAPPINESS.
"BUT THEN YOU TOOK OFF TO SAVE THE MULTIVERSE.
AND WHEN OUR DEADBEAT DAD RETURNED FROM THE DEAD, DID YOU EVER COME TO SEE US?! CHECK IN ON US?!
NOPE!
"UNCLE EOBARD AT LEAST CARED ENOUGH TO PAY US A VISIT!
"SAVED OUR LIVES! AND SHOWED US HOW A REAL FLASH SHOULD ACT."
I DON'T KNOW WHAT THAWNE TOLD YOU, BUT WE DON'T HAVE TO FIGHT. I CAN HELP YOU.
WHAT?
WE ALREADY GOT ALL THE HELP WE NEED...

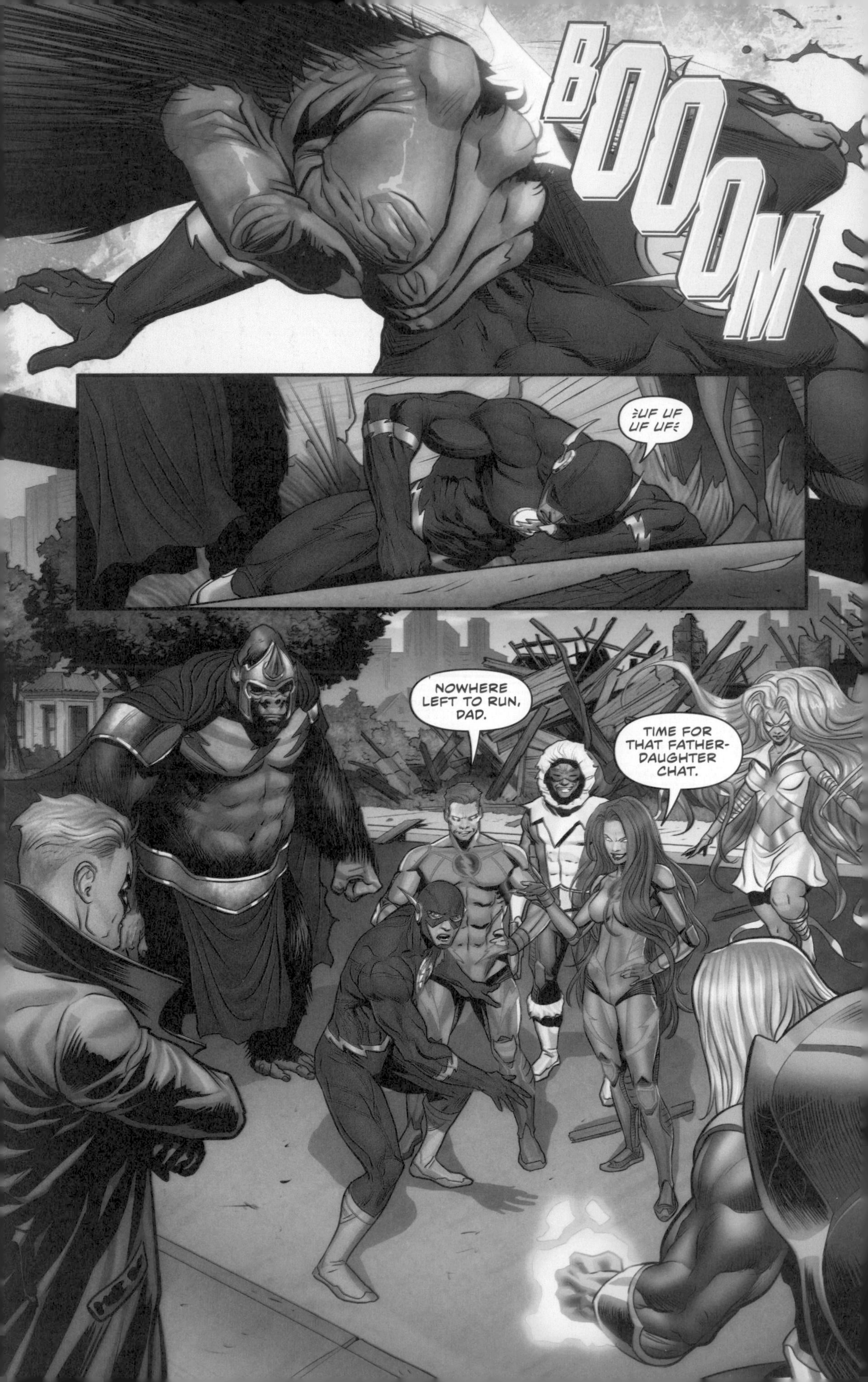
BOOOOM
UF UF UF UF
NOWHERE LEFT TO RUN, DAD.
TIME FOR THAT FATHER-DAUGHTER CHAT.

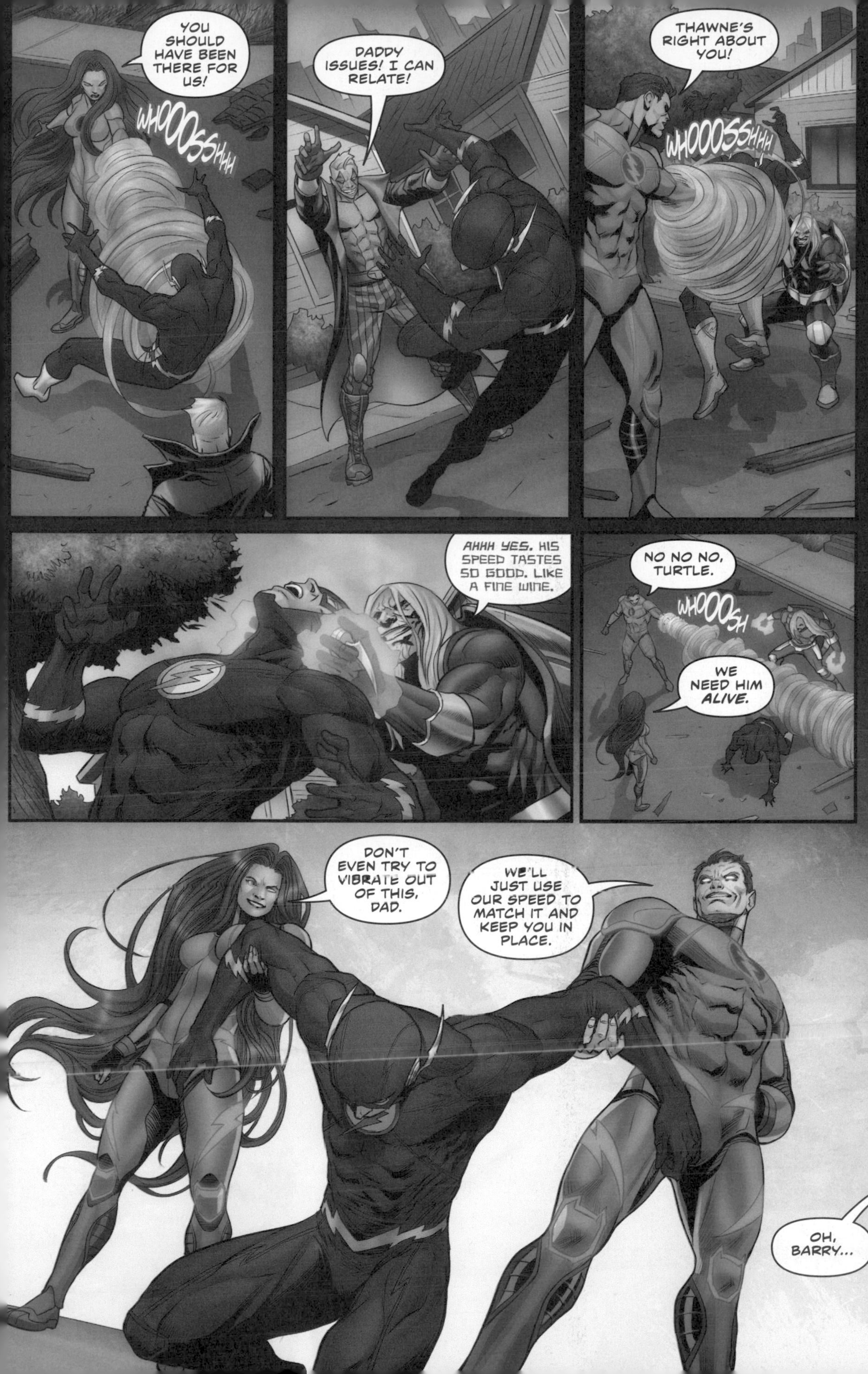

YOU SHOULD HAVE BEEN THERE FOR US!
WHOOOSSHHH
DADDY ISSUES! I CAN RELATE!
THAWNE'S RIGHT ABOUT YOU!
WHOOOSSHHH
AHHH YES. HIS SPEED TASTES SO GOOD. LIKE A FINE WINE.
NO NO NO, TURTLE.
WHOOOSH
WE NEED HIM ALIVE.
DON'T EVEN TRY TO VIBRATE OUT OF THIS, DAD.
WE'LL JUST USE OUR SPEED TO MATCH IT AND KEEP YOU IN PLACE.
OH, BARRY...

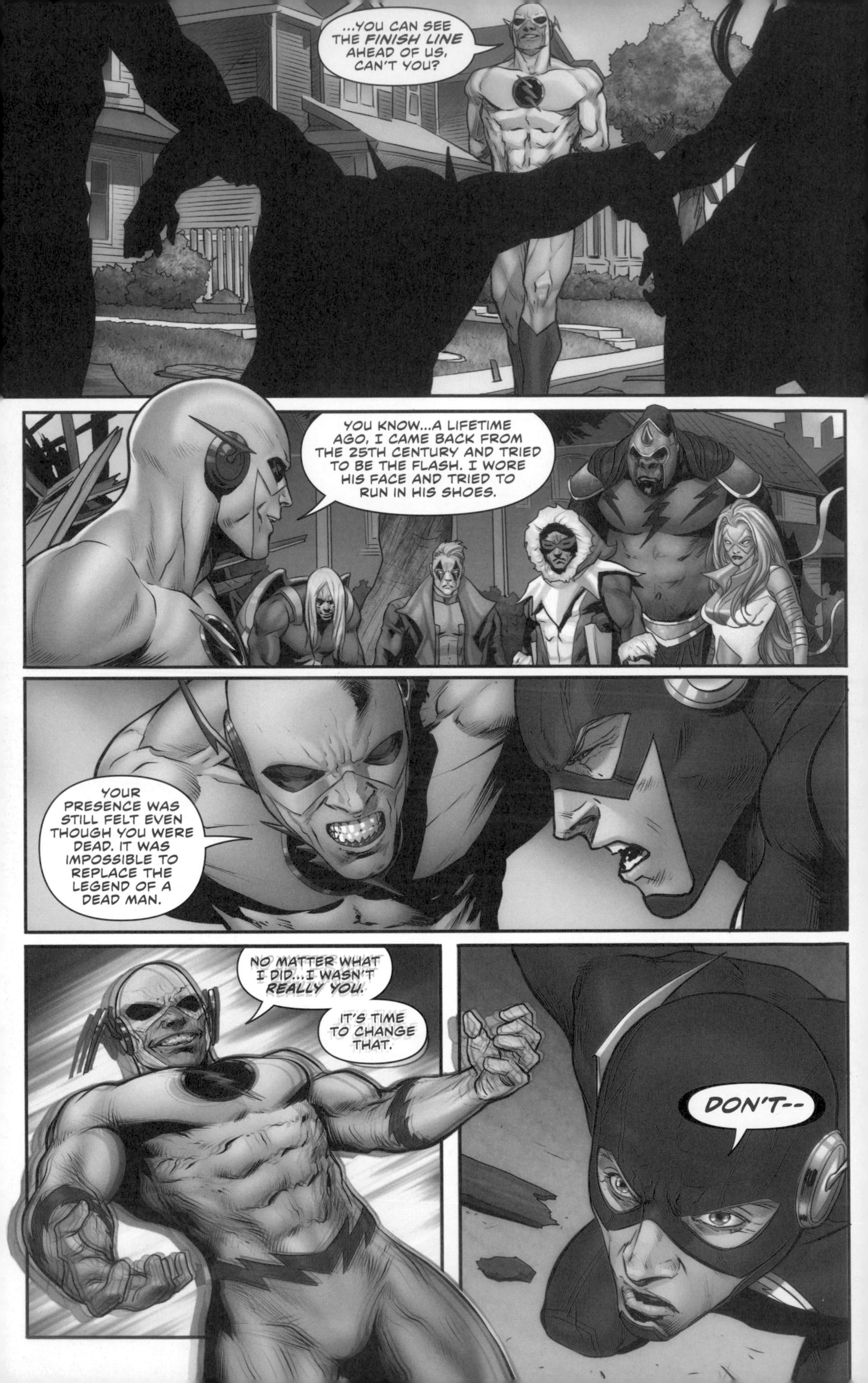
...YOU CAN SEE THE FINISH LINE AHEAD OF US, CAN'T YOU?
YOU KNOW...A LIFETIME AGO, I CAME BACK FROM THE 25TH CENTURY AND TRIED TO BE THE FLASH. I WORE HIS FACE AND TRIED TO RUN IN HIS SHOES.
YOUR PRESENCE WAS STILL FELT EVEN THOUGH YOU WERE DEAD. IT WAS IMPOSSIBLE TO REPLACE THE LEGEND OF A DEAD MAN.
NO MATTER WHAT I DID...I WASN'T REALLY YOU.
IT'S TIME TO CHANGE THAT.
DON'T--

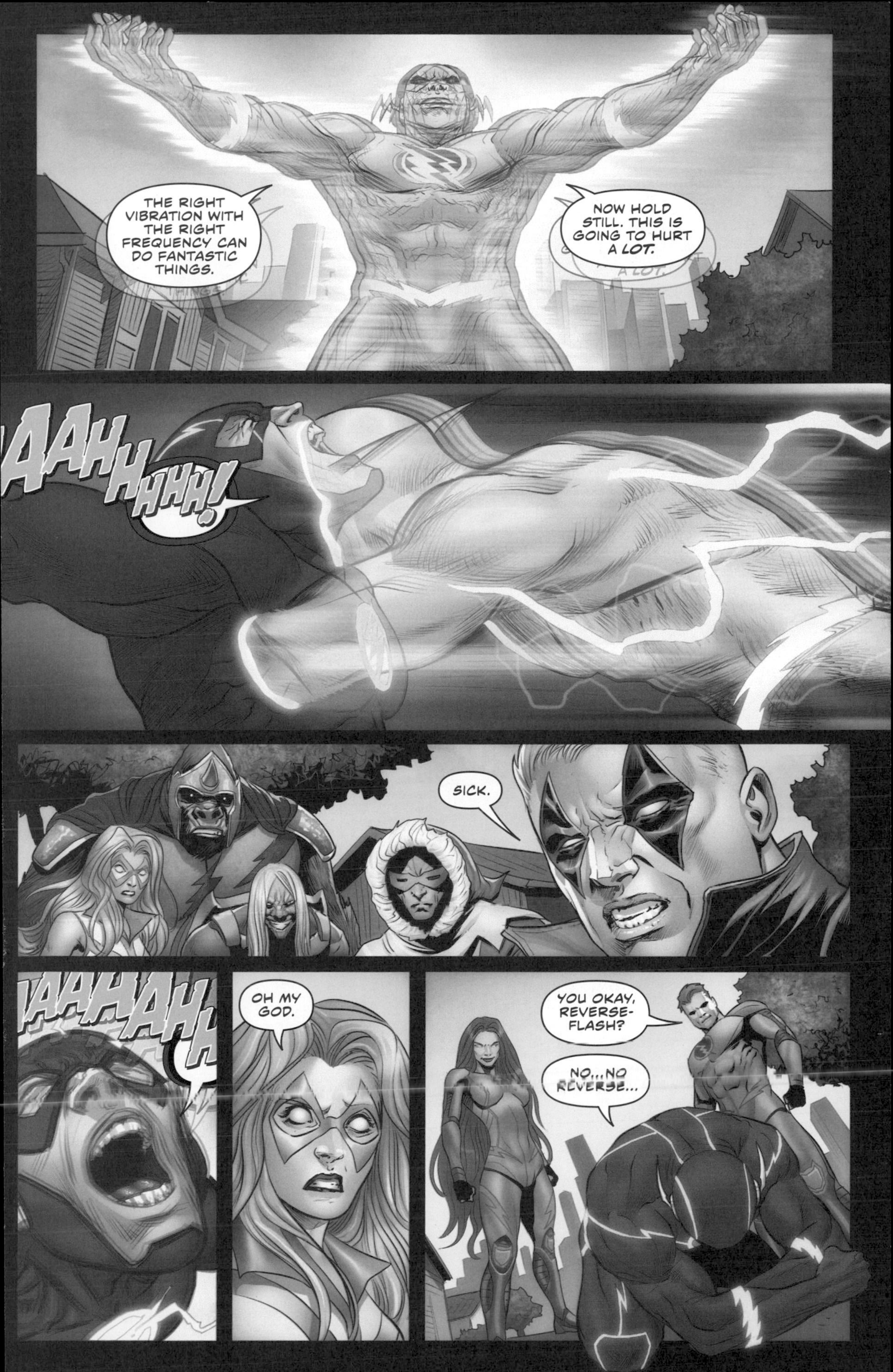
THE RIGHT VIBRATION WITH THE RIGHT FREQUENCY CAN DO FANTASTIC THINGS.
NOW HOLD STILL. THIS IS GOING TO HURT A LOT.
AAHHHHH!
SICK.
AAAAAHH
OH MY GOD.
YOU OKAY, REVERSE-FLASH?
NO...NO REVERSE...

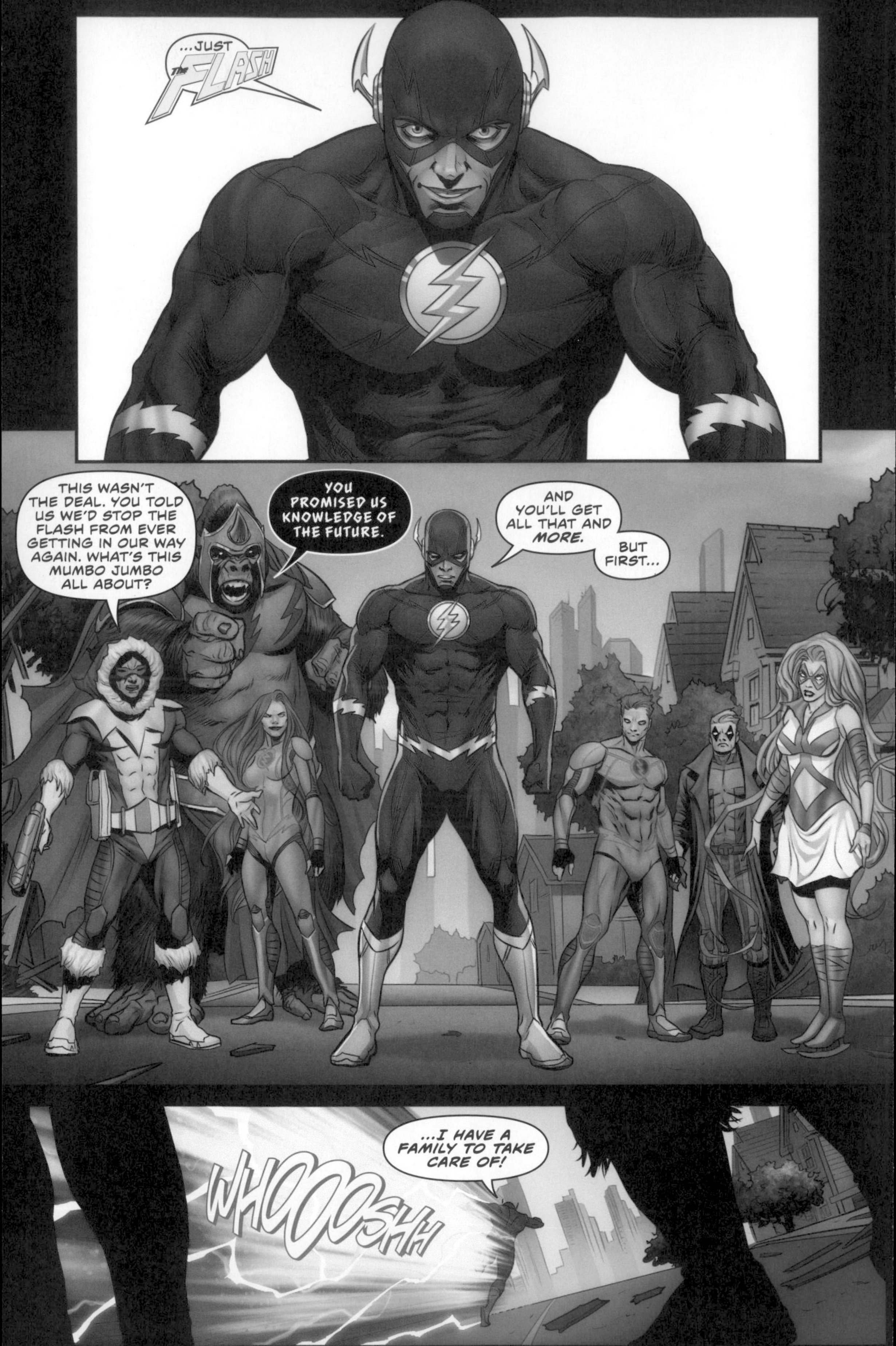
...JUST THE FLASH
THIS WASN'T THE DEAL. YOU TOLD US WE'D STOP THE FLASH FROM EVER GETTING IN OUR WAY AGAIN. WHAT'S THIS MUMBO JUMBO ALL ABOUT?
YOU PROMISED US KNOWLEDGE OF THE FUTURE.
AND YOU'LL GET ALL THAT AND MORE.
BUT FIRST...
...I HAVE A FAMILY TO TAKE CARE OF!
WHOOOOSHH

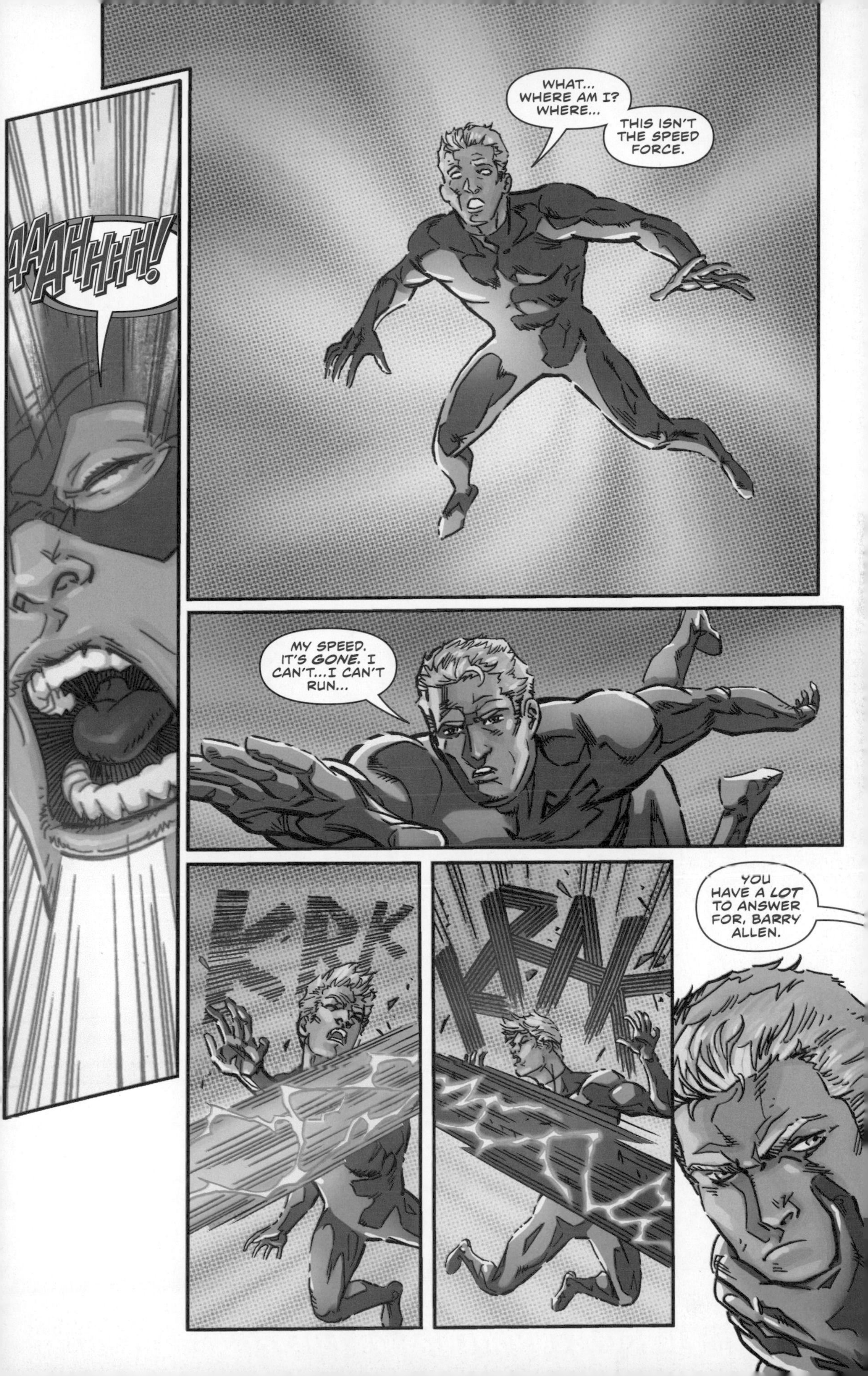
AAAHHHH!
WHAT... WHERE AM I? WHERE...
THIS ISN'T THE SPEED FORCE.
MY SPEED. IT'S *GONE*. I CAN'T...I CAN'T RUN...
KRK
KRAK
YOU HAVE A *LOT* TO ANSWER FOR, BARRY ALLEN.

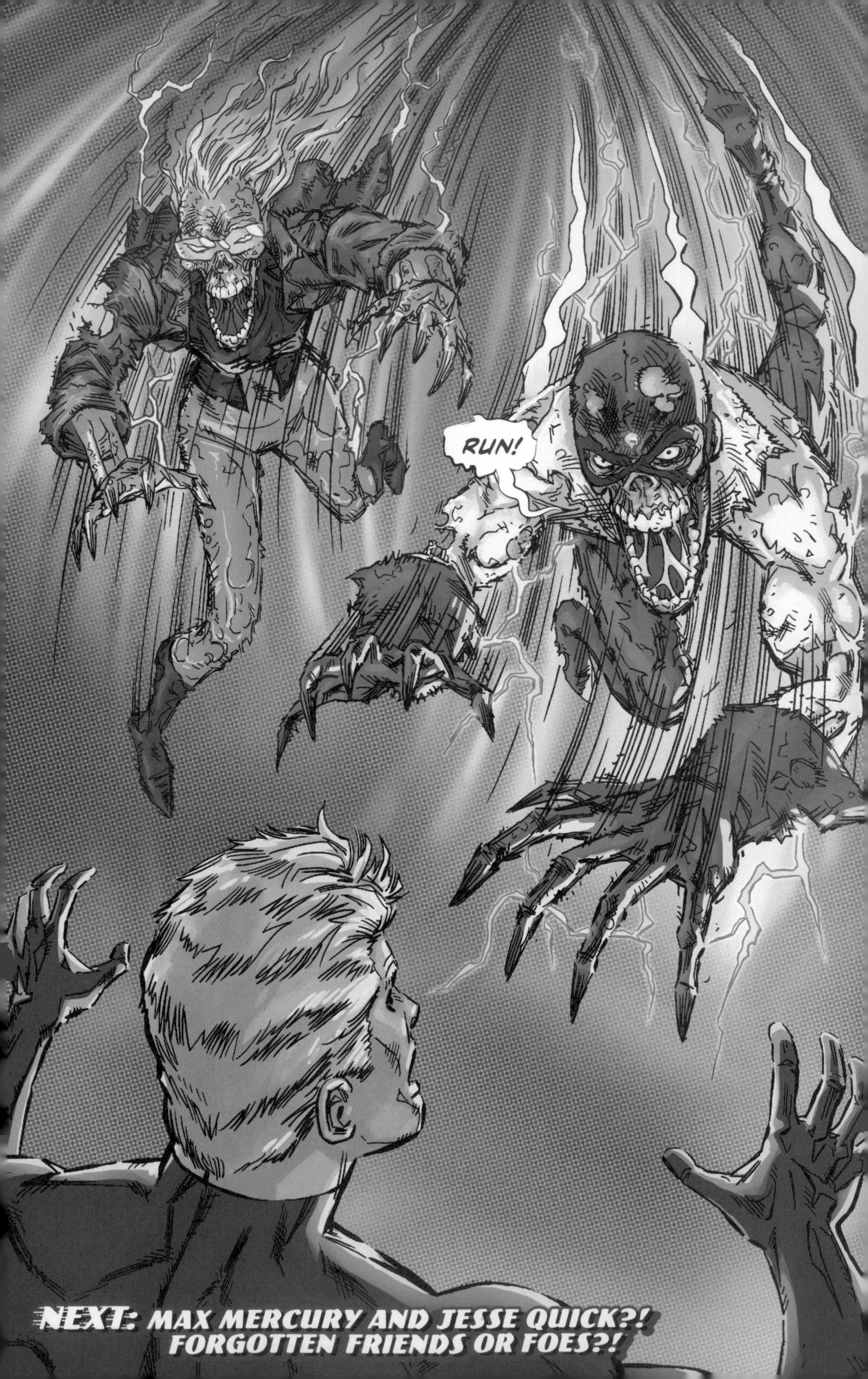
RUN!
NEXT: MAX MERCURY AND JESSE QUICK?! FORGOTTEN FRIENDS OR FOES?!

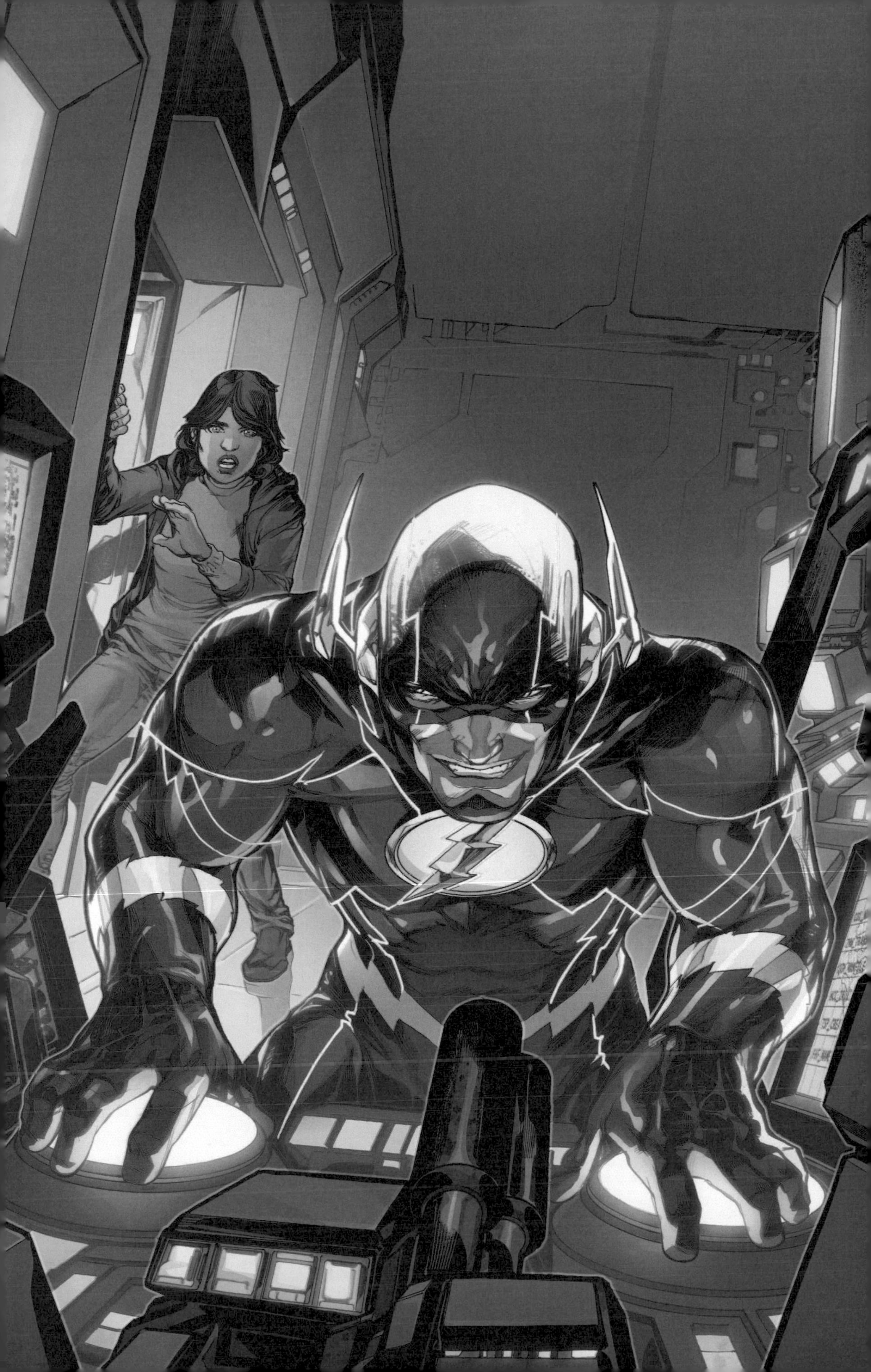

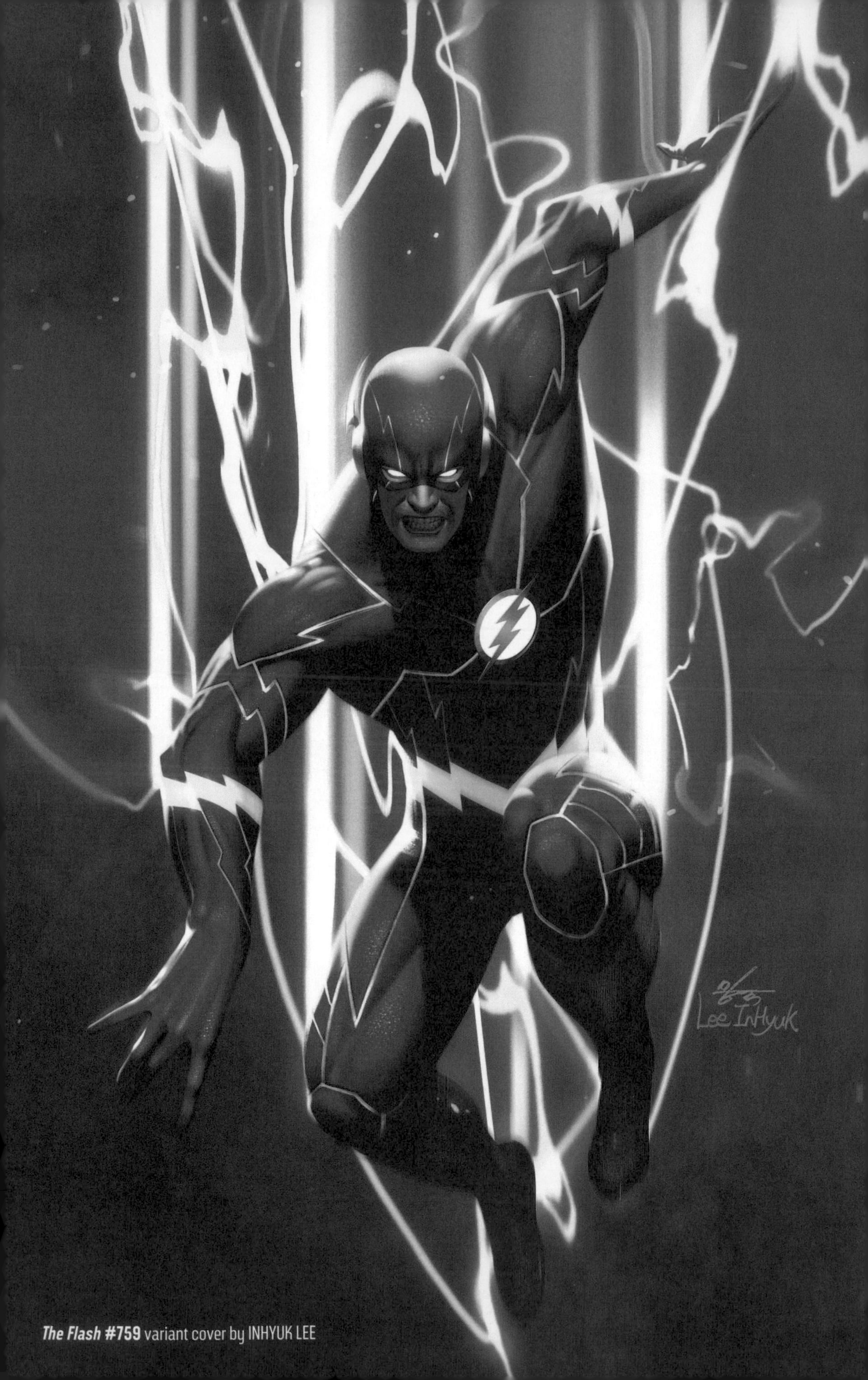
Lee InHyuk

***The Flash* #759** variant cover by INHYUK LEE

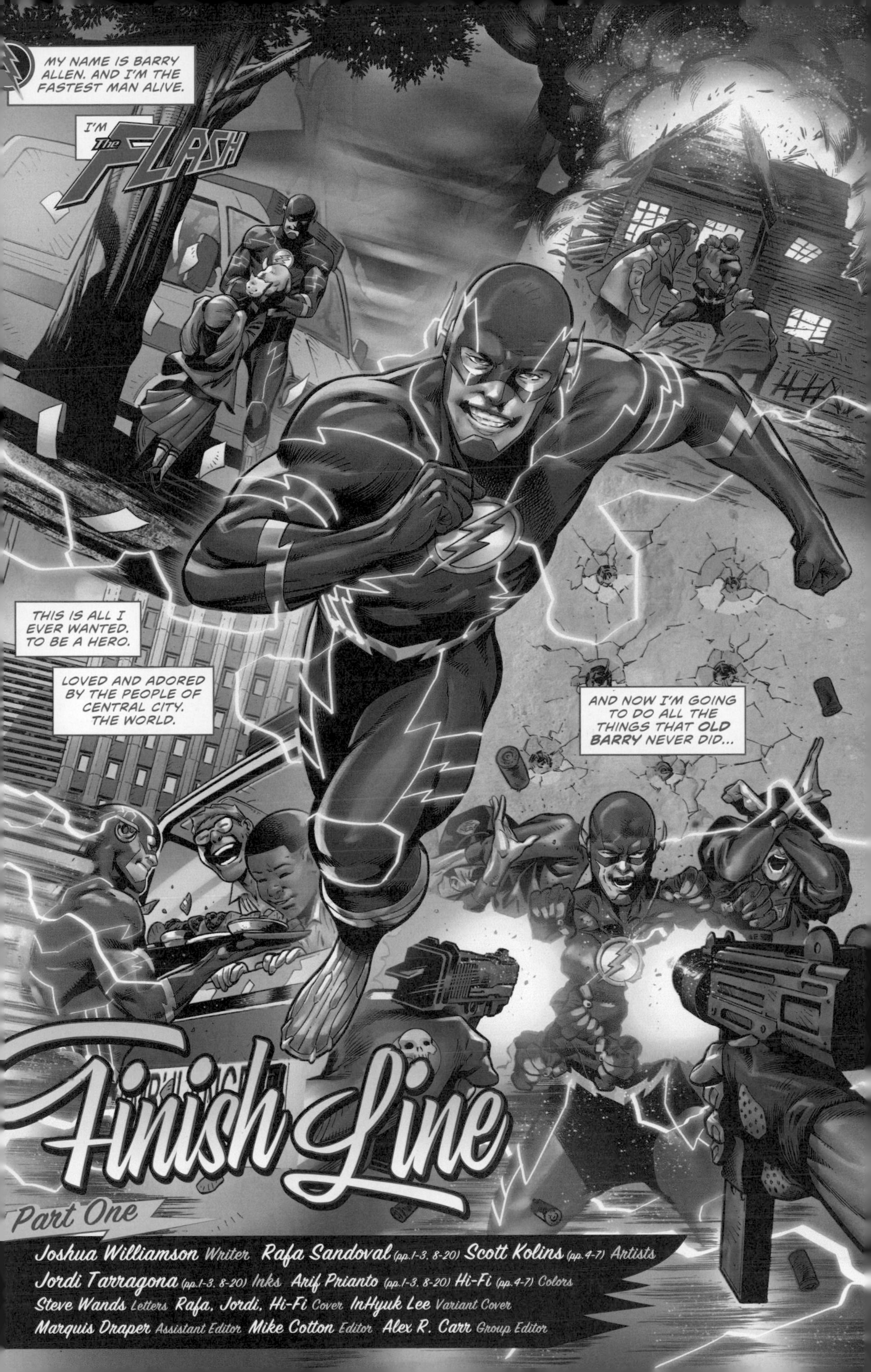
MY NAME IS BARRY ALLEN. AND I'M THE FASTEST MAN ALIVE.
I'M The FLASH
THIS IS ALL I EVER WANTED. TO BE A HERO.
LOVED AND ADORED BY THE PEOPLE OF CENTRAL CITY. THE WORLD.
AND NOW I'M GOING TO DO ALL THE THINGS THAT OLD BARRY NEVER DID...
Finish Line
Part One
Joshua Williamson Writer Rafa Sandoval (pp.1-3, 8-20) Scott Kolins (pp.4-7) Artists
Jordi Tarragona (pp.1-3, 8-20) Inks Arif Prianto (pp.1-3, 8-20) Hi-Fi (pp.4-7) Colors
Steve Wands Letters Rafa, Jordi, Hi-Fi Cover InHyuk Lee Variant Cover
Marquis Draper Assistant Editor Mike Cotton Editor Alex R. Carr Group Editor

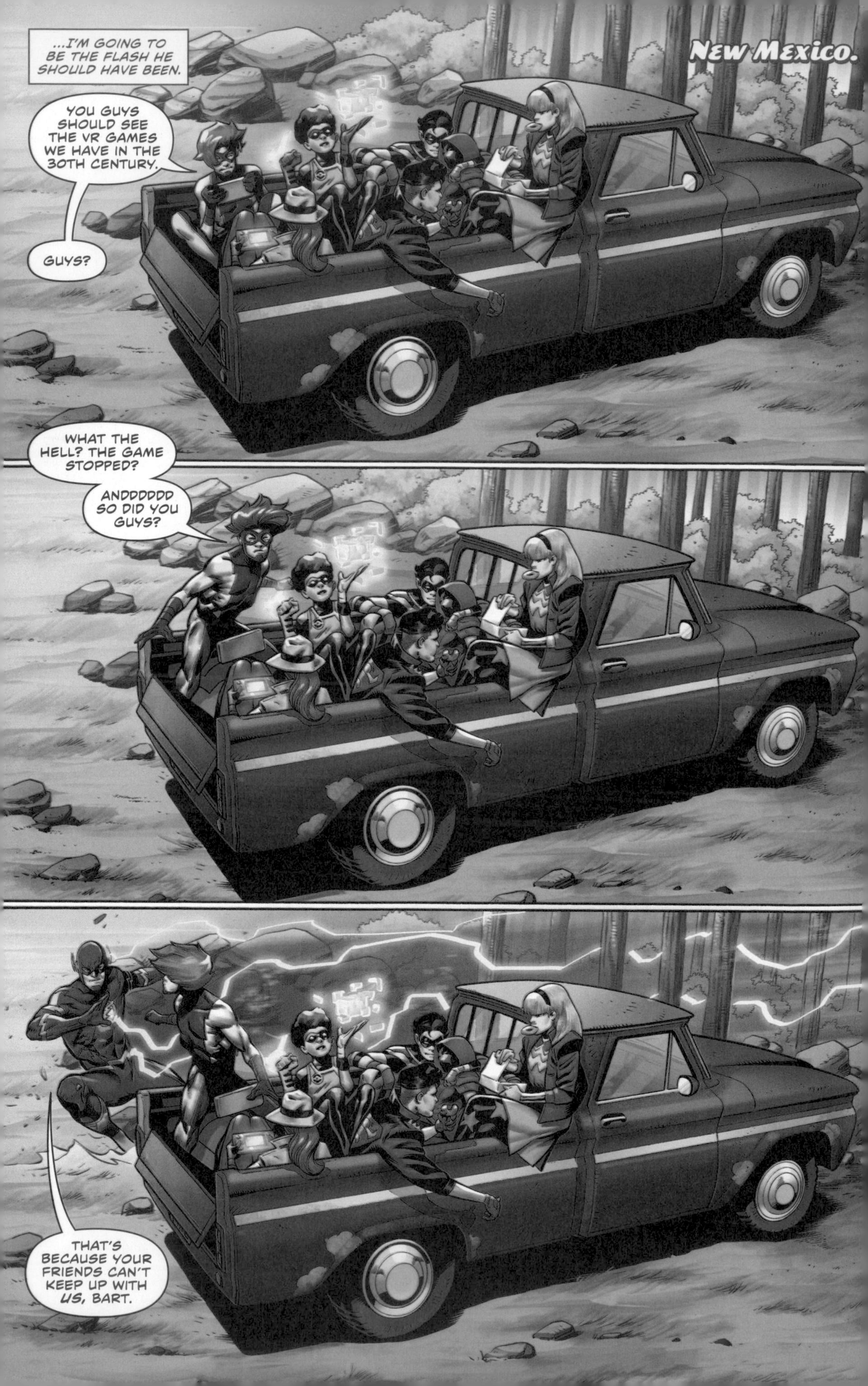

...I'M GOING TO BE THE FLASH HE SHOULD HAVE BEEN.
New Mexico.
YOU GUYS SHOULD SEE THE VR GAMES WE HAVE IN THE 30TH CENTURY.
GUYS?
WHAT THE HELL? THE GAME STOPPED?
ANDDDDDD SO DID YOU GUYS?
THAT'S BECAUSE YOUR FRIENDS CAN'T KEEP UP WITH US, BART.

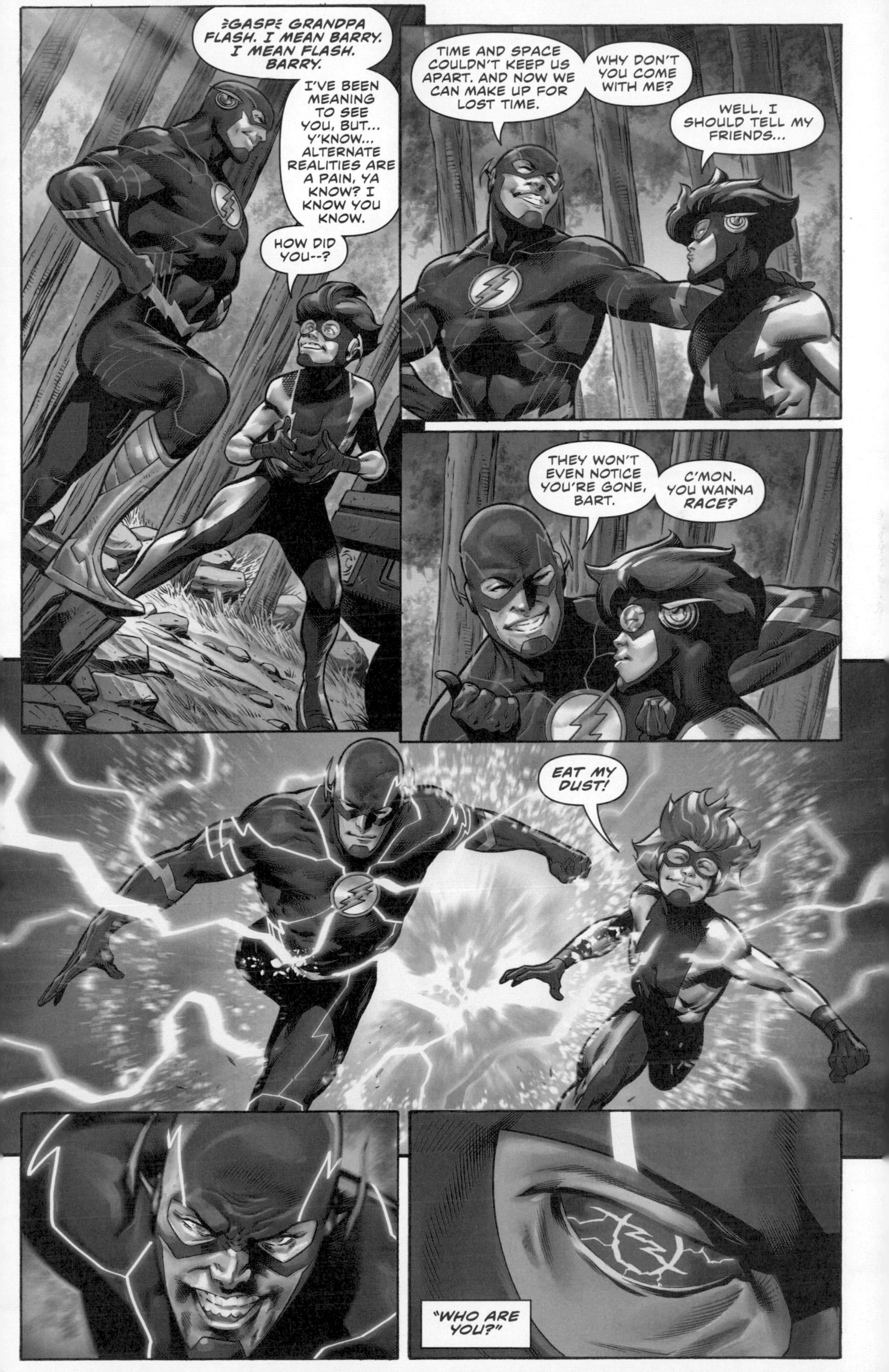

≈GASP≈ GRANDPA FLASH. I MEAN BARRY. I MEAN FLASH. BARRY.
I'VE BEEN MEANING TO SEE YOU, BUT... Y'KNOW... ALTERNATE REALITIES ARE A PAIN, YA KNOW? I KNOW YOU KNOW.
HOW DID YOU--?
TIME AND SPACE COULDN'T KEEP US APART. AND NOW WE CAN MAKE UP FOR LOST TIME.
WHY DON'T YOU COME WITH ME?
WELL, I SHOULD TELL MY FRIENDS...
THEY WON'T EVEN NOTICE YOU'RE GONE, BART.
C'MON. YOU WANNA RACE?
EAT MY DUST!
"WHO ARE YOU?"

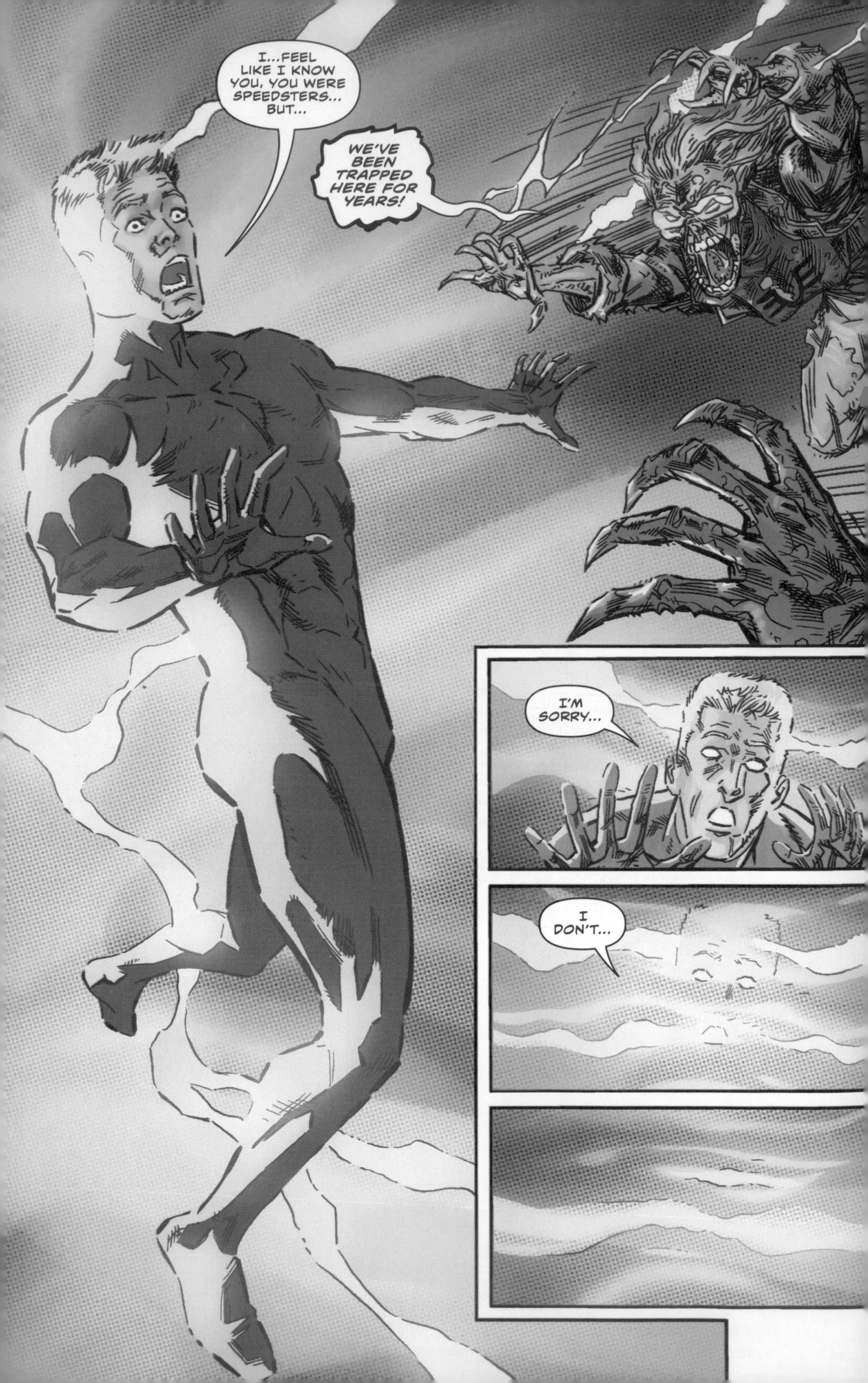
I...FEEL LIKE I KNOW YOU, YOU WERE SPEEDSTERS... BUT...
WE'VE BEEN TRAPPED HERE FOR YEARS!
I'M SORRY...
I DON'T...

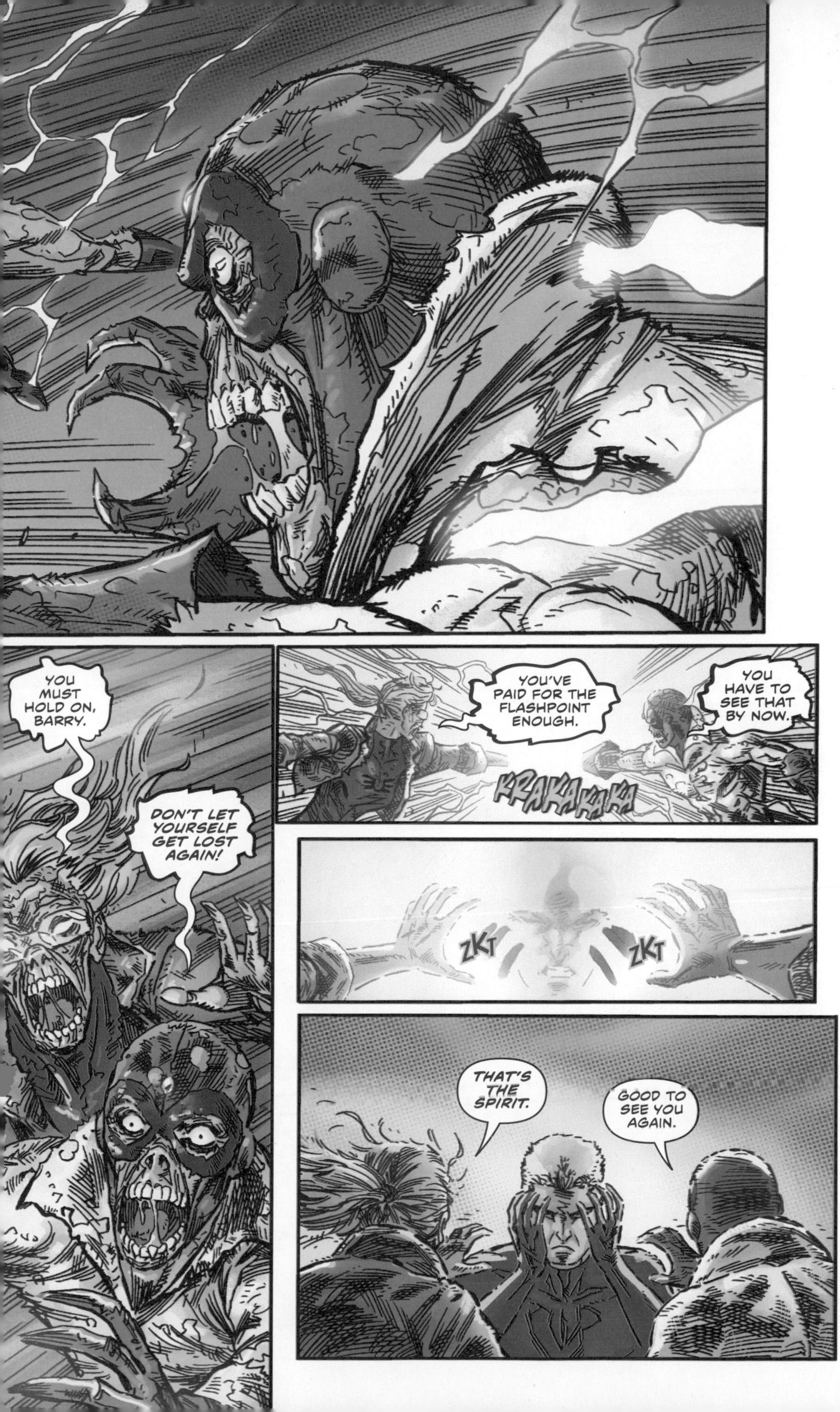
YOU MUST HOLD ON, BARRY.
DON'T LET YOURSELF GET LOST AGAIN!
YOU'VE PAID FOR THE FLASHPOINT ENOUGH.
YOU HAVE TO SEE THAT BY NOW.
KRAKAKAKA
ZKT
ZKT
THAT'S THE SPIRIT.
GOOD TO SEE YOU AGAIN.

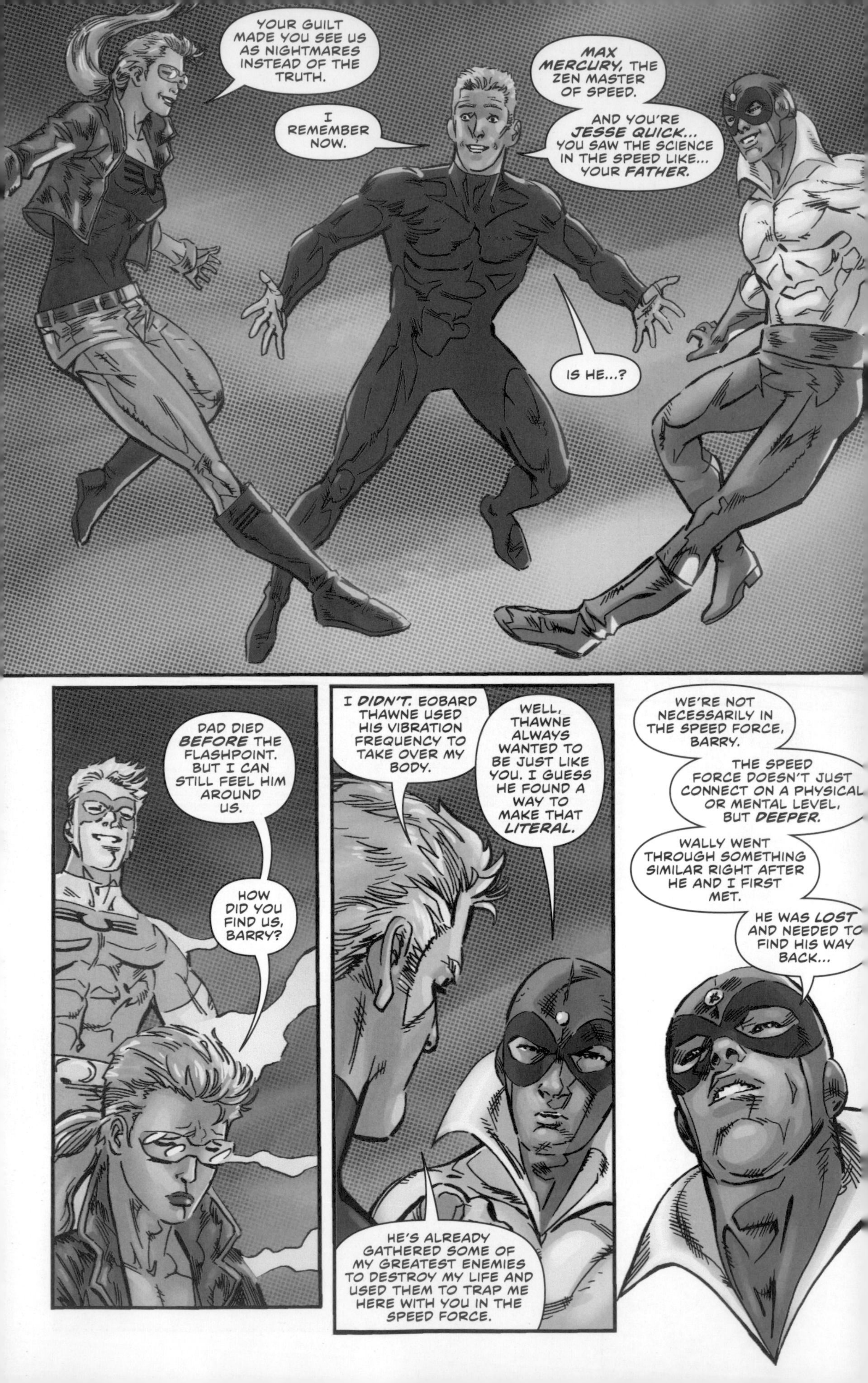

YOUR GUILT MADE YOU SEE US AS NIGHTMARES INSTEAD OF THE TRUTH.
I REMEMBER NOW.
MAX MERCURY, THE ZEN MASTER OF SPEED.
AND YOU'RE JESSE QUICK... YOU SAW THE SCIENCE IN THE SPEED LIKE... YOUR FATHER.
IS HE...?
DAD DIED BEFORE THE FLASHPOINT. BUT I CAN STILL FEEL HIM AROUND US.
HOW DID YOU FIND US, BARRY?
I DIDN'T. EOBARD THAWNE USED HIS VIBRATION FREQUENCY TO TAKE OVER MY BODY.
WELL, THAWNE ALWAYS WANTED TO BE JUST LIKE YOU. I GUESS HE FOUND A WAY TO MAKE THAT LITERAL.
HE'S ALREADY GATHERED SOME OF MY GREATEST ENEMIES TO DESTROY MY LIFE AND USED THEM TO TRAP ME HERE WITH YOU IN THE SPEED FORCE.
WE'RE NOT NECESSARILY IN THE SPEED FORCE, BARRY.
THE SPEED FORCE DOESN'T JUST CONNECT ON A PHYSICAL OR MENTAL LEVEL, BUT DEEPER.
WALLY WENT THROUGH SOMETHING SIMILAR RIGHT AFTER HE AND I FIRST MET.
HE WAS LOST AND NEEDED TO FIND HIS WAY BACK...

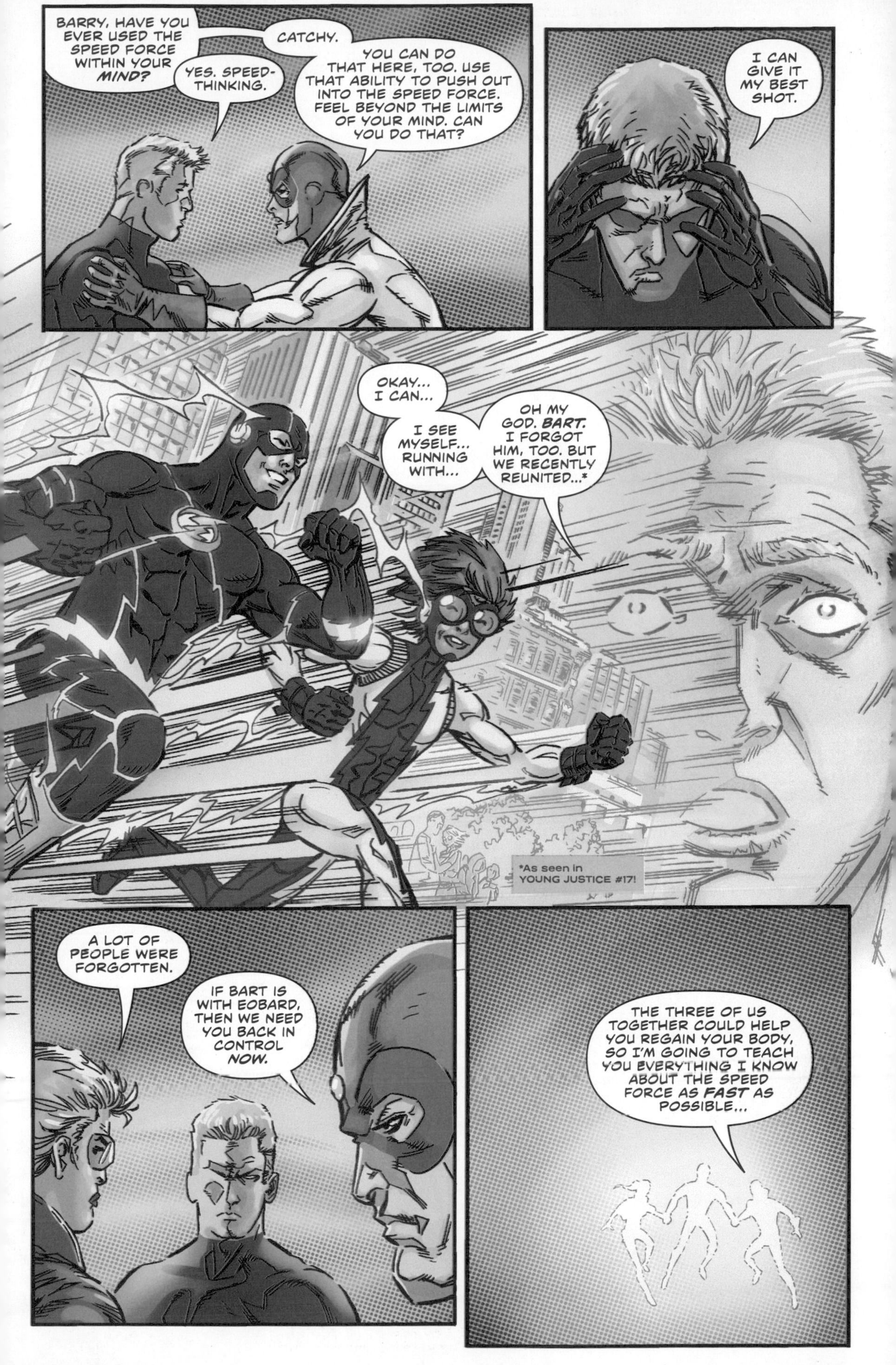
BARRY, HAVE YOU EVER USED THE SPEED FORCE WITHIN YOUR *MIND?*
YES. SPEED-THINKING.
CATCHY.
YOU CAN DO THAT HERE, TOO. USE THAT ABILITY TO PUSH OUT INTO THE SPEED FORCE. FEEL BEYOND THE LIMITS OF YOUR MIND. CAN YOU DO THAT?
I CAN GIVE IT MY BEST SHOT.
OKAY... I CAN...
I SEE MYSELF... RUNNING WITH...
OH MY GOD. *BART.* I FORGOT HIM, TOO. BUT WE RECENTLY REUNITED...*
*As seen in YOUNG JUSTICE #17!
A LOT OF PEOPLE WERE FORGOTTEN.
IF BART IS WITH EOBARD, THEN WE NEED YOU BACK IN CONTROL *NOW.*
THE THREE OF US TOGETHER COULD HELP YOU REGAIN YOUR BODY, SO I'M GOING TO TEACH YOU EVERYTHING I KNOW ABOUT THE SPEED FORCE AS *FAST* AS POSSIBLE...

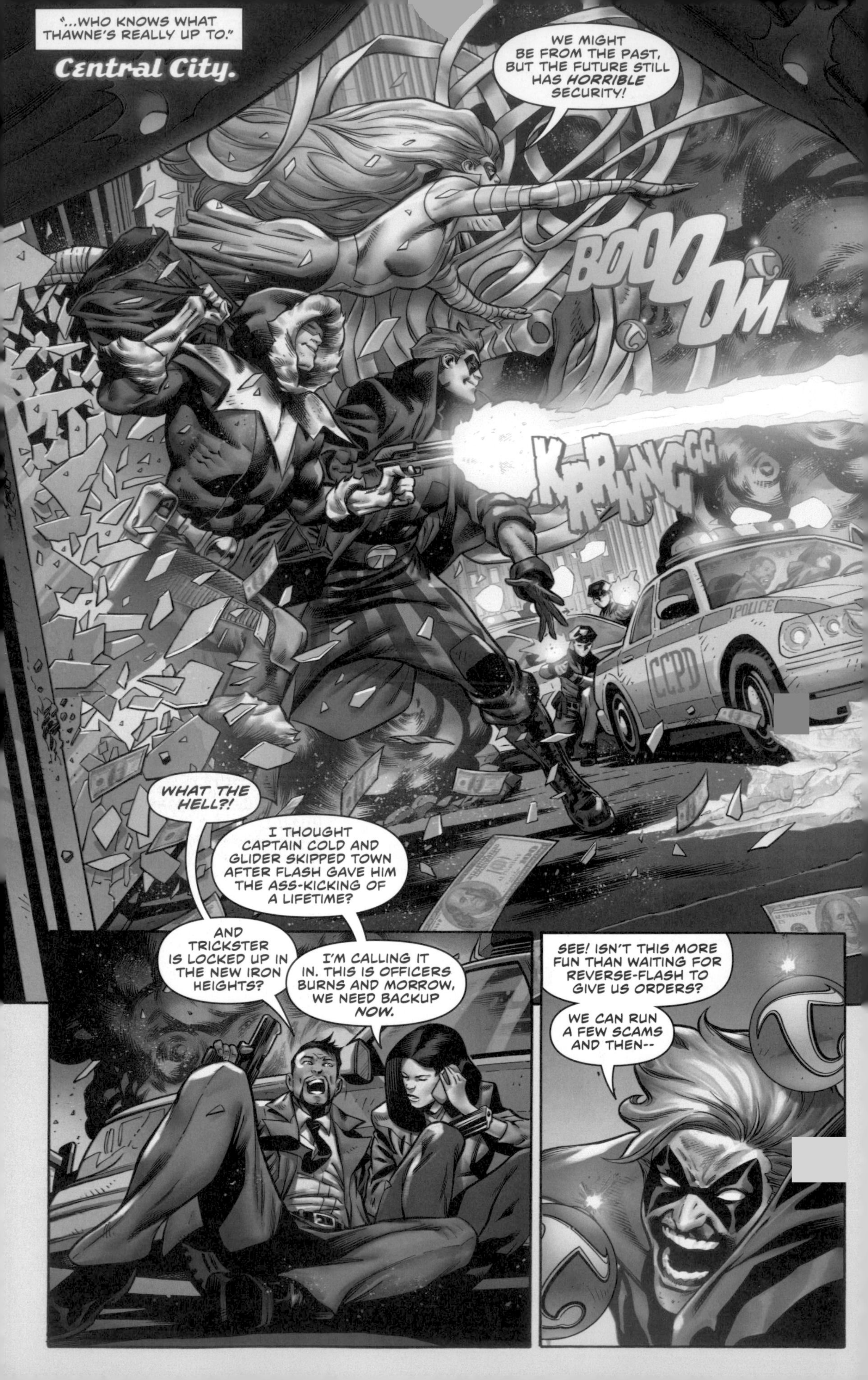
"...WHO KNOWS WHAT THAWNE'S REALLY UP TO."
Central City.
WE MIGHT BE FROM THE PAST, BUT THE FUTURE STILL HAS HORRIBLE SECURITY!
BOOOOOM
KRANNGG
WHAT THE HELL?!
I THOUGHT CAPTAIN COLD AND GLIDER SKIPPED TOWN AFTER FLASH GAVE HIM THE ASS-KICKING OF A LIFETIME?
AND TRICKSTER IS LOCKED UP IN THE NEW IRON HEIGHTS?
I'M CALLING IT IN. THIS IS OFFICERS BURNS AND MORROW, WE NEED BACKUP NOW.
SEE! ISN'T THIS MORE FUN THAN WAITING FOR REVERSE-FLASH TO GIVE US ORDERS?
WE CAN RUN A FEW SCAMS AND THEN--

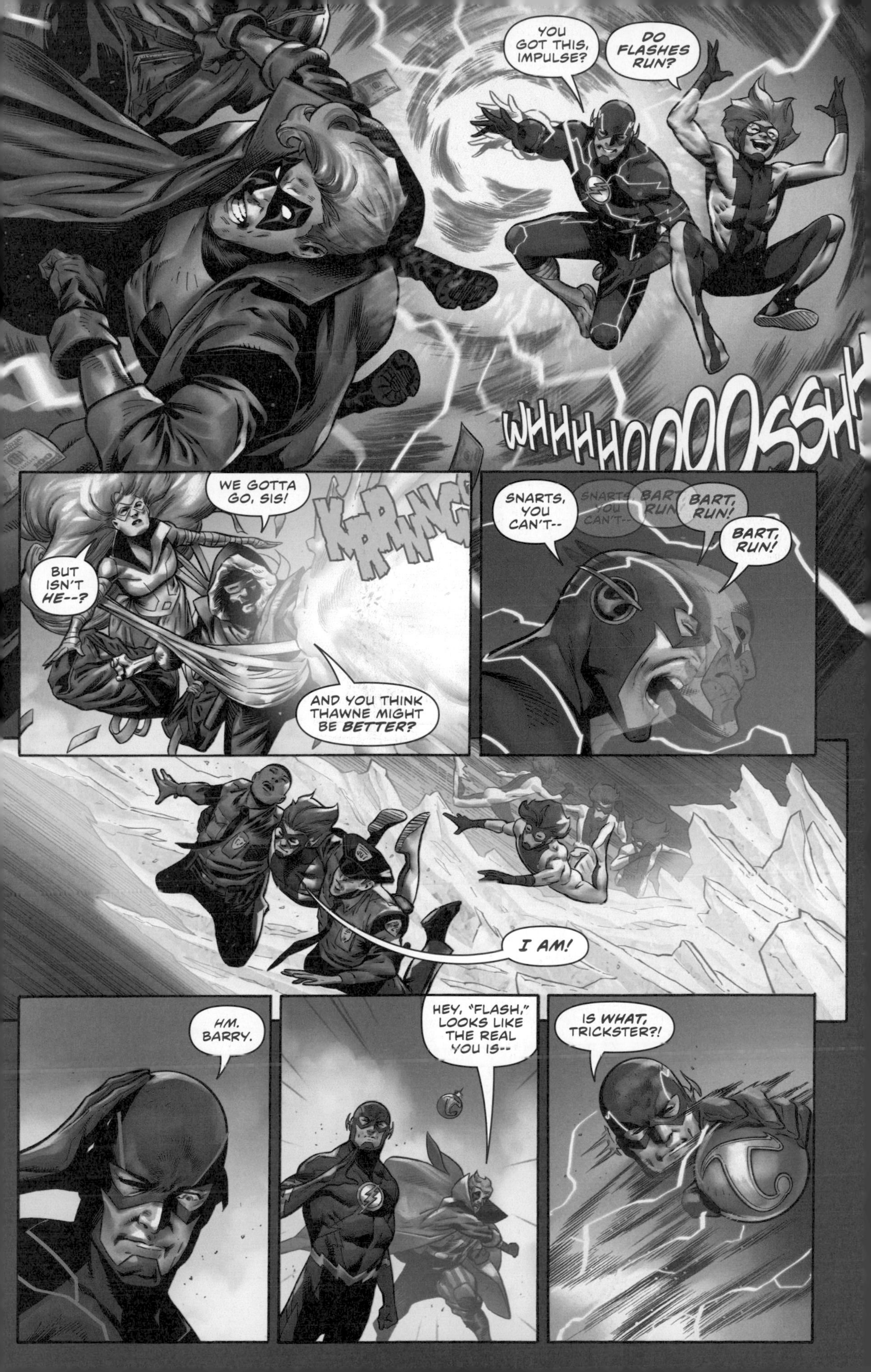

YOU GOT THIS, IMPULSE?
DO FLASHES RUN?
WHHHHOOOOOSSH
WE GOTTA GO, SIS!
KRANNG
BUT ISN'T HE--?
AND YOU THINK THAWNE MIGHT BE BETTER?
SNARTS, YOU CAN'T--
SNARTS, YOU CAN'T--
BART, RUN!
BART, RUN!
BART, RUN!
I AM!
HM. BARRY.
HEY, "FLASH," LOOKS LIKE THE REAL YOU IS--
IS WHAT, TRICKSTER?!

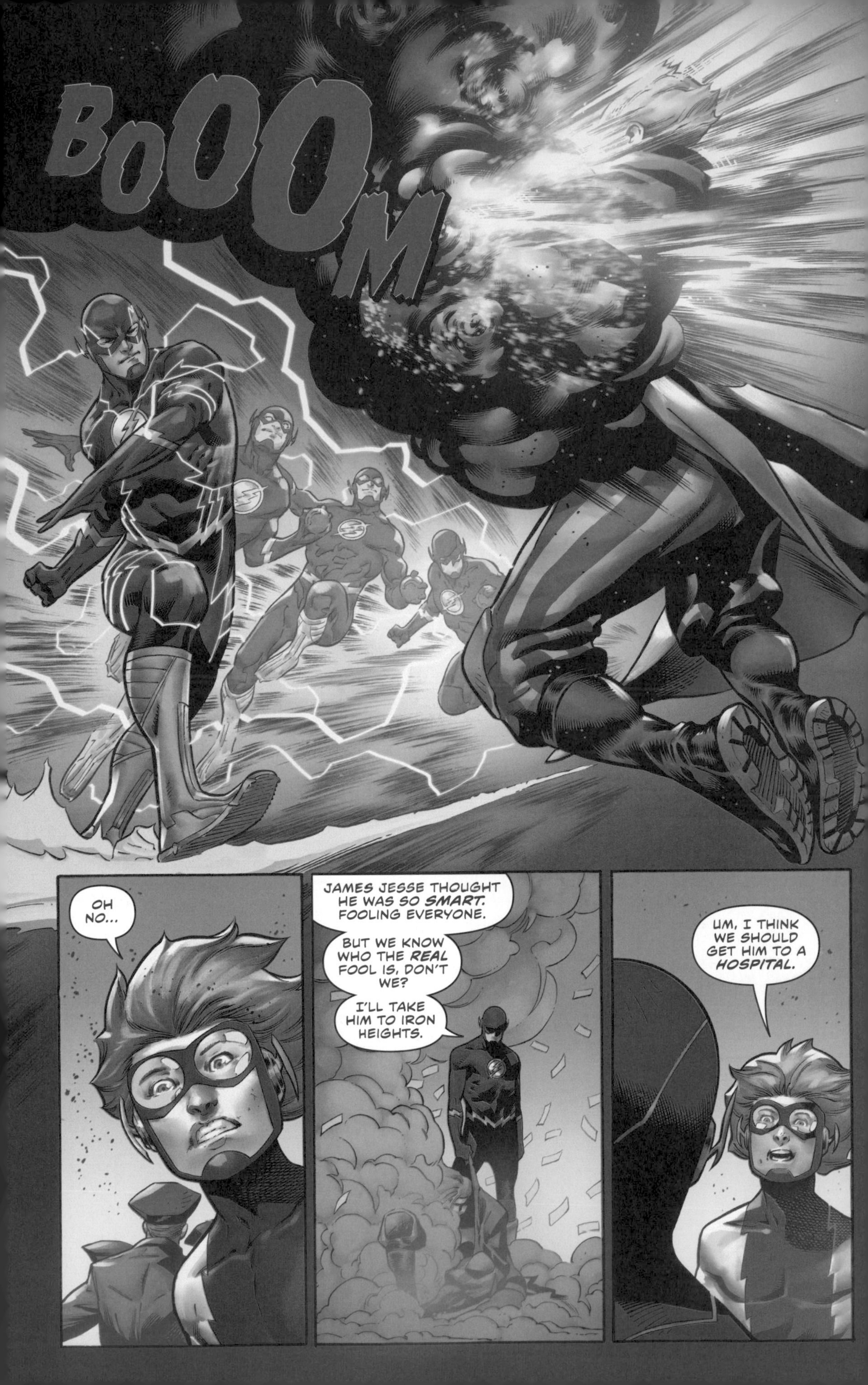
BOOOOM
OH NO...
JAMES JESSE THOUGHT HE WAS SO SMART. FOOLING EVERYONE.
BUT WE KNOW WHO THE REAL FOOL IS, DON'T WE?
I'LL TAKE HIM TO IRON HEIGHTS.
UM, I THINK WE SHOULD GET HIM TO A HOSPITAL.

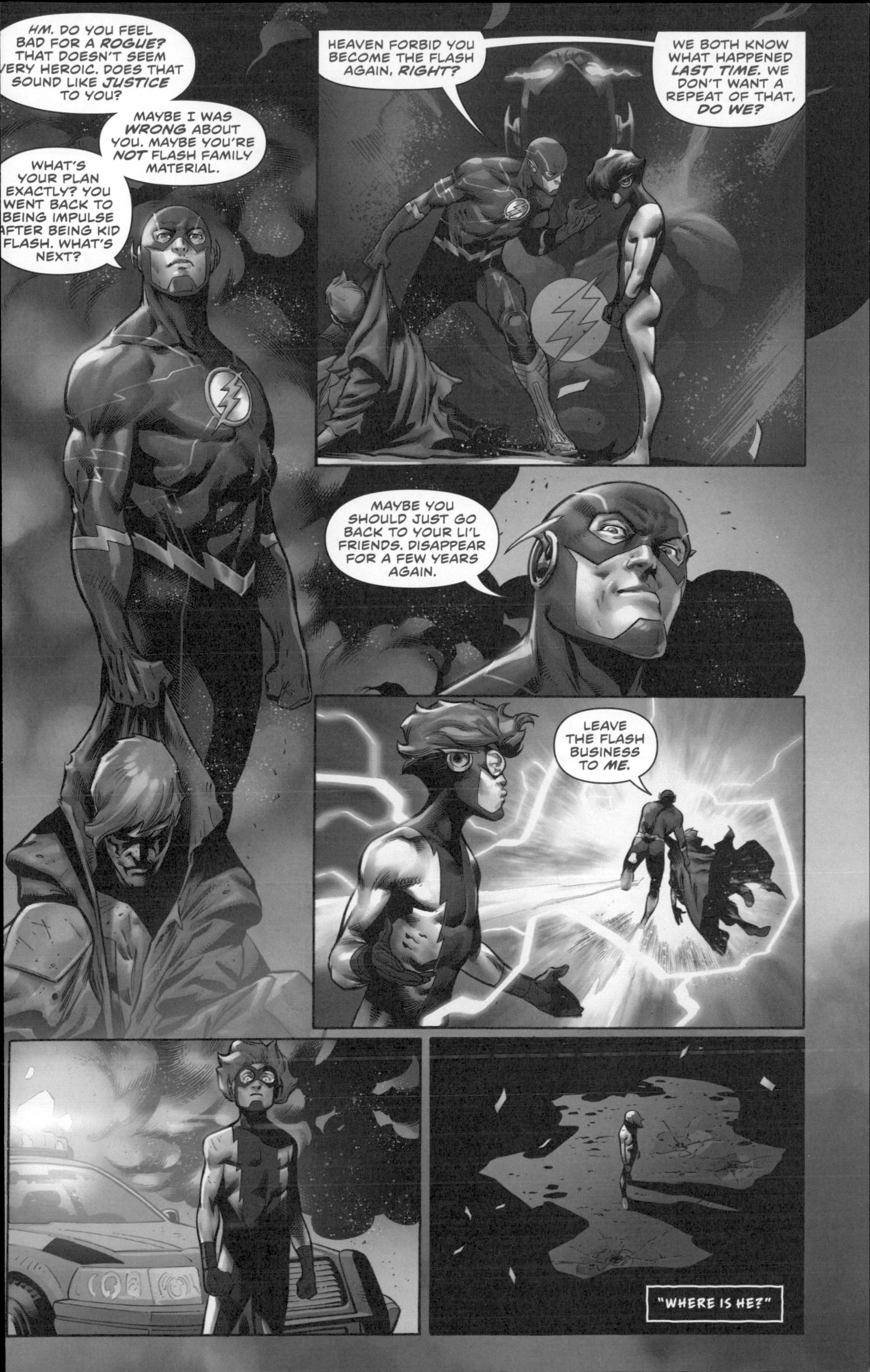

HM. DO YOU FEEL BAD FOR A *ROGUE?* THAT DOESN'T SEEM VERY HEROIC. DOES THAT SOUND LIKE *JUSTICE* TO YOU?
MAYBE I WAS *WRONG* ABOUT YOU. MAYBE YOU'RE *NOT* FLASH FAMILY MATERIAL.
WHAT'S YOUR PLAN EXACTLY? YOU WENT BACK TO BEING IMPULSE AFTER BEING KID FLASH. WHAT'S NEXT?
HEAVEN FORBID YOU BECOME THE FLASH AGAIN, *RIGHT?*
WE BOTH KNOW WHAT HAPPENED *LAST TIME.* WE DON'T WANT A REPEAT OF THAT, *DO WE?*
MAYBE YOU SHOULD JUST GO BACK TO YOUR LI'L FRIENDS. DISAPPEAR FOR A FEW YEARS AGAIN.
LEAVE THE FLASH BUSINESS TO *ME.*
"WHERE IS HE?"

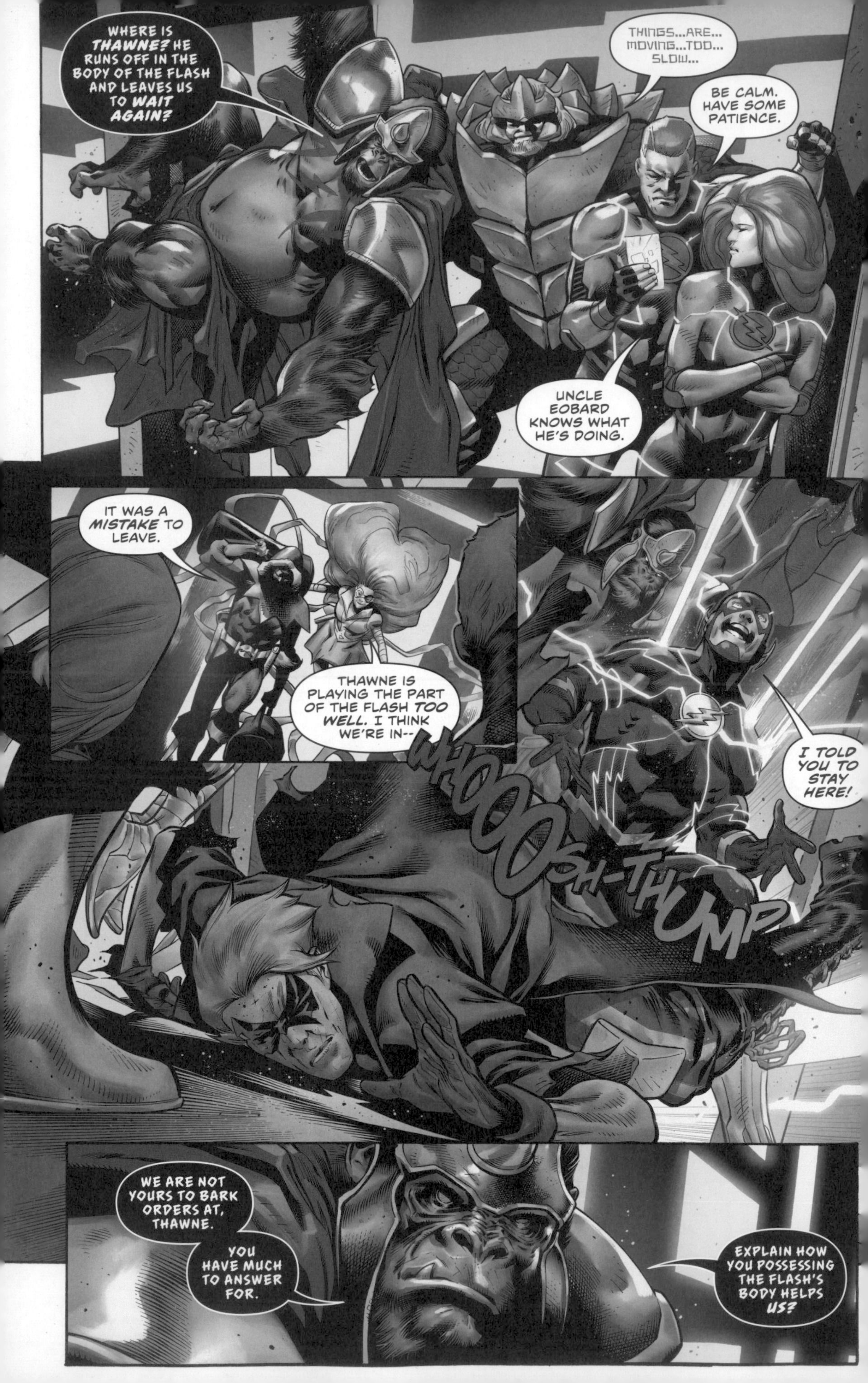
WHERE IS THAWNE? HE RUNS OFF IN THE BODY OF THE FLASH AND LEAVES US TO WAIT AGAIN?
THINGS...ARE... MOVING...TOO... SLOW...
BE CALM. HAVE SOME PATIENCE.
UNCLE EOBARD KNOWS WHAT HE'S DOING.
IT WAS A MISTAKE TO LEAVE.
THAWNE IS PLAYING THE PART OF THE FLASH TOO WELL. I THINK WE'RE IN--
WHOOOOSH-THUMP
I TOLD YOU TO STAY HERE!
WE ARE NOT YOURS TO BARK ORDERS AT, THAWNE.
YOU HAVE MUCH TO ANSWER FOR.
EXPLAIN HOW YOU POSSESSING THE FLASH'S BODY HELPS US?

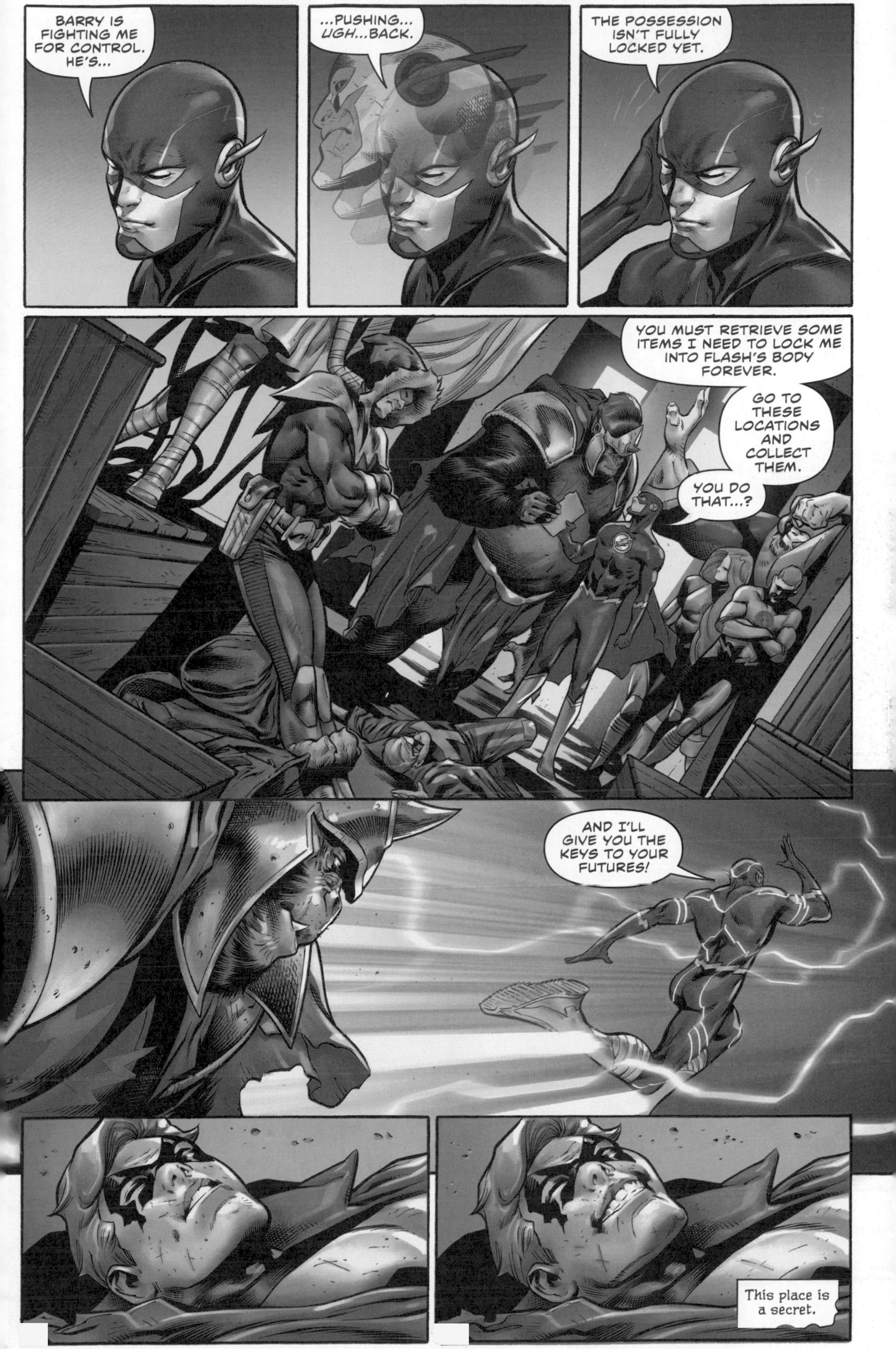
BARRY IS FIGHTING ME FOR CONTROL. HE'S...
...PUSHING... UGH...BACK.
THE POSSESSION ISN'T FULLY LOCKED YET.
YOU MUST RETRIEVE SOME ITEMS I NEED TO LOCK ME INTO FLASH'S BODY FOREVER.
GO TO THESE LOCATIONS AND COLLECT THEM.
YOU DO THAT...?
AND I'LL GIVE YOU THE KEYS TO YOUR FUTURES!
This place is a secret.

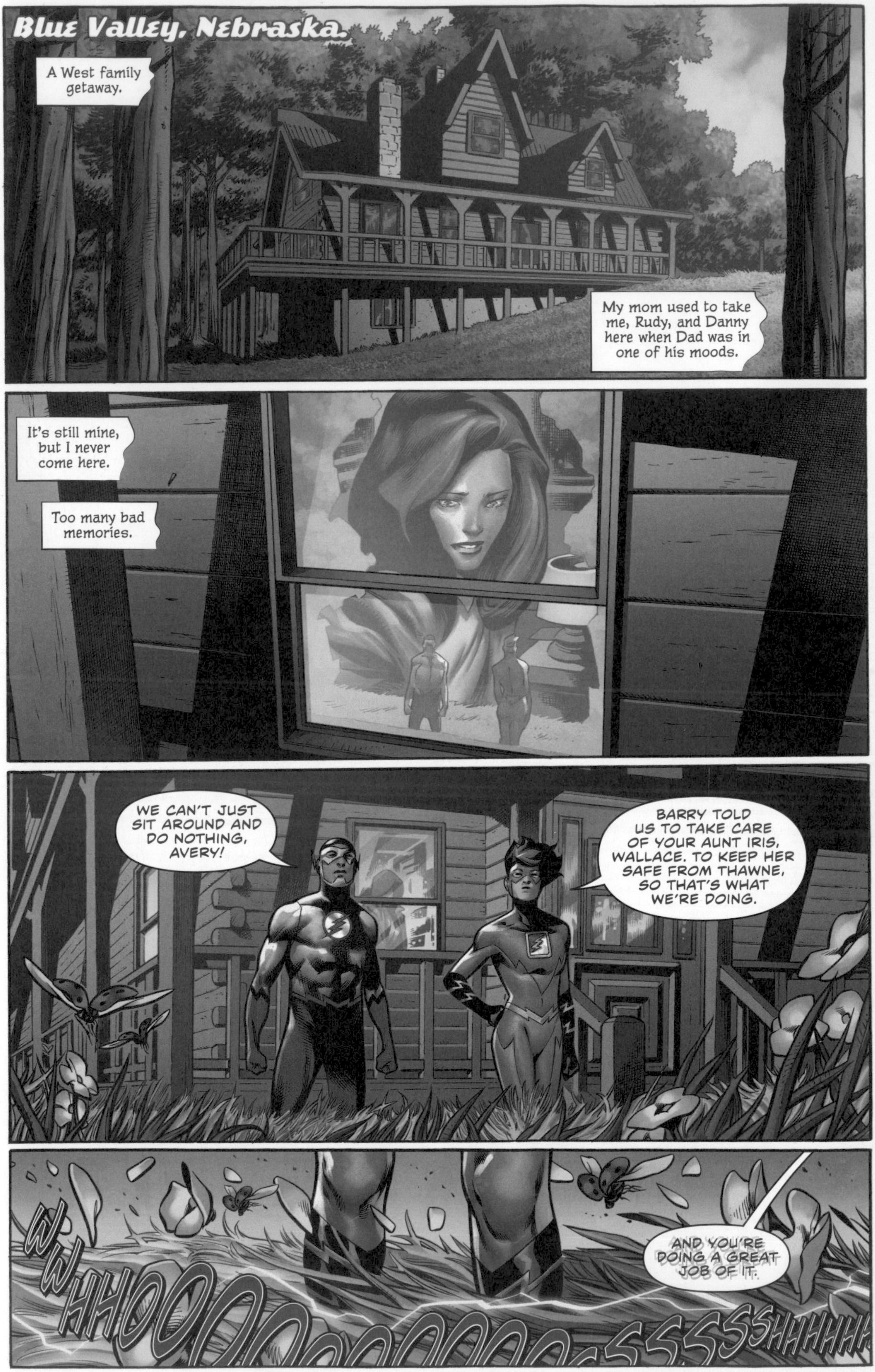
Blue Valley, Nebraska.
A West family getaway.
My mom used to take me, Rudy, and Danny here when Dad was in one of his moods.
It's still mine, but I never come here.
Too many bad memories.
WE CAN'T JUST SIT AROUND AND DO NOTHING, AVERY!
BARRY TOLD US TO TAKE CARE OF YOUR AUNT IRIS, WALLACE. TO KEEP HER SAFE FROM THAWNE, SO THAT'S WHAT WE'RE DOING.
AND YOU'RE DOING A GREAT JOB OF IT.
WWHHOOOOOOOOOOOOSSSSSHHHHHH

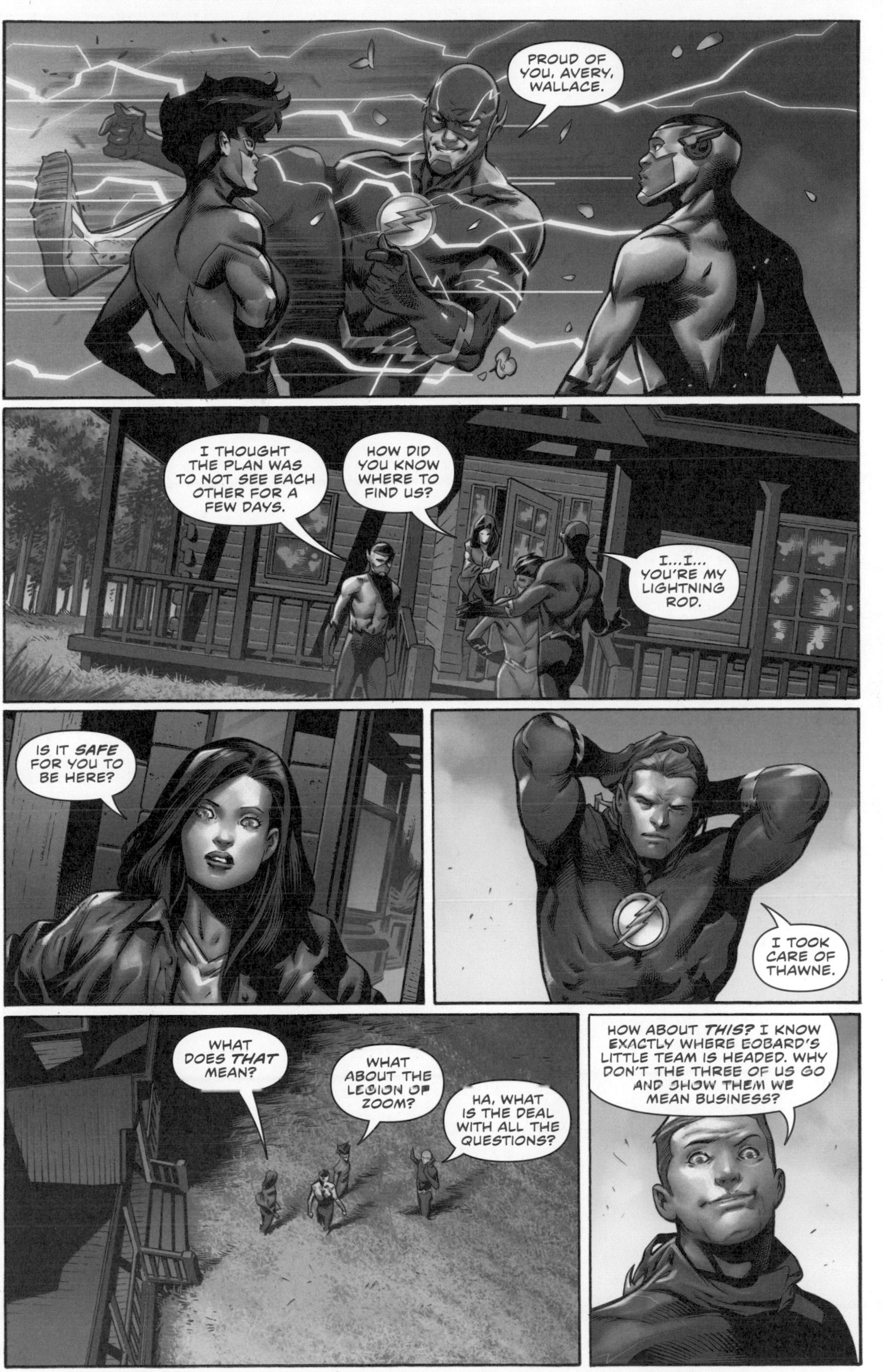
PROUD OF YOU, AVERY, WALLACE.
I THOUGHT THE PLAN WAS TO NOT SEE EACH OTHER FOR A FEW DAYS.
HOW DID YOU KNOW WHERE TO FIND US?
I...I... YOU'RE MY LIGHTNING ROD.
IS IT SAFE FOR YOU TO BE HERE?
I TOOK CARE OF THAWNE.
WHAT DOES THAT MEAN?
WHAT ABOUT THE LEGION OF ZOOM?
HA, WHAT IS THE DEAL WITH ALL THE QUESTIONS?
HOW ABOUT THIS? I KNOW EXACTLY WHERE EOBARD'S LITTLE TEAM IS HEADED. WHY DON'T THE THREE OF US GO AND SHOW THEM WE MEAN BUSINESS?

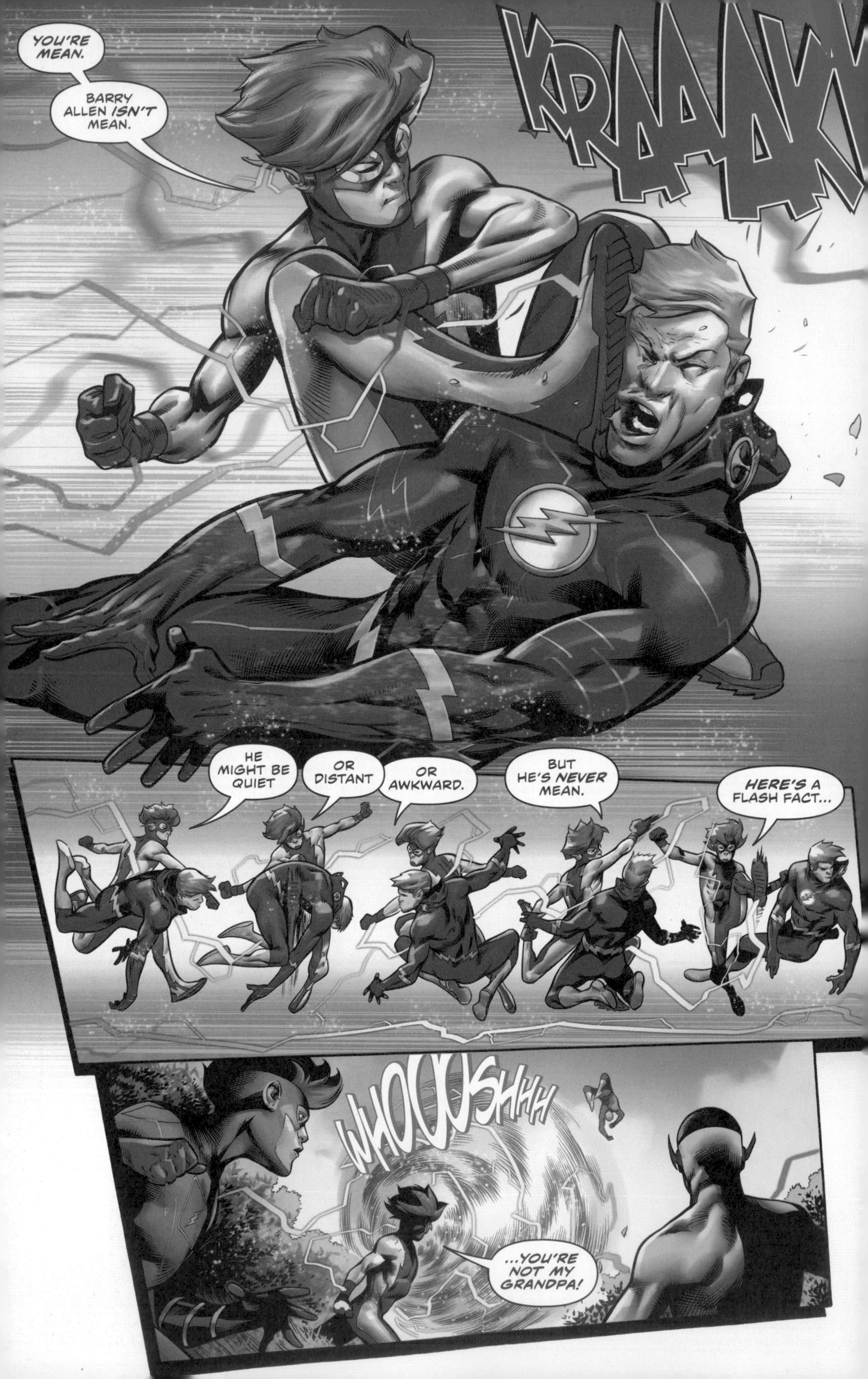

YOU'RE MEAN.
BARRY ALLEN ISN'T MEAN.
KRAAAKK
HE MIGHT BE QUIET
OR DISTANT
OR AWKWARD.
BUT HE'S NEVER MEAN.
HERE'S A FLASH FACT...
WHOOOSHHH
...YOU'RE NOT MY GRANDPA!

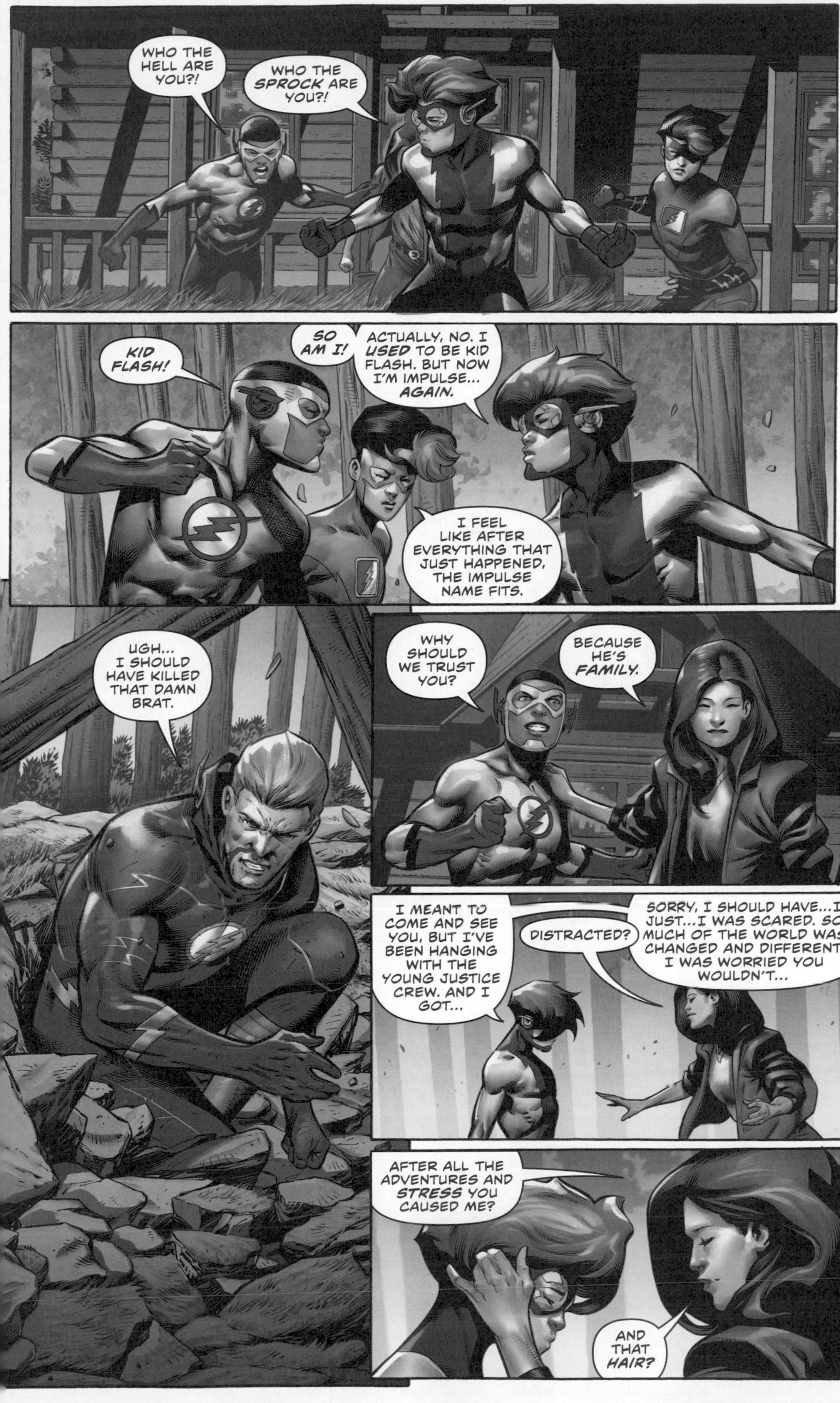
WHO THE HELL ARE YOU?!
WHO THE SPROCK ARE YOU?!
KID FLASH!
SO AM I!
ACTUALLY, NO. I USED TO BE KID FLASH. BUT NOW I'M IMPULSE... AGAIN.
I FEEL LIKE AFTER EVERYTHING THAT JUST HAPPENED, THE IMPULSE NAME FITS.
UGH... I SHOULD HAVE KILLED THAT DAMN BRAT.
WHY SHOULD WE TRUST YOU?
BECAUSE HE'S FAMILY.
I MEANT TO COME AND SEE YOU, BUT I'VE BEEN HANGING WITH THE YOUNG JUSTICE CREW. AND I GOT...
DISTRACTED?
SORRY, I SHOULD HAVE...I JUST...I WAS SCARED. SO MUCH OF THE WORLD WAS CHANGED AND DIFFERENT, I WAS WORRIED YOU WOULDN'T...
AFTER ALL THE ADVENTURES AND STRESS YOU CAUSED ME?
AND THAT HAIR?

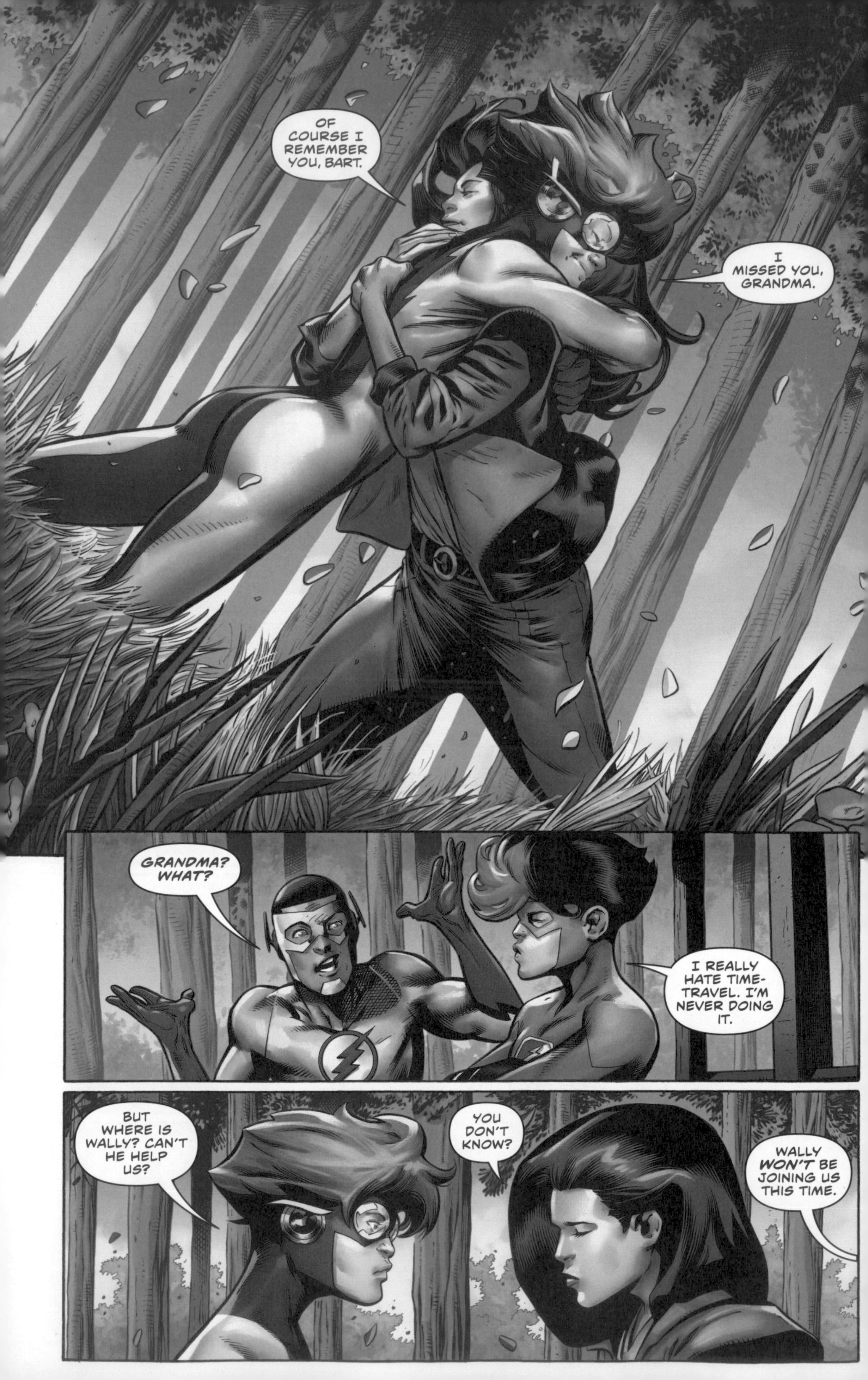
OF COURSE I REMEMBER YOU, BART.
I MISSED YOU, GRANDMA.
GRANDMA? WHAT?
I REALLY HATE TIME-TRAVEL. I'M NEVER DOING IT.
BUT WHERE IS WALLY? CAN'T HE HELP US?
YOU DON'T KNOW?
WALLY *WON'T* BE JOINING US THIS TIME.

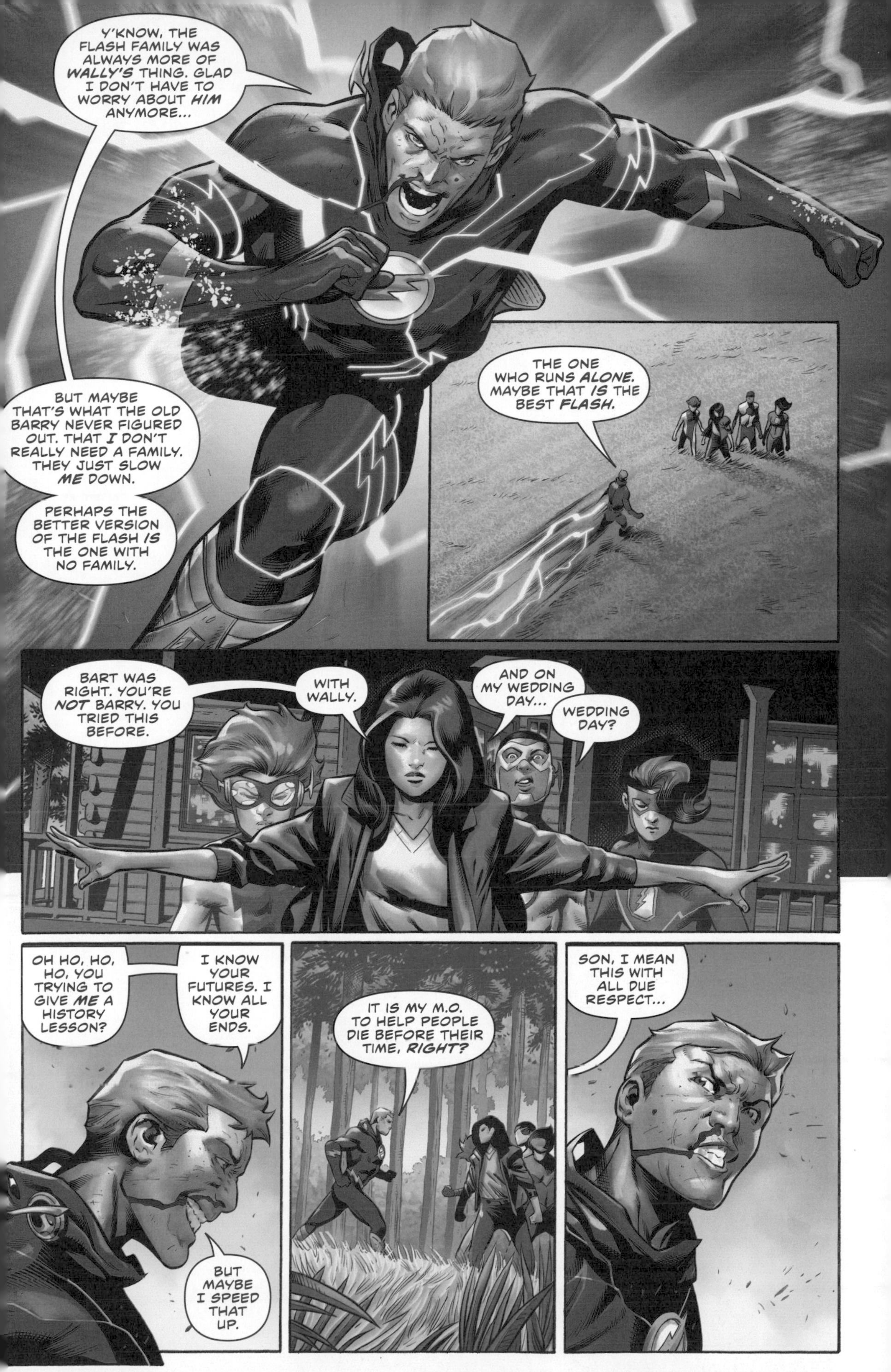

Y'KNOW, THE FLASH FAMILY WAS ALWAYS MORE OF WALLY'S THING. GLAD I DON'T HAVE TO WORRY ABOUT HIM ANYMORE...
BUT MAYBE THAT'S WHAT THE OLD BARRY NEVER FIGURED OUT. THAT I DON'T REALLY NEED A FAMILY. THEY JUST SLOW ME DOWN.
PERHAPS THE BETTER VERSION OF THE FLASH IS THE ONE WITH NO FAMILY.
THE ONE WHO RUNS ALONE. MAYBE THAT IS THE BEST FLASH.
BART WAS RIGHT. YOU'RE NOT BARRY. YOU TRIED THIS BEFORE.
WITH WALLY.
AND ON MY WEDDING DAY...
WEDDING DAY?
OH HO, HO, HO, YOU TRYING TO GIVE ME A HISTORY LESSON?
I KNOW YOUR FUTURES. I KNOW ALL YOUR ENDS.
BUT MAYBE I SPEED THAT UP.
IT IS MY M.O. TO HELP PEOPLE DIE BEFORE THEIR TIME, RIGHT?
SON, I MEAN THIS WITH ALL DUE RESPECT...

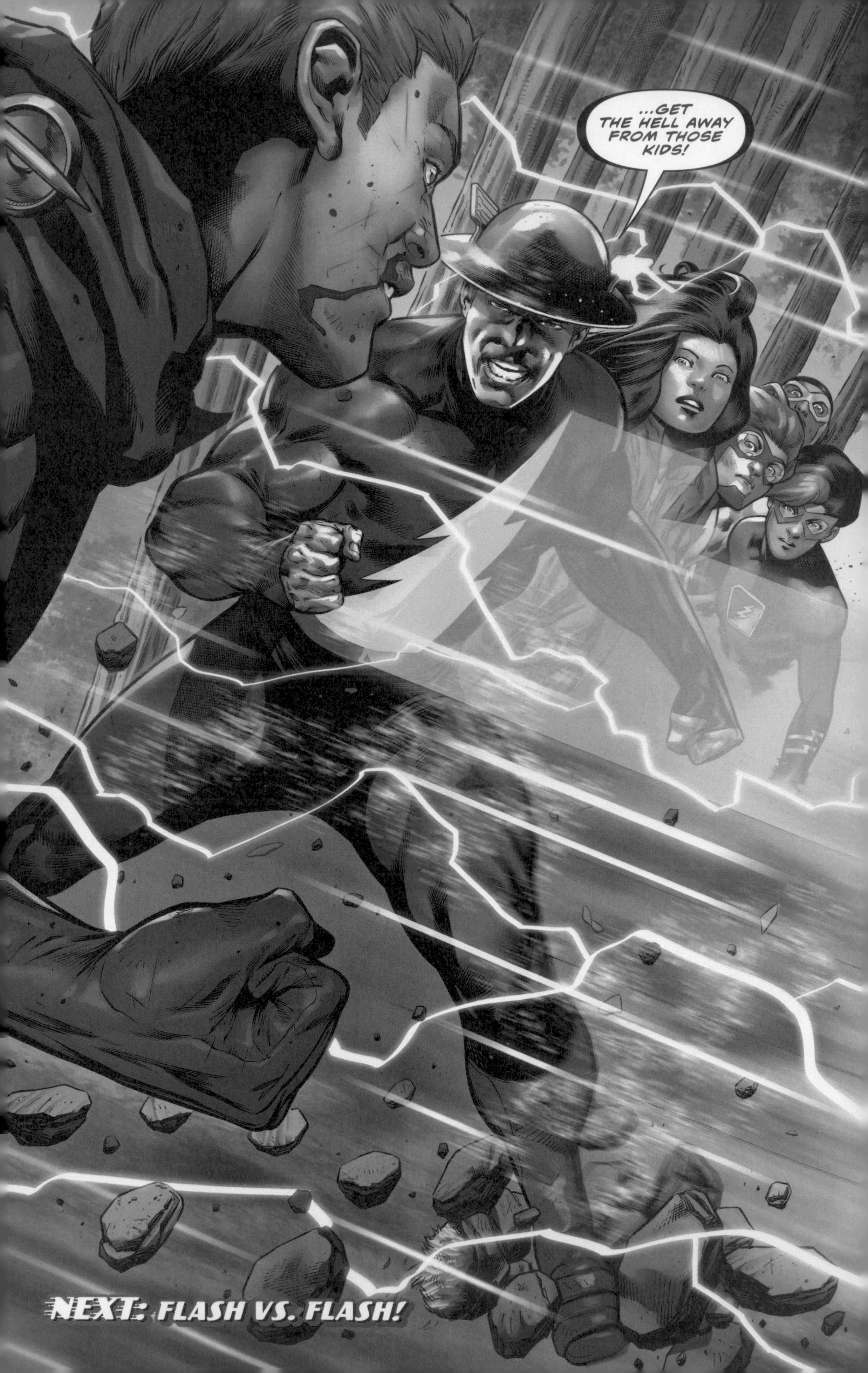
...GET THE HELL AWAY FROM THOSE KIDS!
NEXT: FLASH VS. FLASH!

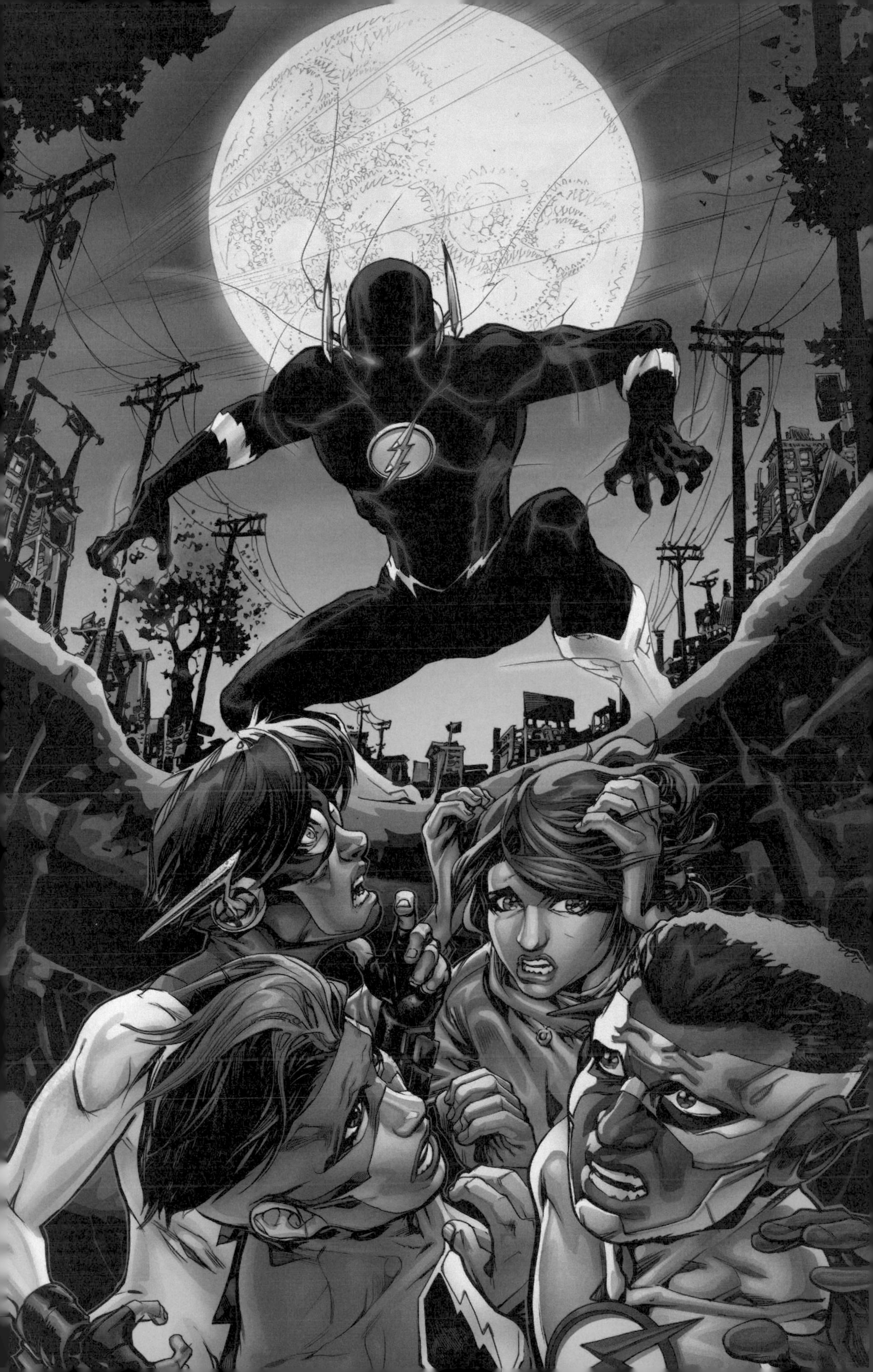

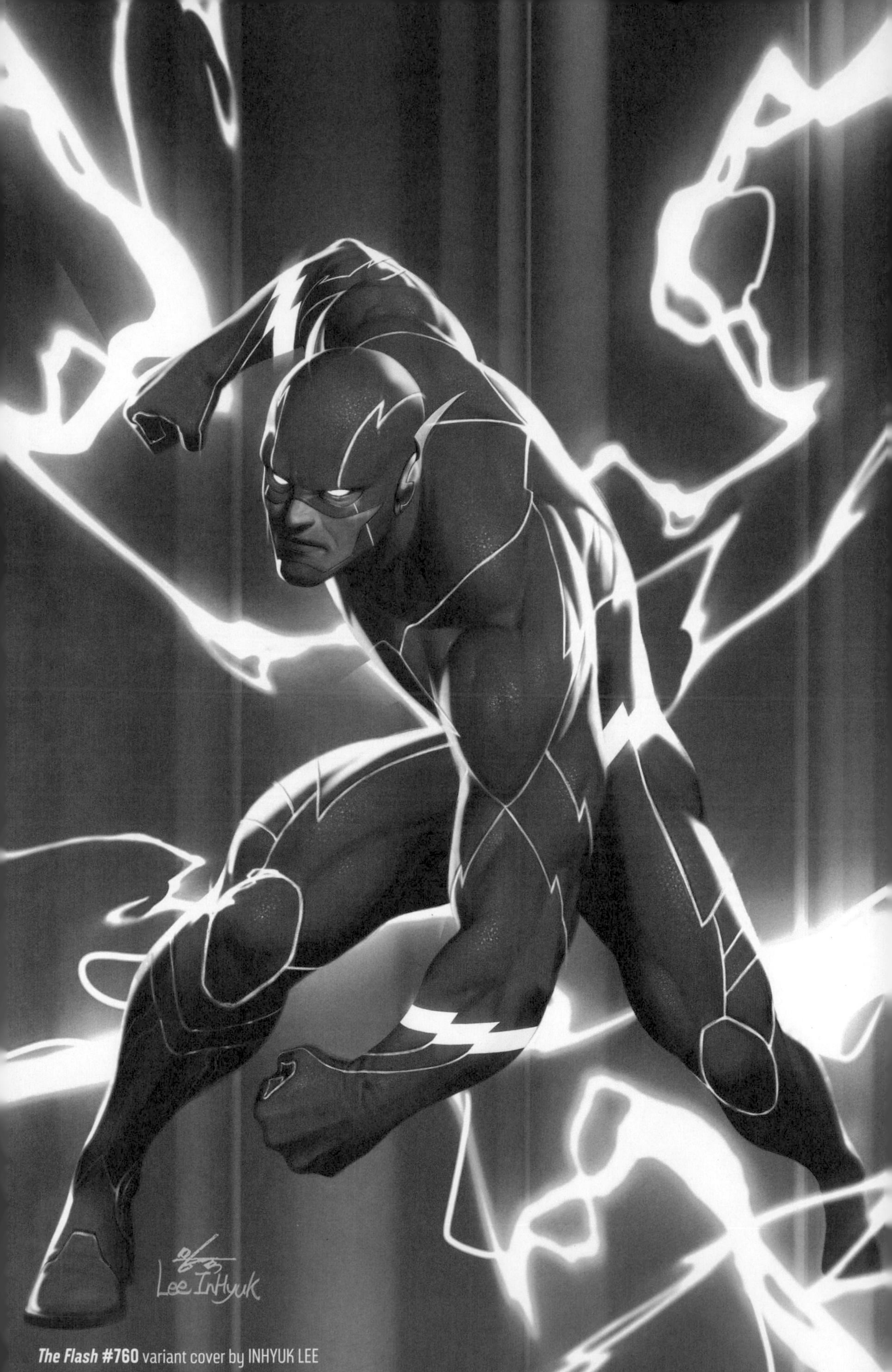
Lee InHyuk

***The Flash* #760** variant cover by INHYUK LEE

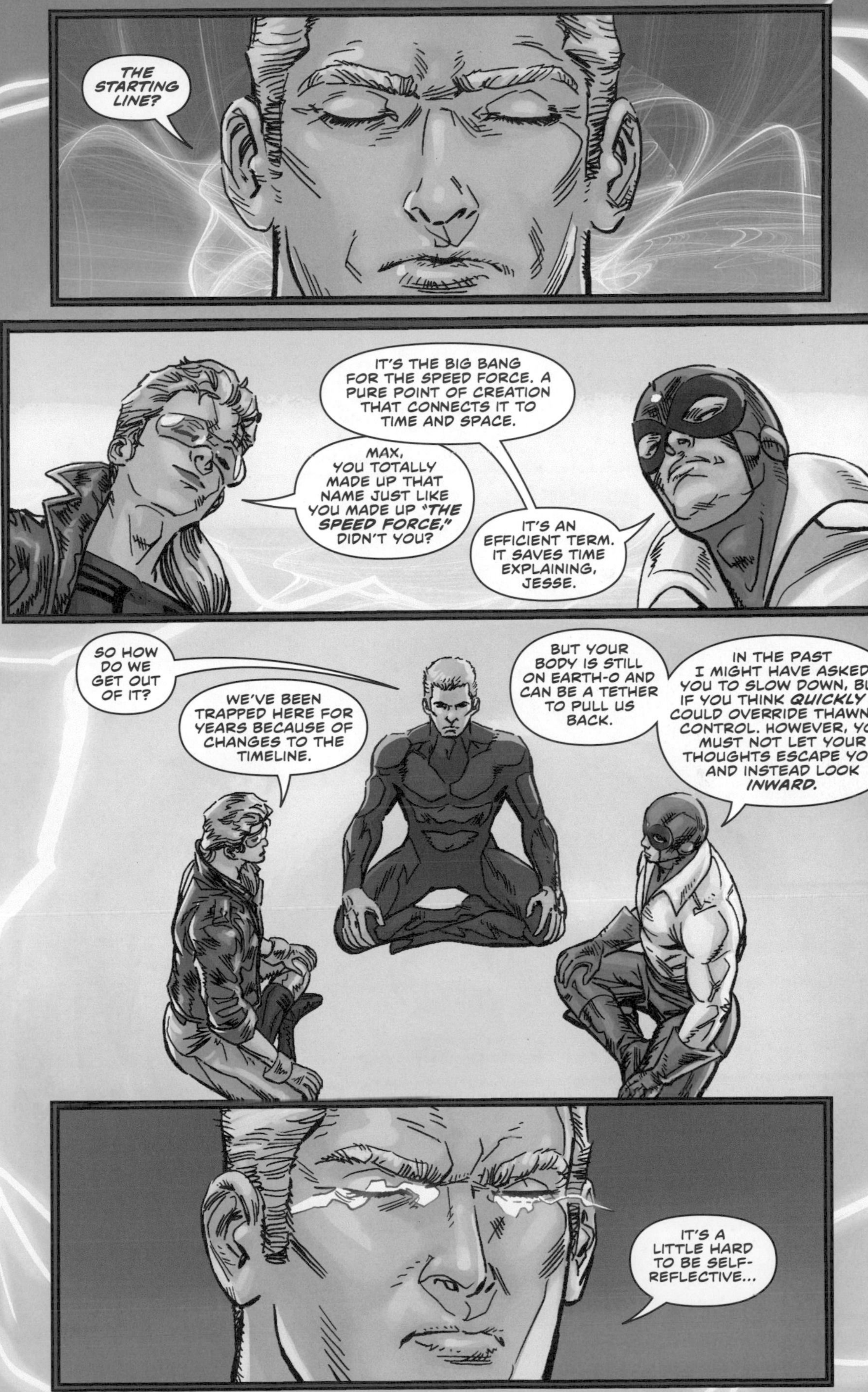
THE STARTING LINE?
IT'S THE BIG BANG FOR THE SPEED FORCE. A PURE POINT OF CREATION THAT CONNECTS IT TO TIME AND SPACE.
MAX, YOU TOTALLY MADE UP THAT NAME JUST LIKE YOU MADE UP "THE SPEED FORCE," DIDN'T YOU?
IT'S AN EFFICIENT TERM. IT SAVES TIME EXPLAINING, JESSE.
SO HOW DO WE GET OUT OF IT?
WE'VE BEEN TRAPPED HERE FOR YEARS BECAUSE OF CHANGES TO THE TIMELINE.
BUT YOUR BODY IS STILL ON EARTH-0 AND CAN BE A TETHER TO PULL US BACK.
IN THE PAST I MIGHT HAVE ASKED YOU TO SLOW DOWN, BUT IF YOU THINK QUICKLY IT COULD OVERRIDE THAWNE'S CONTROL. HOWEVER, YOU MUST NOT LET YOUR THOUGHTS ESCAPE YOU, AND INSTEAD LOOK INWARD.
IT'S A LITTLE HARD TO BE SELF-REFLECTIVE...

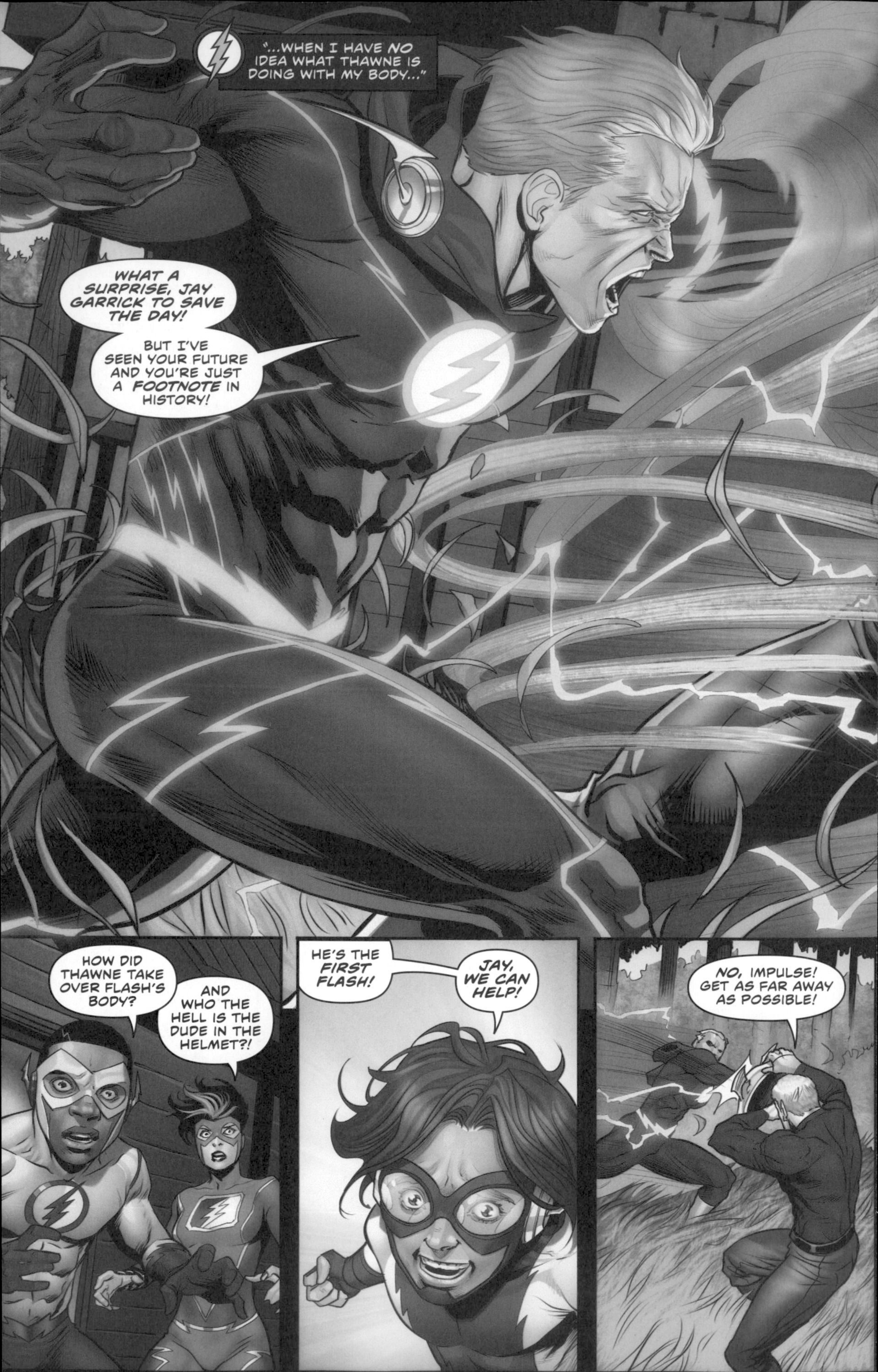
"...WHEN I HAVE NO IDEA WHAT THAWNE IS DOING WITH MY BODY..."
WHAT A SURPRISE, JAY GARRICK TO SAVE THE DAY!
BUT I'VE SEEN YOUR FUTURE AND YOU'RE JUST A FOOTNOTE IN HISTORY!
HOW DID THAWNE TAKE OVER FLASH'S BODY?
AND WHO THE HELL IS THE DUDE IN THE HELMET?!
HE'S THE FIRST FLASH!
JAY, WE CAN HELP!
NO, IMPULSE! GET AS FAR AWAY AS POSSIBLE!

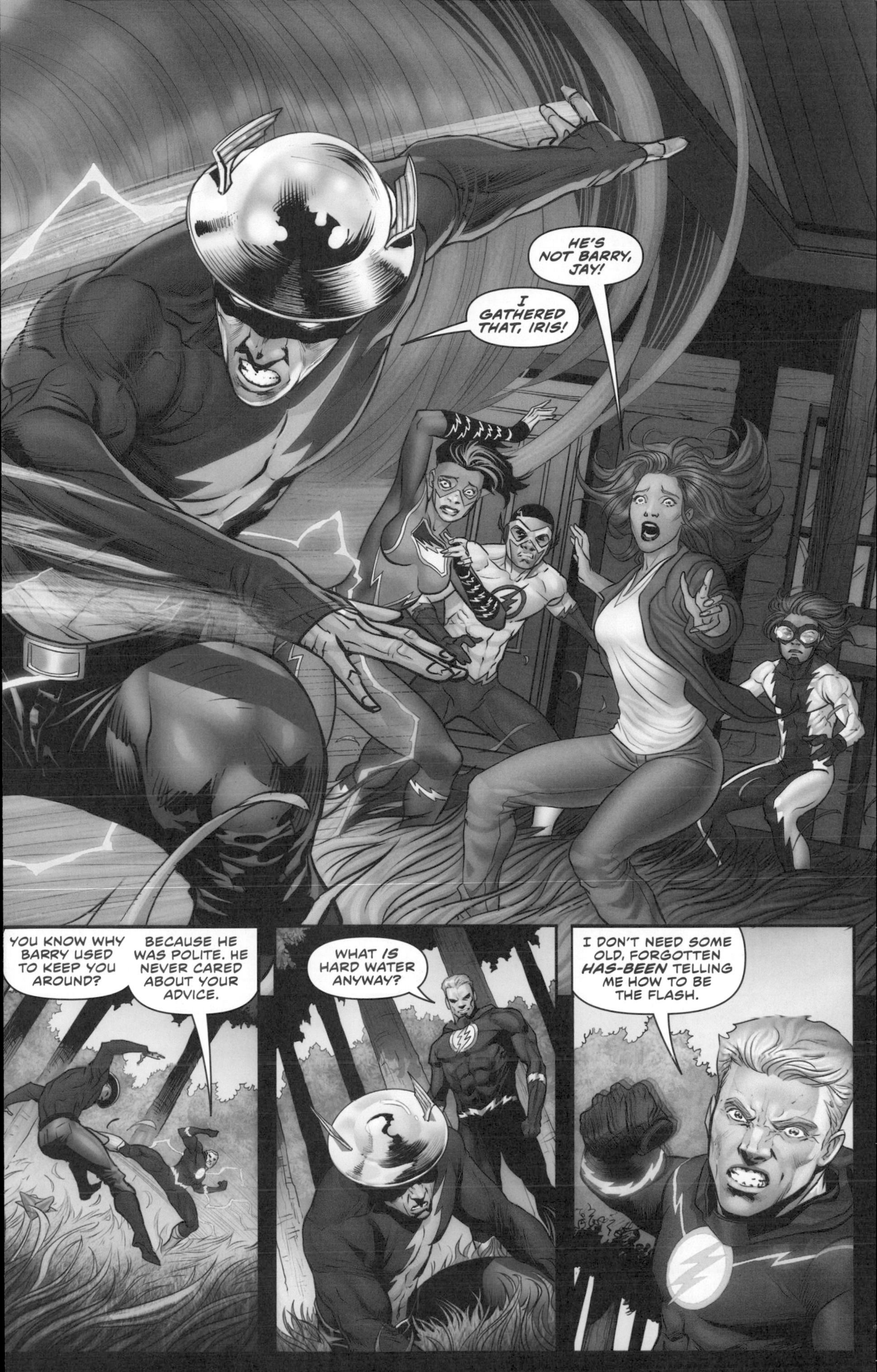

HE'S NOT BARRY, JAY!
I GATHERED THAT, IRIS!
YOU KNOW WHY BARRY USED TO KEEP YOU AROUND?
BECAUSE HE WAS POLITE. HE NEVER CARED ABOUT YOUR ADVICE.
WHAT *IS* HARD WATER ANYWAY?
I DON'T NEED SOME OLD, FORGOTTEN ***HAS-BEEN*** TELLING ME HOW TO BE THE FLASH.

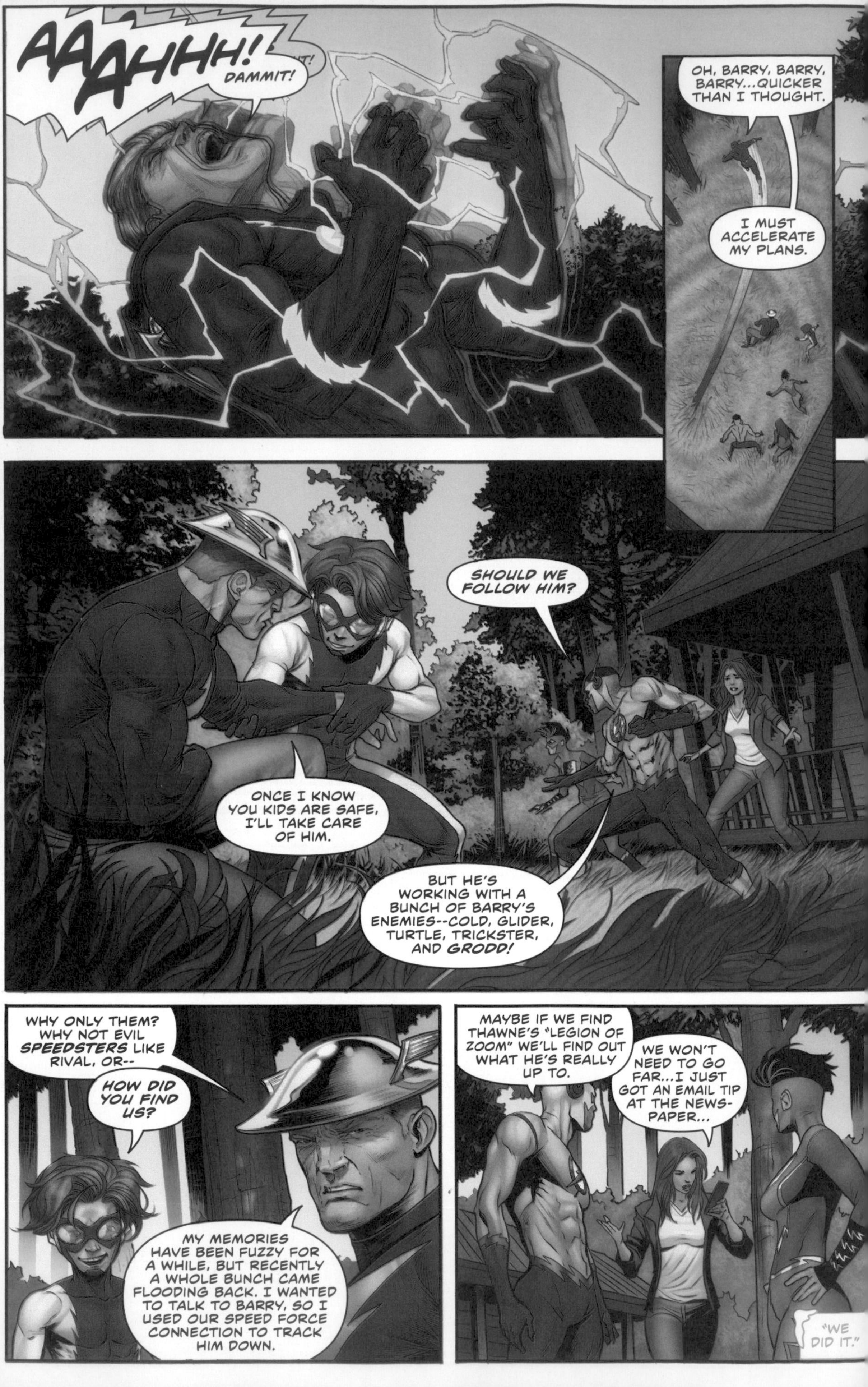
AAAHHH!
DAMMIT!
OH, BARRY, BARRY, BARRY...QUICKER THAN I THOUGHT.
I MUST ACCELERATE MY PLANS.
SHOULD WE FOLLOW HIM?
ONCE I KNOW YOU KIDS ARE SAFE, I'LL TAKE CARE OF HIM.
BUT HE'S WORKING WITH A BUNCH OF BARRY'S ENEMIES--COLD, GLIDER, TURTLE, TRICKSTER, AND GRODD!
WHY ONLY THEM? WHY NOT EVIL SPEEDSTERS LIKE RIVAL, OR--
HOW DID YOU FIND US?
MY MEMORIES HAVE BEEN FUZZY FOR A WHILE, BUT RECENTLY A WHOLE BUNCH CAME FLOODING BACK. I WANTED TO TALK TO BARRY, SO I USED OUR SPEED FORCE CONNECTION TO TRACK HIM DOWN.
MAYBE IF WE FIND THAWNE'S "LEGION OF ZOOM" WE'LL FIND OUT WHAT HE'S REALLY UP TO.
WE WON'T NEED TO GO FAR...I JUST GOT AN EMAIL TIP AT THE NEWS-PAPER...
"WE DID IT."

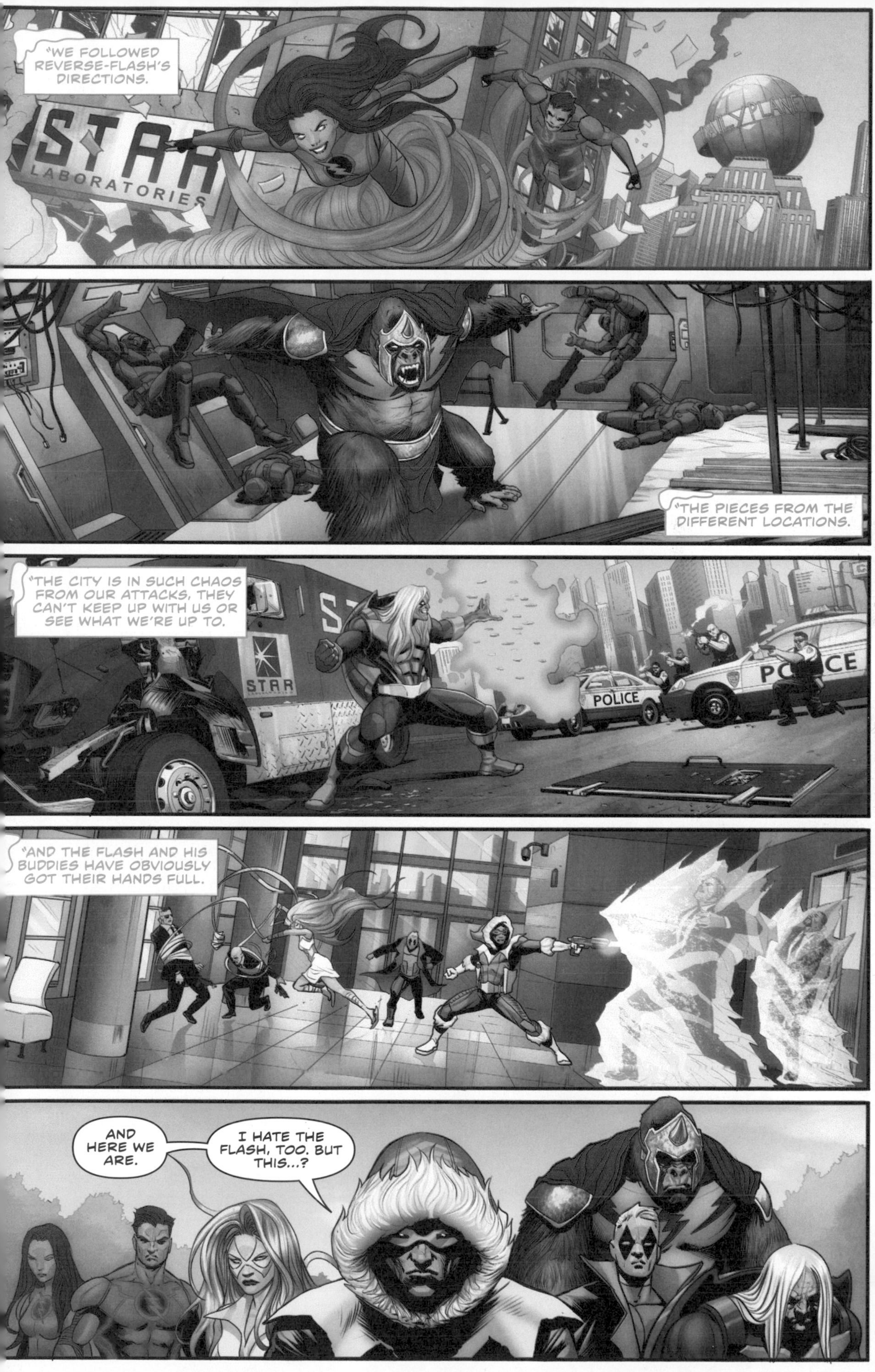
"WE FOLLOWED REVERSE-FLASH'S DIRECTIONS.
"THE PIECES FROM THE DIFFERENT LOCATIONS.
"THE CITY IS IN SUCH CHAOS FROM OUR ATTACKS, THEY CAN'T KEEP UP WITH US OR SEE WHAT WE'RE UP TO.
"AND THE FLASH AND HIS BUDDIES HAVE OBVIOUSLY GOT THEIR HANDS FULL.
AND HERE WE ARE.
I HATE THE FLASH, TOO. BUT THIS...?

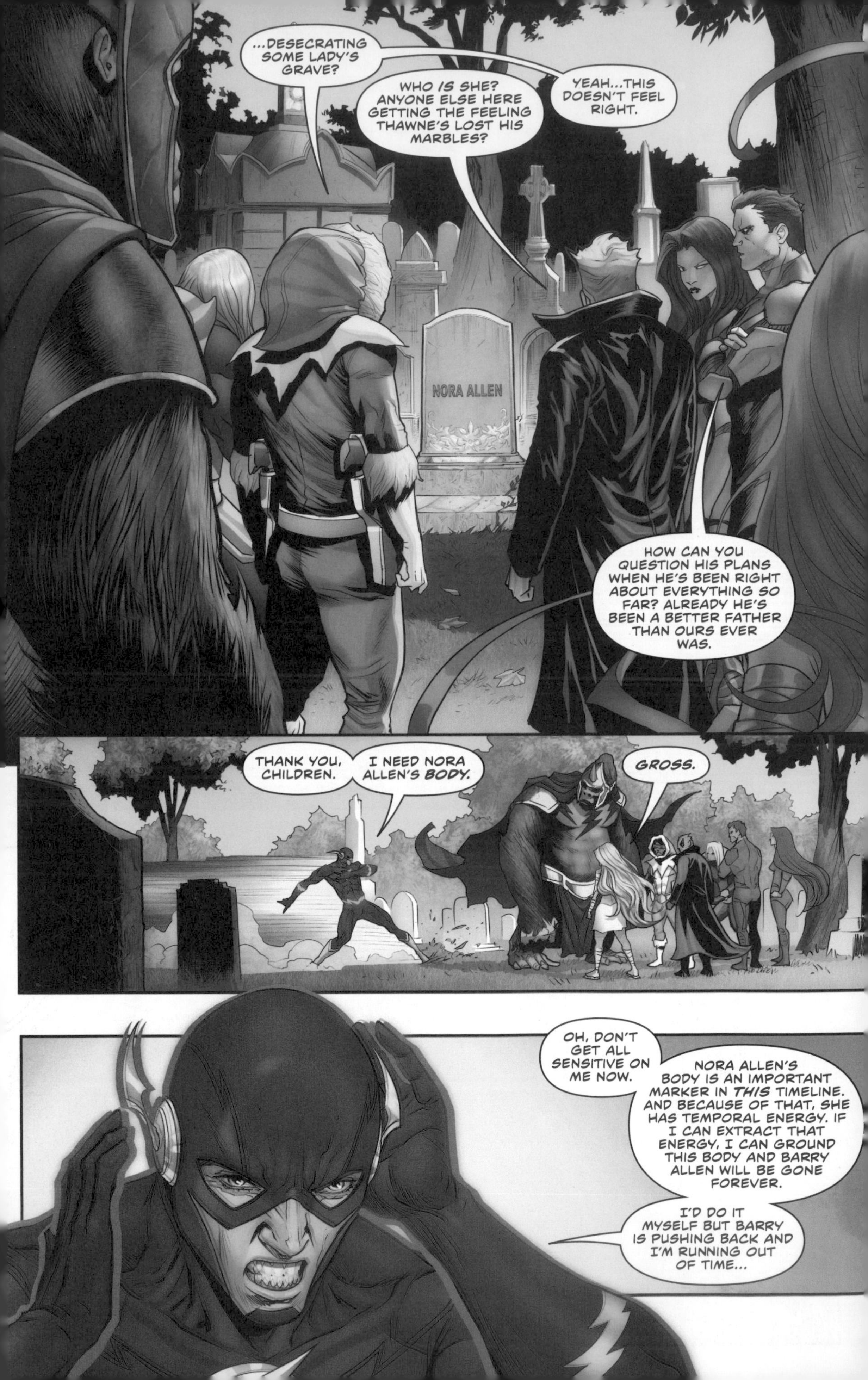
...DESECRATING SOME LADY'S GRAVE?
YEAH...THIS DOESN'T FEEL RIGHT.
WHO *IS* SHE? ANYONE ELSE HERE GETTING THE FEELING THAWNE'S LOST HIS MARBLES?
NORA ALLEN
HOW CAN YOU QUESTION HIS PLANS WHEN HE'S BEEN RIGHT ABOUT EVERYTHING SO FAR? ALREADY HE'S BEEN A BETTER FATHER THAN OURS EVER WAS.
THANK YOU, CHILDREN.
I NEED NORA ALLEN'S *BODY.*
GROSS.
OH, DON'T GET ALL SENSITIVE ON ME NOW.
NORA ALLEN'S BODY IS AN IMPORTANT MARKER IN *THIS* TIMELINE. AND BECAUSE OF THAT, SHE HAS TEMPORAL ENERGY. IF I CAN EXTRACT THAT ENERGY, I CAN GROUND THIS BODY AND BARRY ALLEN WILL BE GONE FOREVER.
I'D DO IT MYSELF BUT BARRY IS PUSHING BACK AND I'M RUNNING OUT OF TIME...

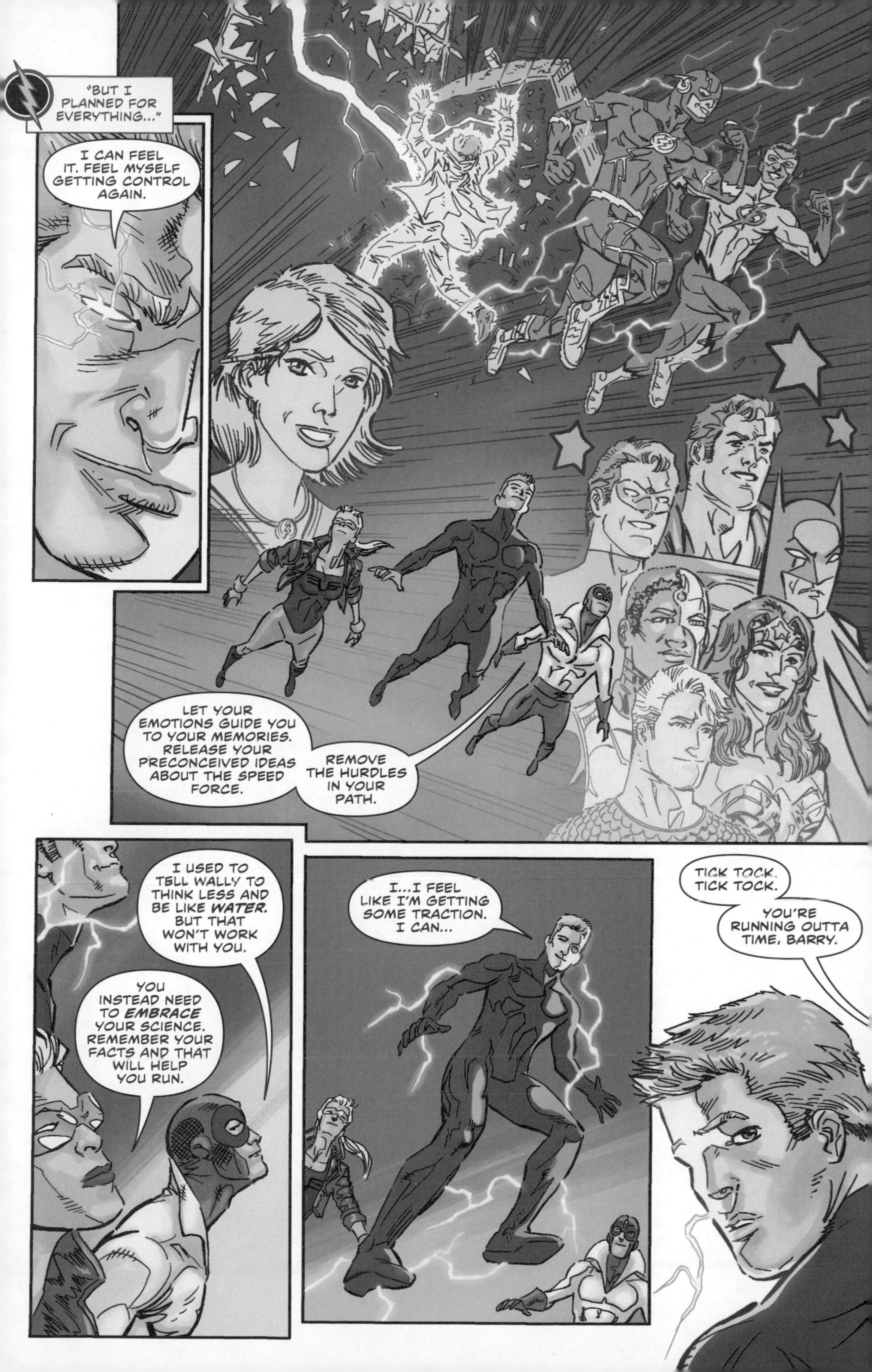
"BUT I PLANNED FOR EVERYTHING..."
I CAN FEEL IT. FEEL MYSELF GETTING CONTROL AGAIN.
LET YOUR EMOTIONS GUIDE YOU TO YOUR MEMORIES. RELEASE YOUR PRECONCEIVED IDEAS ABOUT THE SPEED FORCE.
REMOVE THE HURDLES IN YOUR PATH.
I USED TO TELL WALLY TO THINK LESS AND BE LIKE *WATER.* BUT THAT WON'T WORK WITH YOU.
YOU INSTEAD NEED TO *EMBRACE* YOUR SCIENCE. REMEMBER YOUR FACTS AND THAT WILL HELP YOU RUN.
I...I FEEL LIKE I'M GETTING SOME TRACTION. I CAN...
TICK TOCK. TICK TOCK.
YOU'RE RUNNING OUTTA TIME, BARRY.

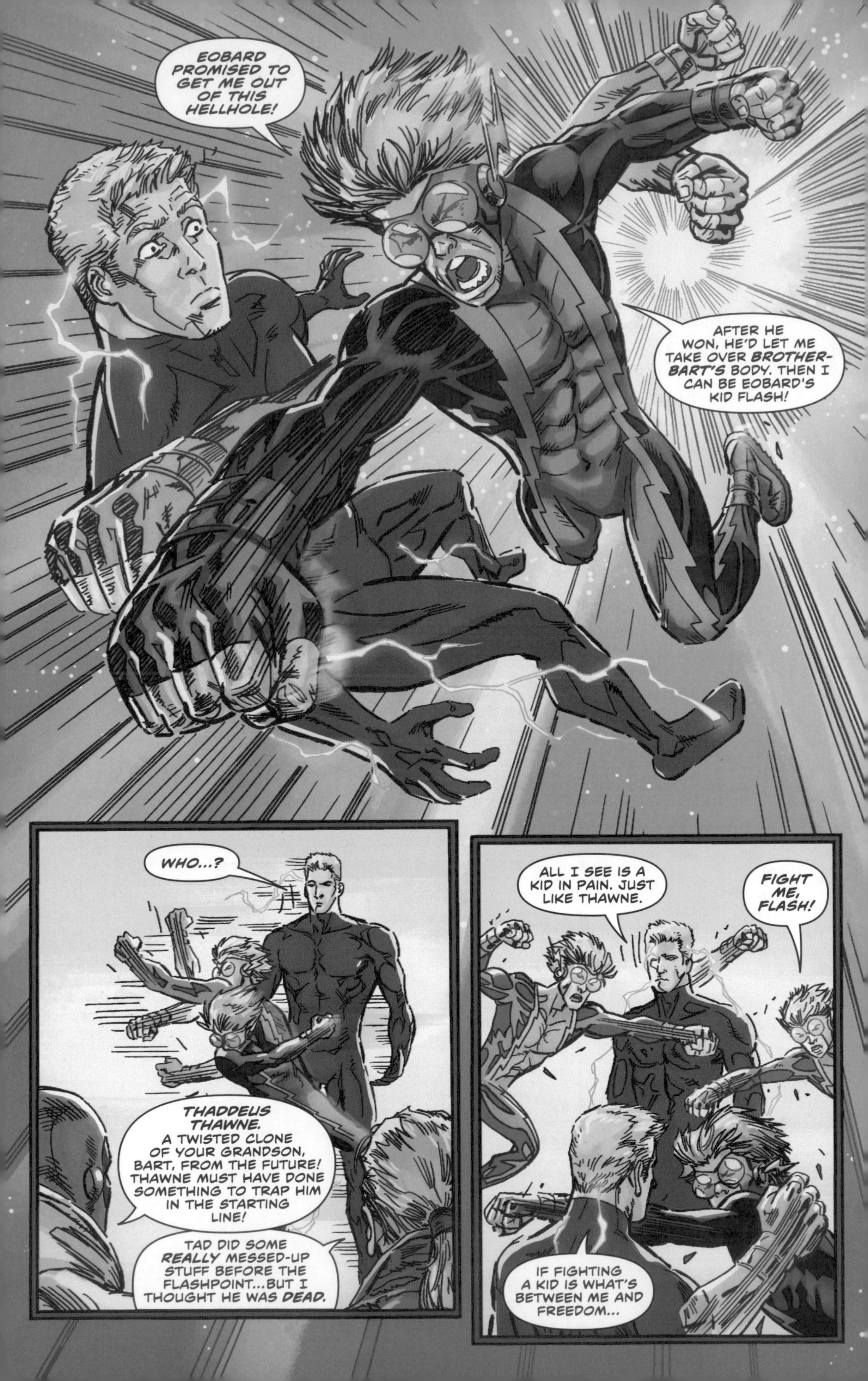
EOBARD PROMISED TO GET ME OUT OF THIS HELLHOLE!
AFTER HE WON, HE'D LET ME TAKE OVER BROTHER-BART'S BODY. THEN I CAN BE EOBARD'S KID FLASH!
WHO...?
THADDEUS THAWNE. A TWISTED CLONE OF YOUR GRANDSON, BART, FROM THE FUTURE! THAWNE MUST HAVE DONE SOMETHING TO TRAP HIM IN THE STARTING LINE!
TAD DID SOME REALLY MESSED-UP STUFF BEFORE THE FLASHPOINT...BUT I THOUGHT HE WAS DEAD.
ALL I SEE IS A KID IN PAIN. JUST LIKE THAWNE.
FIGHT ME, FLASH!
IF FIGHTING A KID IS WHAT'S BETWEEN ME AND FREEDOM...

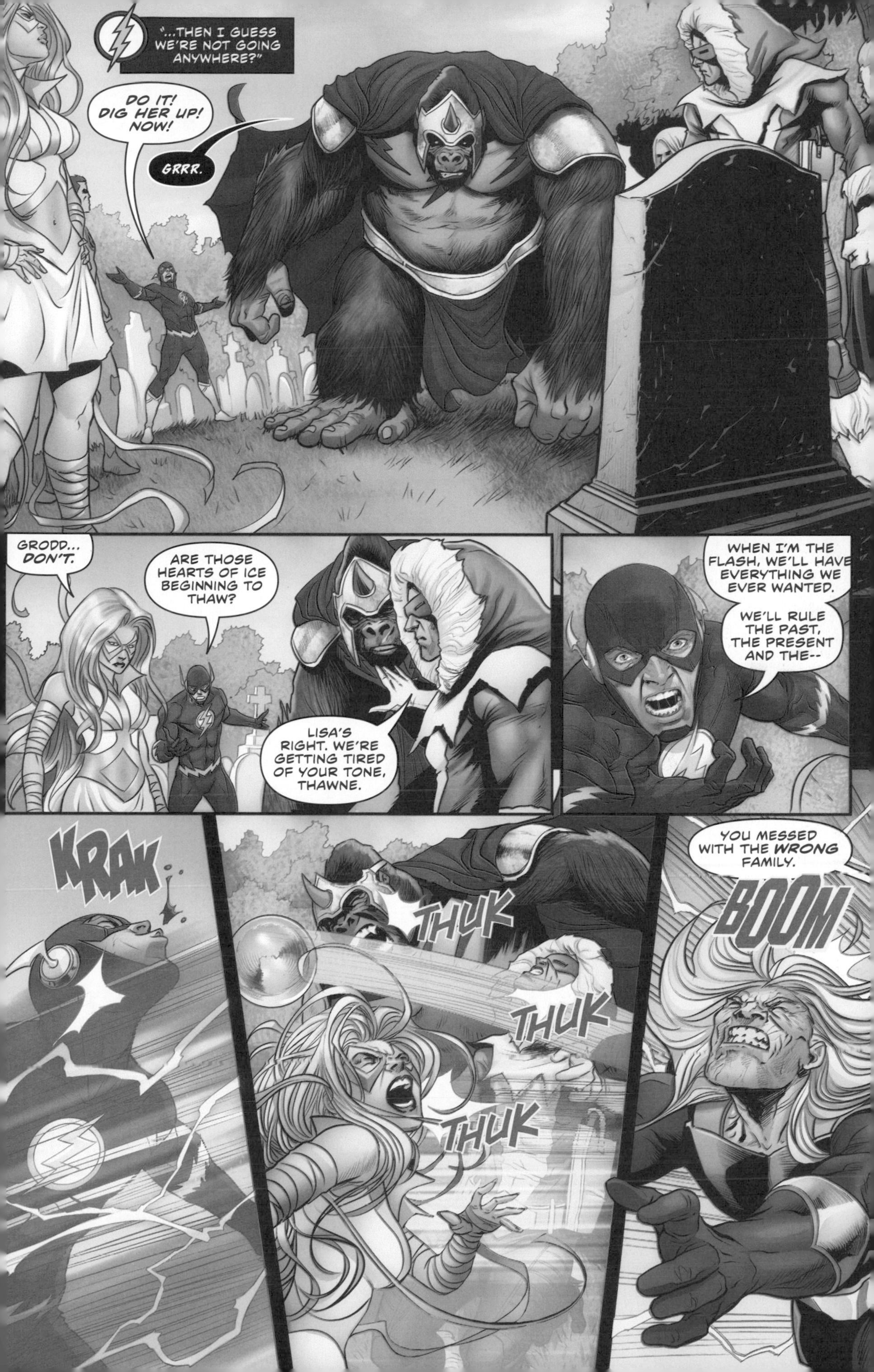
"...THEN I GUESS WE'RE NOT GOING ANYWHERE?"
DO IT! DIG HER UP! NOW!
GRRR.
GRODD... DON'T.
ARE THOSE HEARTS OF ICE BEGINNING TO THAW?
LISA'S RIGHT. WE'RE GETTING TIRED OF YOUR TONE, THAWNE.
WHEN I'M THE FLASH, WE'LL HAVE EVERYTHING WE EVER WANTED.
WE'LL RULE THE PAST, THE PRESENT AND THE--
KRAK
THUK
THUK
THUK
YOU MESSED WITH THE WRONG FAMILY.
BOOM

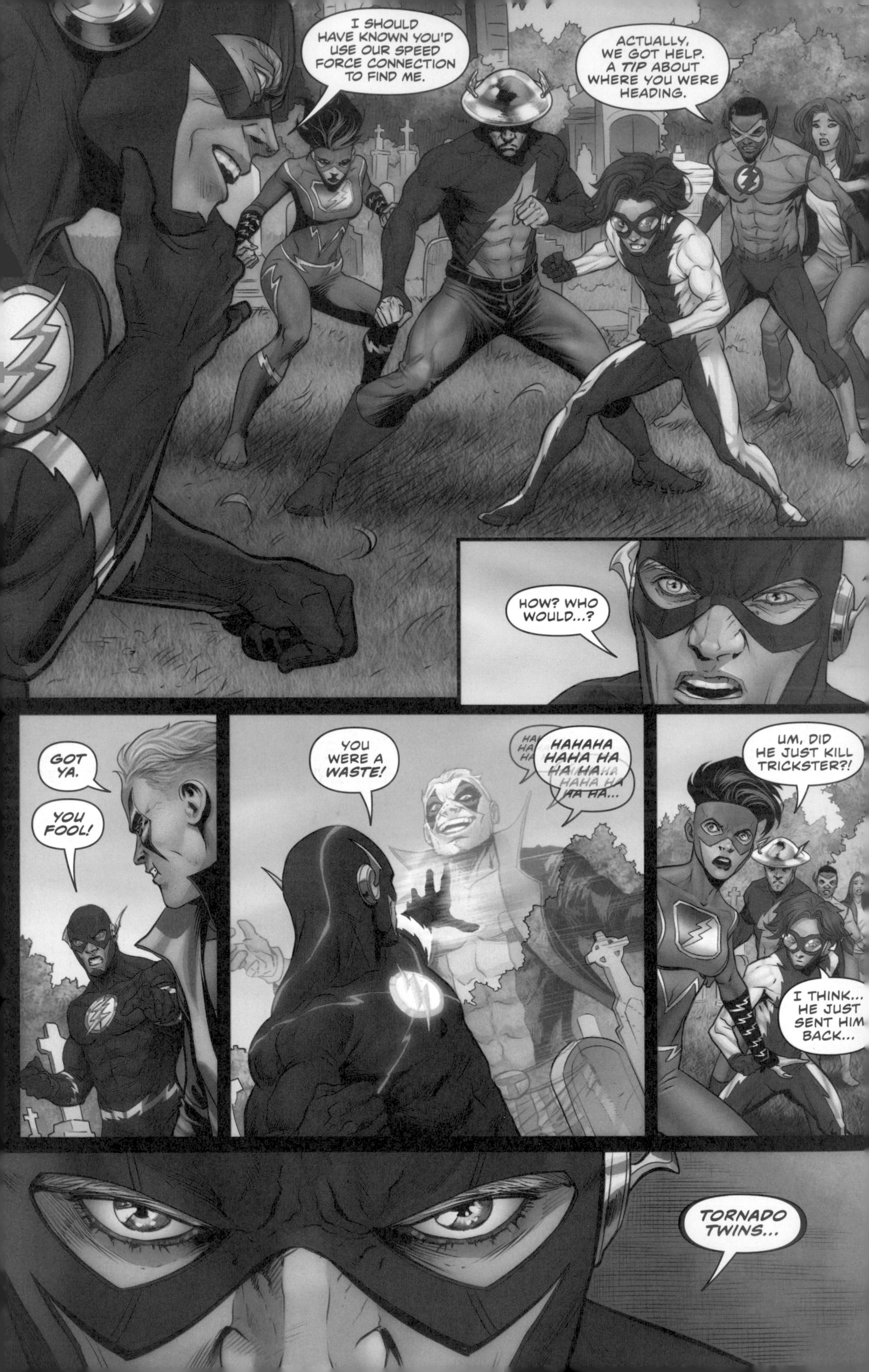
I SHOULD HAVE KNOWN YOU'D USE OUR SPEED FORCE CONNECTION TO FIND ME.
ACTUALLY, WE GOT HELP. A *TIP* ABOUT WHERE YOU WERE HEADING.
HOW? WHO WOULD...?
GOT YA.
YOU FOOL!
YOU WERE A *WASTE!*
HAHAHA HAHA HA HA HA...
UM, DID HE JUST KILL TRICKSTER?!
I THINK... HE JUST SENT HIM BACK...
TORNADO TWINS...

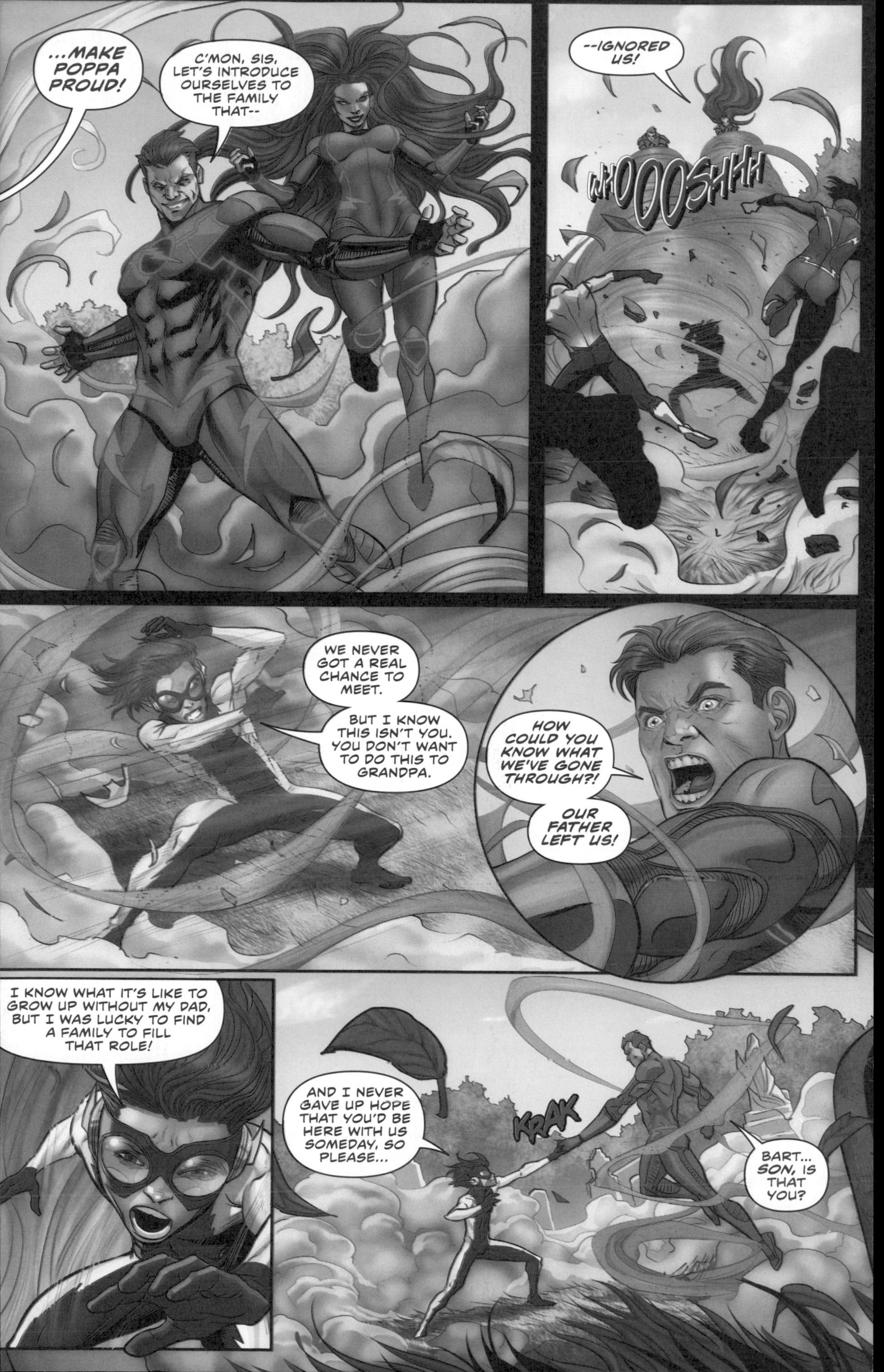
...MAKE POPPA PROUD!
C'MON, SIS, LET'S INTRODUCE OURSELVES TO THE FAMILY THAT--
--IGNORED US!
WHOOOOSHHH
WE NEVER GOT A REAL CHANCE TO MEET.
BUT I KNOW THIS ISN'T YOU. YOU DON'T WANT TO DO THIS TO GRANDPA.
HOW COULD YOU KNOW WHAT WE'VE GONE THROUGH?!
OUR FATHER LEFT US!
I KNOW WHAT IT'S LIKE TO GROW UP WITHOUT MY DAD, BUT I WAS LUCKY TO FIND A FAMILY TO FILL THAT ROLE!
AND I NEVER GAVE UP HOPE THAT YOU'D BE HERE WITH US SOMEDAY, SO PLEASE...
KRAK
BART... SON, IS THAT YOU?

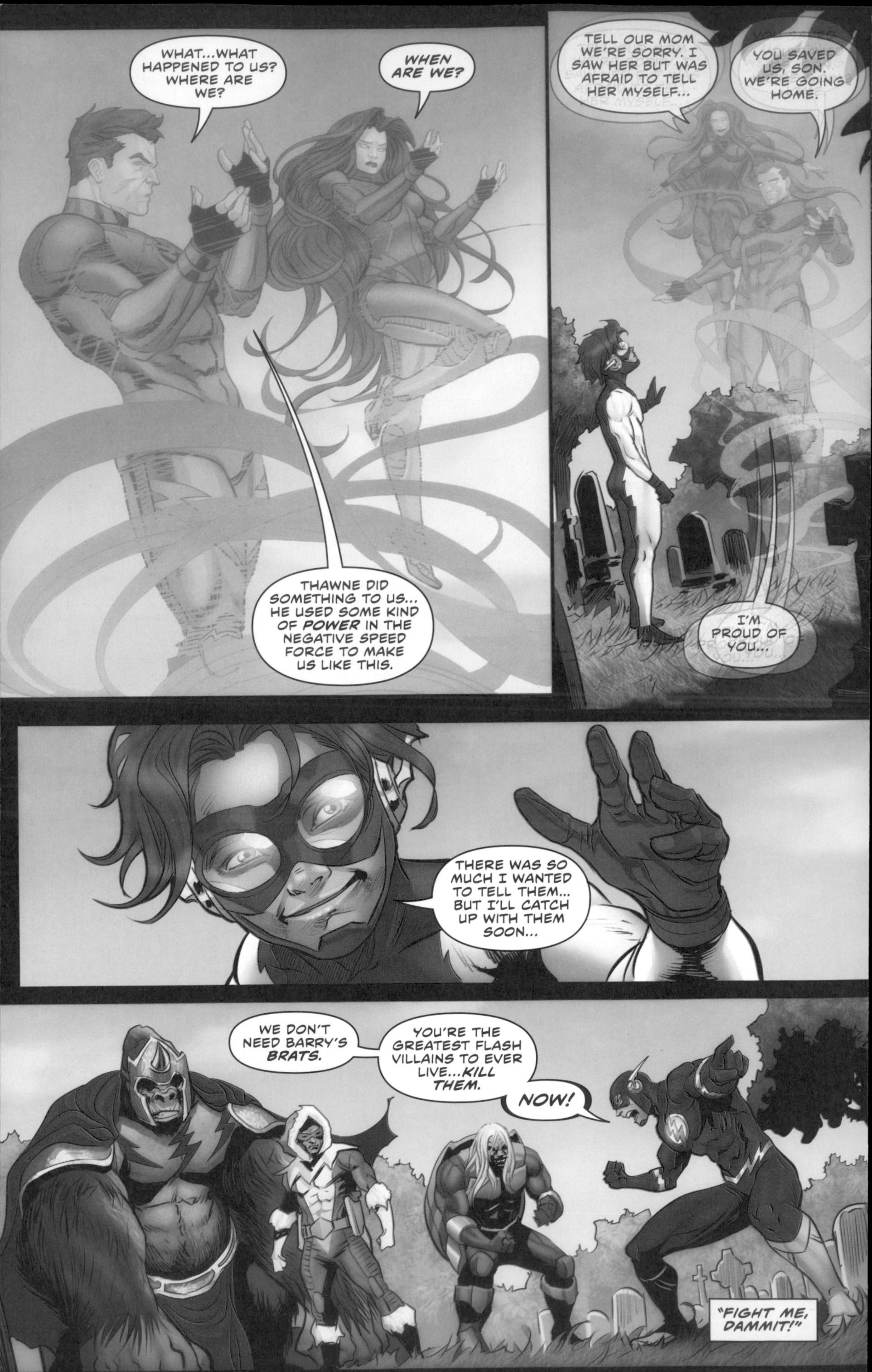
WHAT...WHAT HAPPENED TO US? WHERE ARE WE?
WHEN ARE WE?
THAWNE DID SOMETHING TO US... HE USED SOME KIND OF POWER IN THE NEGATIVE SPEED FORCE TO MAKE US LIKE THIS.
TELL OUR MOM WE'RE SORRY. I SAW HER BUT WAS AFRAID TO TELL HER MYSELF...
YOU SAVED US, SON. WE'RE GOING HOME.
I'M PROUD OF YOU...
THERE WAS SO MUCH I WANTED TO TELL THEM... BUT I'LL CATCH UP WITH THEM SOON...
WE DON'T NEED BARRY'S BRATS.
YOU'RE THE GREATEST FLASH VILLAINS TO EVER LIVE...KILL THEM.
NOW!
"FIGHT ME, DAMMIT!"

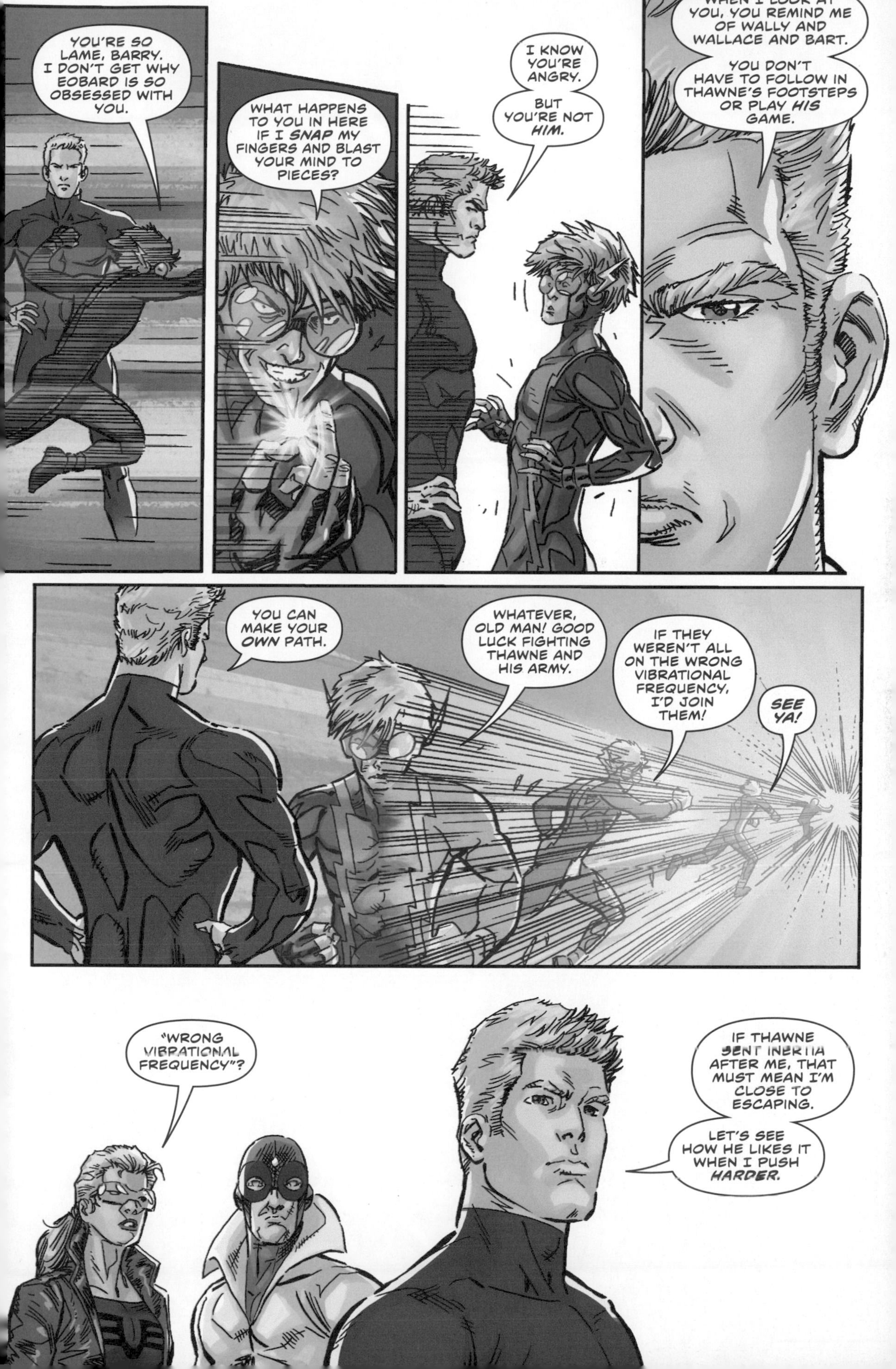
YOU'RE SO LAME, BARRY. I DON'T GET WHY EOBARD IS SO OBSESSED WITH YOU.
WHAT HAPPENS TO YOU IN HERE IF I SNAP MY FINGERS AND BLAST YOUR MIND TO PIECES?
I KNOW YOU'RE ANGRY.
BUT YOU'RE NOT HIM.
WHEN I LOOK AT YOU, YOU REMIND ME OF WALLY AND WALLACE AND BART.
YOU DON'T HAVE TO FOLLOW IN THAWNE'S FOOTSTEPS OR PLAY HIS GAME.
YOU CAN MAKE YOUR OWN PATH.
WHATEVER, OLD MAN! GOOD LUCK FIGHTING THAWNE AND HIS ARMY.
IF THEY WEREN'T ALL ON THE WRONG VIBRATIONAL FREQUENCY, I'D JOIN THEM!
SEE YA!
"WRONG VIBRATIONAL FREQUENCY"?
IF THAWNE SENT INERTIA AFTER ME, THAT MUST MEAN I'M CLOSE TO ESCAPING.
LET'S SEE HOW HE LIKES IT WHEN I PUSH HARDER.

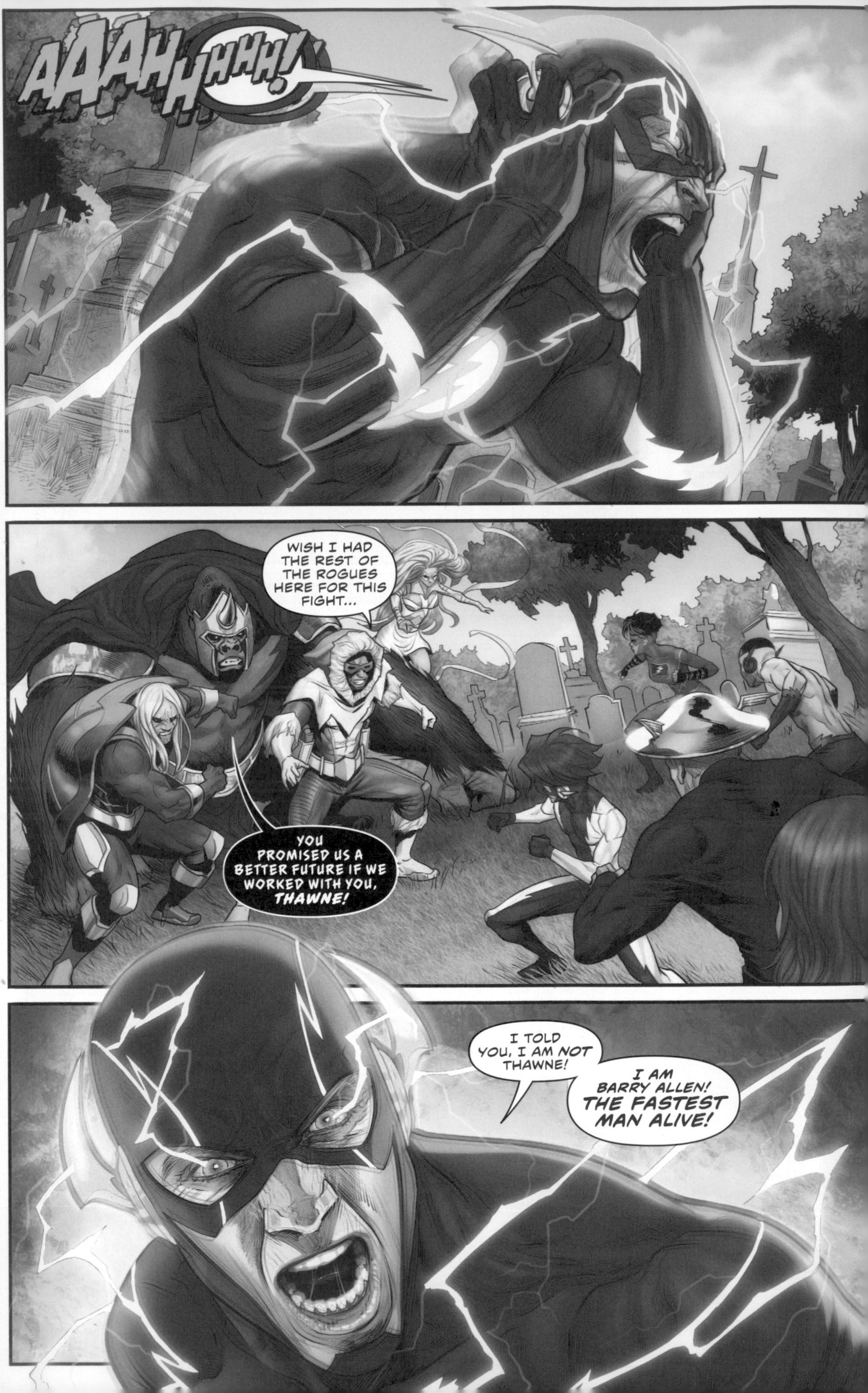
AAAHHHHH!
WISH I HAD THE REST OF THE ROGUES HERE FOR THIS FIGHT...
YOU PROMISED US A BETTER FUTURE IF WE WORKED WITH YOU, THAWNE!
I TOLD YOU, I AM NOT THAWNE!
I AM BARRY ALLEN! THE FASTEST MAN ALIVE!

AHHHHHH!

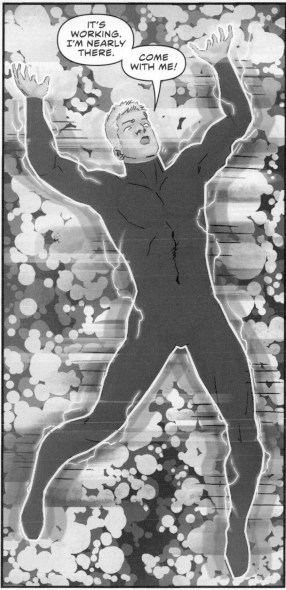

IT'S WORKING. I'M NEARLY THERE.

COME WITH ME!

I DON'T THINK WE CAN.

BUT WHEN YOU GET THERE, DON'T HESITATE TO *KICK HIS ASS.*

GIVE HIM A FEW PUNCHES FOR ME.

NO, YOU'VE BEEN GONE FROM OUR LIVES LONG ENOUGH AND I REFUSE TO LET ANYONE ELSE BE TRAPPED HERE!

KRAKAKA

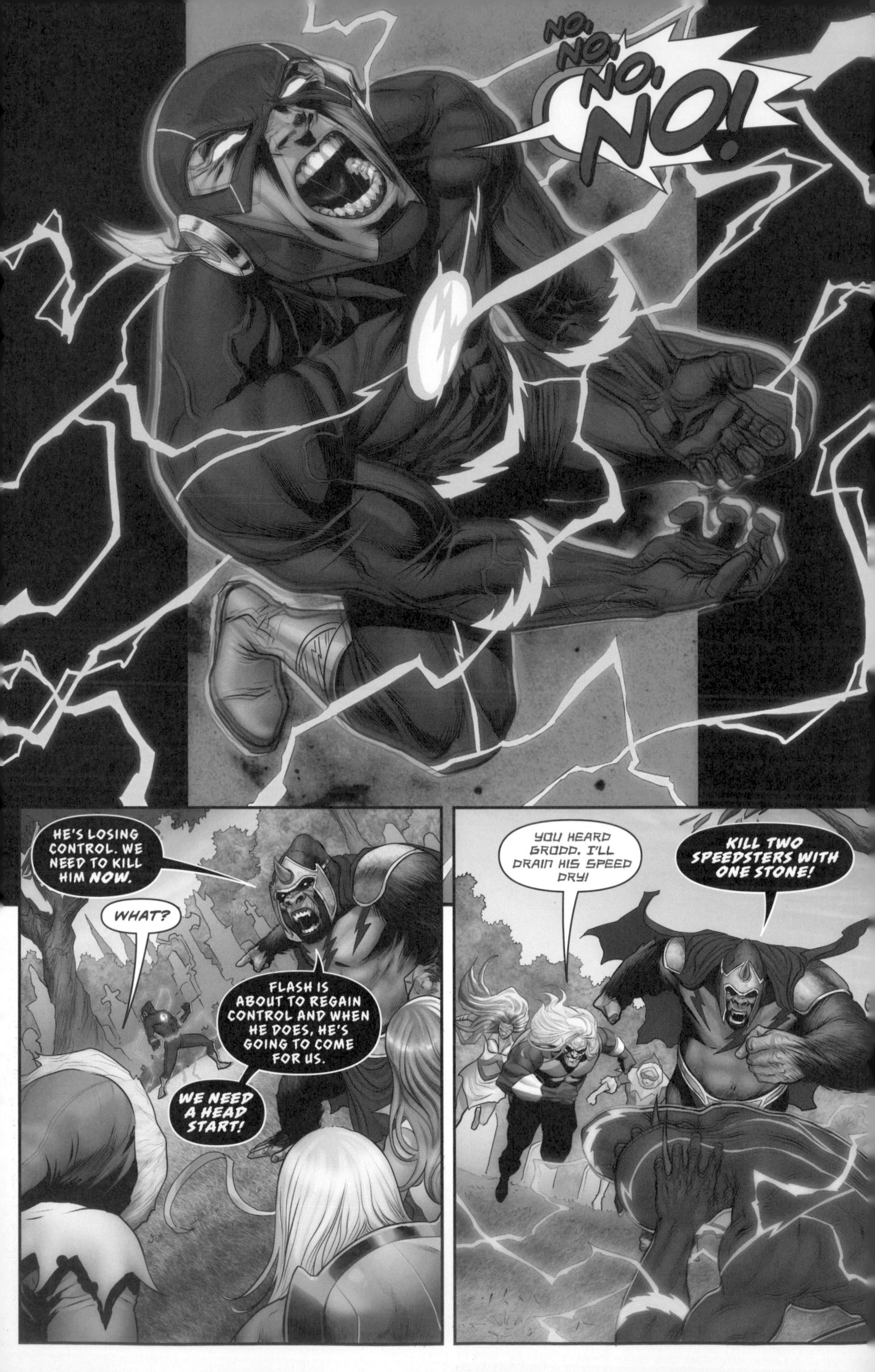
NO, NO, NO, NO!
HE'S LOSING CONTROL. WE NEED TO KILL HIM NOW.
WHAT?
FLASH IS ABOUT TO REGAIN CONTROL AND WHEN HE DOES, HE'S GOING TO COME FOR US.
WE NEED A HEAD START!
YOU HEARD GRODD. I'LL DRAIN HIS SPEED DRY!
KILL TWO SPEEDSTERS WITH ONE STONE!

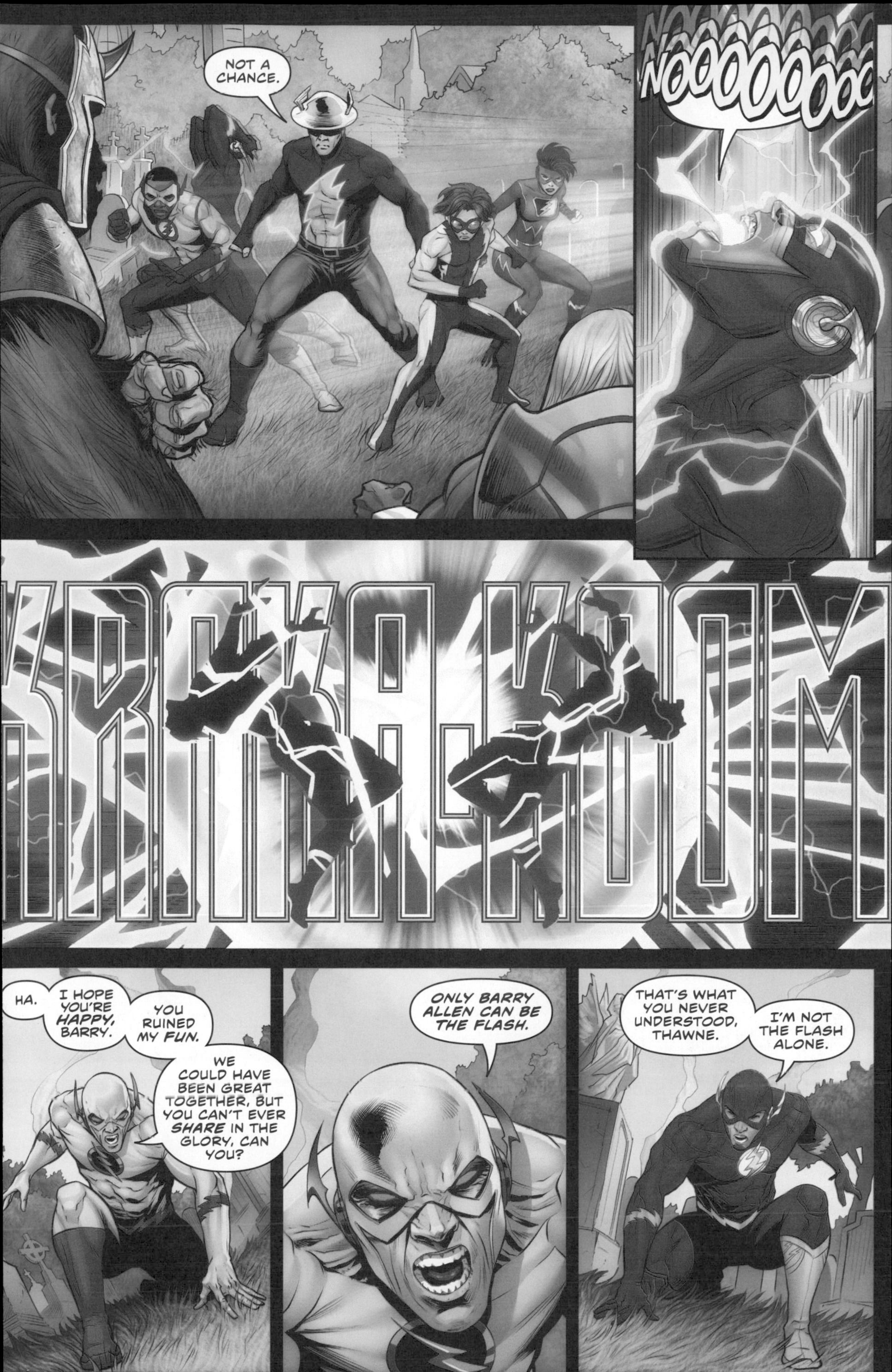
NOT A CHANCE.
NOOOOOOOO
KRAKA-KOOM
HA.
I HOPE YOU'RE HAPPY, BARRY.
YOU RUINED MY FUN.
WE COULD HAVE BEEN GREAT TOGETHER, BUT YOU CAN'T EVER SHARE IN THE GLORY, CAN YOU?
ONLY BARRY ALLEN CAN BE THE FLASH.
THAT'S WHAT YOU NEVER UNDERSTOOD, THAWNE.
I'M NOT THE FLASH ALONE.

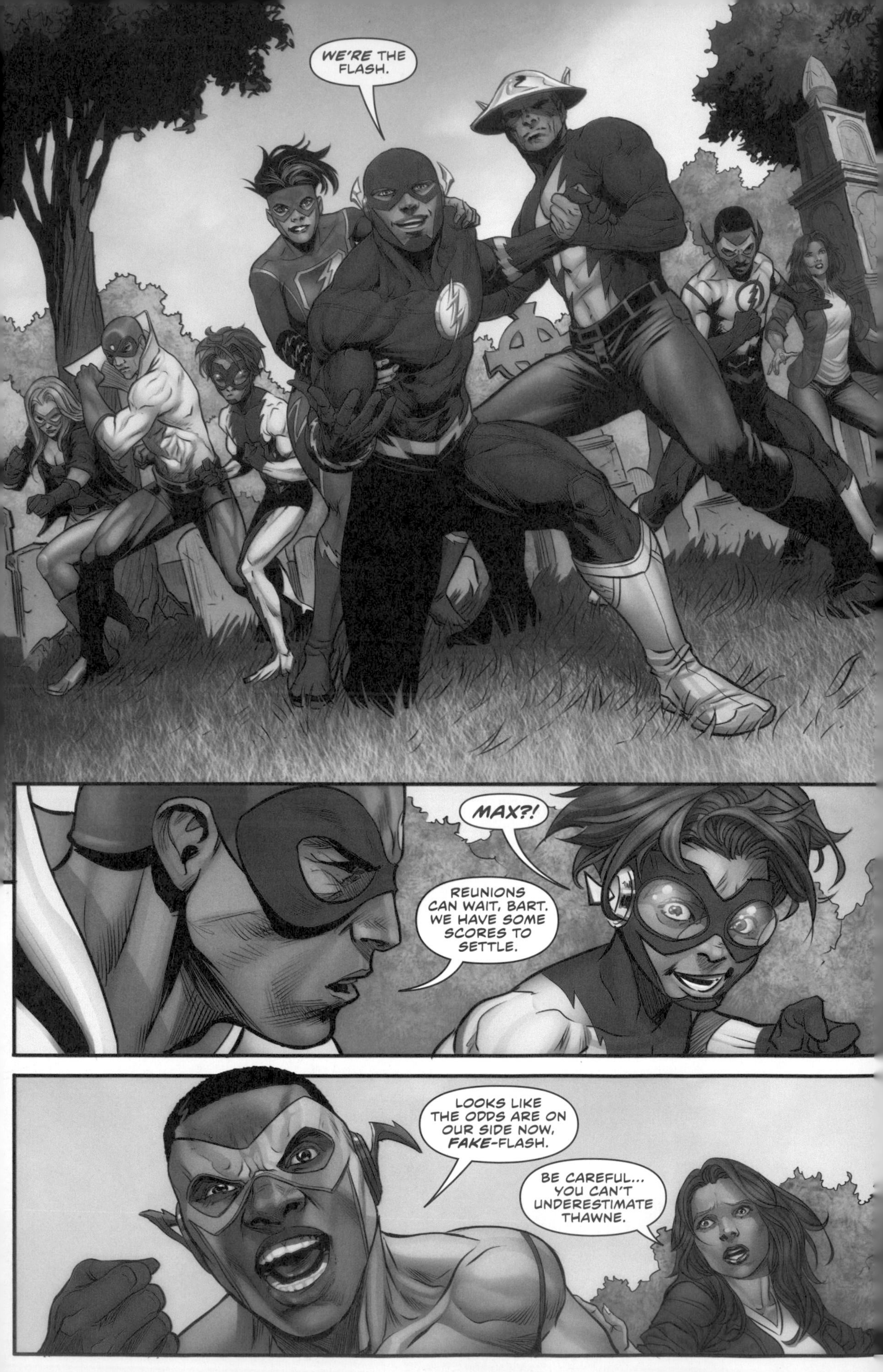
WE'RE THE FLASH.
MAX?!
REUNIONS CAN WAIT, BART. WE HAVE SOME SCORES TO SETTLE.
LOOKS LIKE THE ODDS ARE ON OUR SIDE NOW, FAKE-FLASH.
BE CAREFUL... YOU CAN'T UNDERESTIMATE THAWNE.

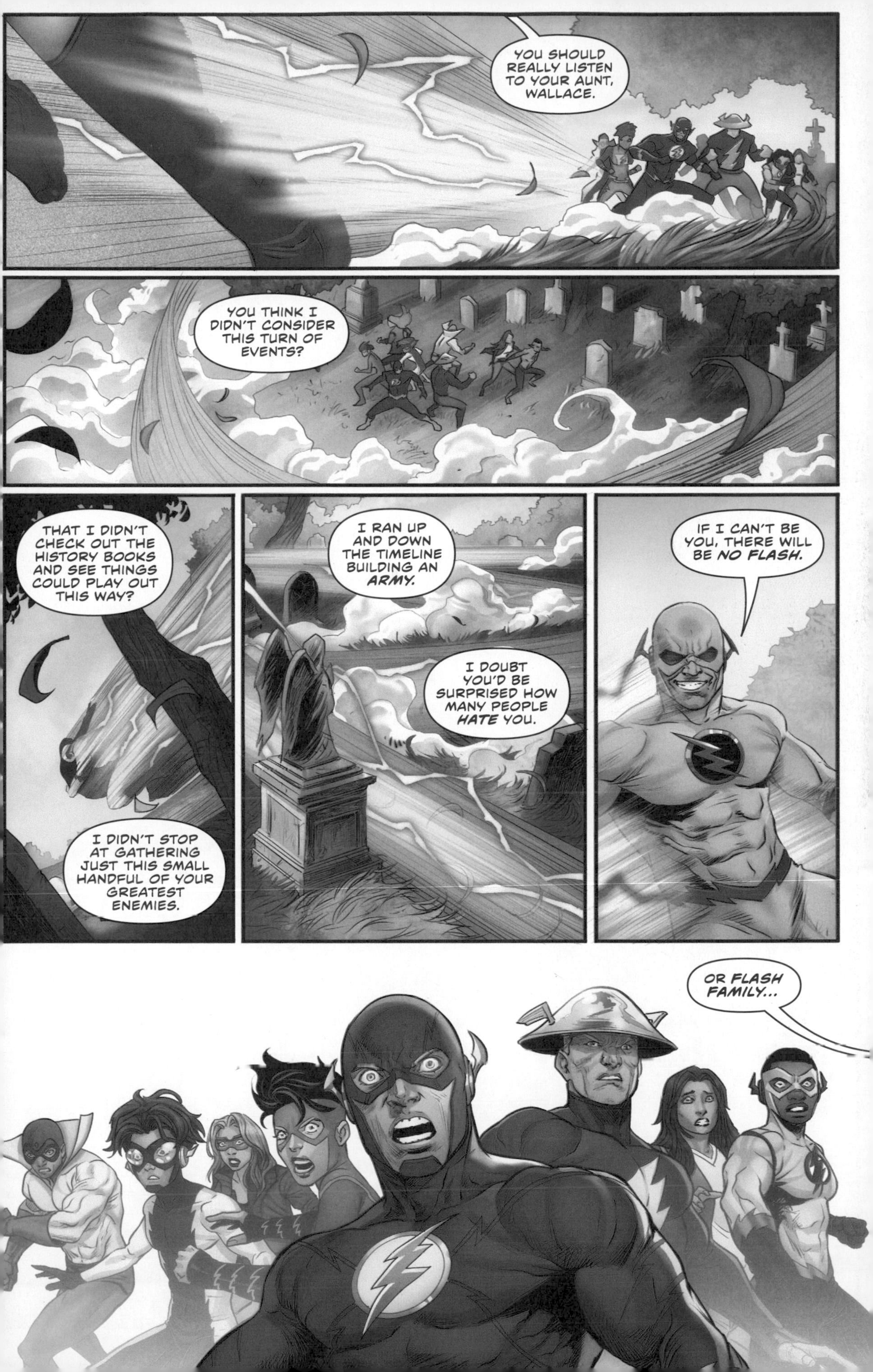
YOU SHOULD REALLY LISTEN TO YOUR AUNT, WALLACE.
YOU THINK I DIDN'T CONSIDER THIS TURN OF EVENTS?
THAT I DIDN'T CHECK OUT THE HISTORY BOOKS AND SEE THINGS COULD PLAY OUT THIS WAY?
I DIDN'T STOP AT GATHERING JUST THIS SMALL HANDFUL OF YOUR GREATEST ENEMIES.
I RAN UP AND DOWN THE TIMELINE BUILDING AN *ARMY.*
I DOUBT YOU'D BE SURPRISED HOW MANY PEOPLE *HATE* YOU.
IF I CAN'T BE YOU, THERE WILL BE *NO FLASH.*
OR *FLASH* FAMILY...

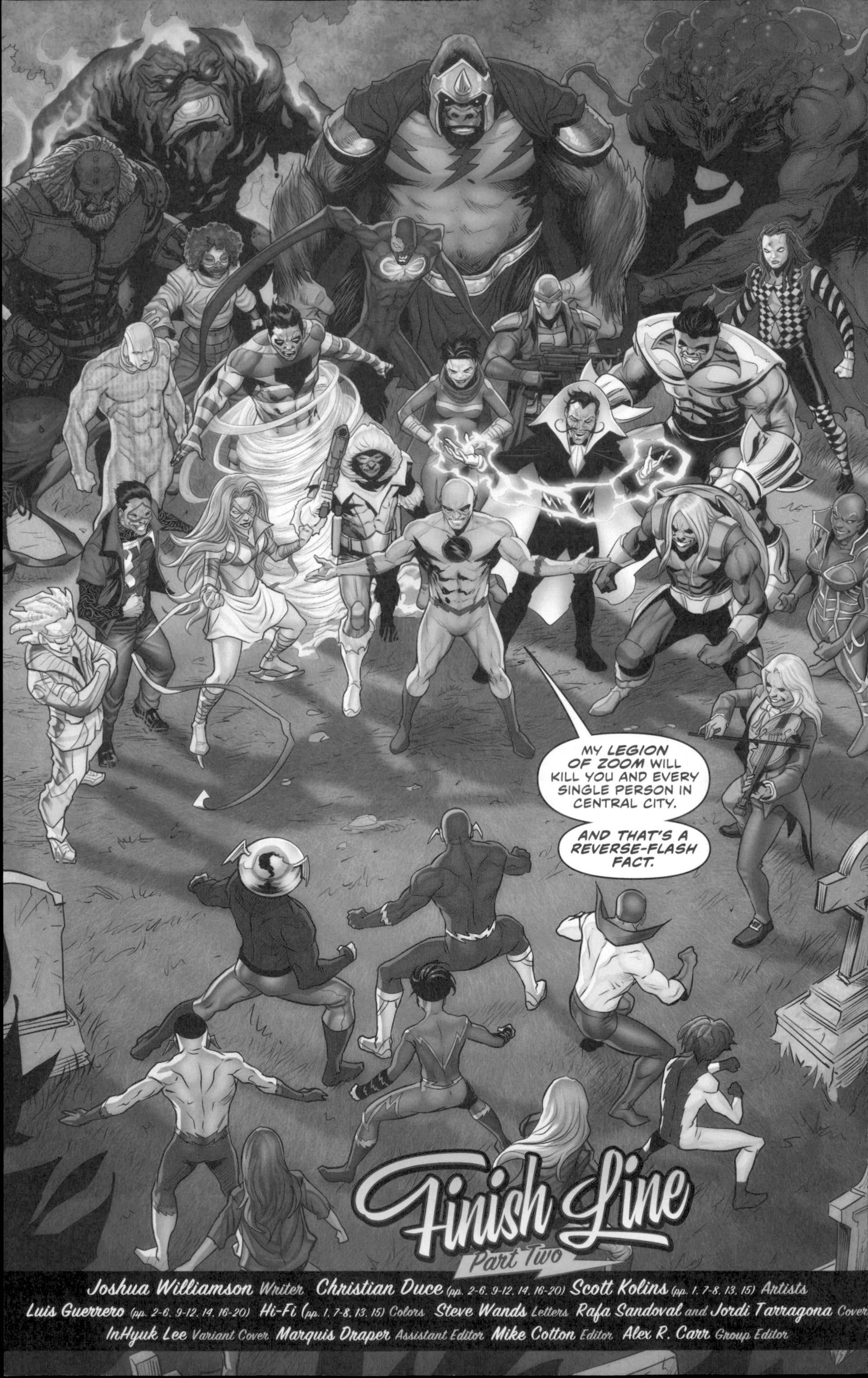
MY LEGION OF ZOOM WILL KILL YOU AND EVERY SINGLE PERSON IN CENTRAL CITY.
AND THAT'S A REVERSE-FLASH FACT.
Finish Line
Part Two
Joshua Williamson Writer Christian Duce (pp. 2-6, 9-12, 14, 16-20) Scott Kolins (pp. 1, 7-8, 13, 15) Artists
Luis Guerrero (pp. 2-6, 9-12, 14, 16-20) Hi-Fi (pp. 1, 7-8, 13, 15) Colors Steve Wands Letters Rafa Sandoval and Jordi Tarragona Cover
InHyuk Lee Variant Cover Marquis Draper Assistant Editor Mike Cotton Editor Alex R. Carr Group Editor

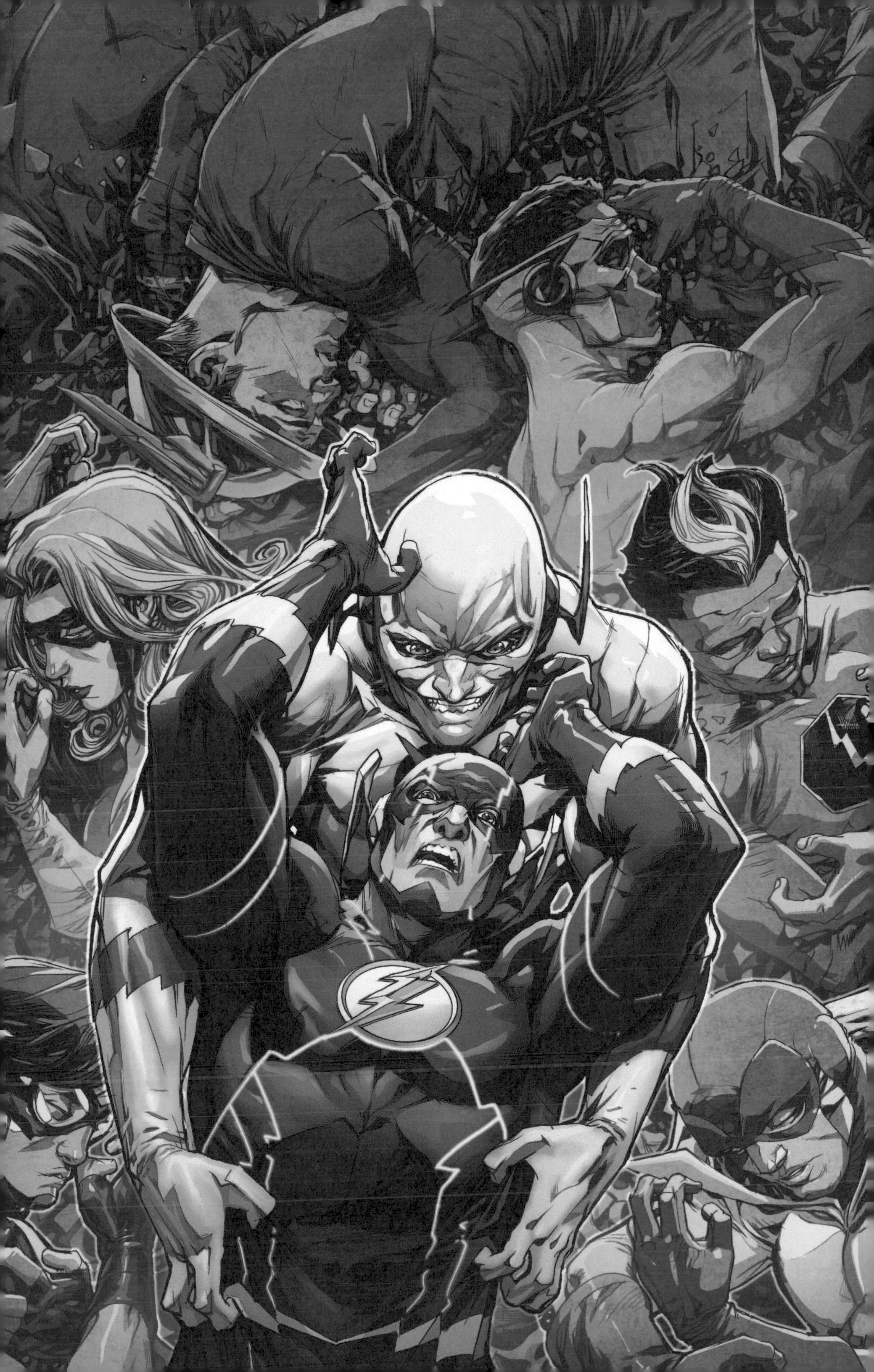

The Flash **#761** variant cover by INHYUK LEE

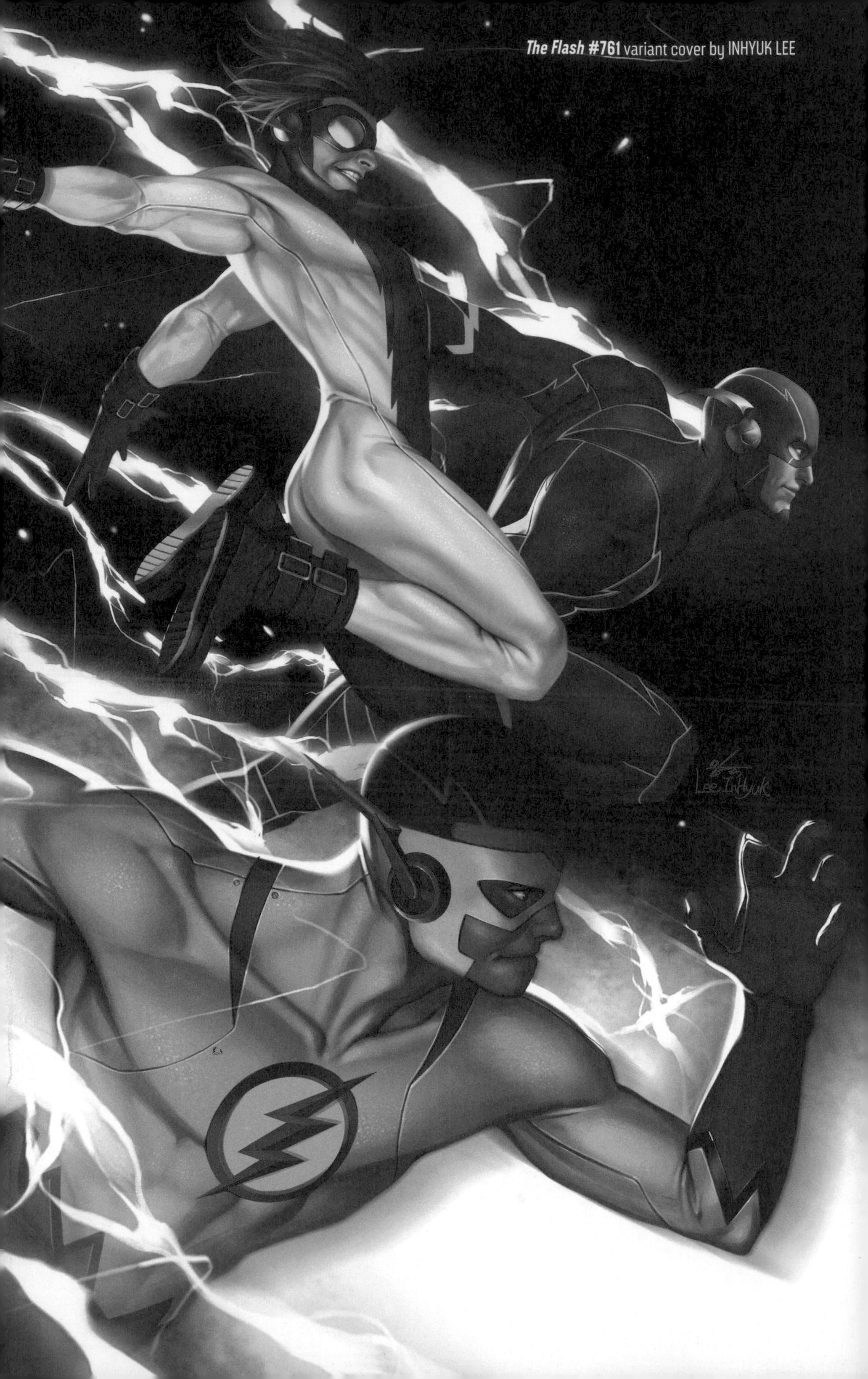
Lee InHyuk

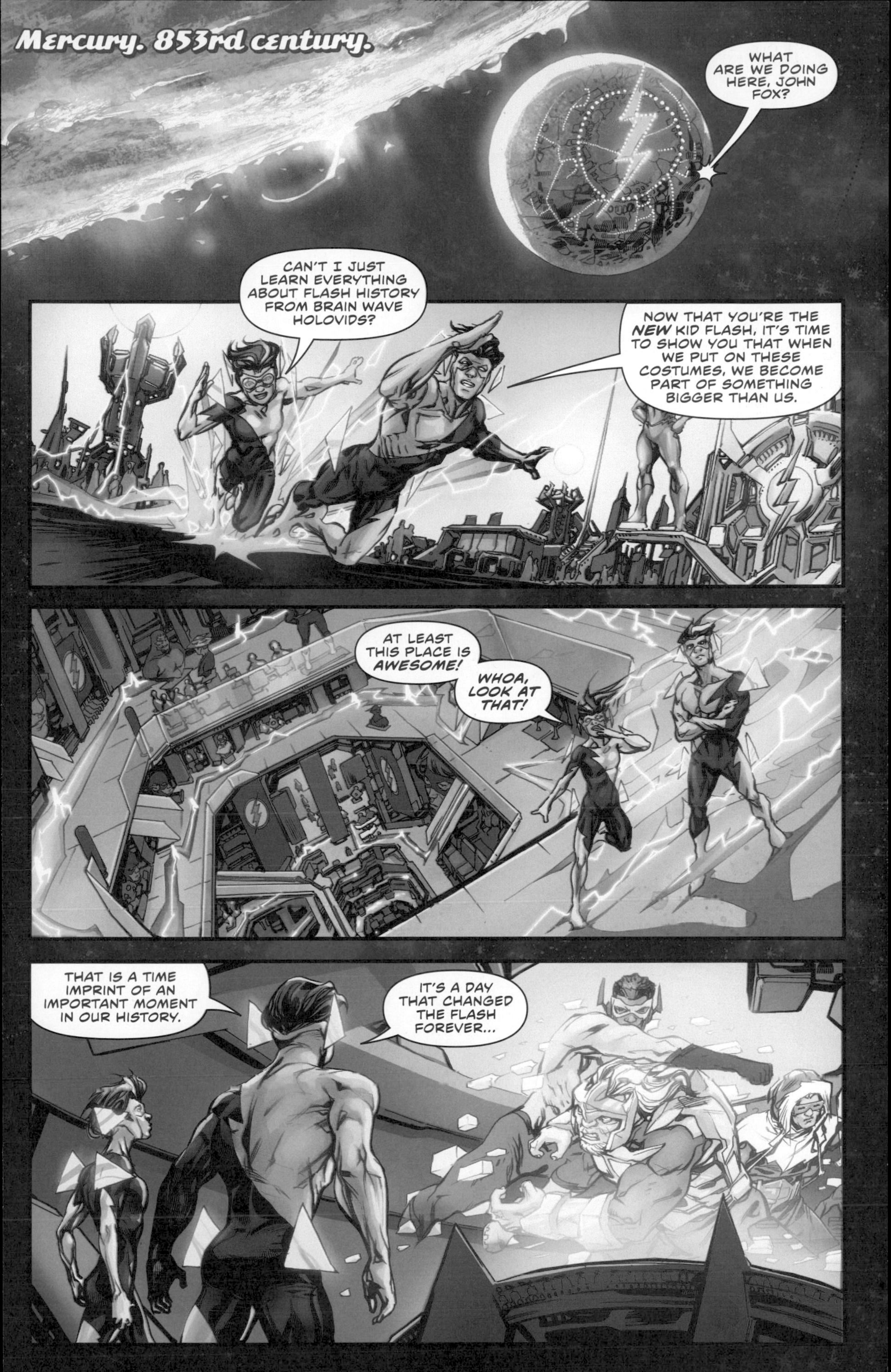
Mercury. 853rd century.
WHAT ARE WE DOING HERE, JOHN FOX?
CAN'T I JUST LEARN EVERYTHING ABOUT FLASH HISTORY FROM BRAIN WAVE HOLOVIDS?
NOW THAT YOU'RE THE NEW KID FLASH, IT'S TIME TO SHOW YOU THAT WHEN WE PUT ON THESE COSTUMES, WE BECOME PART OF SOMETHING BIGGER THAN US.
AT LEAST THIS PLACE IS AWESOME!
WHOA, LOOK AT THAT!
THAT IS A TIME IMPRINT OF AN IMPORTANT MOMENT IN OUR HISTORY.
IT'S A DAY THAT CHANGED THE FLASH FOREVER...

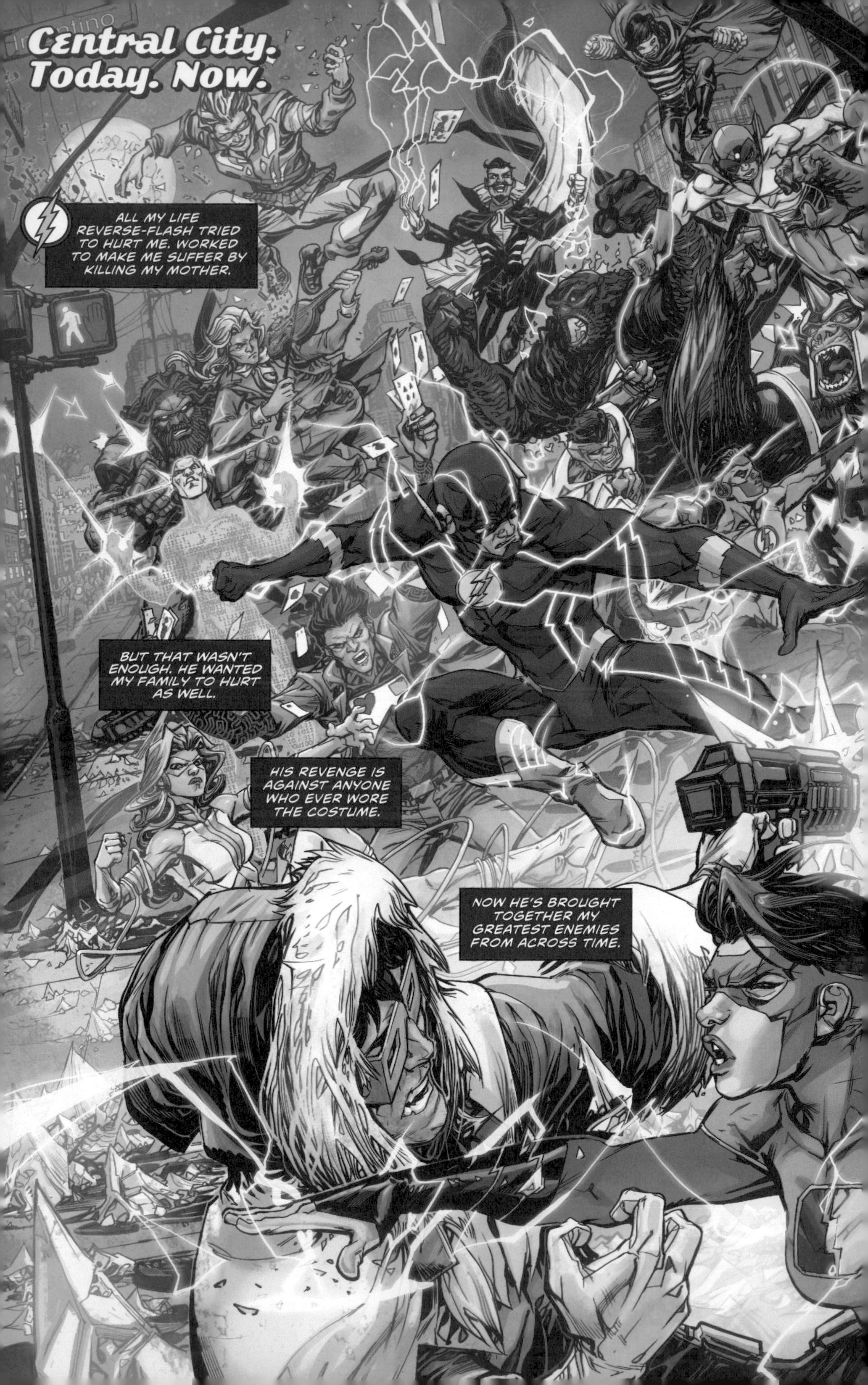
Central City. Today. Now.
ALL MY LIFE REVERSE-FLASH TRIED TO HURT ME. WORKED TO MAKE ME SUFFER BY KILLING MY MOTHER.
BUT THAT WASN'T ENOUGH. HE WANTED MY FAMILY TO HURT AS WELL.
HIS REVENGE IS AGAINST ANYONE WHO EVER WORE THE COSTUME.
NOW HE'S BROUGHT TOGETHER MY GREATEST ENEMIES FROM ACROSS TIME.

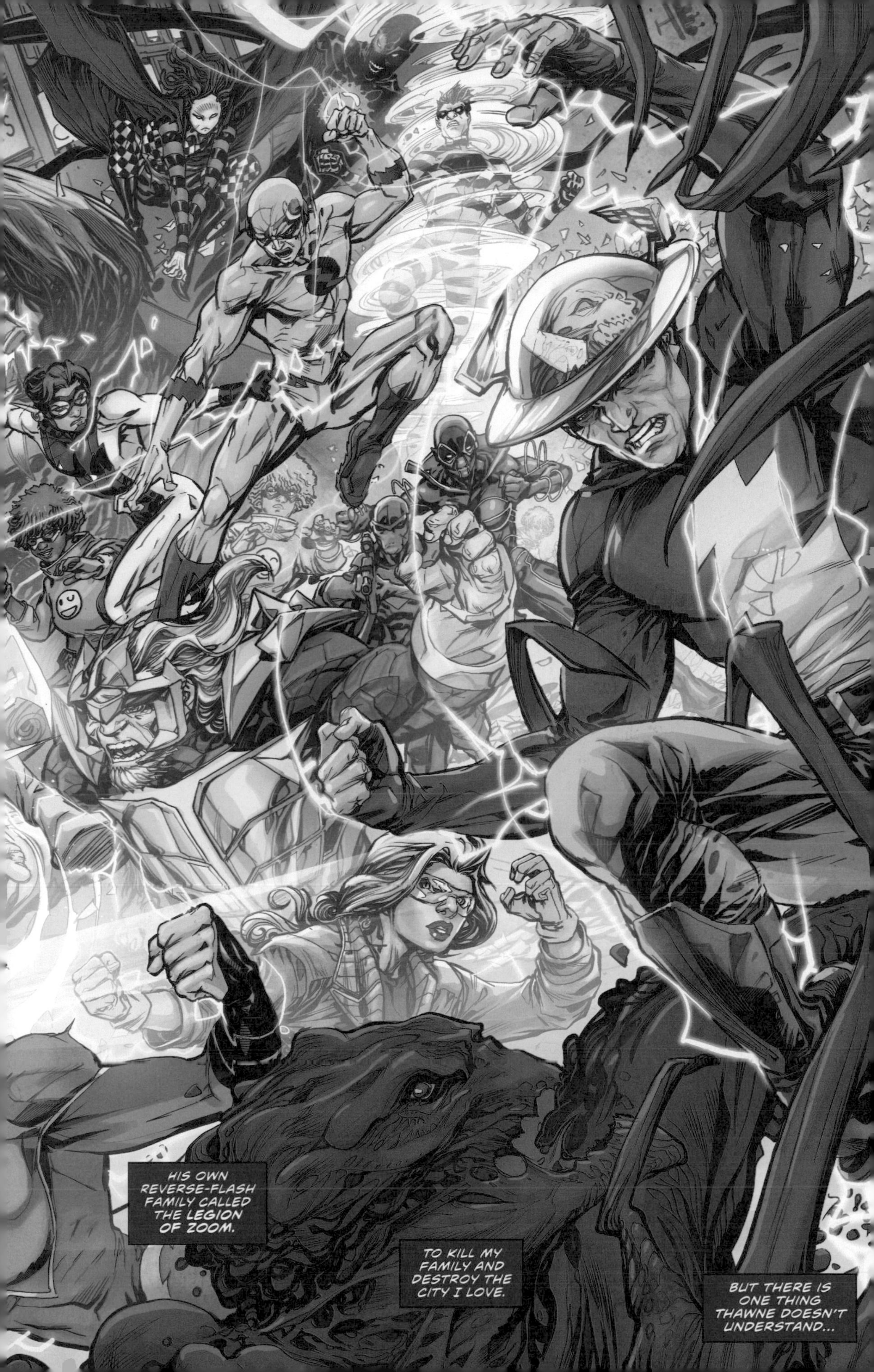
HIS OWN REVERSE-FLASH FAMILY CALLED THE LEGION OF ZOOM.
TO KILL MY FAMILY AND DESTROY THE CITY I LOVE.
BUT THERE IS ONE THING THAWNE DOESN'T UNDERSTAND...

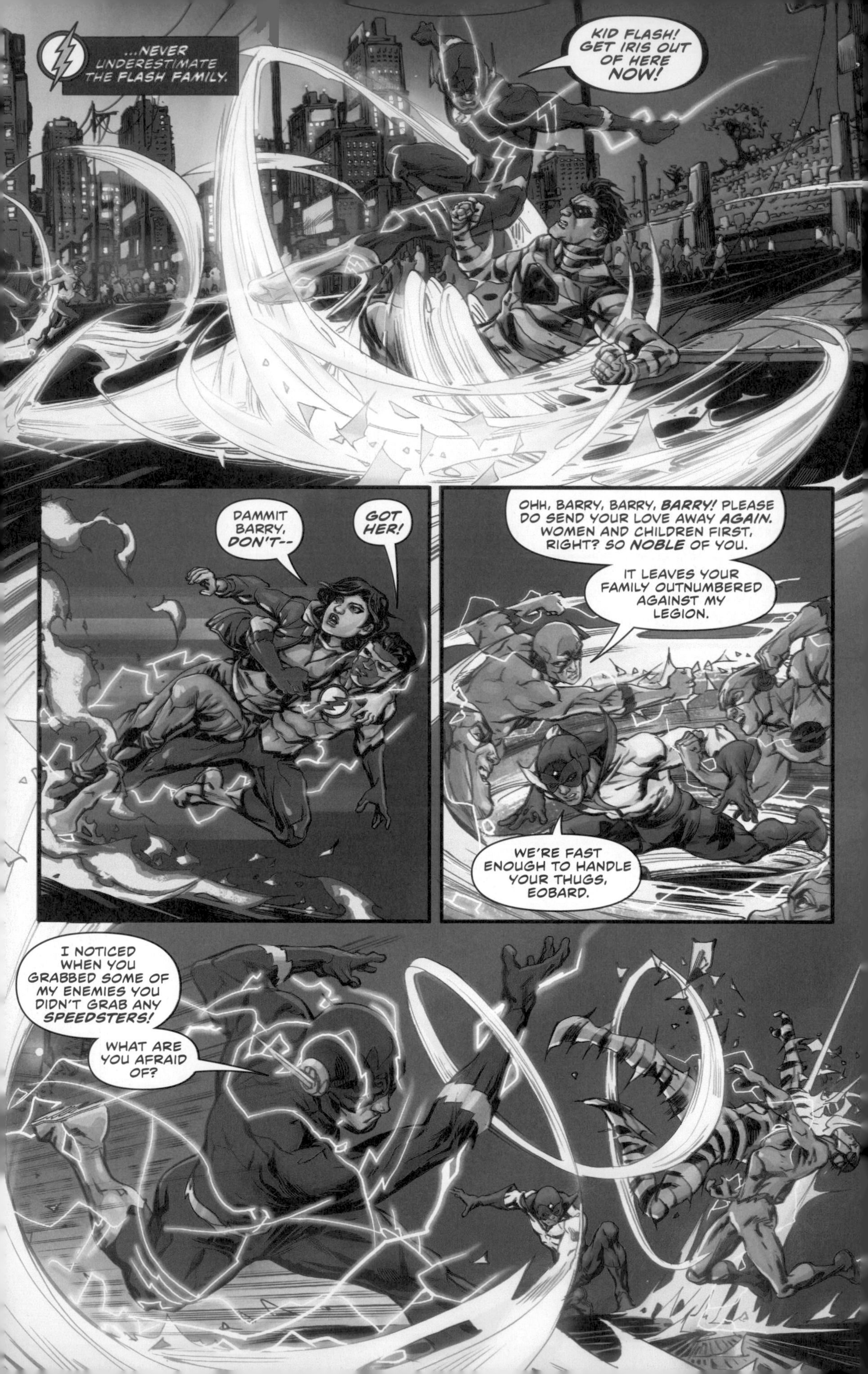
...NEVER UNDERESTIMATE THE FLASH FAMILY.
KID FLASH! GET IRIS OUT OF HERE NOW!
DAMMIT BARRY, DON'T--
GOT HER!
OHH, BARRY, BARRY, BARRY! PLEASE DO SEND YOUR LOVE AWAY AGAIN. WOMEN AND CHILDREN FIRST, RIGHT? SO NOBLE OF YOU.
IT LEAVES YOUR FAMILY OUTNUMBERED AGAINST MY LEGION.
WE'RE FAST ENOUGH TO HANDLE YOUR THUGS, EOBARD.
I NOTICED WHEN YOU GRABBED SOME OF MY ENEMIES YOU DIDN'T GRAB ANY SPEEDSTERS!
WHAT ARE YOU AFRAID OF?

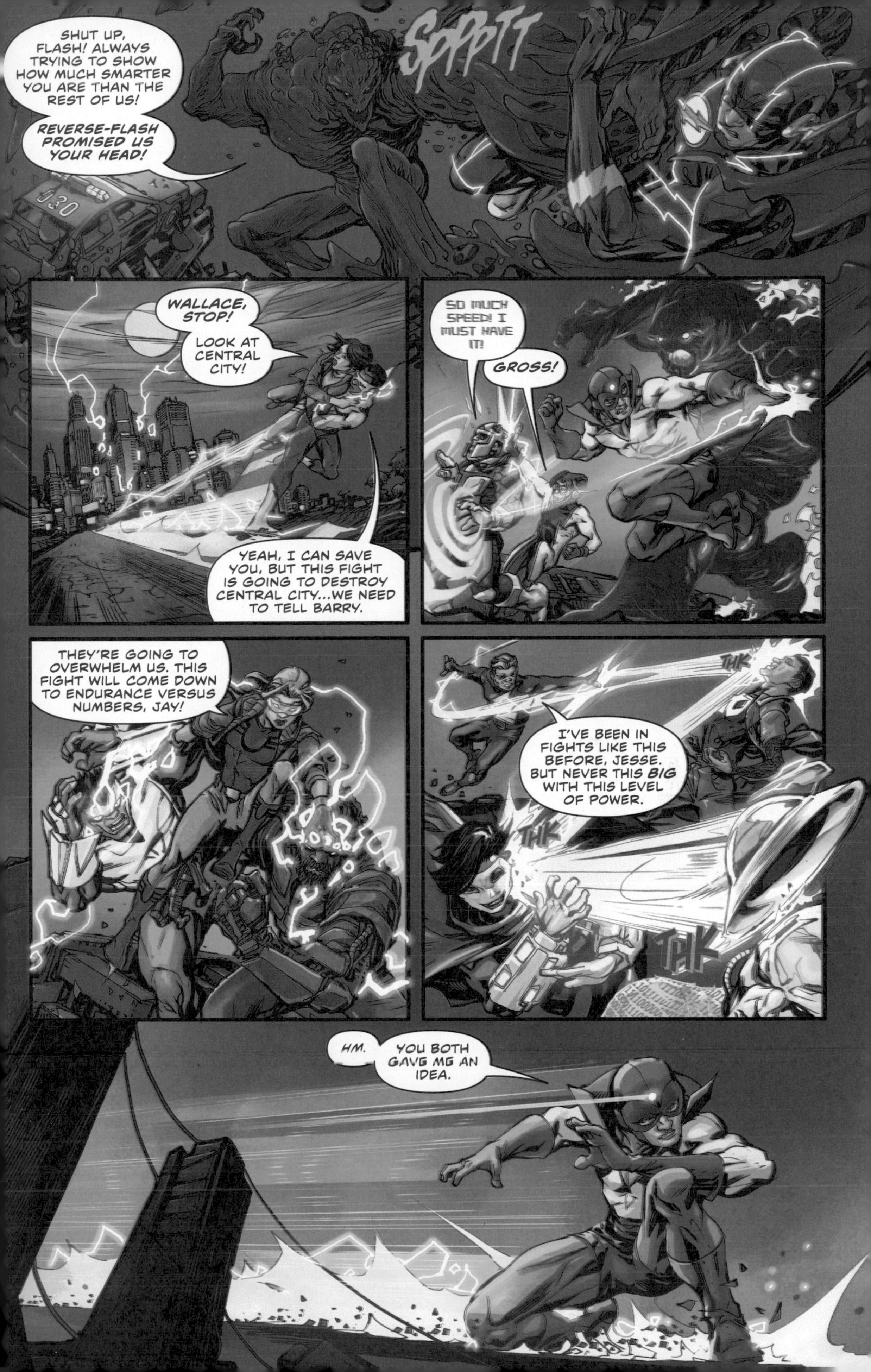
SHUT UP, FLASH! ALWAYS TRYING TO SHOW HOW MUCH SMARTER YOU ARE THAN THE REST OF US!
REVERSE-FLASH PROMISED US YOUR HEAD!
SPPPTT
WALLACE, STOP!
LOOK AT CENTRAL CITY!
YEAH, I CAN SAVE YOU, BUT THIS FIGHT IS GOING TO DESTROY CENTRAL CITY...WE NEED TO TELL BARRY.
SO MUCH SPEED! I MUST HAVE IT!
GROSS!
THEY'RE GOING TO OVERWHELM US. THIS FIGHT WILL COME DOWN TO ENDURANCE VERSUS NUMBERS, JAY!
THK
I'VE BEEN IN FIGHTS LIKE THIS BEFORE, JESSE. BUT NEVER THIS *BIG* WITH THIS LEVEL OF POWER.
THK
THK
HM.
YOU BOTH GAVE ME AN IDEA.

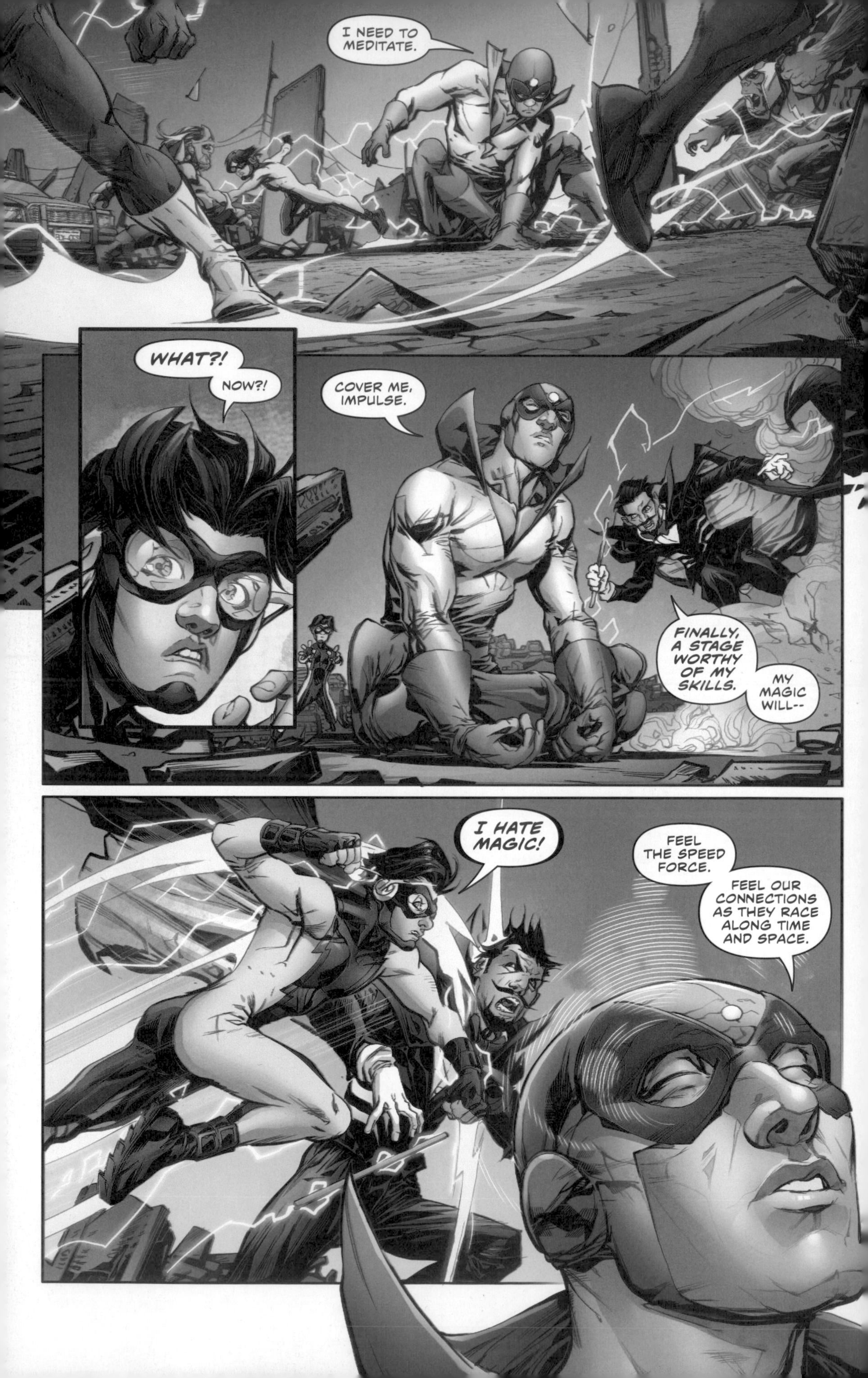

I NEED TO MEDITATE.
WHAT?!
NOW?!
COVER ME, IMPULSE.
FINALLY, A STAGE WORTHY OF MY SKILLS.
MY MAGIC WILL--
I HATE MAGIC!
FEEL THE SPEED FORCE.
FEEL OUR CONNECTIONS AS THEY RACE ALONG TIME AND SPACE.

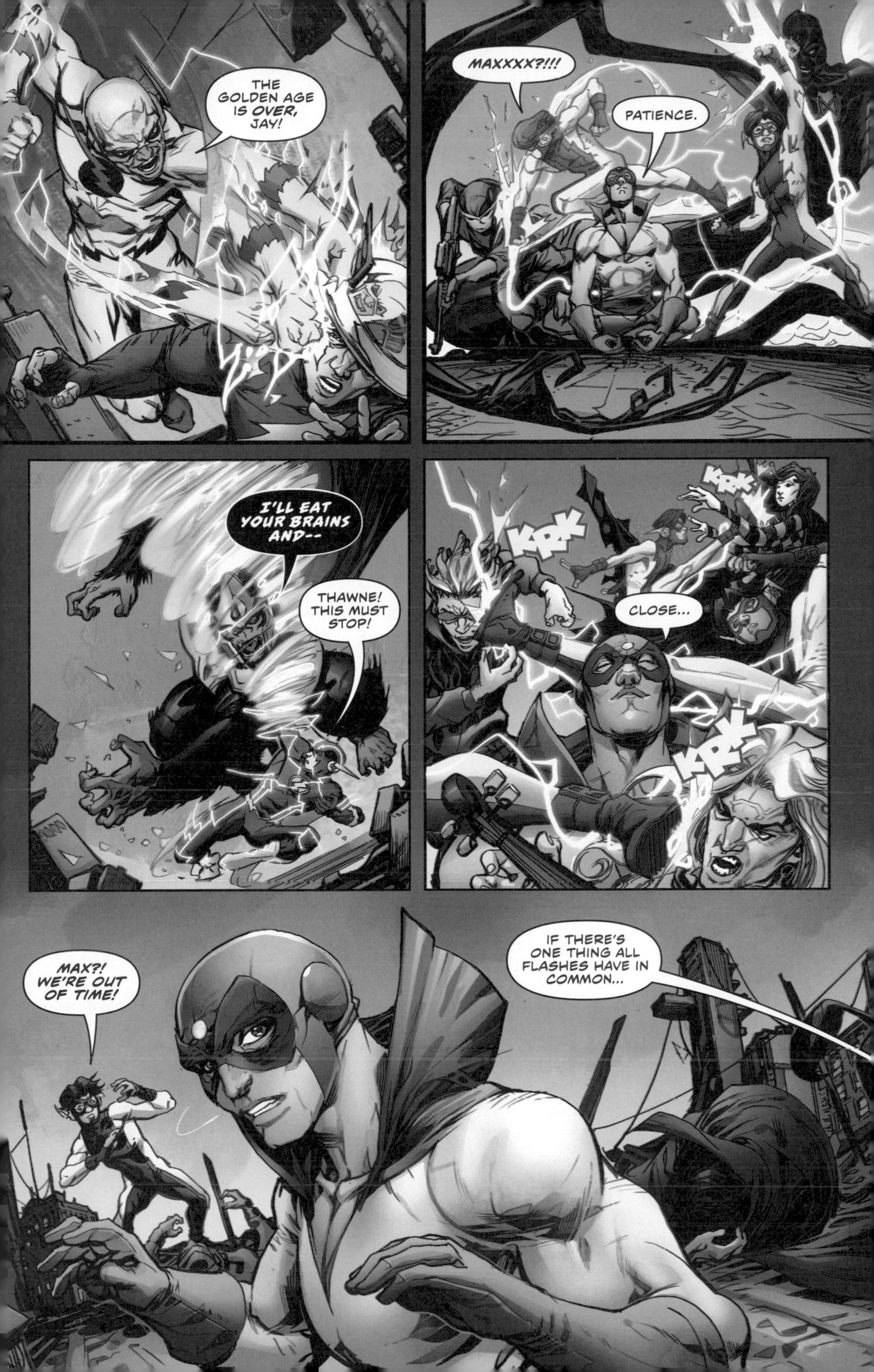
THE GOLDEN AGE IS OVER, JAY!
MAXXXX?!!!
PATIENCE.
I'LL EAT YOUR BRAINS AND--
THAWNE! THIS MUST STOP!
KRK
KRK
CLOSE...
KRK
MAX?! WE'RE OUT OF TIME!
IF THERE'S ONE THING ALL FLASHES HAVE IN COMMON...

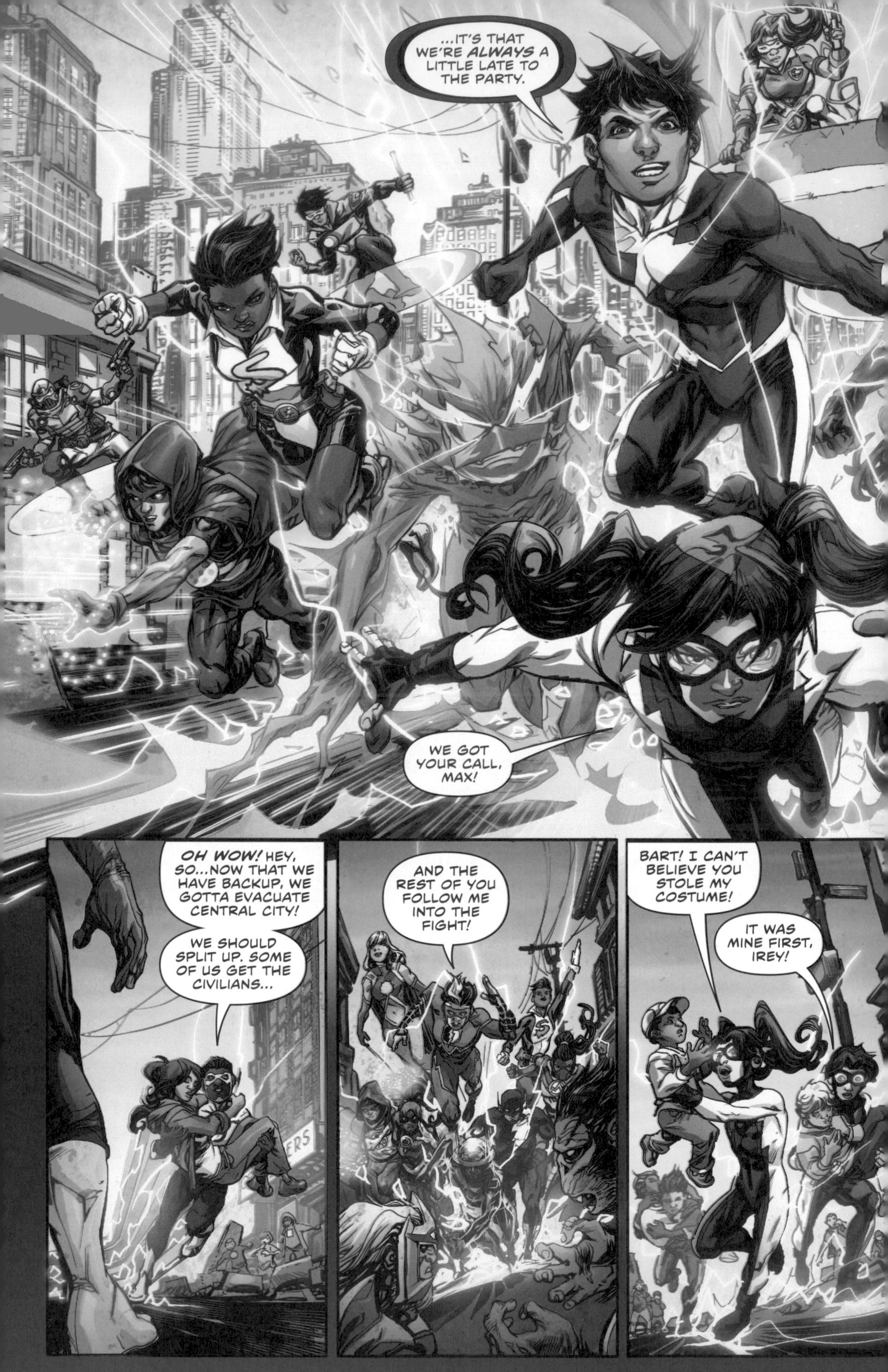
...IT'S THAT WE'RE ALWAYS A LITTLE LATE TO THE PARTY.
WE GOT YOUR CALL, MAX!
OH WOW! HEY, SO...NOW THAT WE HAVE BACKUP, WE GOTTA EVACUATE CENTRAL CITY!
WE SHOULD SPLIT UP. SOME OF US GET THE CIVILIANS...
AND THE REST OF YOU FOLLOW ME INTO THE FIGHT!
BART! I CAN'T BELIEVE YOU STOLE MY COSTUME!
IT WAS MINE FIRST, IREY!

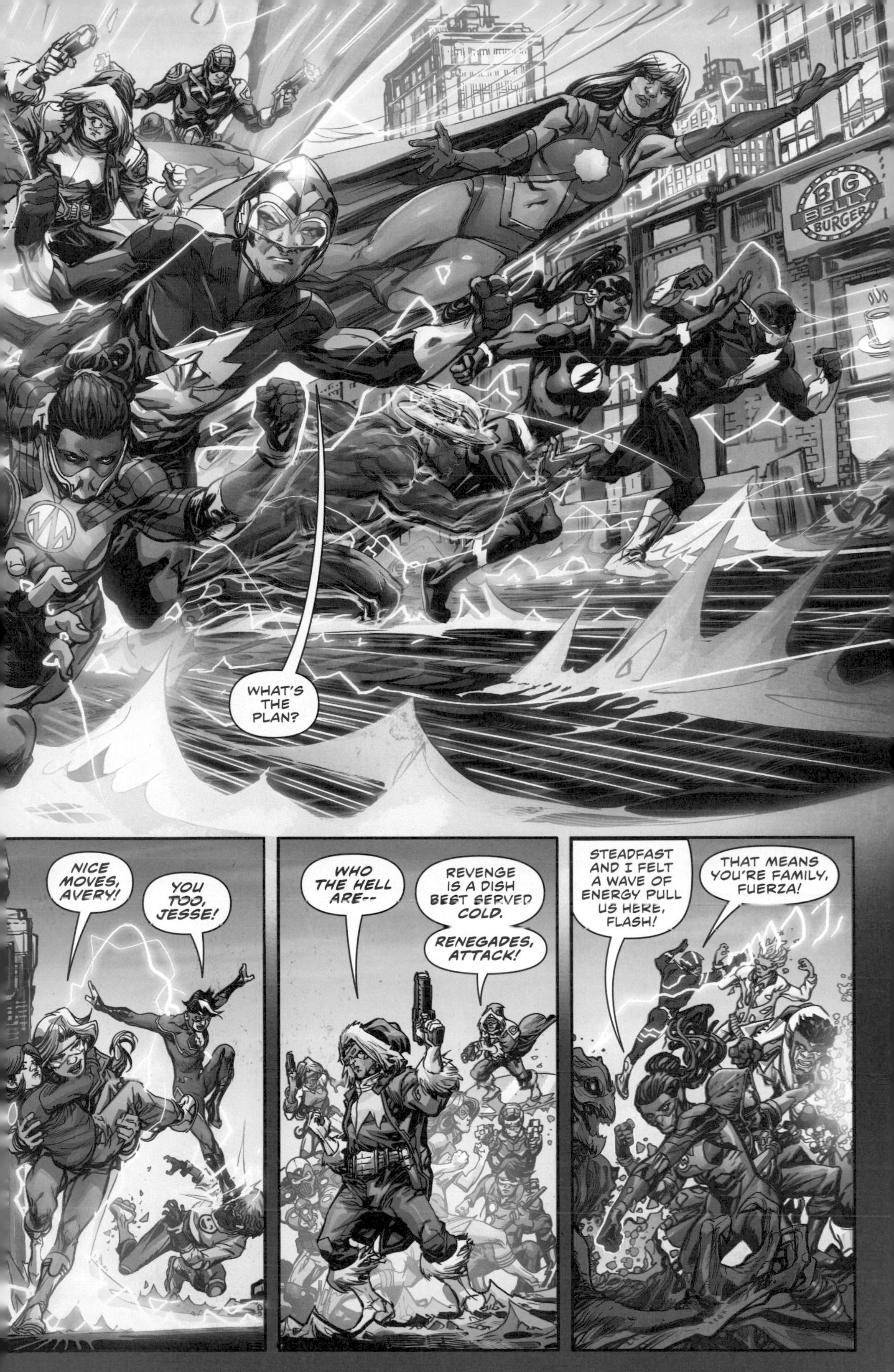
WHAT'S THE PLAN?
NICE MOVES, AVERY!
YOU TOO, JESSE!
WHO THE HELL ARE--
REVENGE IS A DISH BEST SERVED COLD.
RENEGADES, ATTACK!
STEADFAST AND I FELT A WAVE OF ENERGY PULL US HERE, FLASH!
THAT MEANS YOU'RE FAMILY, FUERZA!
BIG BELLY BURGER

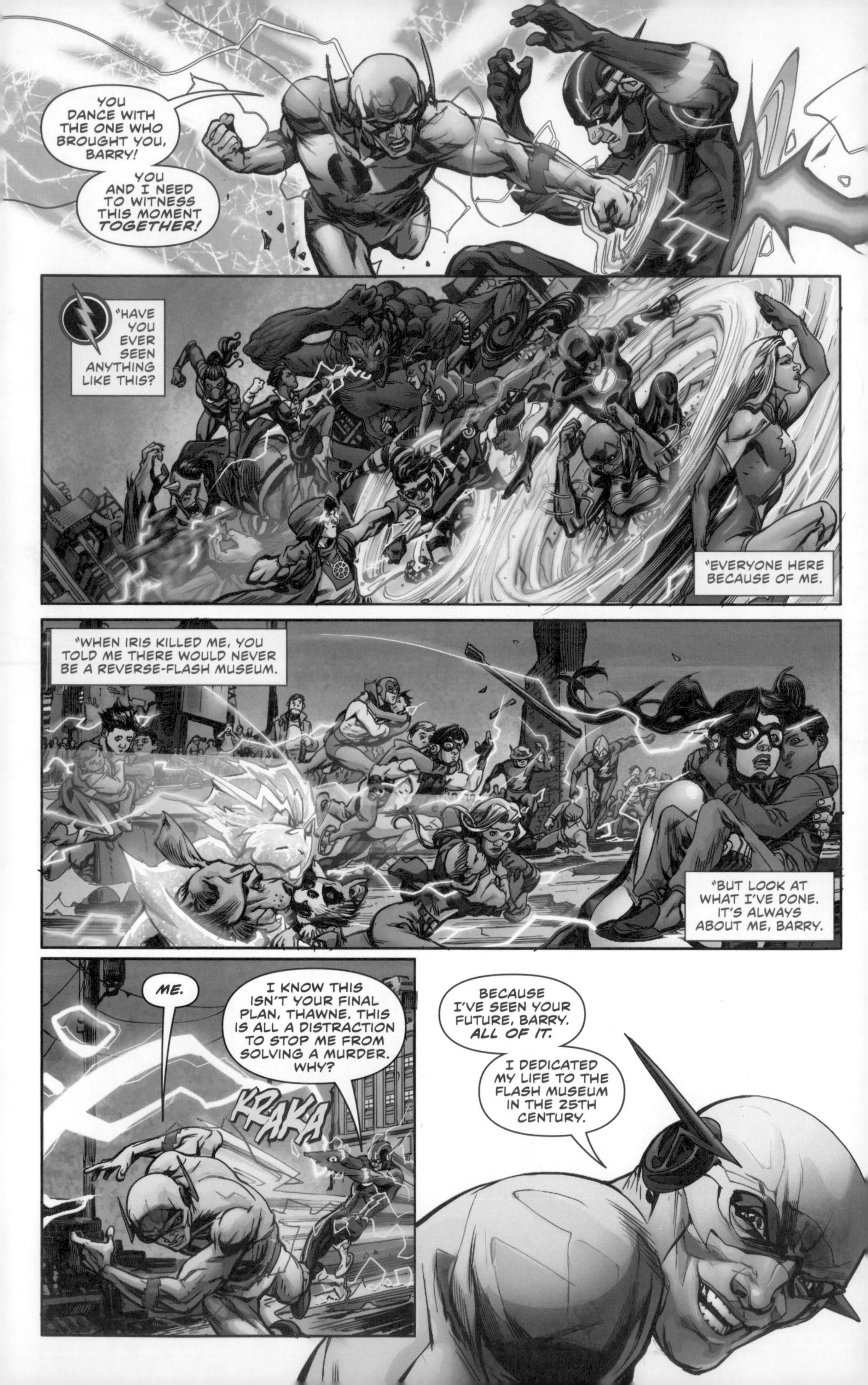
YOU DANCE WITH THE ONE WHO BROUGHT YOU, BARRY!
YOU AND I NEED TO WITNESS THIS MOMENT *TOGETHER!*
"HAVE YOU EVER SEEN ANYTHING LIKE THIS?
"EVERYONE HERE BECAUSE OF ME.
"WHEN IRIS KILLED ME, YOU TOLD ME THERE WOULD NEVER BE A REVERSE-FLASH MUSEUM.
"BUT LOOK AT WHAT I'VE DONE. IT'S ALWAYS ABOUT ME, BARRY.
ME.
I KNOW THIS ISN'T YOUR FINAL PLAN, THAWNE. THIS IS ALL A DISTRACTION TO STOP ME FROM SOLVING A MURDER. WHY?
KRAKA
BECAUSE I'VE SEEN YOUR FUTURE, BARRY. *ALL OF IT.*
I DEDICATED MY LIFE TO THE FLASH MUSEUM IN THE 25TH CENTURY.

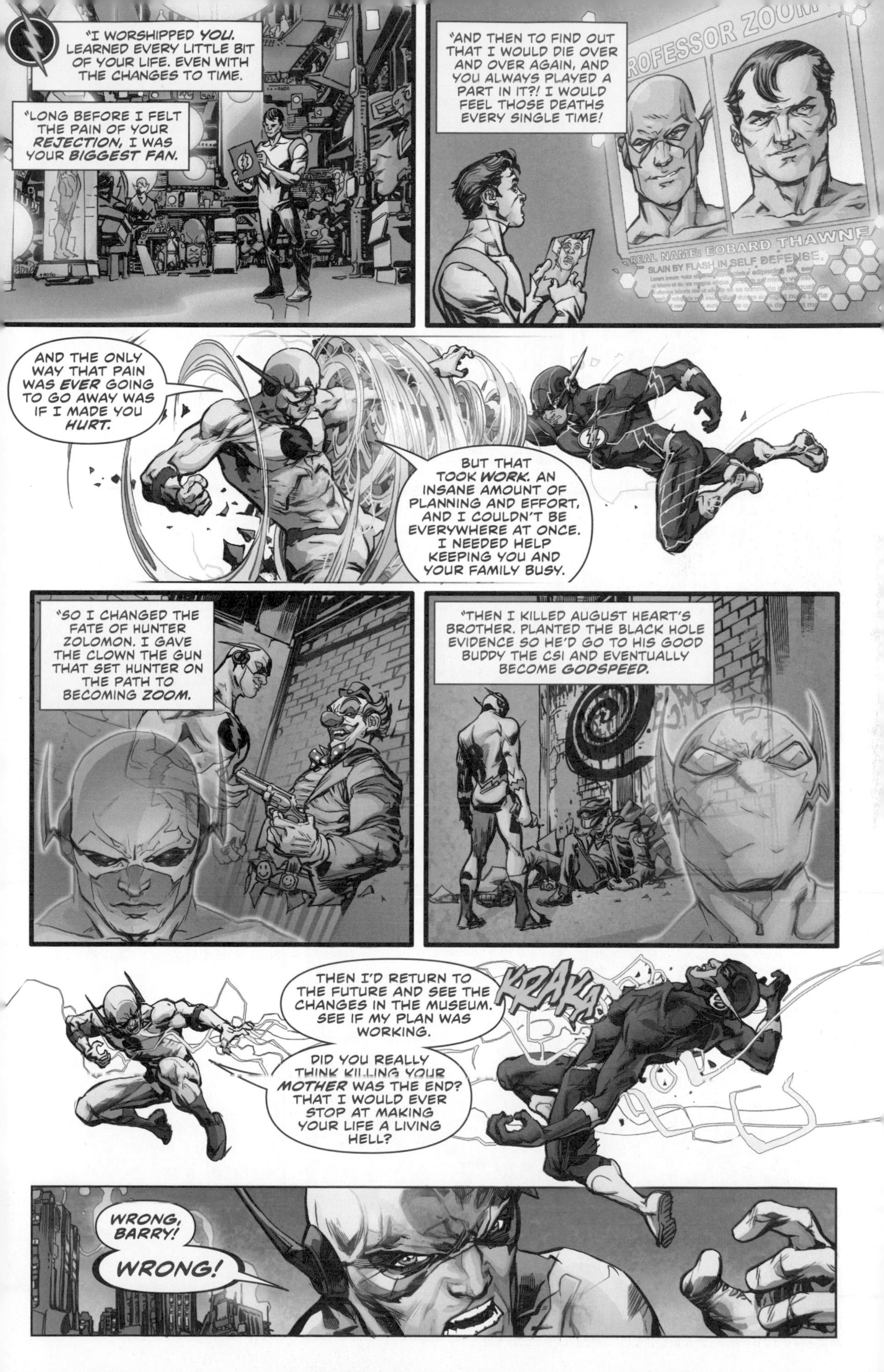
"I WORSHIPPED YOU. LEARNED EVERY LITTLE BIT OF YOUR LIFE. EVEN WITH THE CHANGES TO TIME.
"LONG BEFORE I FELT THE PAIN OF YOUR REJECTION, I WAS YOUR BIGGEST FAN.
"AND THEN TO FIND OUT THAT I WOULD DIE OVER AND OVER AGAIN, AND YOU ALWAYS PLAYED A PART IN IT?! I WOULD FEEL THOSE DEATHS EVERY SINGLE TIME!
PROFESSOR ZOOM
REAL NAME: EOBARD THAWNE
SLAIN BY FLASH IN SELF DEFENSE,
AND THE ONLY WAY THAT PAIN WAS EVER GOING TO GO AWAY WAS IF I MADE YOU HURT.
BUT THAT TOOK WORK. AN INSANE AMOUNT OF PLANNING AND EFFORT, AND I COULDN'T BE EVERYWHERE AT ONCE. I NEEDED HELP KEEPING YOU AND YOUR FAMILY BUSY.
"SO I CHANGED THE FATE OF HUNTER ZOLOMON. I GAVE THE CLOWN THE GUN THAT SET HUNTER ON THE PATH TO BECOMING ZOOM.
"THEN I KILLED AUGUST HEART'S BROTHER. PLANTED THE BLACK HOLE EVIDENCE SO HE'D GO TO HIS GOOD BUDDY THE CSI AND EVENTUALLY BECOME GODSPEED.
THEN I'D RETURN TO THE FUTURE AND SEE THE CHANGES IN THE MUSEUM. SEE IF MY PLAN WAS WORKING.
KRAKA
DID YOU REALLY THINK KILLING YOUR MOTHER WAS THE END? THAT I WOULD EVER STOP AT MAKING YOUR LIFE A LIVING HELL?
WRONG, BARRY!
WRONG!

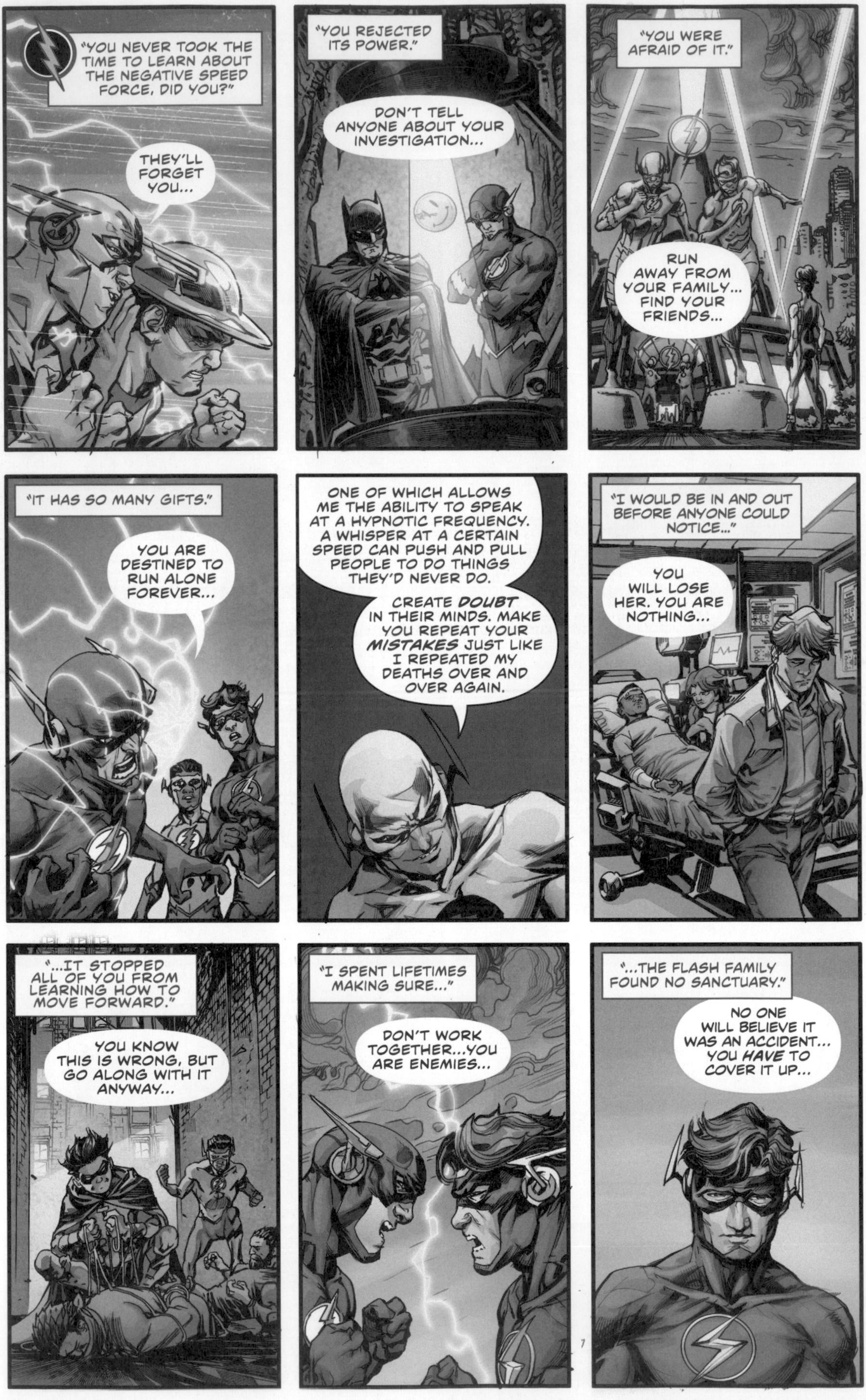
"YOU NEVER TOOK THE TIME TO LEARN ABOUT THE NEGATIVE SPEED FORCE, DID YOU?"
THEY'LL FORGET YOU...
"YOU REJECTED ITS POWER."
DON'T TELL ANYONE ABOUT YOUR INVESTIGATION...
"YOU WERE AFRAID OF IT."
RUN AWAY FROM YOUR FAMILY... FIND YOUR FRIENDS...
"IT HAS SO MANY GIFTS."
YOU ARE DESTINED TO RUN ALONE FOREVER...
ONE OF WHICH ALLOWS ME THE ABILITY TO SPEAK AT A HYPNOTIC FREQUENCY. A WHISPER AT A CERTAIN SPEED CAN PUSH AND PULL PEOPLE TO DO THINGS THEY'D NEVER DO.
CREATE *DOUBT* IN THEIR MINDS. MAKE YOU REPEAT YOUR *MISTAKES* JUST LIKE I REPEATED MY DEATHS OVER AND OVER AGAIN.
"I WOULD BE IN AND OUT BEFORE ANYONE COULD NOTICE..."
YOU WILL LOSE HER. YOU ARE NOTHING...
"...IT STOPPED ALL OF YOU FROM LEARNING HOW TO MOVE FORWARD."
YOU KNOW THIS IS WRONG, BUT GO ALONG WITH IT ANYWAY...
"I SPENT LIFETIMES MAKING SURE..."
DON'T WORK TOGETHER...YOU ARE ENEMIES...
"...THE FLASH FAMILY FOUND NO SANCTUARY."
NO ONE WILL BELIEVE IT WAS AN ACCIDENT... YOU *HAVE* TO COVER IT UP...

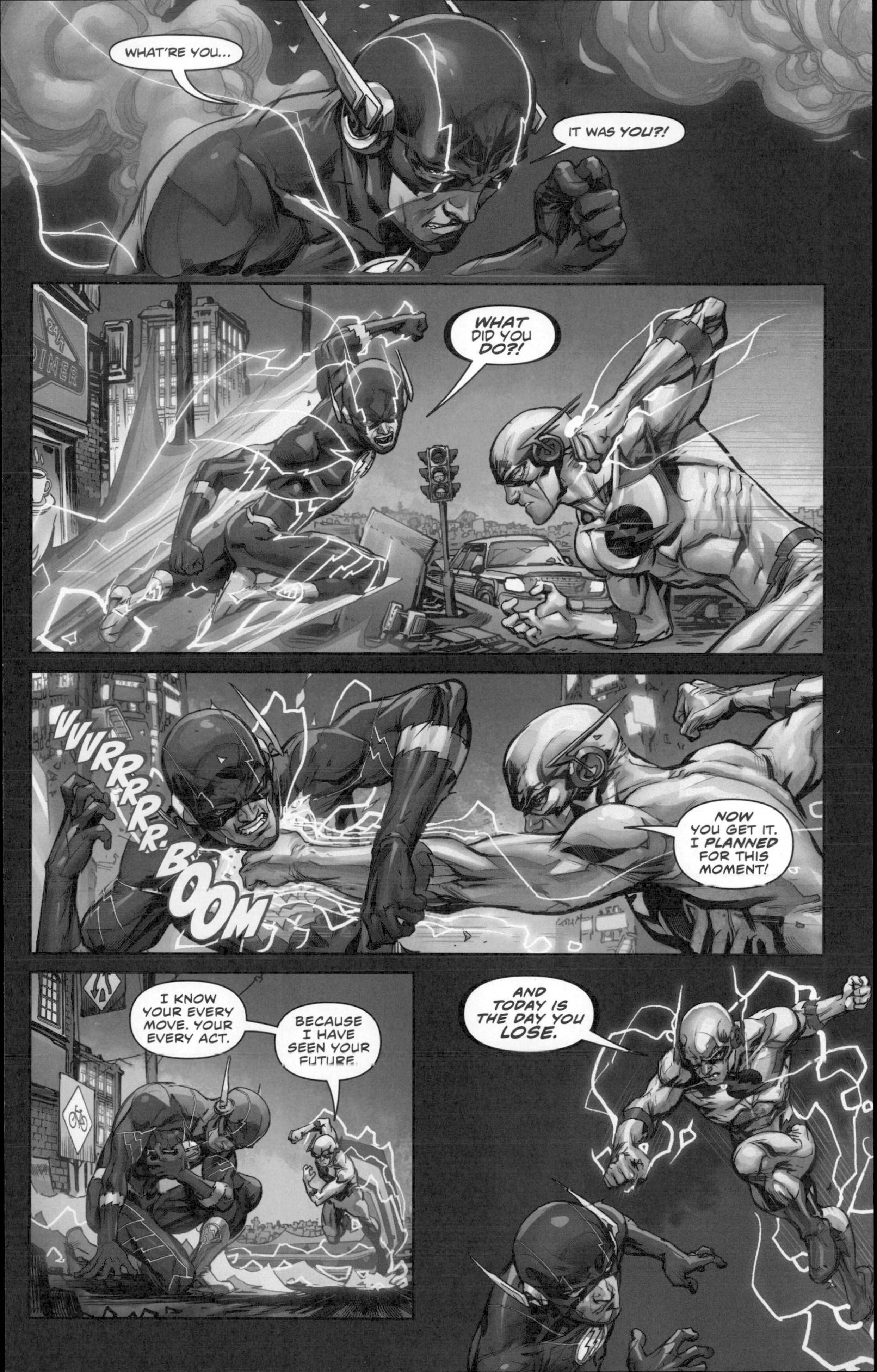
WHAT'RE YOU...
IT WAS YOU?!
WHAT DID YOU DO?!
24/7 DINER
VVVRRRRR-BOOM
NOW YOU GET IT. I PLANNED FOR THIS MOMENT!
I KNOW YOUR EVERY MOVE. YOUR EVERY ACT.
BECAUSE I HAVE SEEN YOUR FUTURE.
AND TODAY IS THE DAY YOU LOSE.

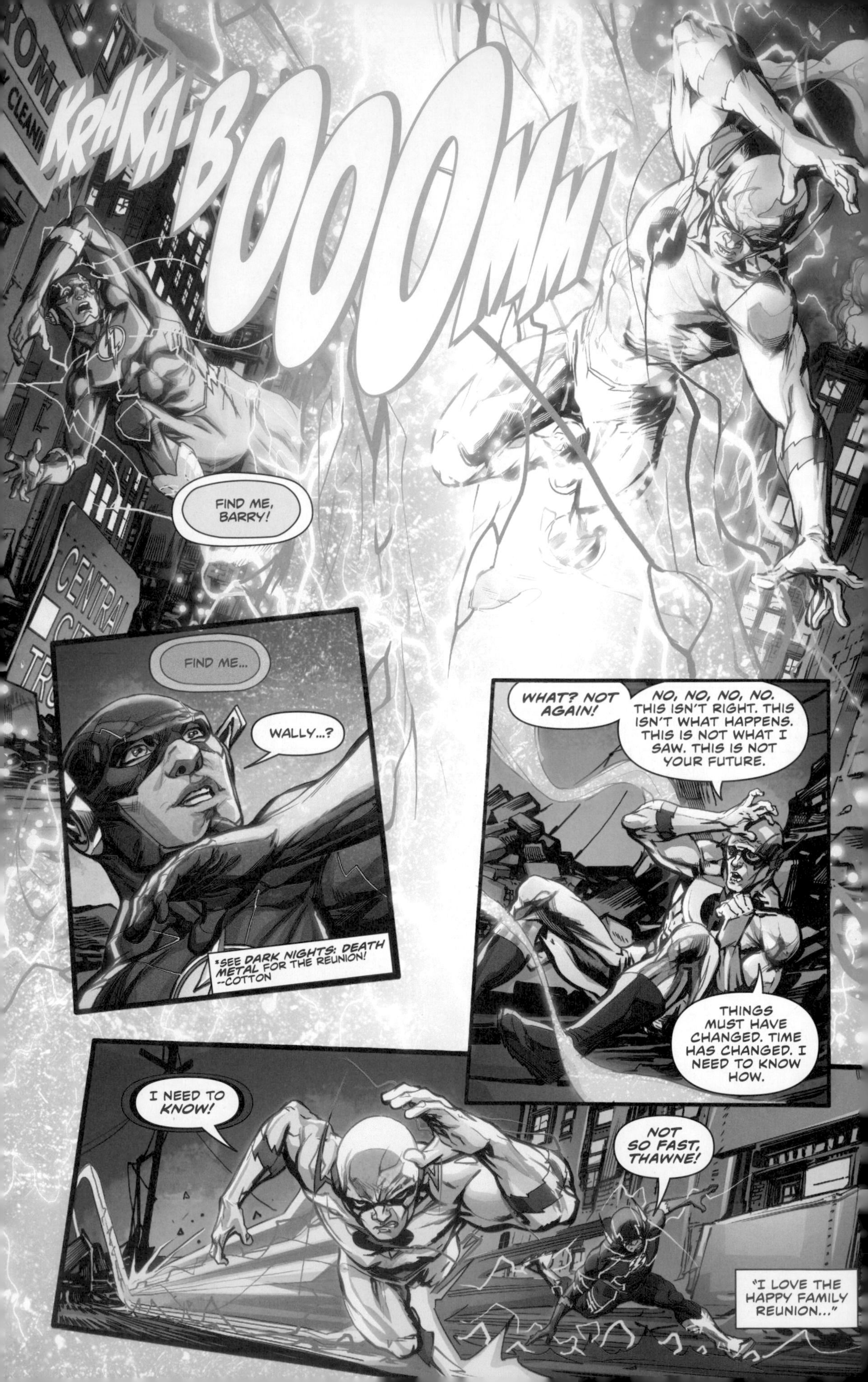
KRAKA-BOOOOMMM
FIND ME, BARRY!
FIND ME...
WALLY...?
*SEE DARK NIGHTS: DEATH METAL FOR THE REUNION! --COTTON
WHAT? NOT AGAIN!
NO, NO, NO, NO. THIS ISN'T RIGHT. THIS ISN'T WHAT HAPPENS. THIS IS NOT WHAT I SAW. THIS IS NOT YOUR FUTURE.
THINGS MUST HAVE CHANGED. TIME HAS CHANGED. I NEED TO KNOW HOW.
I NEED TO KNOW!
NOT SO FAST, THAWNE!
"I LOVE THE HAPPY FAMILY REUNION..."

...BUT CENTRAL CITY CAN'T TAKE MUCH MORE OF THIS!

NONE OF THESE VILLAINS ARE FROM THE HERE AND NOW, RIGHT? SO HOW DO WE SEND THEM BACK TO THEIR OWN TIMES *QUICK?*

HEARD MY NAME!

LISTEN, WHEN THAWNE WAS INSIDE BARRY'S BODY, WE LEARNED THAT NONE OF THESE VILLAINS ARE ON THE CORRECT VIBRATIONAL FREQUENCY.

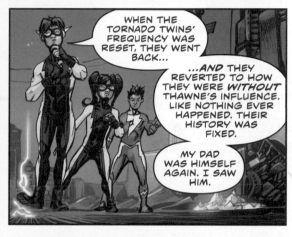

WHEN THE TORNADO TWINS' FREQUENCY WAS RESET, THEY WENT BACK...

...*AND THEY* REVERTED TO HOW THEY WERE *WITHOUT* THAWNE'S INFLUENCE. LIKE NOTHING EVER HAPPENED. THEIR HISTORY WAS FIXED.

MY DAD WAS HIMSELF AGAIN. I SAW HIM.

IS THAT WHY THAWNE DIDN'T BRING ANY SPEEDSTERS?

PLEASE TELL ME YOU HAVE A PLAN.

YES. NO. MAYBE.

UH, OKAY, SO TIME-TRAVEL. IT'S PRETTY WACKY AND I'VE DONE A LOT OF IT. AND THESE BAD GUYS ARE ALL ON A DIFFERENT VIBRATIONAL FREQUENCY.

ISN'T THAT HOW THE FLASH TRAVELS THROUGH TIME?

YEAH, HE CONTROLS HIS *VIBRATIONS.*

THIS REMINDS ME OF WHEN BARRY, WALLY, AND I WERE IN A SIMILAR PICKLE, WE HAD TO--

JAY.

THE KIDS ARE CLOSE, OLD-TIMER. LET THEM FIGURE IT OUT.

WHAT IF WE RAN AROUND THE BAD GUYS--

--CREATING A *CORRECT* SHOCK WAVE FREQUENCY--

--THAT SENDS THEM BACK HOME *AND* RESETS THEM.

THEY WON'T EVEN REMEMBER THIS HAPPENED!

WE JUST GOTTA GET THE SCIENCE RIGHT!

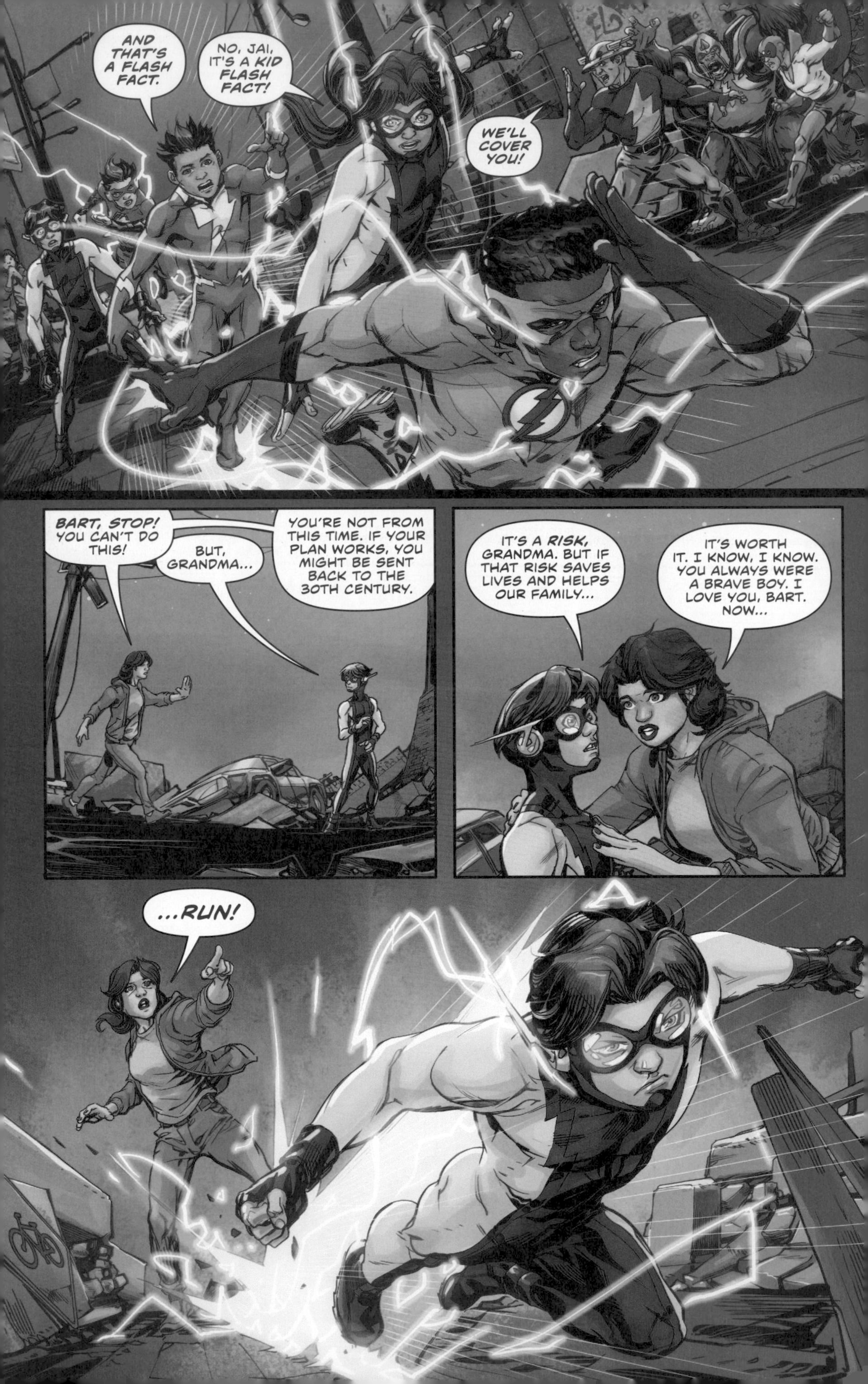
AND THAT'S A FLASH FACT.
NO, JAI, IT'S A KID FLASH FACT!
WE'LL COVER YOU!
BART, STOP! YOU CAN'T DO THIS!
BUT, GRANDMA...
YOU'RE NOT FROM THIS TIME. IF YOUR PLAN WORKS, YOU MIGHT BE SENT BACK TO THE 30TH CENTURY.
IT'S A RISK, GRANDMA. BUT IF THAT RISK SAVES LIVES AND HELPS OUR FAMILY...
IT'S WORTH IT. I KNOW, I KNOW. YOU ALWAYS WERE A BRAVE BOY. I LOVE YOU, BART. NOW...
...RUN!

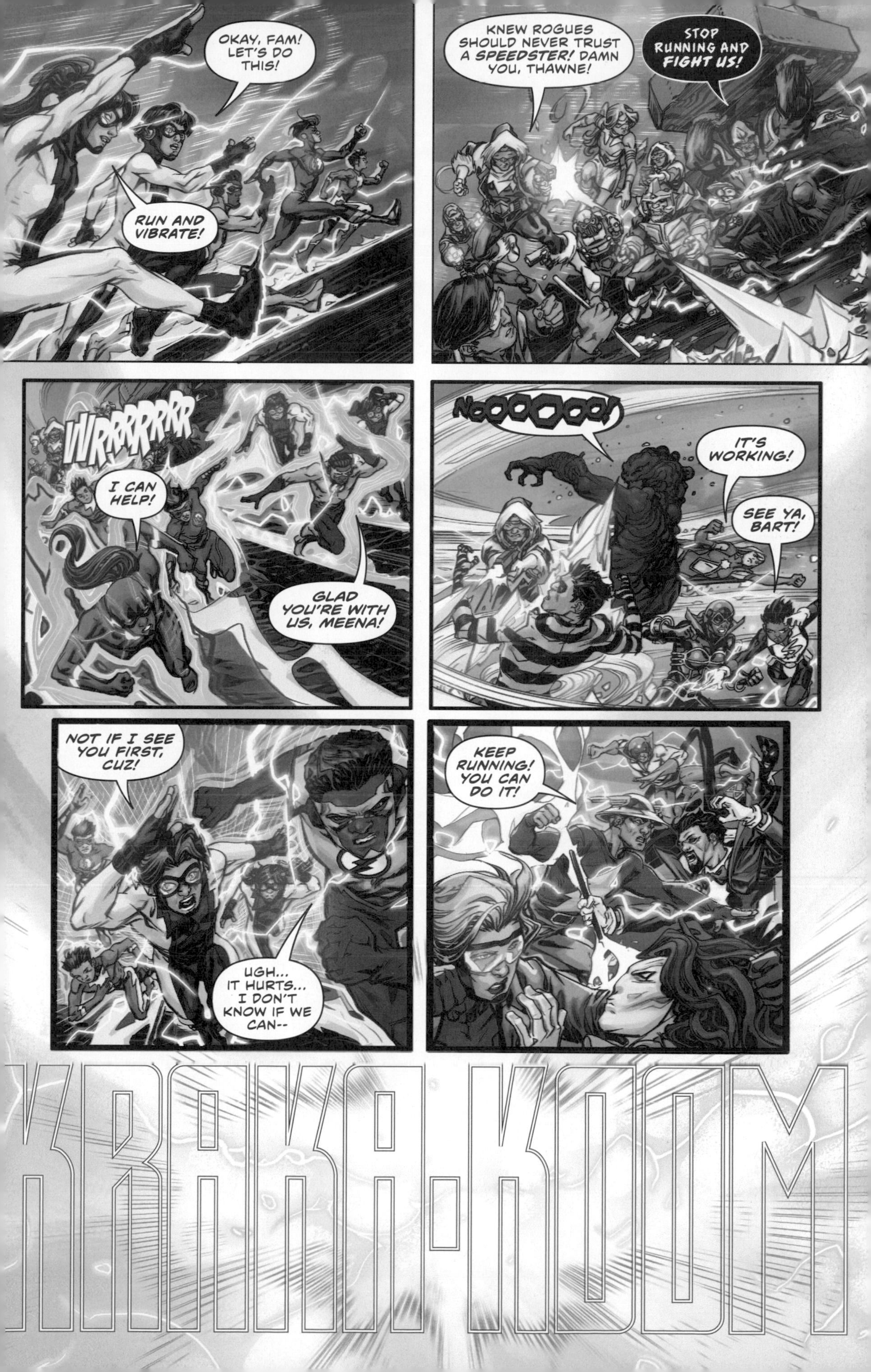
OKAY, FAM! LET'S DO THIS!
RUN AND VIBRATE!
KNEW ROGUES SHOULD NEVER TRUST A SPEEDSTER! DAMN YOU, THAWNE!
STOP RUNNING AND FIGHT US!
WRRRRRRR
I CAN HELP!
GLAD YOU'RE WITH US, MEENA!
NOOOOOO!
IT'S WORKING!
SEE YA, BART!
NOT IF I SEE YOU FIRST, CUZ!
UGH... IT HURTS... I DON'T KNOW IF WE CAN--
KEEP RUNNING! YOU CAN DO IT!
KRAKA-KOOM

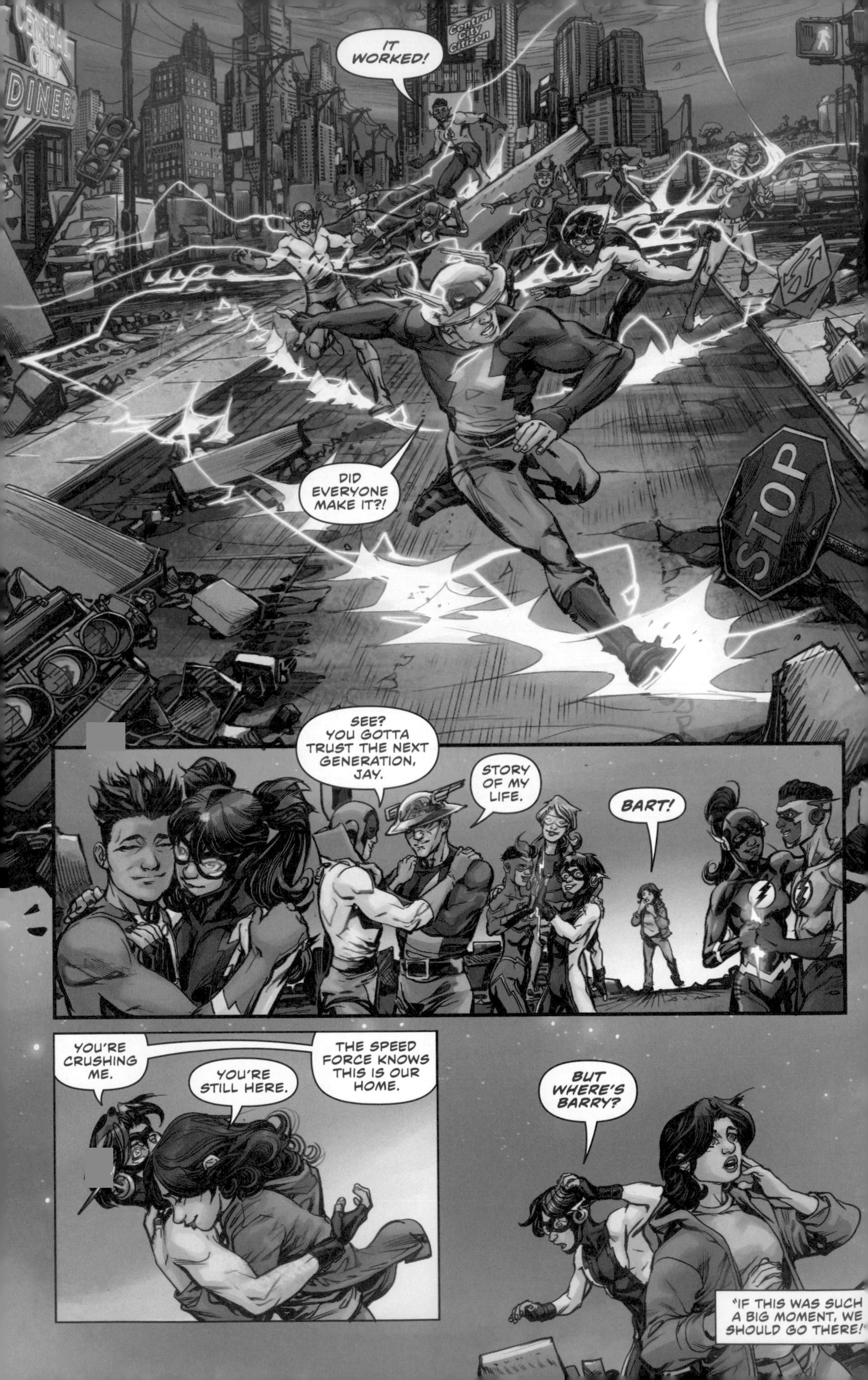
CENTRAL CITY DINER
Central City Citizen
IT WORKED!
DID EVERYONE MAKE IT?!
STOP
SEE? YOU GOTTA TRUST THE NEXT GENERATION, JAY.
STORY OF MY LIFE.
BART!
YOU'RE CRUSHING ME.
YOU'RE STILL HERE.
THE SPEED FORCE KNOWS THIS IS OUR HOME.
BUT WHERE'S BARRY?
"IF THIS WAS SUCH A BIG MOMENT, WE SHOULD GO THERE!"

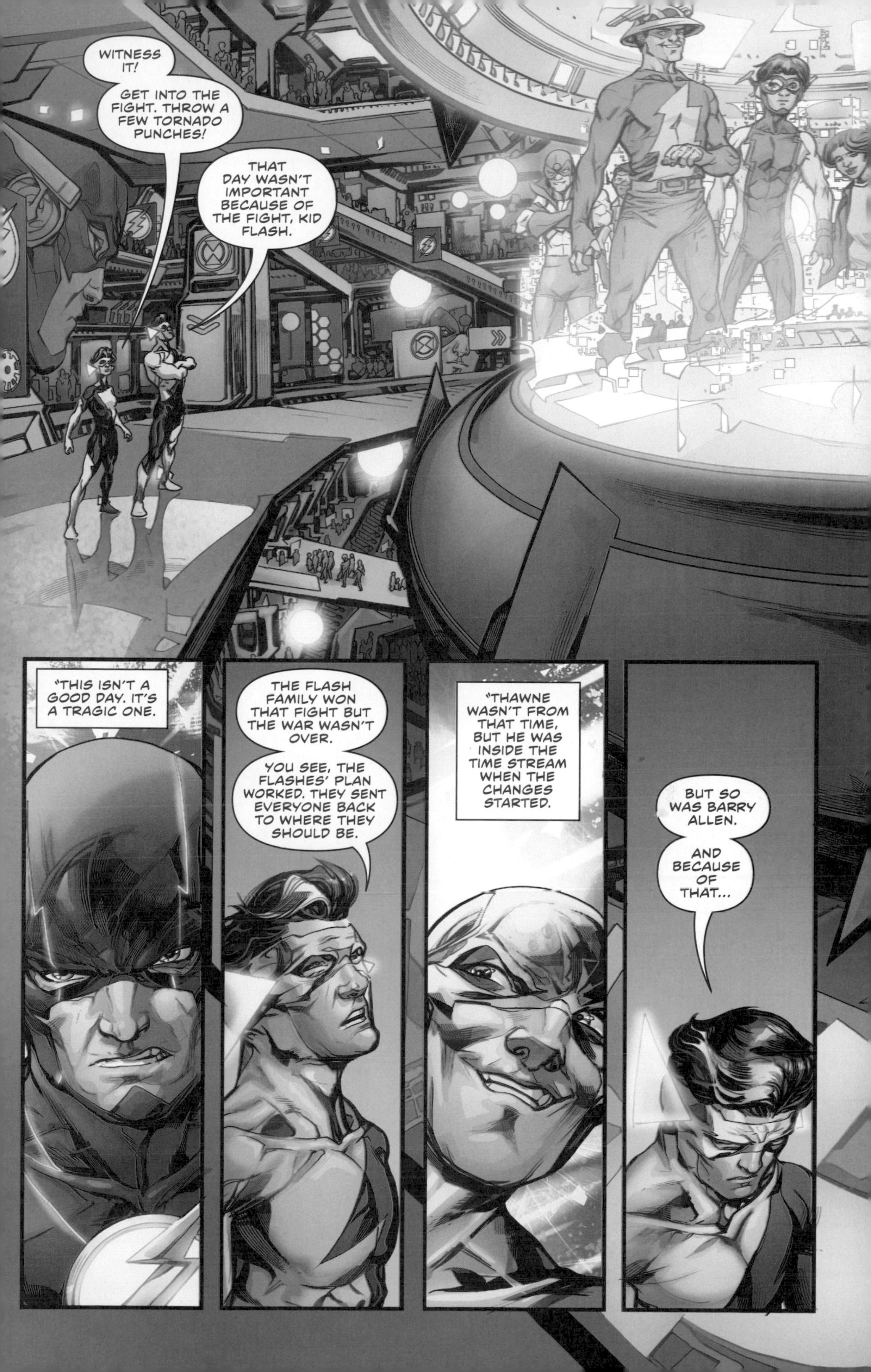
WITNESS IT!
GET INTO THE FIGHT. THROW A FEW TORNADO PUNCHES!
THAT DAY WASN'T IMPORTANT BECAUSE OF THE FIGHT, KID FLASH.
"THIS ISN'T A GOOD DAY. IT'S A TRAGIC ONE.
THE FLASH FAMILY WON THAT FIGHT BUT THE WAR WASN'T OVER.
YOU SEE, THE FLASHES' PLAN WORKED. THEY SENT EVERYONE BACK TO WHERE THEY SHOULD BE.
"THAWNE WASN'T FROM THAT TIME, BUT HE WAS INSIDE THE TIME STREAM WHEN THE CHANGES STARTED.
BUT SO WAS BARRY ALLEN.
AND BECAUSE OF THAT...

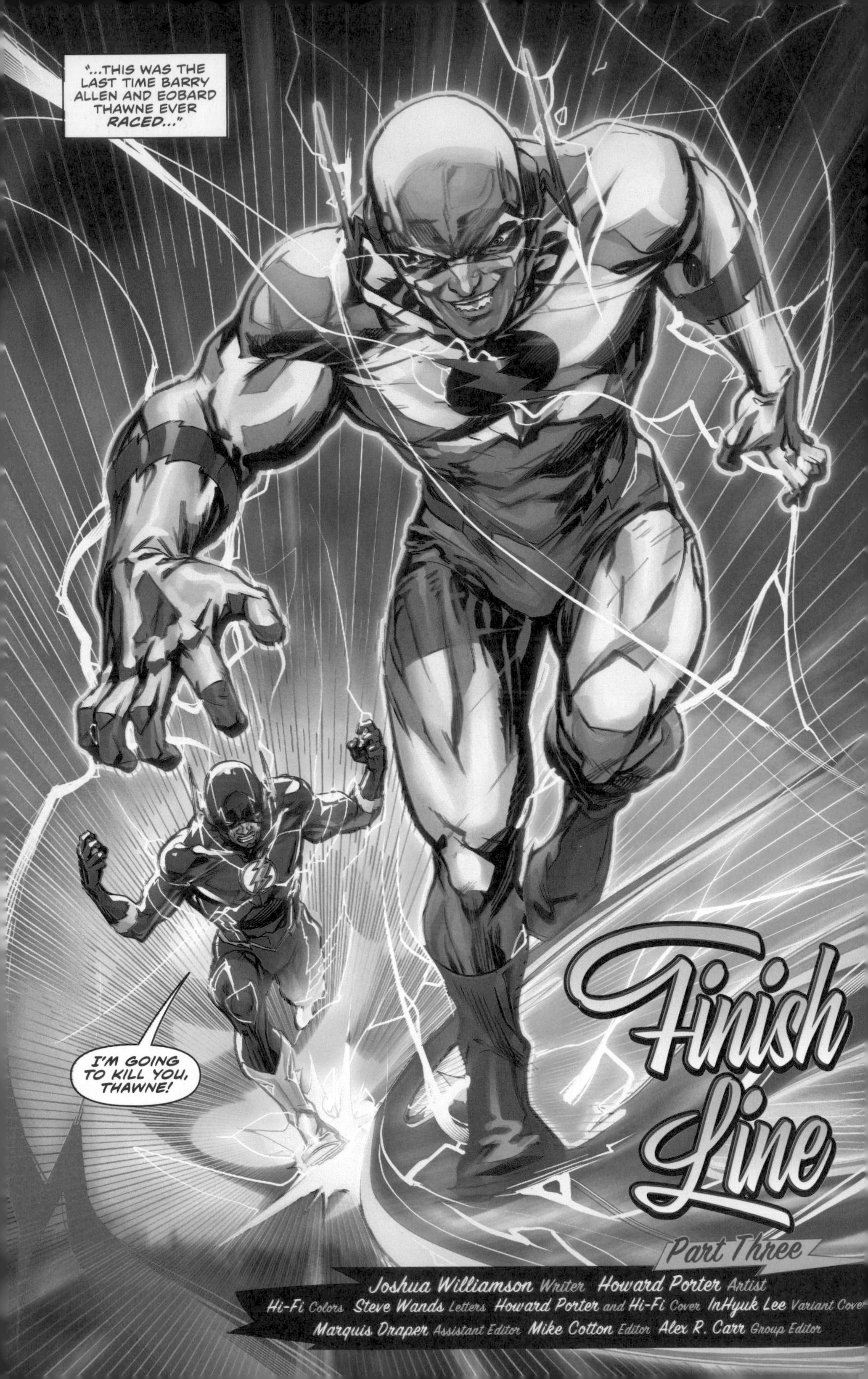
"...THIS WAS THE LAST TIME BARRY ALLEN AND EOBARD THAWNE EVER RACED..."
I'M GOING TO KILL YOU, THAWNE!
Finish Line
Part Three
Joshua Williamson Writer Howard Porter Artist
Hi-Fi Colors Steve Wands Letters Howard Porter and Hi-Fi Cover InHyuk Lee Variant Cover
Marquis Draper Assistant Editor Mike Cotton Editor Alex R. Carr Group Editor

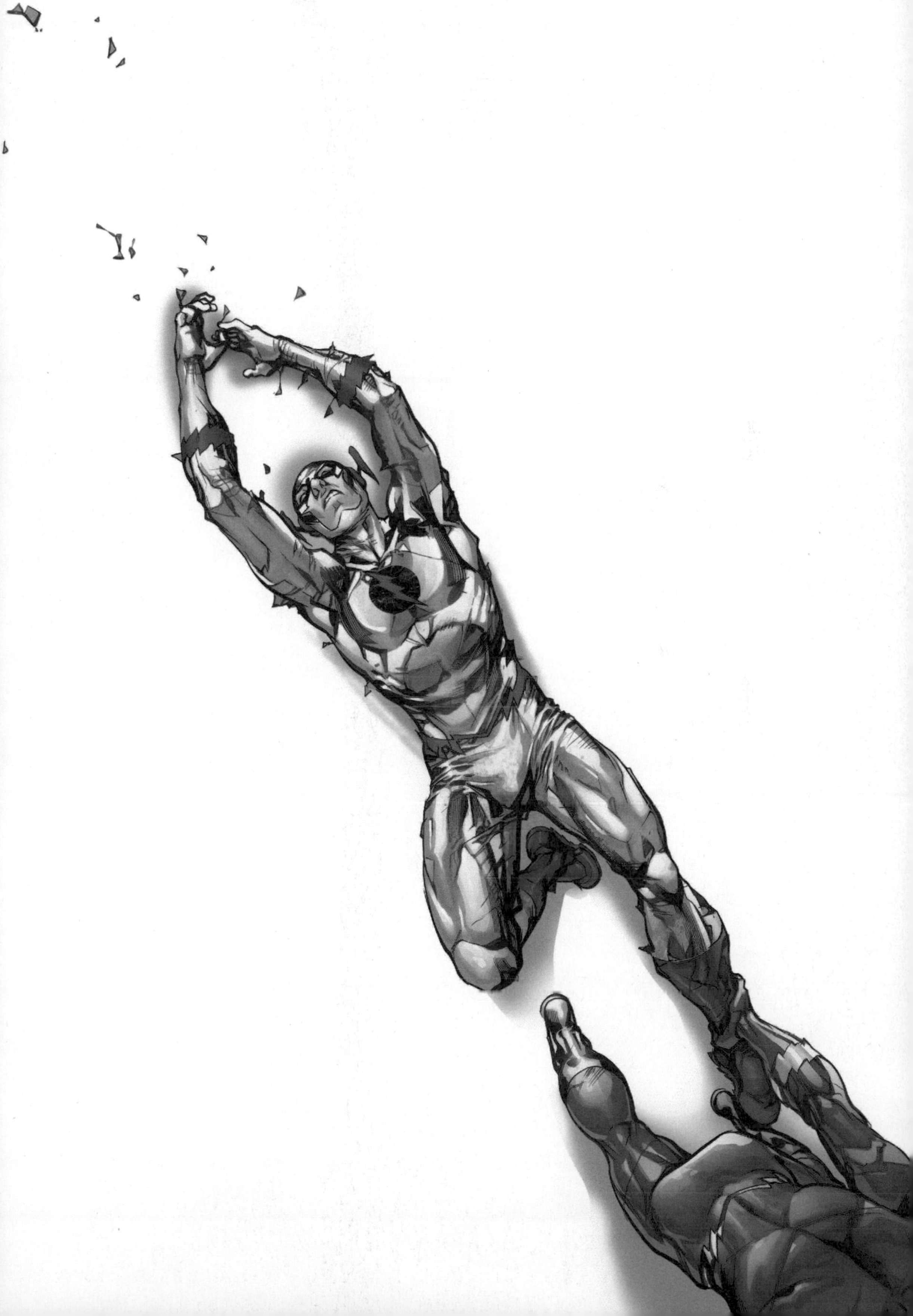

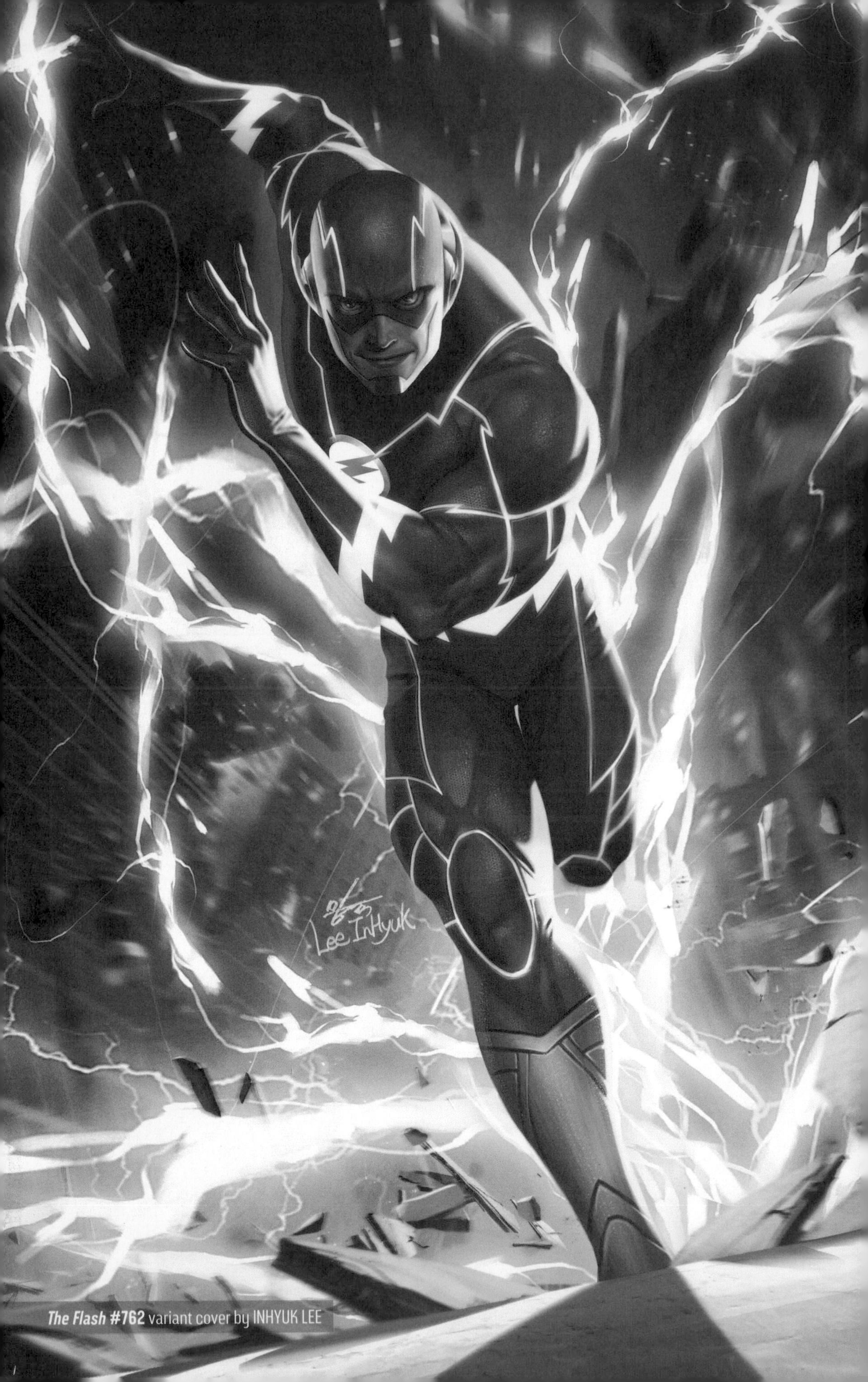
Lee InHyuk

***The Flash* #762** variant cover by INHYUK LEE

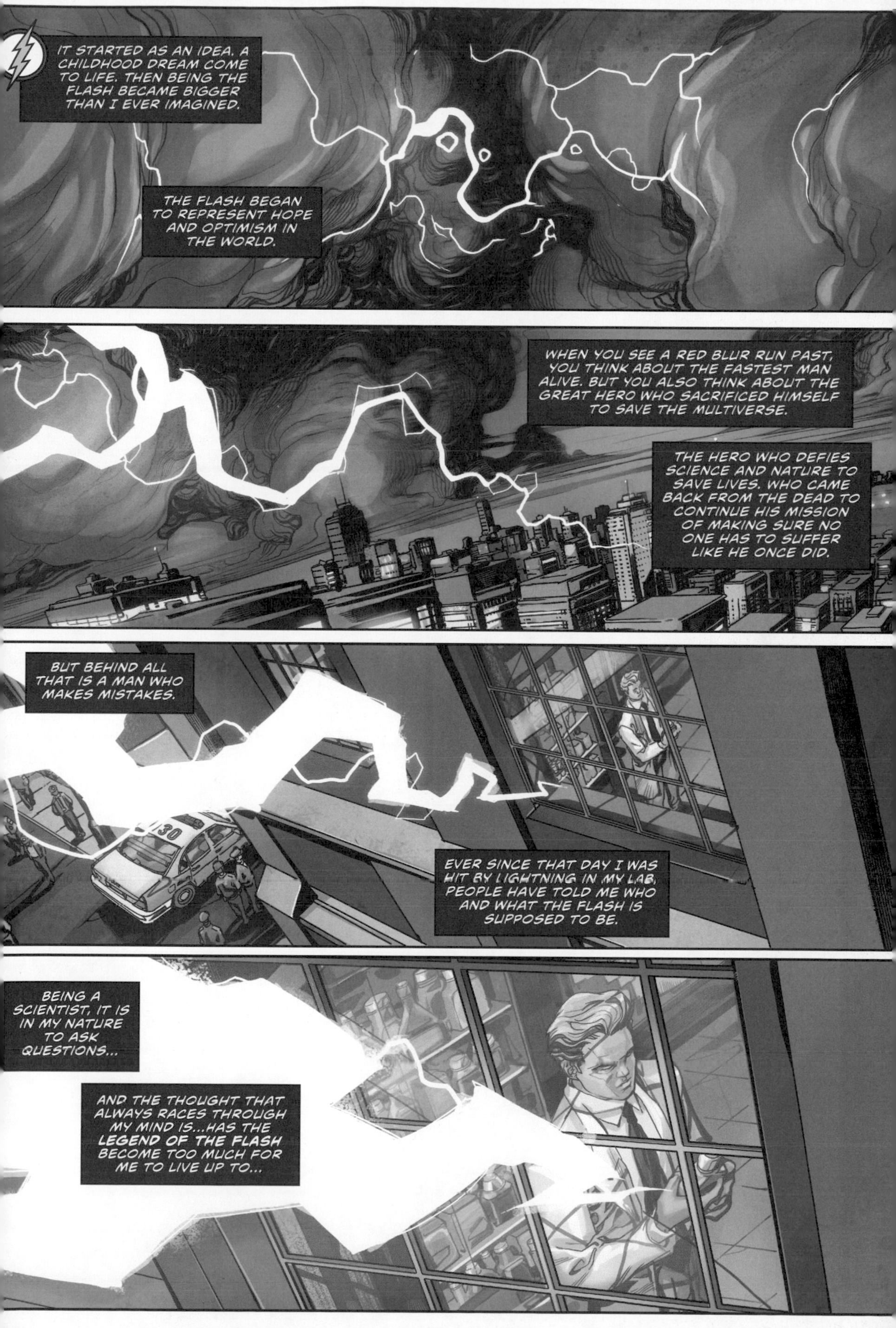
IT STARTED AS AN IDEA. A CHILDHOOD DREAM COME TO LIFE. THEN BEING THE FLASH BECAME BIGGER THAN I EVER IMAGINED.
THE FLASH BEGAN TO REPRESENT HOPE AND OPTIMISM IN THE WORLD.
WHEN YOU SEE A RED BLUR RUN PAST, YOU THINK ABOUT THE FASTEST MAN ALIVE. BUT YOU ALSO THINK ABOUT THE GREAT HERO WHO SACRIFICED HIMSELF TO SAVE THE MULTIVERSE.
THE HERO WHO DEFIES SCIENCE AND NATURE TO SAVE LIVES. WHO CAME BACK FROM THE DEAD TO CONTINUE HIS MISSION OF MAKING SURE NO ONE HAS TO SUFFER LIKE HE ONCE DID.
BUT BEHIND ALL THAT IS A MAN WHO MAKES MISTAKES.
30
EVER SINCE THAT DAY I WAS HIT BY LIGHTNING IN MY LAB, PEOPLE HAVE TOLD ME WHO AND WHAT THE FLASH IS SUPPOSED TO BE.
BEING A SCIENTIST, IT IS IN MY NATURE TO ASK QUESTIONS...
AND THE THOUGHT THAT ALWAYS RACES THROUGH MY MIND IS...HAS THE **LEGEND OF THE FLASH** BECOME TOO MUCH FOR ME TO LIVE UP TO...

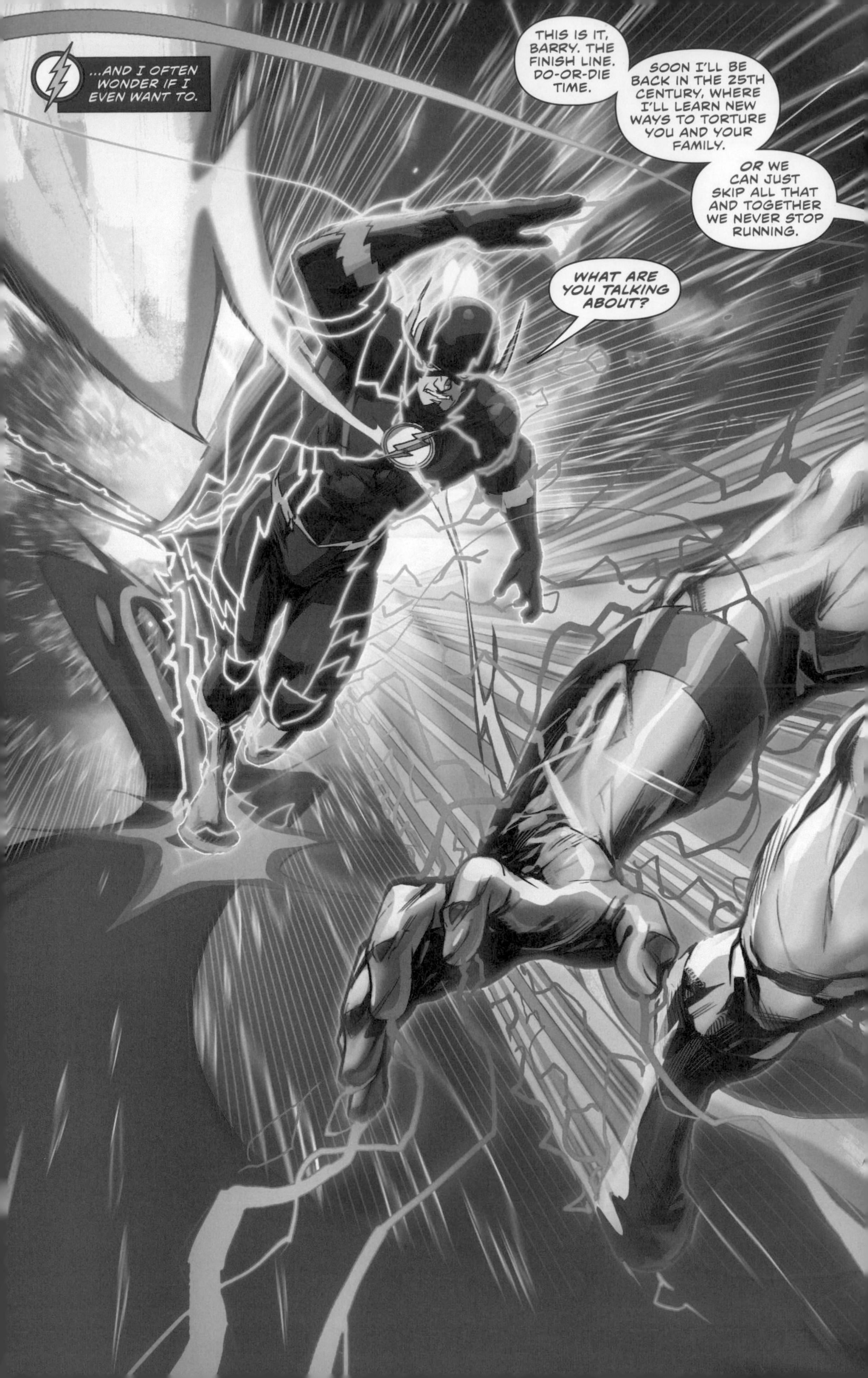
...AND I OFTEN WONDER IF I EVEN WANT TO.
THIS IS IT, BARRY. THE FINISH LINE. DO-OR-DIE TIME.
SOON I'LL BE BACK IN THE 25TH CENTURY, WHERE I'LL LEARN NEW WAYS TO TORTURE YOU AND YOUR FAMILY.
OR WE CAN JUST SKIP ALL THAT AND TOGETHER WE NEVER STOP RUNNING.
WHAT ARE YOU TALKING ABOUT?

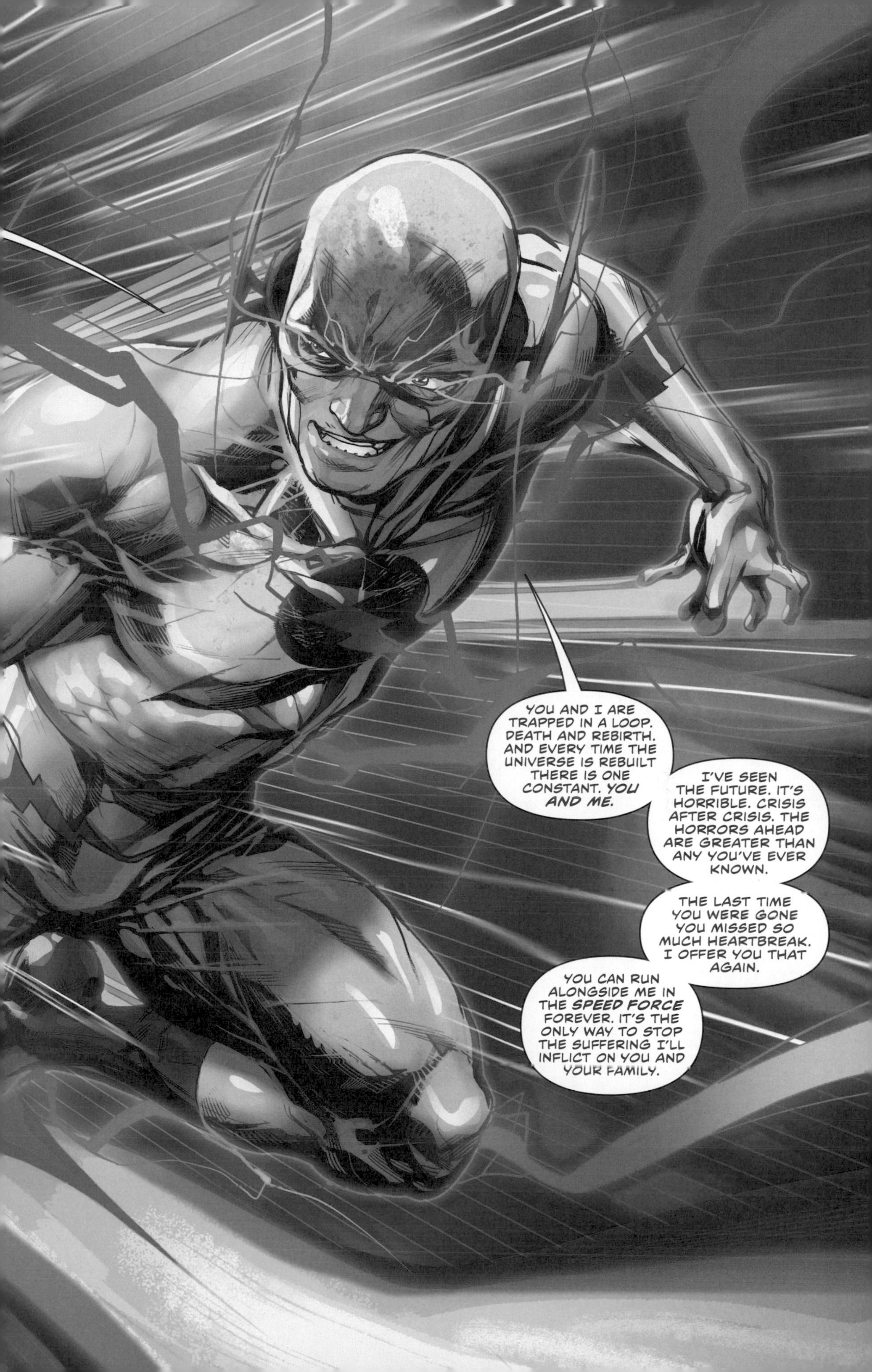
YOU AND I ARE TRAPPED IN A LOOP. DEATH AND REBIRTH. AND EVERY TIME THE UNIVERSE IS REBUILT THERE IS ONE CONSTANT. *YOU AND ME.*
I'VE SEEN THE FUTURE. IT'S HORRIBLE. CRISIS AFTER CRISIS. THE HORRORS AHEAD ARE GREATER THAN ANY YOU'VE EVER KNOWN.
THE LAST TIME YOU WERE GONE YOU MISSED SO MUCH HEARTBREAK. I OFFER YOU THAT AGAIN.
YOU CAN RUN ALONGSIDE ME IN THE *SPEED FORCE* FOREVER. IT'S THE ONLY WAY TO STOP THE SUFFERING I'LL INFLICT ON YOU AND YOUR FAMILY.

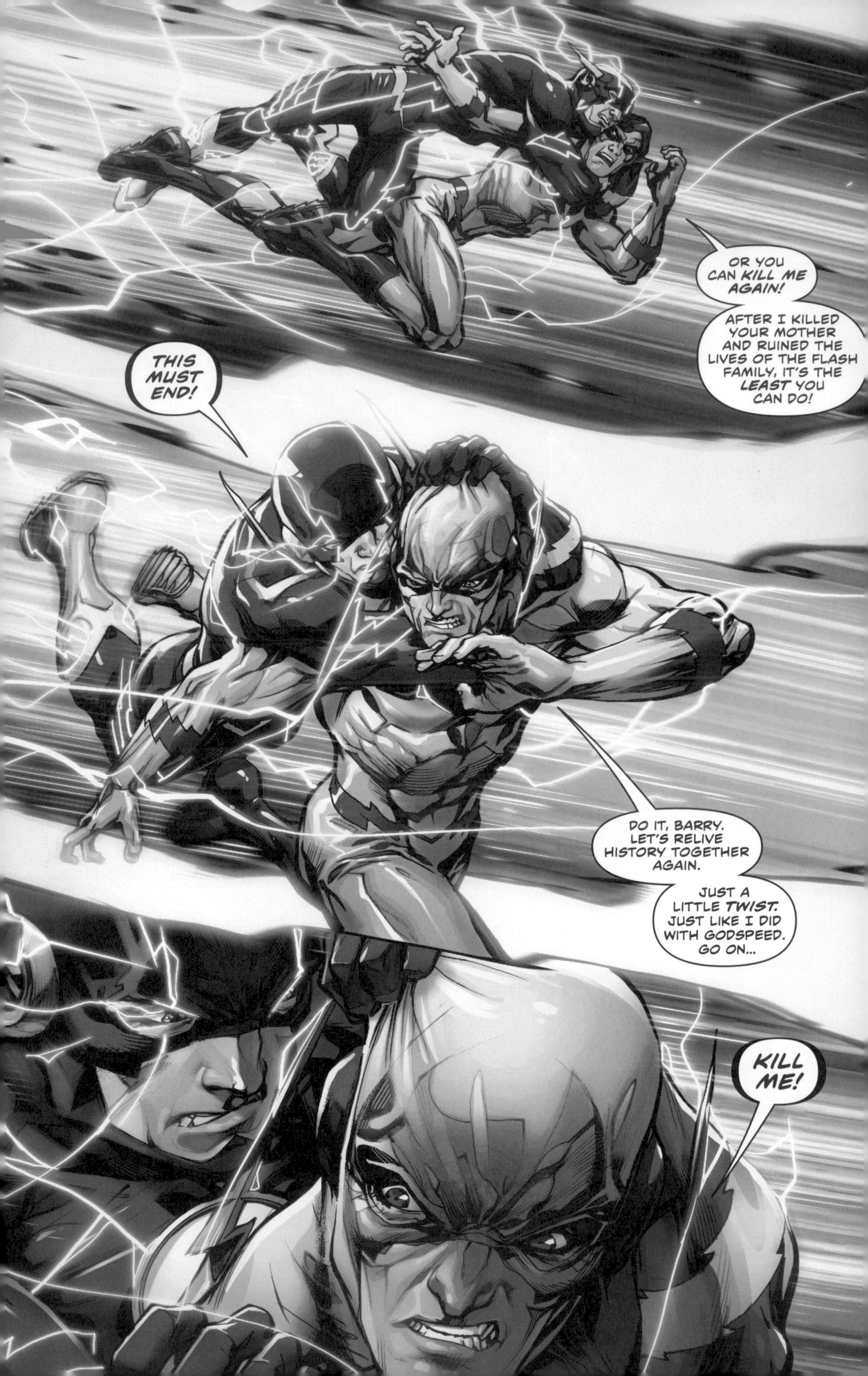
OR YOU CAN KILL ME AGAIN!
AFTER I KILLED YOUR MOTHER AND RUINED THE LIVES OF THE FLASH FAMILY, IT'S THE LEAST YOU CAN DO!
THIS MUST END!
DO IT, BARRY. LET'S RELIVE HISTORY TOGETHER AGAIN.
JUST A LITTLE TWIST. JUST LIKE I DID WITH GODSPEED. GO ON...
KILL ME!

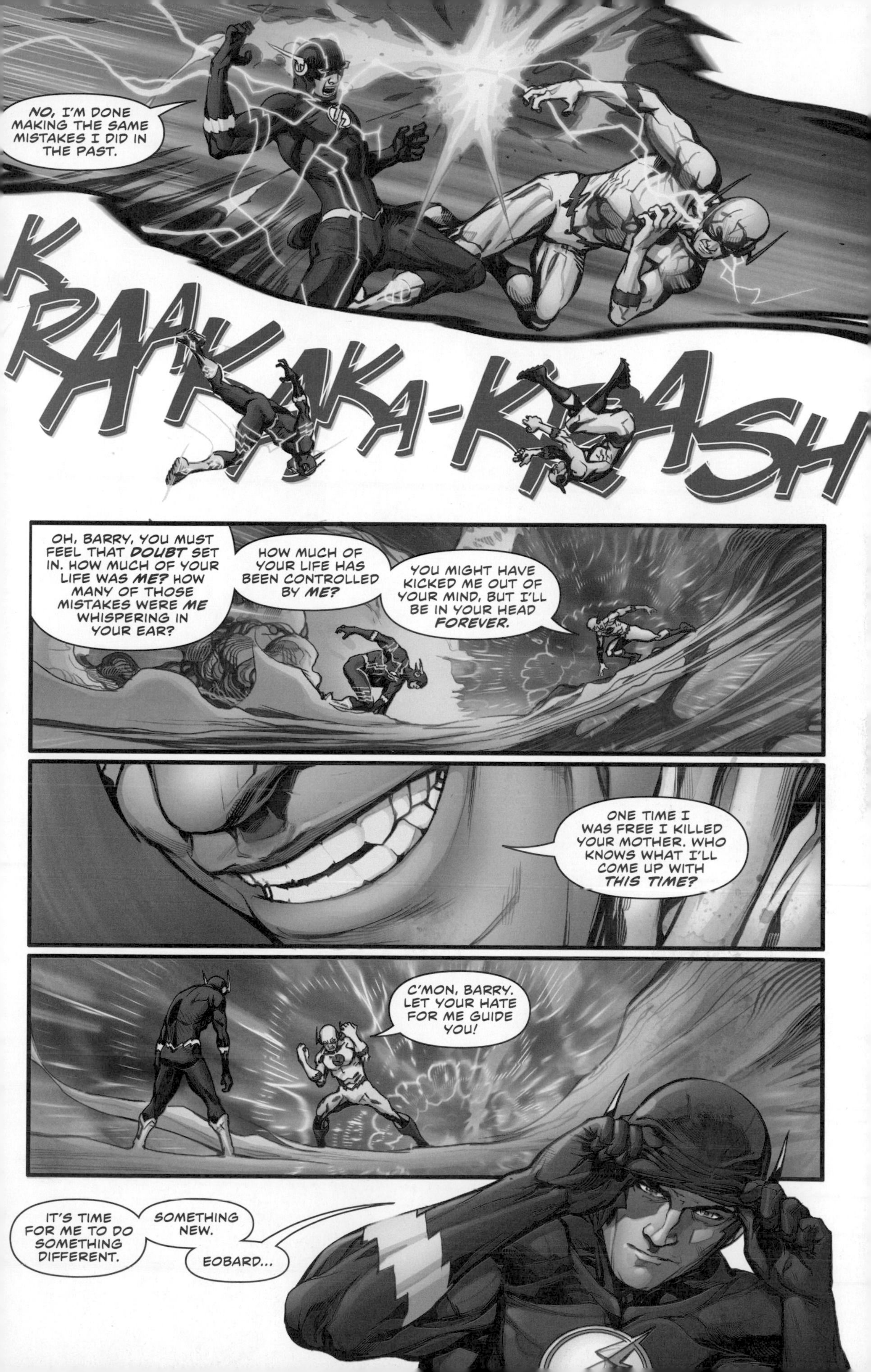
NO, I'M DONE MAKING THE SAME MISTAKES I DID IN THE PAST.
KRAAKAKA-KRASH
OH, BARRY, YOU MUST FEEL THAT DOUBT SET IN. HOW MUCH OF YOUR LIFE WAS ME? HOW MANY OF THOSE MISTAKES WERE ME WHISPERING IN YOUR EAR?
HOW MUCH OF YOUR LIFE HAS BEEN CONTROLLED BY ME?
YOU MIGHT HAVE KICKED ME OUT OF YOUR MIND, BUT I'LL BE IN YOUR HEAD FOREVER.
ONE TIME I WAS FREE I KILLED YOUR MOTHER. WHO KNOWS WHAT I'LL COME UP WITH THIS TIME?
C'MON, BARRY. LET YOUR HATE FOR ME GUIDE YOU!
IT'S TIME FOR ME TO DO SOMETHING DIFFERENT.
SOMETHING NEW.
EOBARD...

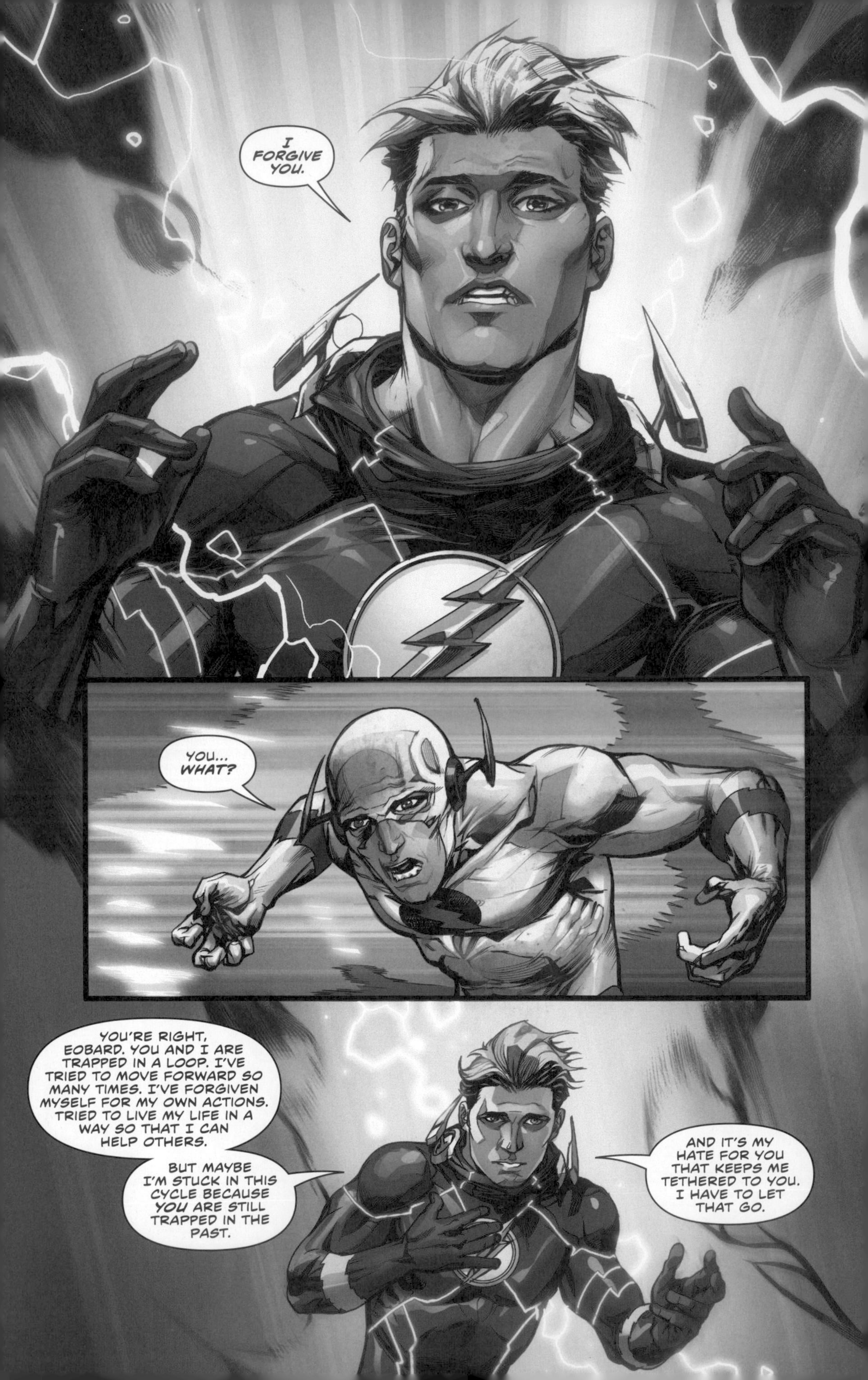
I FORGIVE YOU.
YOU... WHAT?
YOU'RE RIGHT, EOBARD. YOU AND I ARE TRAPPED IN A LOOP. I'VE TRIED TO MOVE FORWARD SO MANY TIMES. I'VE FORGIVEN MYSELF FOR MY OWN ACTIONS. TRIED TO LIVE MY LIFE IN A WAY SO THAT I CAN HELP OTHERS.
BUT MAYBE I'M STUCK IN THIS CYCLE BECAUSE YOU ARE STILL TRAPPED IN THE PAST.
AND IT'S MY HATE FOR YOU THAT KEEPS ME TETHERED TO YOU. I HAVE TO LET THAT GO.

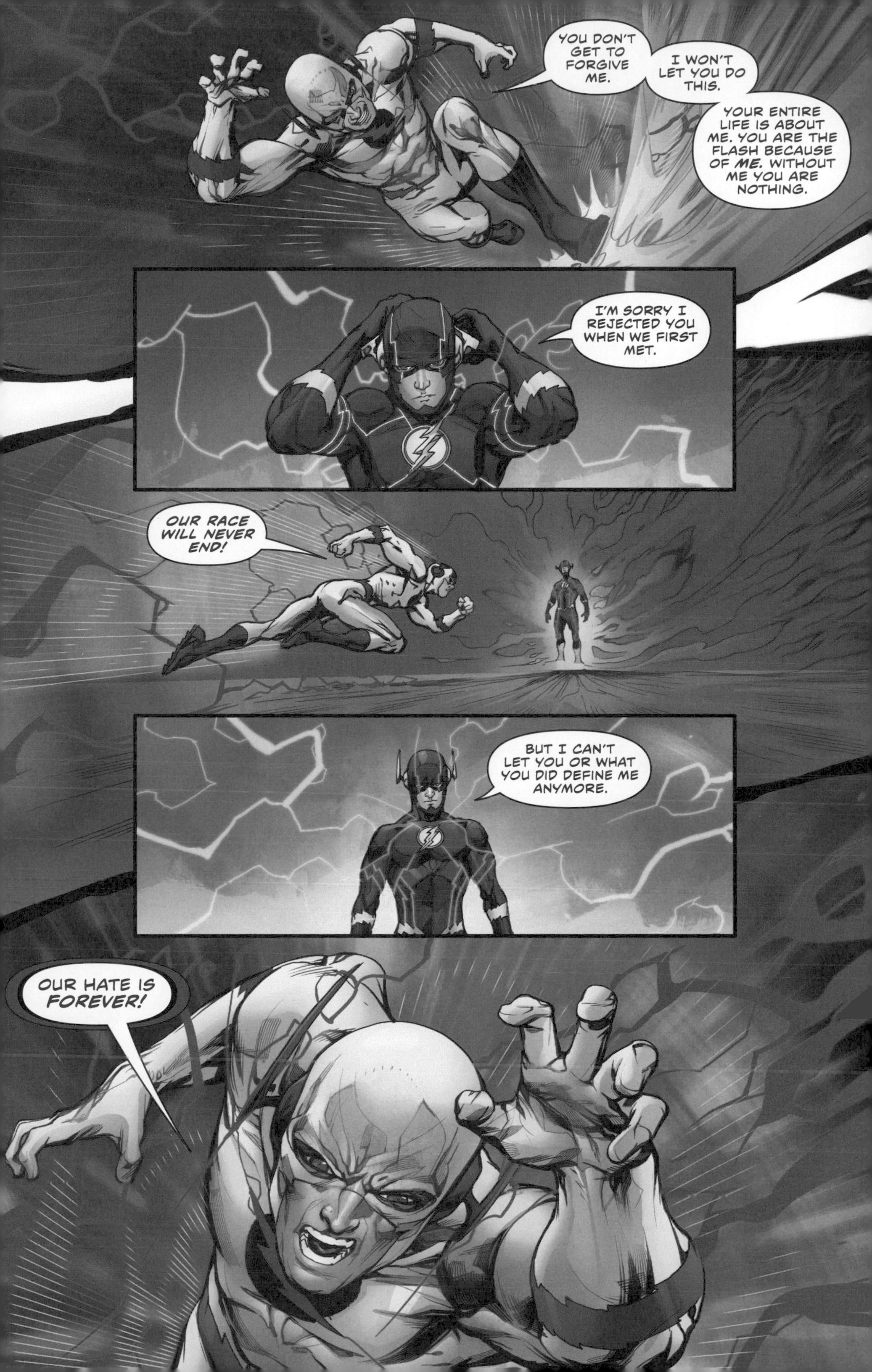
YOU DON'T GET TO FORGIVE ME.
I WON'T LET YOU DO THIS.
YOUR ENTIRE LIFE IS ABOUT ME. YOU ARE THE FLASH BECAUSE OF *ME.* WITHOUT ME YOU ARE NOTHING.
I'M SORRY I REJECTED YOU WHEN WE FIRST MET.
OUR RACE WILL NEVER END!
BUT I CAN'T LET YOU OR WHAT YOU DID DEFINE ME ANYMORE.
OUR HATE IS *FOREVER!*

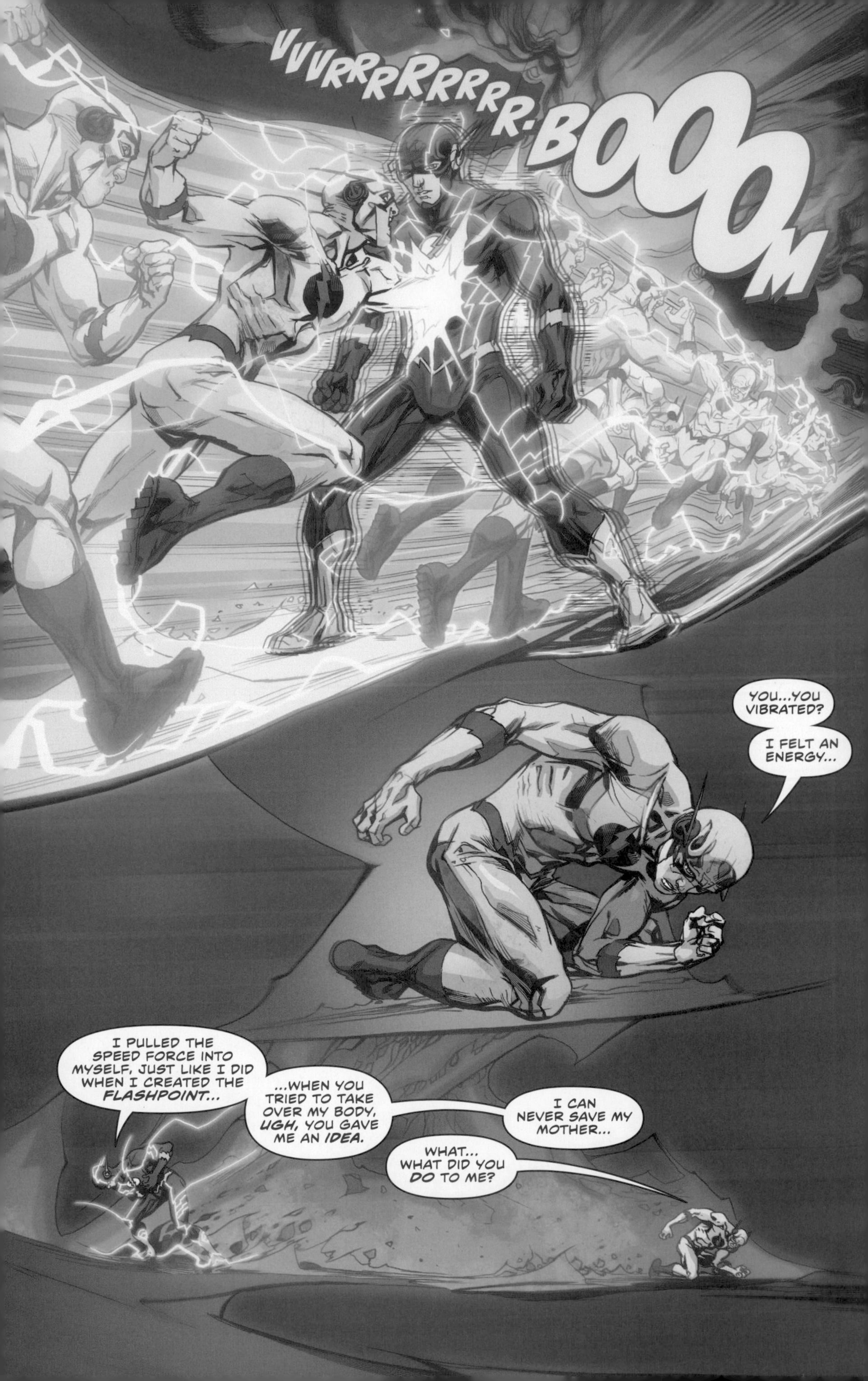
VVVRRRRRRRRR-BOOOOM
YOU...YOU VIBRATED?
I FELT AN ENERGY...
I PULLED THE SPEED FORCE INTO MYSELF, JUST LIKE I DID WHEN I CREATED THE FLASHPOINT...
...WHEN YOU TRIED TO TAKE OVER MY BODY, UGH, YOU GAVE ME AN IDEA.
I CAN NEVER SAVE MY MOTHER...
WHAT... WHAT DID YOU DO TO ME?

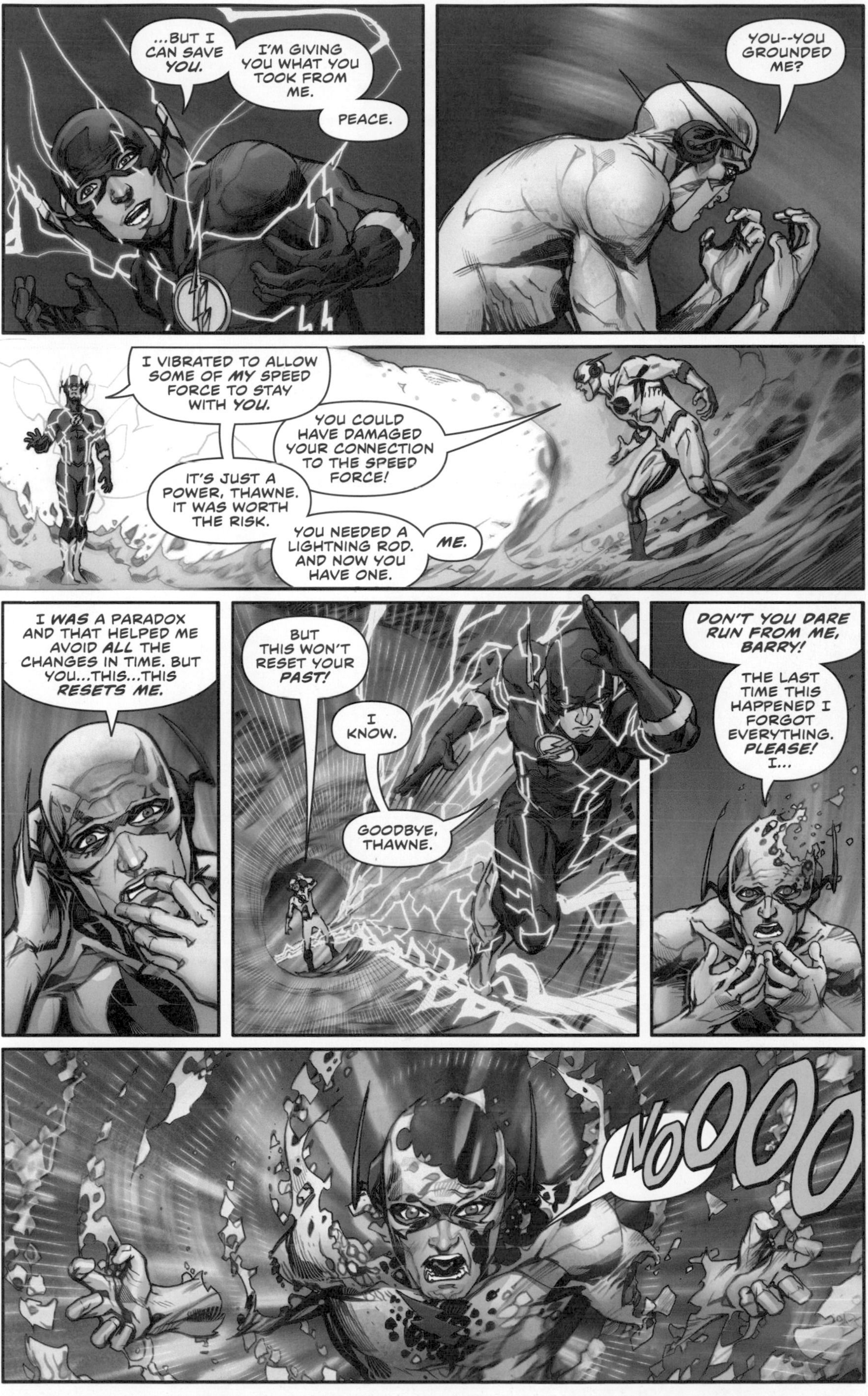
...BUT I CAN SAVE *YOU.*
I'M GIVING YOU WHAT YOU TOOK FROM ME.
PEACE.
YOU--YOU GROUNDED ME?
I VIBRATED TO ALLOW SOME OF *MY* SPEED FORCE TO STAY WITH *YOU.*
YOU COULD HAVE DAMAGED YOUR CONNECTION TO THE SPEED FORCE!
IT'S JUST A POWER, THAWNE. IT WAS WORTH THE RISK.
YOU NEEDED A LIGHTNING ROD. AND NOW YOU HAVE ONE.
ME.
I *WAS* A PARADOX AND THAT HELPED ME AVOID *ALL* THE CHANGES IN TIME. BUT YOU...THIS...THIS *RESETS ME.*
BUT THIS WON'T RESET YOUR *PAST!*
I KNOW.
GOODBYE, THAWNE.
DON'T YOU DARE RUN FROM ME, BARRY!
THE LAST TIME THIS HAPPENED I FORGOT EVERYTHING. *PLEASE!* I...
NOOOOO

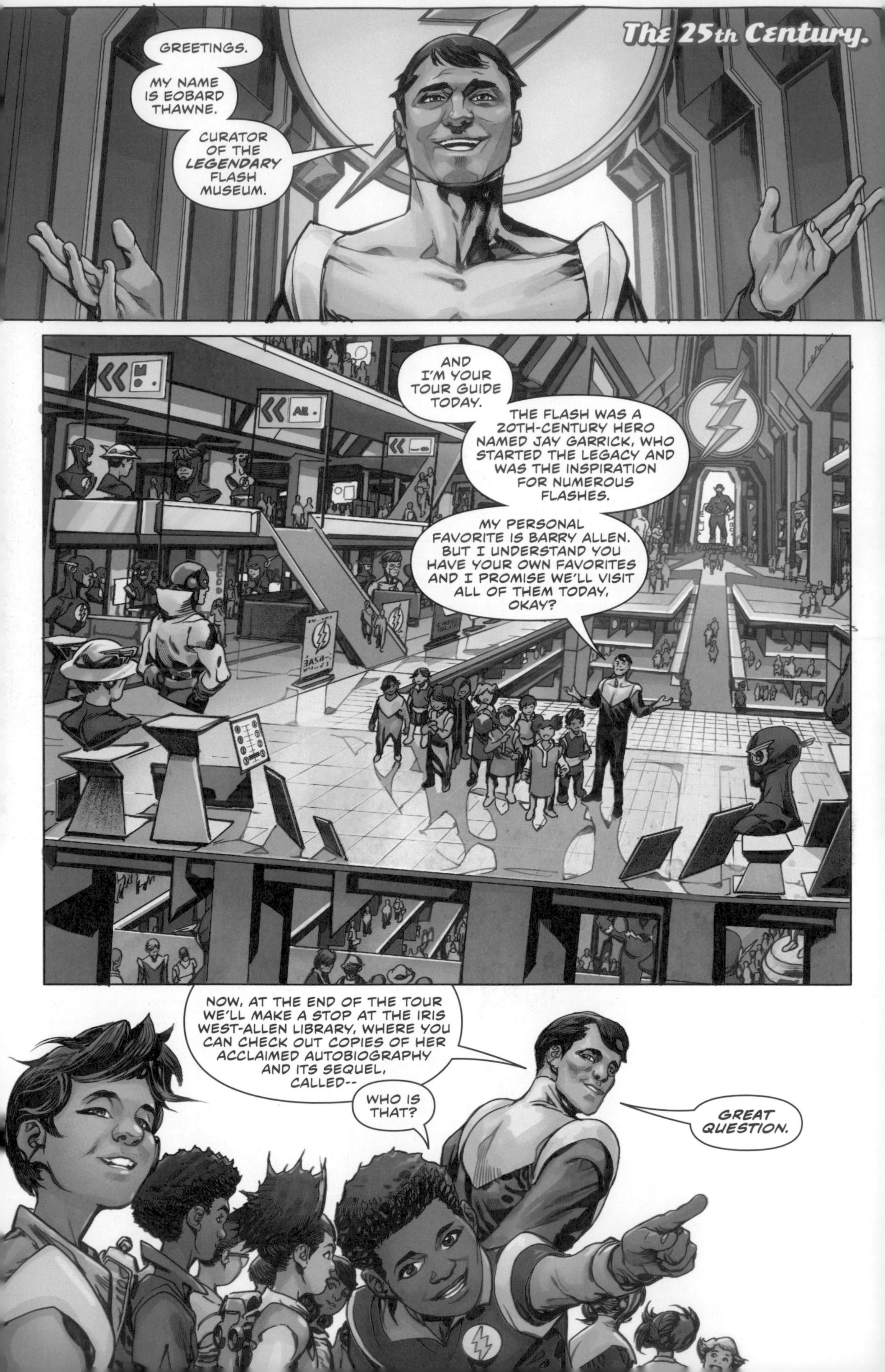
The 25th Century.
GREETINGS.
MY NAME IS EOBARD THAWNE.
CURATOR OF THE *LEGENDARY* FLASH MUSEUM.
AND I'M YOUR TOUR GUIDE TODAY.
THE FLASH WAS A 20TH-CENTURY HERO NAMED JAY GARRICK, WHO STARTED THE LEGACY AND WAS THE INSPIRATION FOR NUMEROUS FLASHES.
MY PERSONAL FAVORITE IS BARRY ALLEN. BUT I UNDERSTAND YOU HAVE YOUR OWN FAVORITES AND I PROMISE WE'LL VISIT ALL OF THEM TODAY, OKAY?
NOW, AT THE END OF THE TOUR WE'LL MAKE A STOP AT THE IRIS WEST-ALLEN LIBRARY, WHERE YOU CAN CHECK OUT COPIES OF HER ACCLAIMED AUTOBIOGRAPHY AND ITS SEQUEL, CALLED--
WHO IS THAT?
GREAT QUESTION.

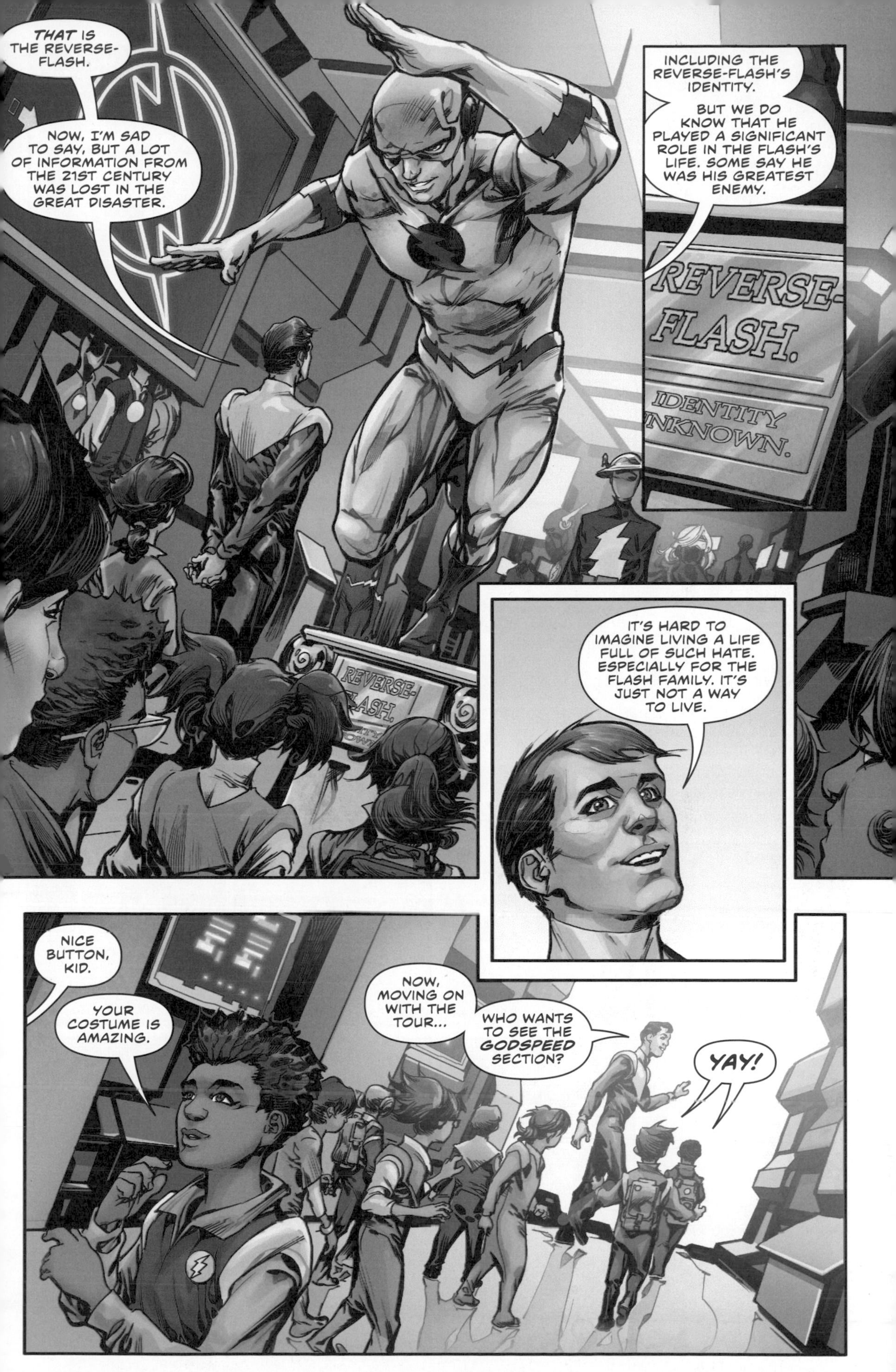
THAT IS THE REVERSE-FLASH.
NOW, I'M SAD TO SAY, BUT A LOT OF INFORMATION FROM THE 21ST CENTURY WAS LOST IN THE GREAT DISASTER.
INCLUDING THE REVERSE-FLASH'S IDENTITY.
BUT WE DO KNOW THAT HE PLAYED A SIGNIFICANT ROLE IN THE FLASH'S LIFE. SOME SAY HE WAS HIS GREATEST ENEMY.
REVERSE-FLASH.
IDENTITY UNKNOWN.
IT'S HARD TO IMAGINE LIVING A LIFE FULL OF SUCH HATE. ESPECIALLY FOR THE FLASH FAMILY. IT'S JUST NOT A WAY TO LIVE.
NICE BUTTON, KID.
YOUR COSTUME IS AMAZING.
NOW, MOVING ON WITH THE TOUR...
WHO WANTS TO SEE THE GODSPEED SECTION?
YAY!

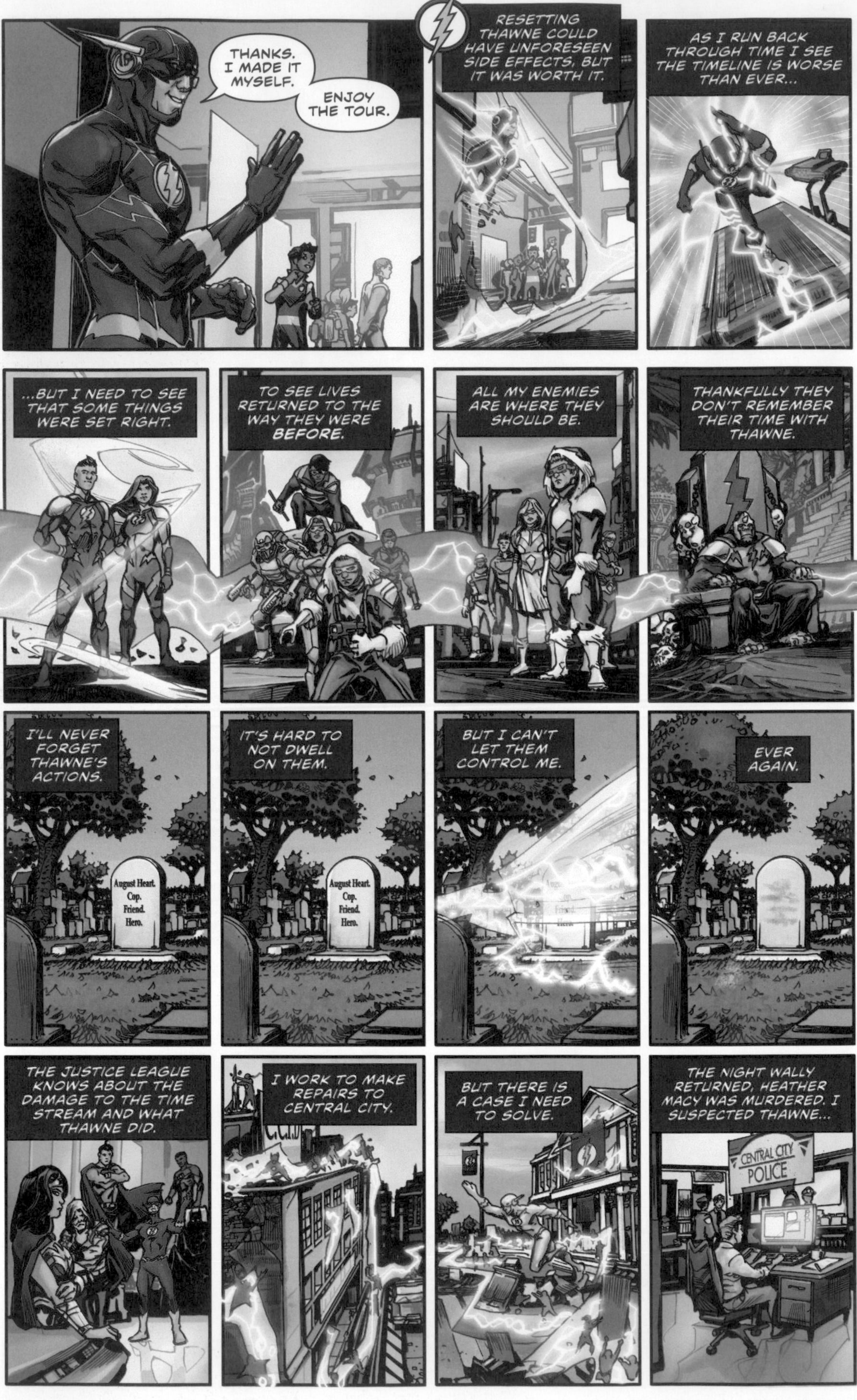
THANKS. I MADE IT MYSELF.
ENJOY THE TOUR.
RESETTING THAWNE COULD HAVE UNFORESEEN SIDE EFFECTS, BUT IT WAS WORTH IT.
AS I RUN BACK THROUGH TIME I SEE THE TIMELINE IS WORSE THAN EVER...
...BUT I NEED TO SEE THAT SOME THINGS WERE SET RIGHT.
TO SEE LIVES RETURNED TO THE WAY THEY WERE BEFORE.
ALL MY ENEMIES ARE WHERE THEY SHOULD BE.
THANKFULLY THEY DON'T REMEMBER THEIR TIME WITH THAWNE.
I'LL NEVER FORGET THAWNE'S ACTIONS.
August Heart. Cop. Friend. Hero.
IT'S HARD TO NOT DWELL ON THEM.
August Heart. Cop. Friend. Hero.
BUT I CAN'T LET THEM CONTROL ME.
EVER AGAIN.
THE JUSTICE LEAGUE KNOWS ABOUT THE DAMAGE TO THE TIME STREAM AND WHAT THAWNE DID.
I WORK TO MAKE REPAIRS TO CENTRAL CITY.
BUT THERE IS A CASE I NEED TO SOLVE.
THE NIGHT WALLY RETURNED, HEATHER MACY WAS MURDERED. I SUSPECTED THAWNE...
CENTRAL CITY POLICE

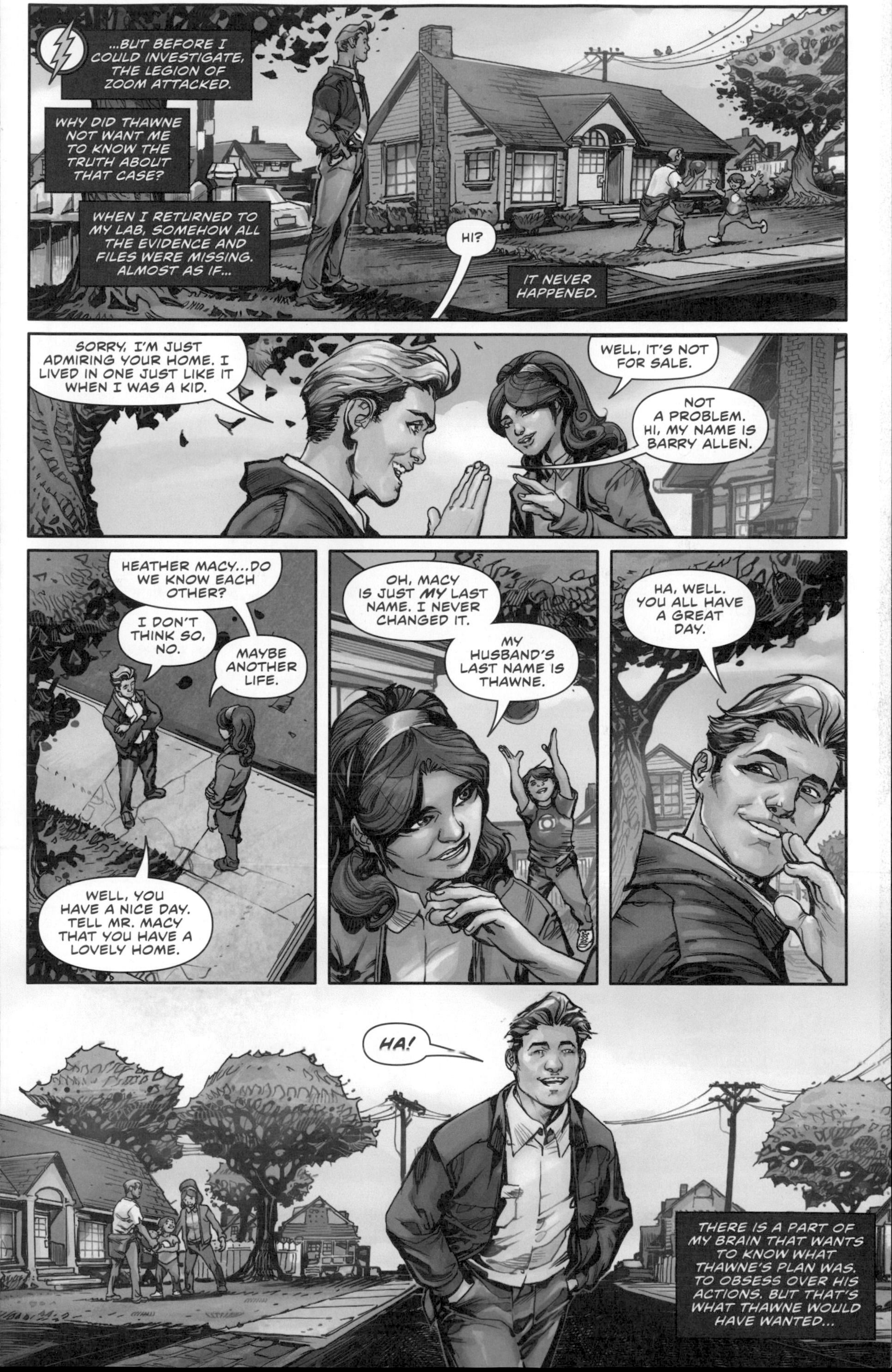
...BUT BEFORE I COULD INVESTIGATE, THE LEGION OF ZOOM ATTACKED.
WHY DID THAWNE NOT WANT ME TO KNOW THE TRUTH ABOUT THAT CASE?
WHEN I RETURNED TO MY LAB, SOMEHOW ALL THE EVIDENCE AND FILES WERE MISSING. ALMOST AS IF...
HI?
IT NEVER HAPPENED.
SORRY, I'M JUST ADMIRING YOUR HOME. I LIVED IN ONE JUST LIKE IT WHEN I WAS A KID.
WELL, IT'S NOT FOR SALE.
NOT A PROBLEM. HI, MY NAME IS BARRY ALLEN.
HEATHER MACY...DO WE KNOW EACH OTHER?
I DON'T THINK SO, NO.
MAYBE ANOTHER LIFE.
WELL, YOU HAVE A NICE DAY. TELL MR. MACY THAT YOU HAVE A LOVELY HOME.
OH, MACY IS JUST MY LAST NAME. I NEVER CHANGED IT.
MY HUSBAND'S LAST NAME IS THAWNE.
HA, WELL. YOU ALL HAVE A GREAT DAY.
HA!
THERE IS A PART OF MY BRAIN THAT WANTS TO KNOW WHAT THAWNE'S PLAN WAS. TO OBSESS OVER HIS ACTIONS. BUT THAT'S WHAT THAWNE WOULD HAVE WANTED...

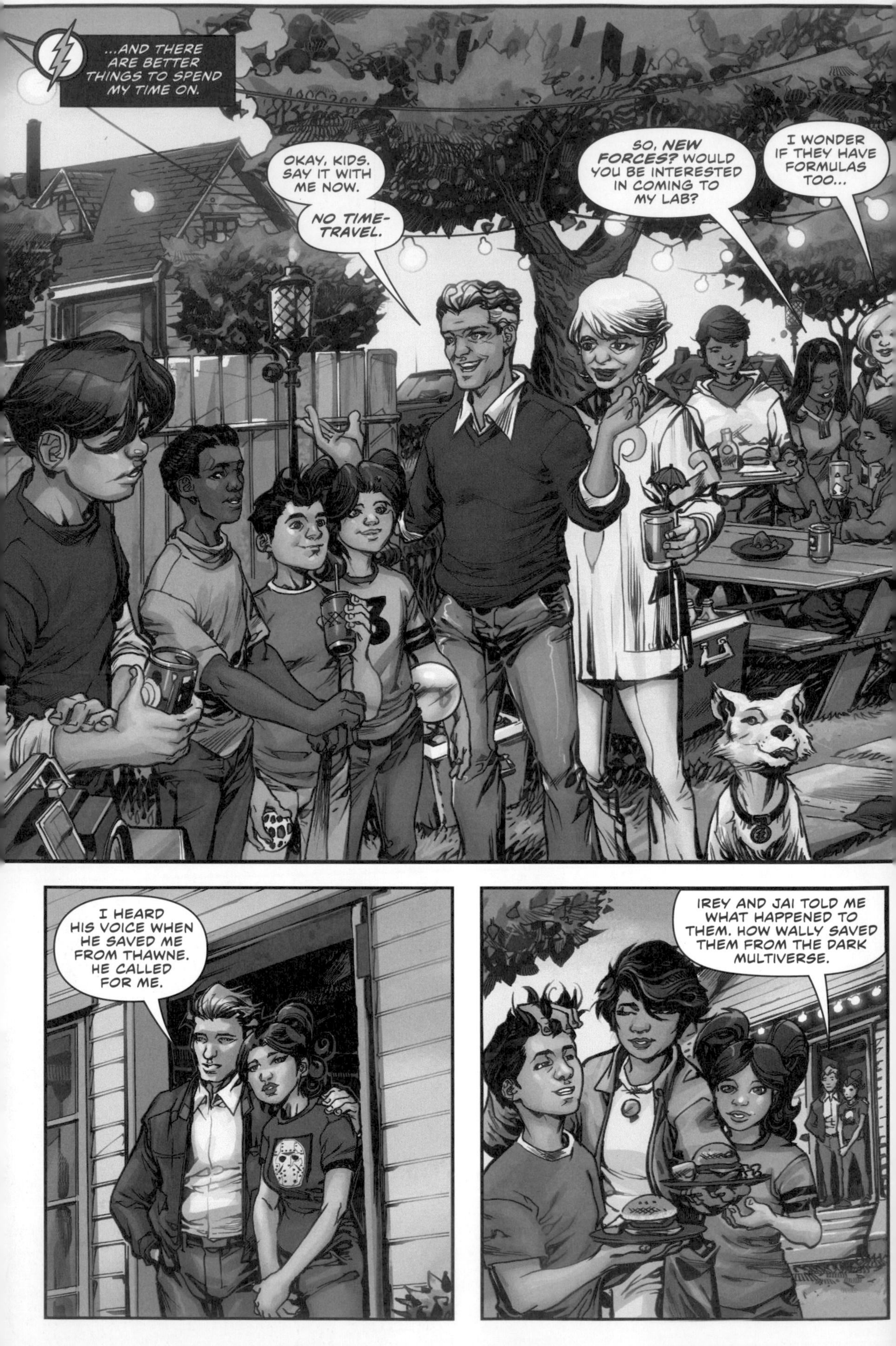
...AND THERE ARE BETTER THINGS TO SPEND MY TIME ON.
OKAY, KIDS. SAY IT WITH ME NOW.
NO TIME-TRAVEL.
SO, NEW FORCES? WOULD YOU BE INTERESTED IN COMING TO MY LAB?
I WONDER IF THEY HAVE FORMULAS TOO...
I HEARD HIS VOICE WHEN HE SAVED ME FROM THAWNE. HE CALLED FOR ME.
IREY AND JAI TOLD ME WHAT HAPPENED TO THEM. HOW WALLY SAVED THEM FROM THE DARK MULTIVERSE.

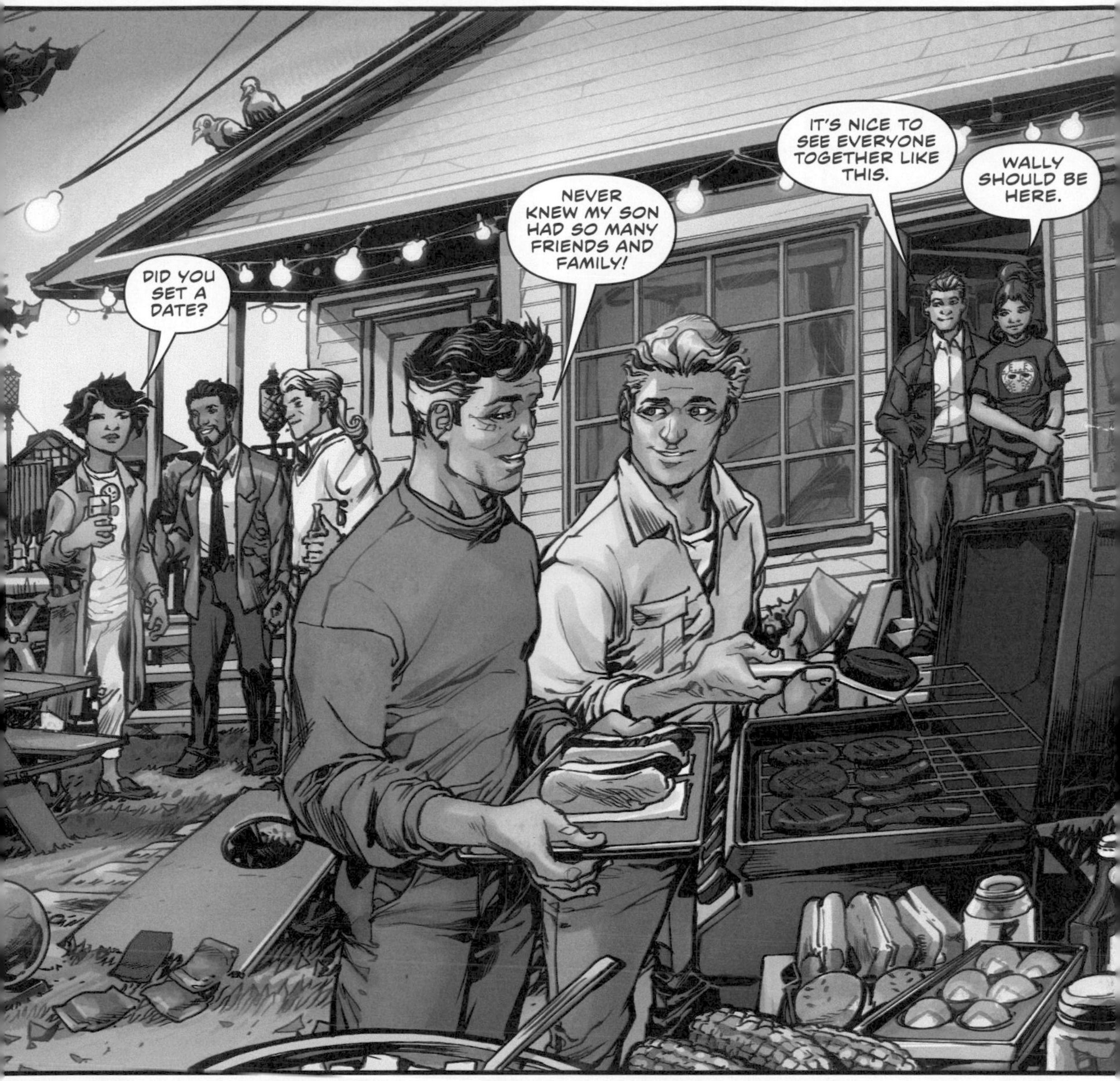
DID YOU SET A DATE?
NEVER KNEW MY SON HAD SO MANY FRIENDS AND FAMILY!
IT'S NICE TO SEE EVERYONE TOGETHER LIKE THIS.
WALLY SHOULD BE HERE.

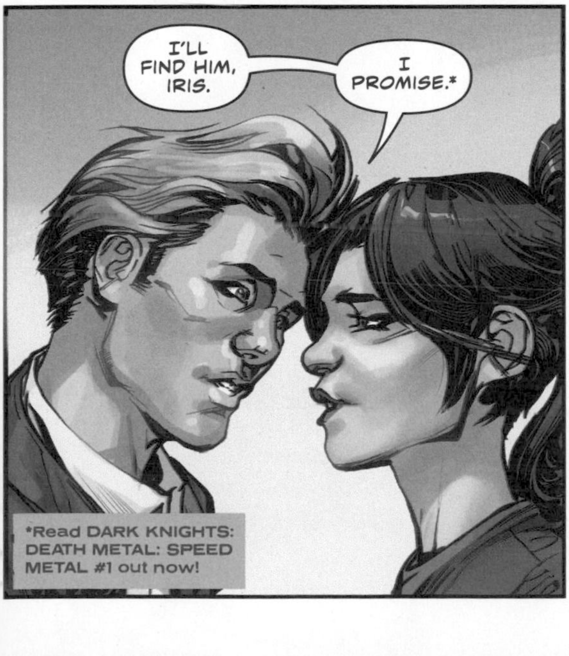
I'LL FIND HIM, IRIS.
I PROMISE.*
*Read DARK KNIGHTS: DEATH METAL: SPEED METAL #1 out now!

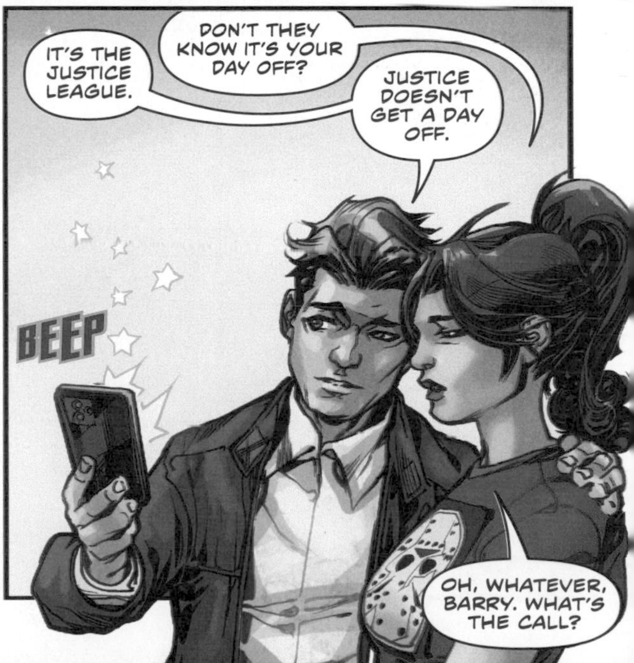
IT'S THE JUSTICE LEAGUE.
DON'T THEY KNOW IT'S YOUR DAY OFF?
JUSTICE DOESN'T GET A DAY OFF.
BEEP
OH, WHATEVER, BARRY. WHAT'S THE CALL?

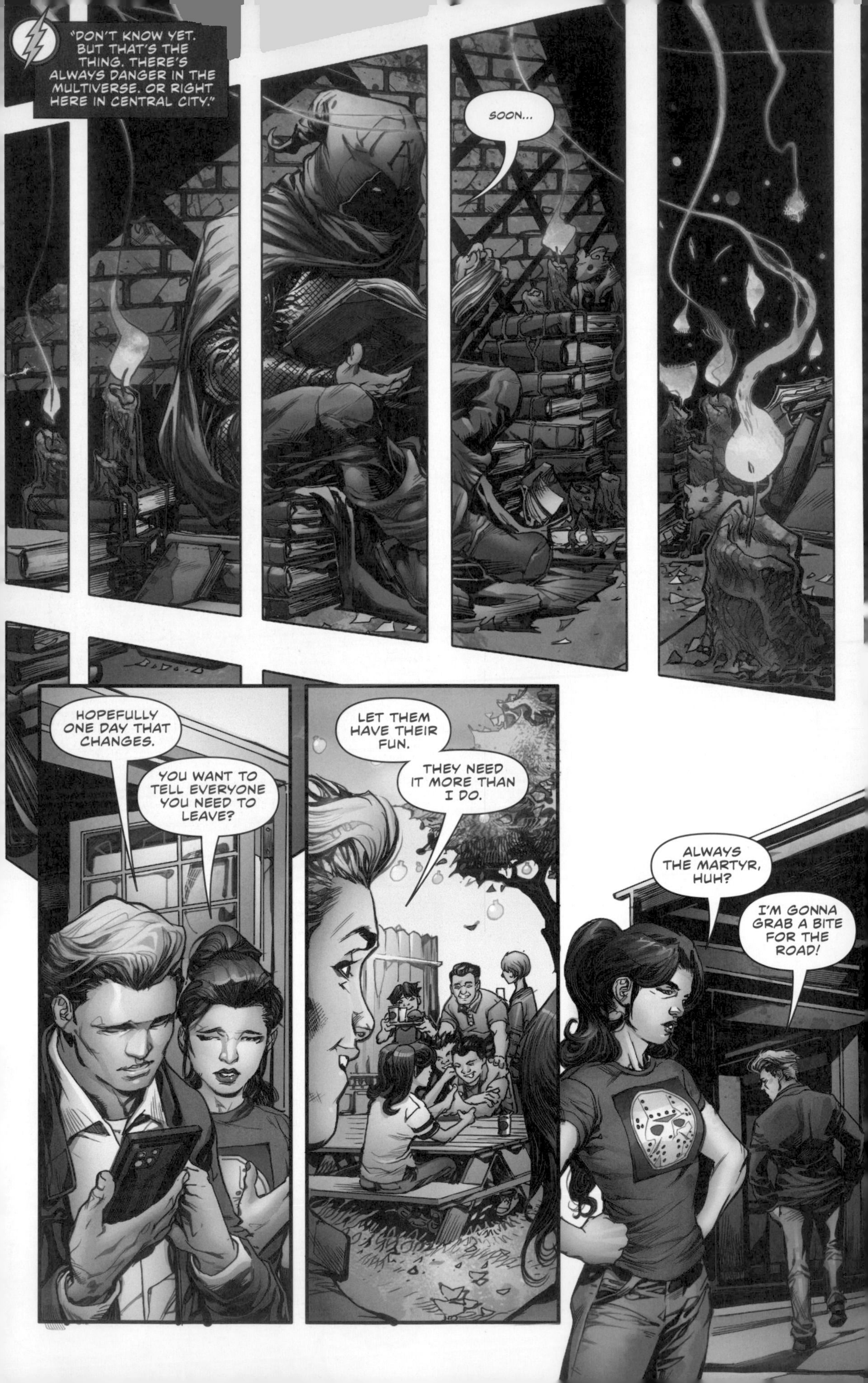
"DON'T KNOW YET. BUT THAT'S THE THING. THERE'S ALWAYS DANGER IN THE MULTIVERSE. OR RIGHT HERE IN CENTRAL CITY."
SOON...
HOPEFULLY ONE DAY THAT CHANGES.
YOU WANT TO TELL EVERYONE YOU NEED TO LEAVE?
LET THEM HAVE THEIR FUN.
THEY NEED IT MORE THAN I DO.
ALWAYS THE MARTYR, HUH?
I'M GONNA GRAB A BITE FOR THE ROAD!

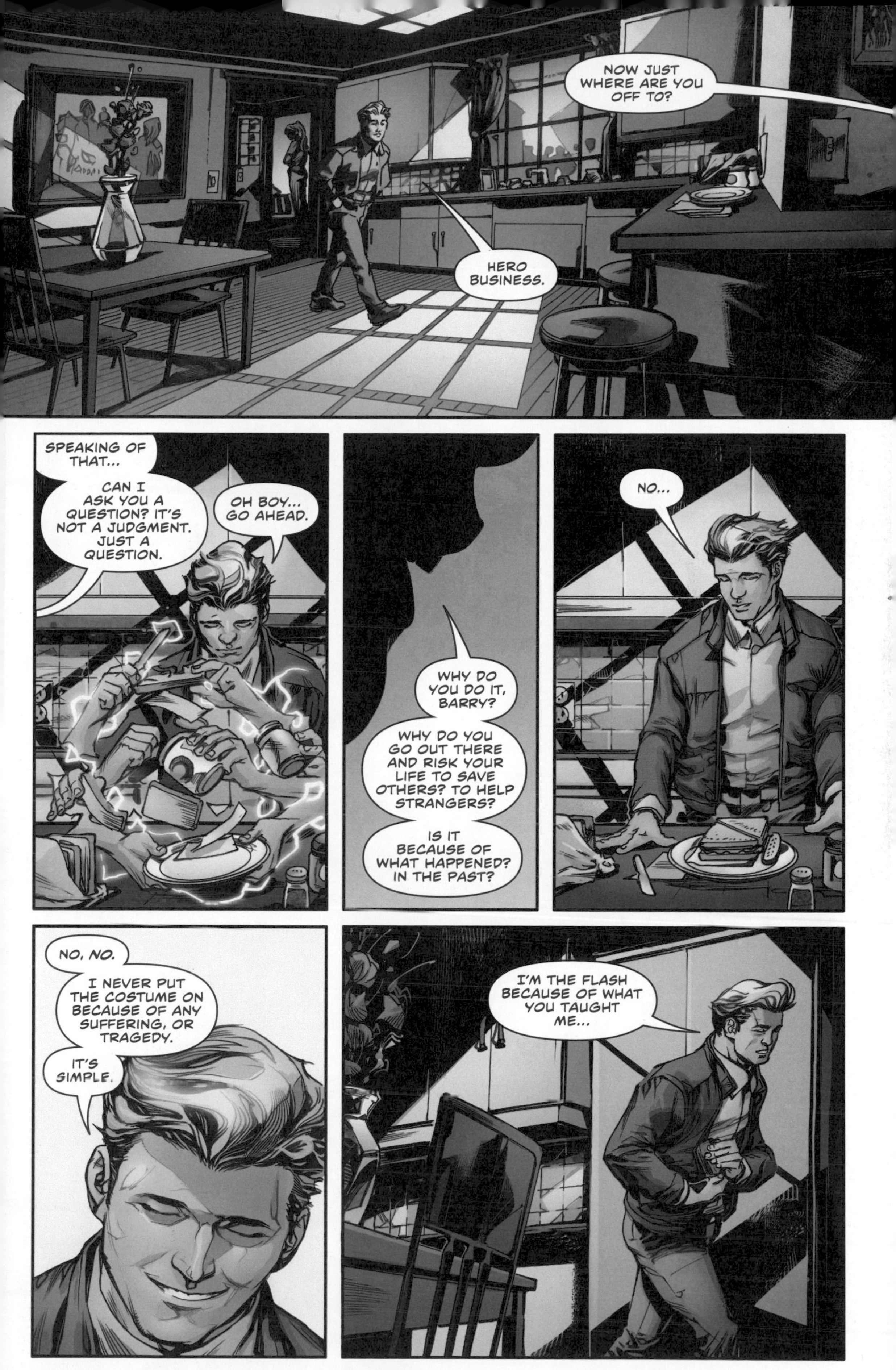
NOW JUST WHERE ARE YOU OFF TO?
HERO BUSINESS.
SPEAKING OF THAT...
CAN I ASK YOU A QUESTION? IT'S NOT A JUDGMENT. JUST A QUESTION.
OH BOY... GO AHEAD.
WHY DO YOU DO IT, BARRY?
WHY DO YOU GO OUT THERE AND RISK YOUR LIFE TO SAVE OTHERS? TO HELP STRANGERS?
IS IT BECAUSE OF WHAT HAPPENED? IN THE PAST?
NO...
NO, NO.
I NEVER PUT THE COSTUME ON BECAUSE OF ANY SUFFERING, OR TRAGEDY.
IT'S SIMPLE.
I'M THE FLASH BECAUSE OF WHAT YOU TAUGHT ME...

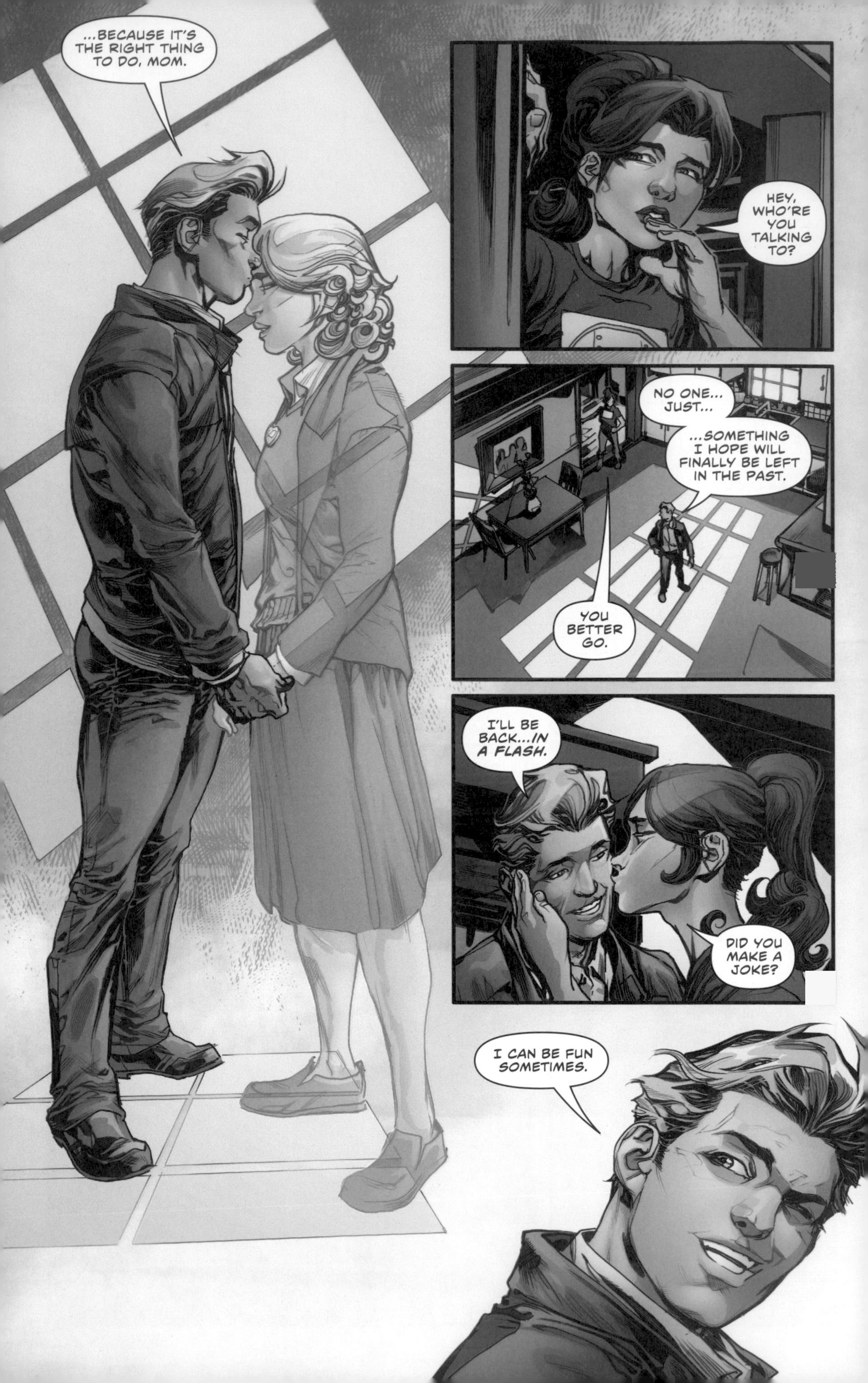
...BECAUSE IT'S THE RIGHT THING TO DO, MOM.
HEY, WHO'RE YOU TALKING TO?
NO ONE... JUST...
...SOMETHING I HOPE WILL FINALLY BE LEFT IN THE PAST.
YOU BETTER GO.
I'LL BE BACK...*IN A FLASH.*
DID YOU MAKE A JOKE?
I CAN BE FUN SOMETIMES.

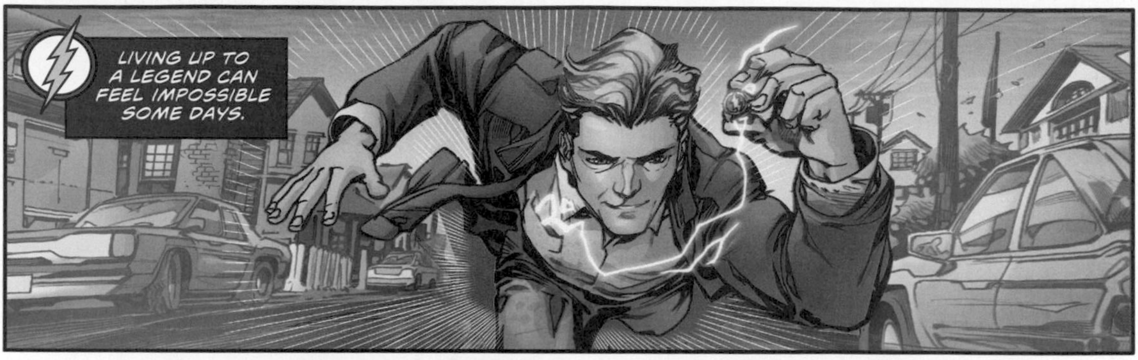
LIVING UP TO A LEGEND CAN FEEL IMPOSSIBLE SOME DAYS.

Story by Joshua Williamson & Howard Porter

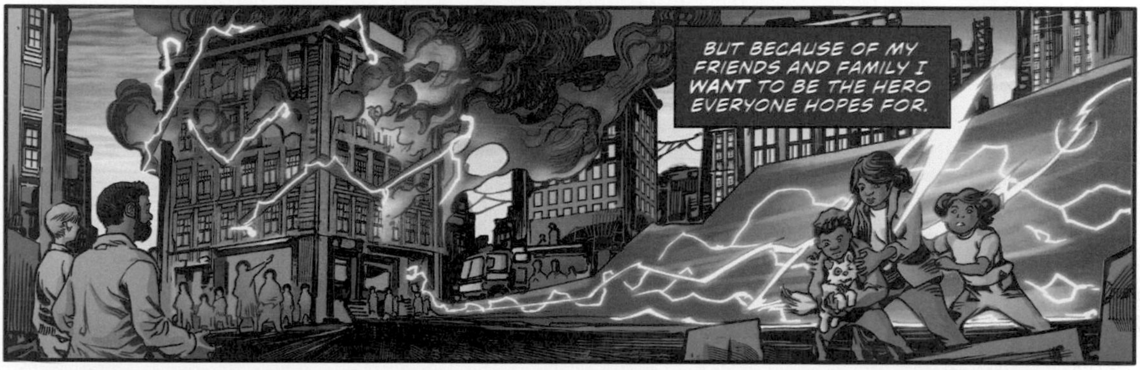
BUT BECAUSE OF MY FRIENDS AND FAMILY I WANT TO BE THE HERO EVERYONE HOPES FOR.

Hi-Fi Colors Steve Wands Letters Howard Porter & Hi-Fi Cover InHyuk Lee Variant Cover
Marquis Draper Assistant Editor Mike Cotton Editor Alex R. Carr Group Editor

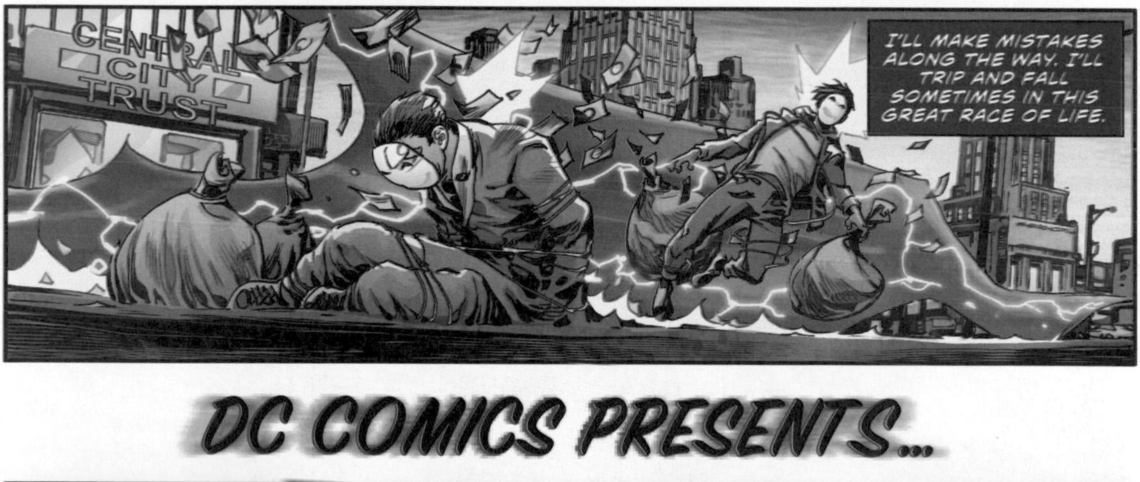
CENTRAL CITY TRUST
I'LL MAKE MISTAKES ALONG THE WAY. I'LL TRIP AND FALL SOMETIMES IN THIS GREAT RACE OF LIFE.

DC COMICS PRESENTS...

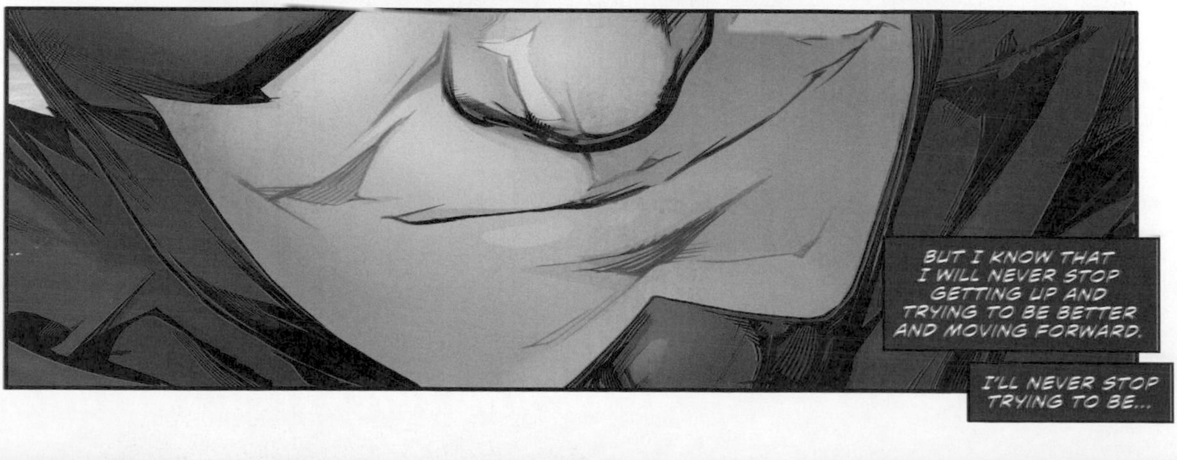
BUT I KNOW THAT I WILL NEVER STOP GETTING UP AND TRYING TO BE BETTER AND MOVING FORWARD.
I'LL NEVER STOP TRYING TO BE...

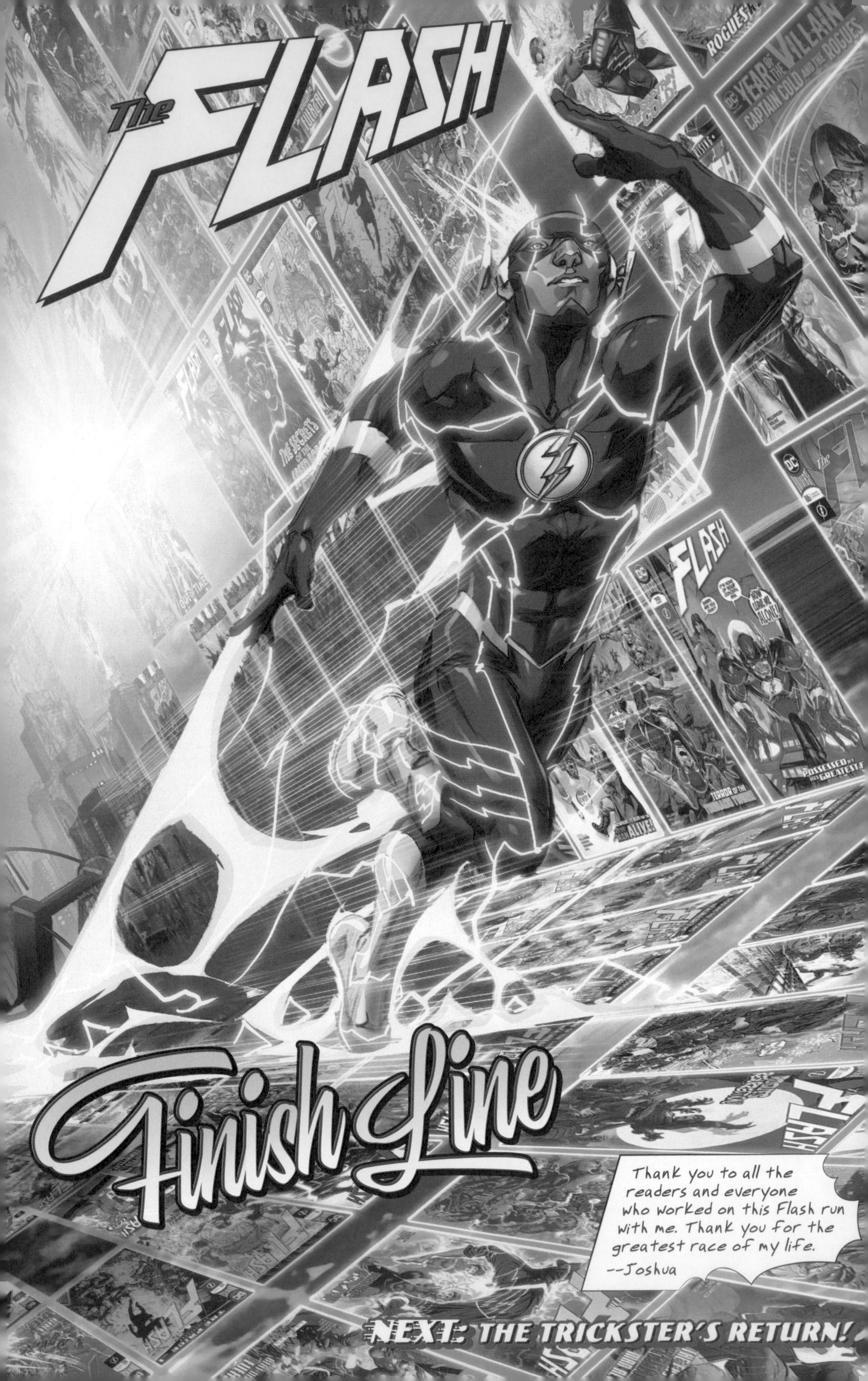
The FLASH
Finish Line
Thank you to all the readers and everyone who worked on this Flash run with me. Thank you for the greatest race of my life.
--Joshua
NEXT: THE TRICKSTER'S RETURN!

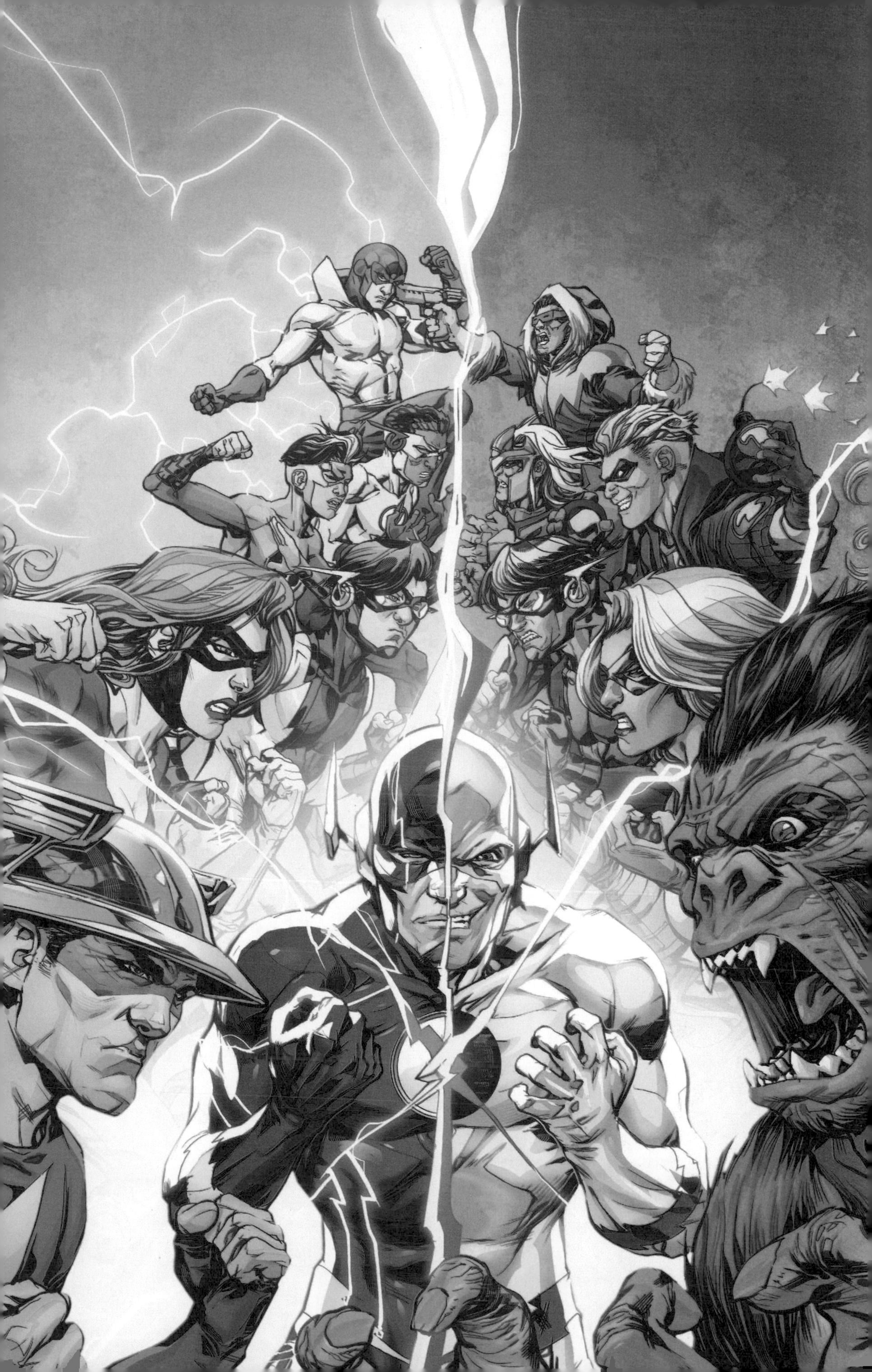

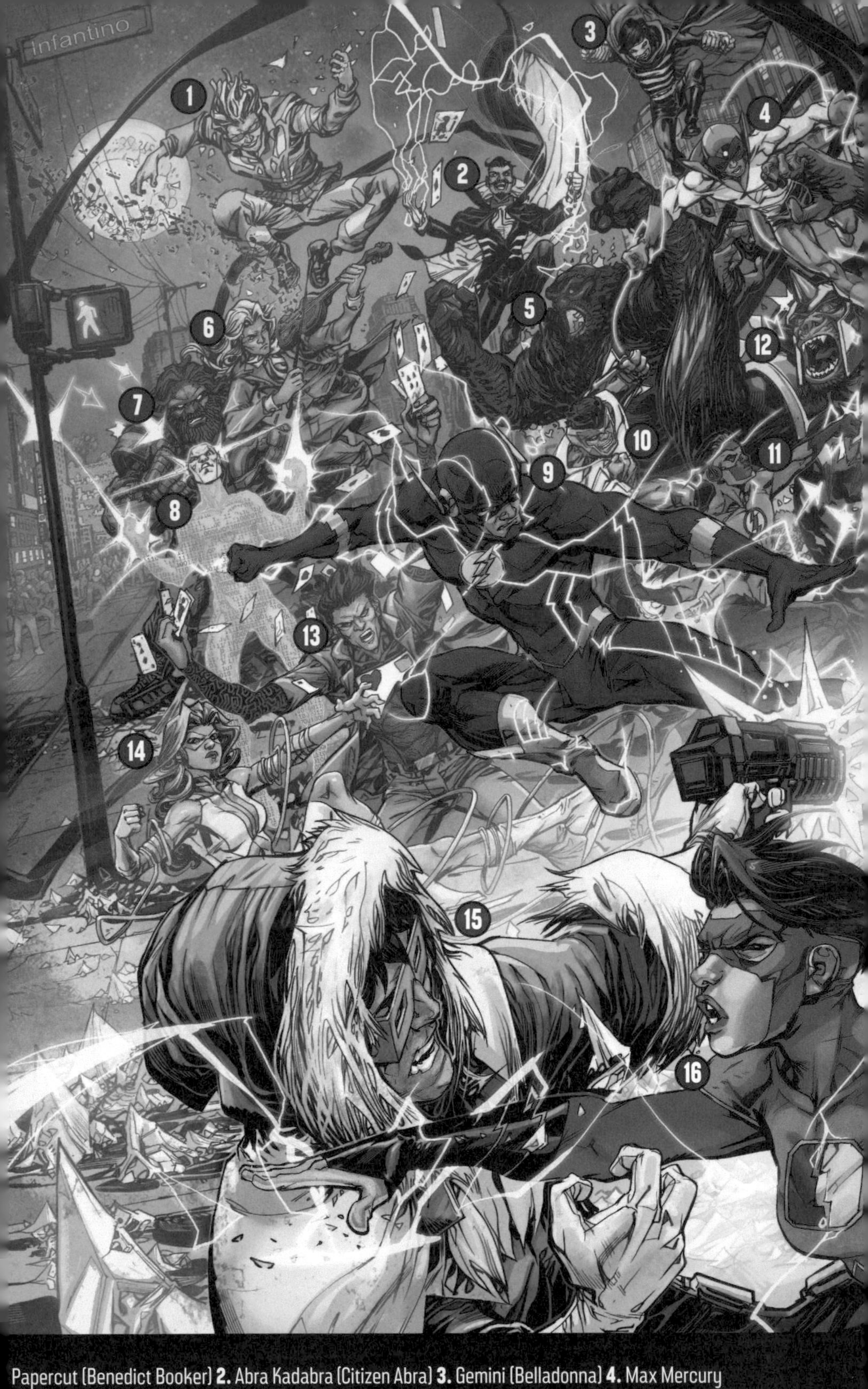
Infantino
1
2
3
4
5
6
7
8
9
10
11
12
13
14
15
16

Papercut (Benedict Booker) **2.** Abra Kadabra (Citizen Abra) **3.** Gemini (Belladonna) **4.** Max Mercury
. Tar Pit (Joseph Monteleone) **6.** Fiddler (Isaac Bowin) **7.** Girder (Tony Woodward) **8.** The Thinker (Clifford DeVoe)
. The Flash (Barry Allen) **10.** Razer **11.** Kid Flash (Wallace West) **12.** Gorilla Grodd **13.** Double Down (Jeremy Tell)
. Golden Glider (Lisa Snart) **15.** Captain Cold (Leonard Snart) **16.** Flash of China (Avery Ho)

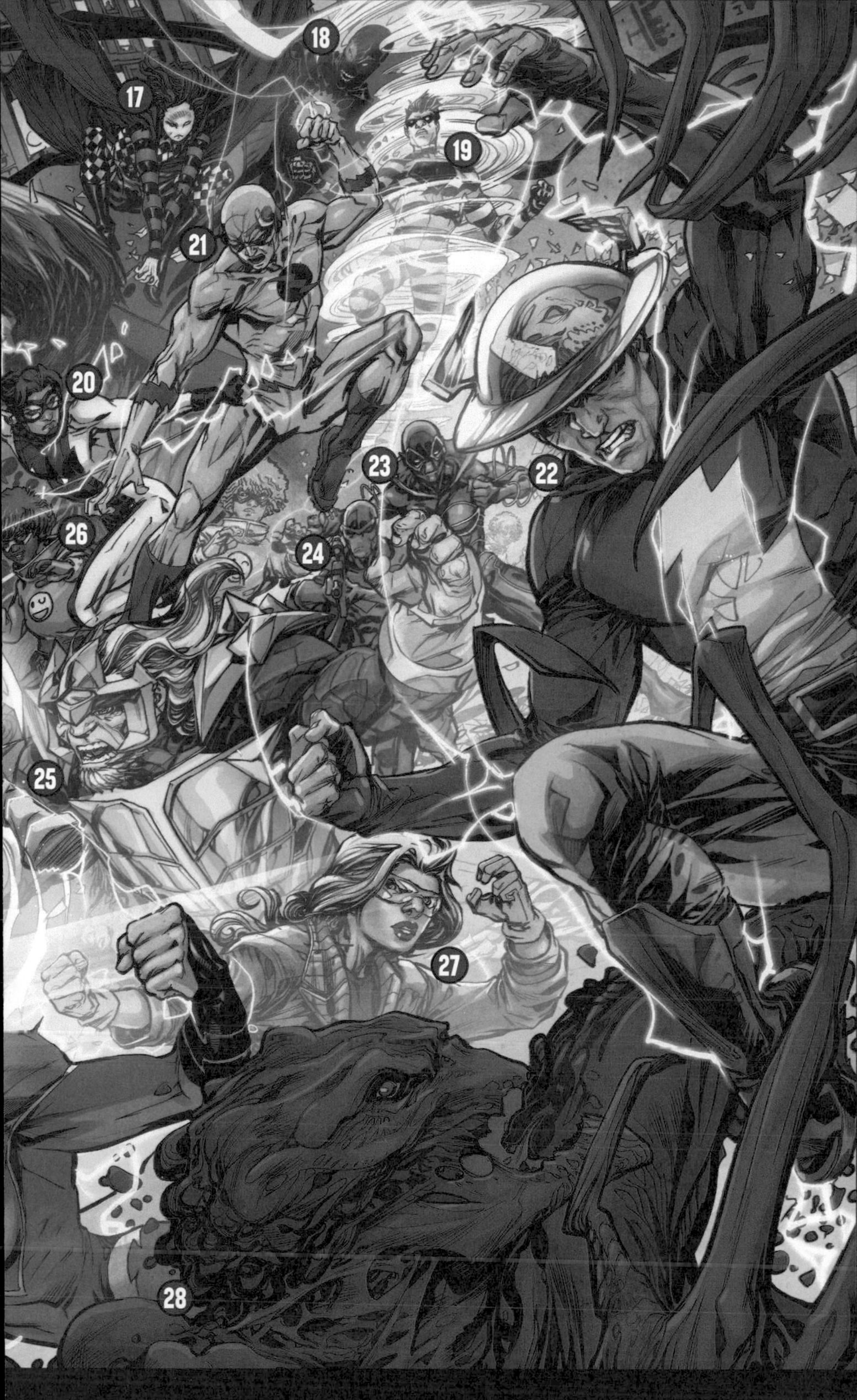
18
17
19
21
20
23
22
26
24
25
27
28

17. Rag Doll (Peter Merkel Jr.) **18.** Folded Man (Xolani) **19.** The Top (Roscoe Dillon) **20.** Impulse (Bart Allen) **21.** Professor Zoom (Eobard Thawne) **22.** The Flash (Jay Garrick) **23.** Blacksmith (Amunet Black) **24.** Plunder (Jared Morillo) **25.** Turtle **26.** Peek-a-Boo (Lashawn Baez) **27.** Jesse Quick (Jesse Chambers) **28.** Bloodwork (Ramsey Rosso)

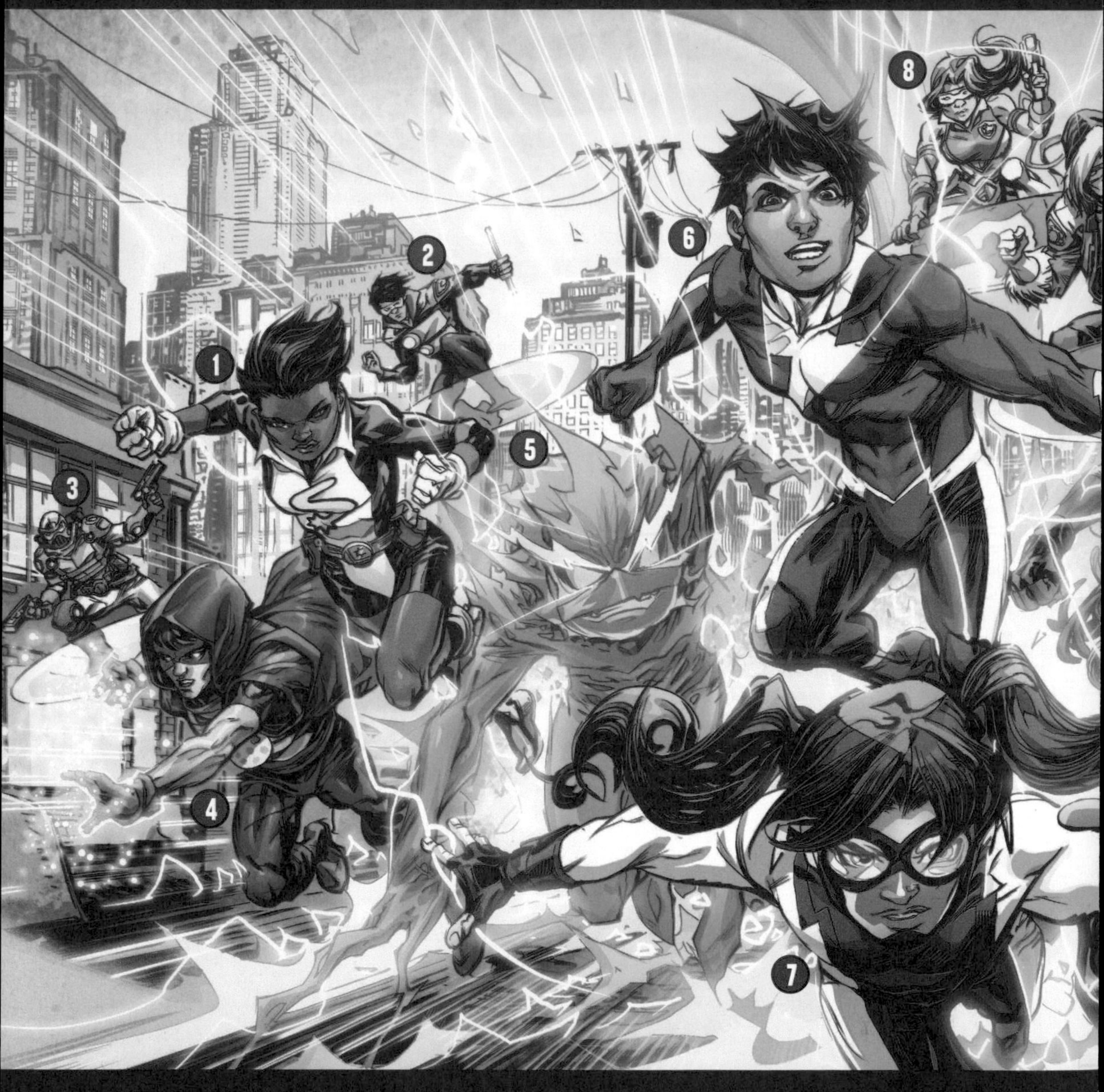
8
6
2
1
5
3
4
7

1. XS (Jenni Ognats) **2.** Weather Warlock **3.** Heatstroke **4.** Steadfast **5.** Krakkl **6.** Jai West **7.** Irey West
8. Golden Guardian **9.** Commander Cold **10.** Mirror Monarch **11.** Flash of Earth-2 (Jay Garrick)
12. Fuerza (Alexa Antigone) **13.** Flash of Earth-9 (Lia Nelson) **14.** Flash of Earth-22 (Wally West)
15. Fast Track (Meena Dhawan) **16.** Dark Flash (Walter West)

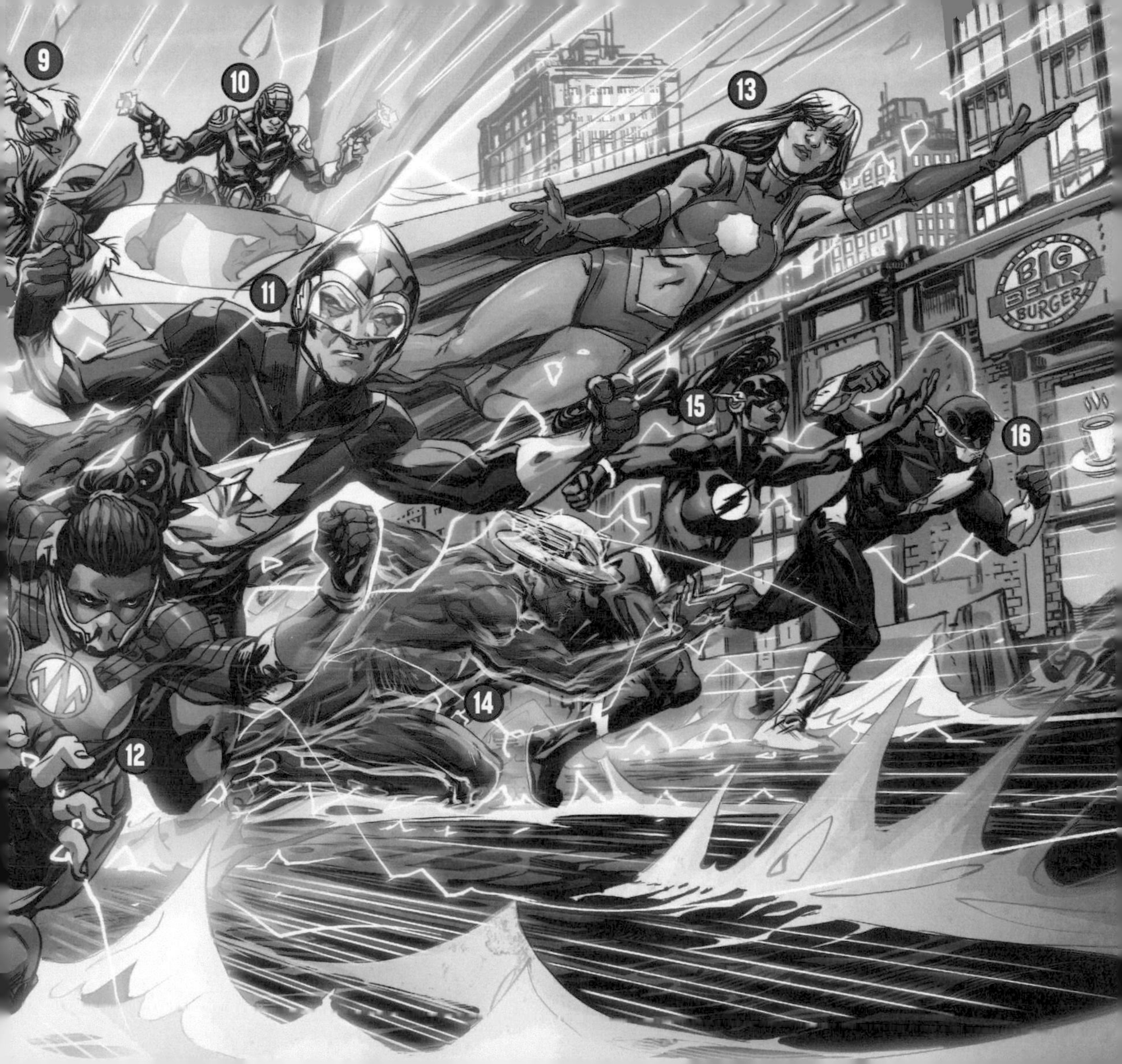
9
10
13
11
BIG BELLY BURGER
15
16
14
12

***The Flash* #757** page 20,
Pencils by Rafa Sandoval,
Inks by Jordi Tarragona

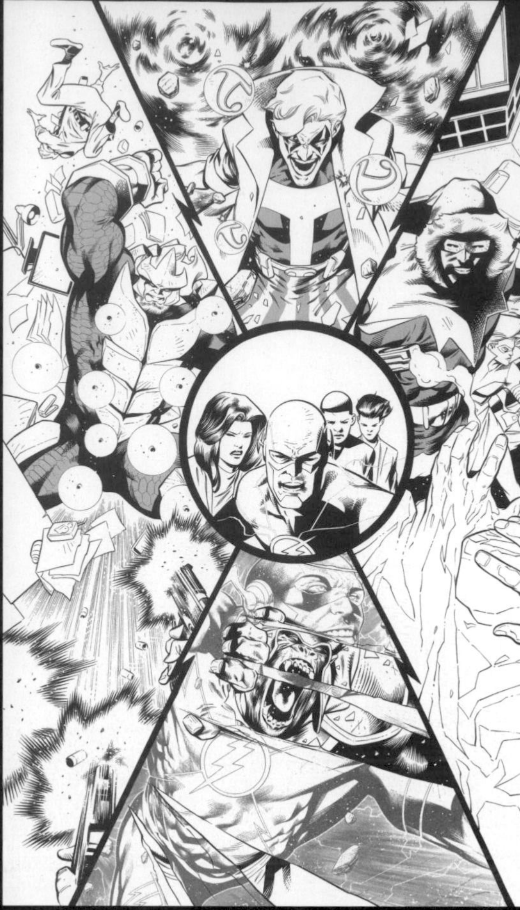

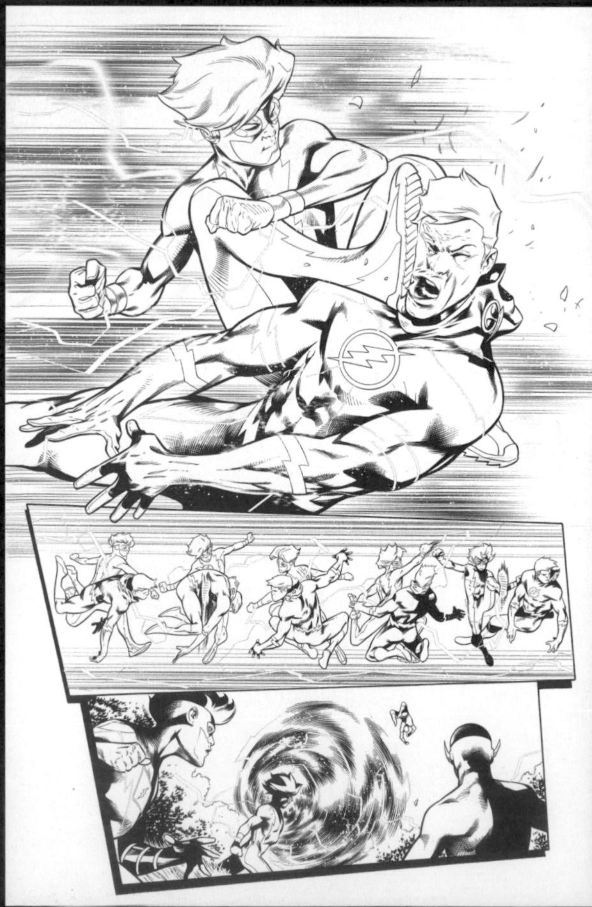

***The Flash* #759** page 16,
Pencils by Rafa Sandoval,
Inks by Jordi Tarragona

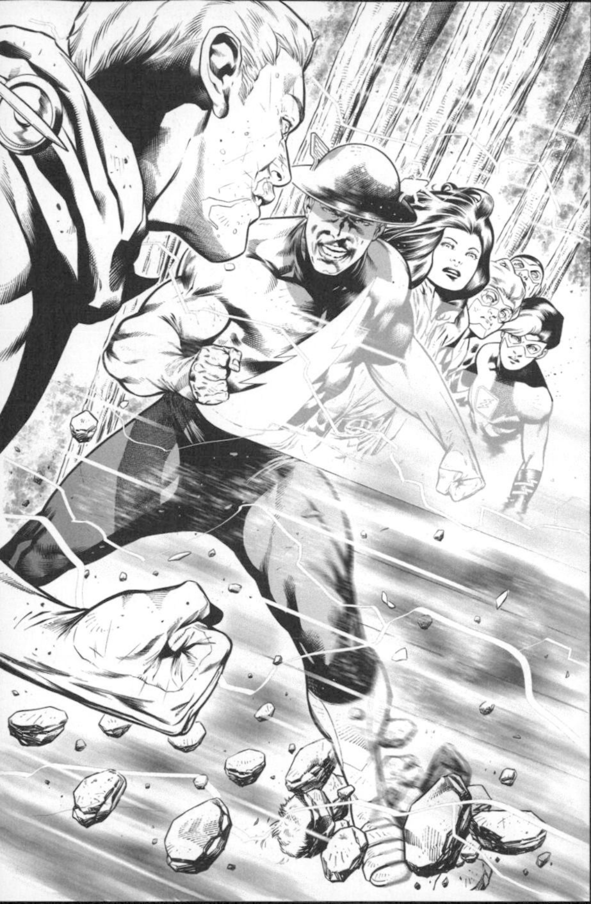

***The Flash* #759** page 20,
Pencils by Rafa Sandoval,
Inks by Jordi Tarragona

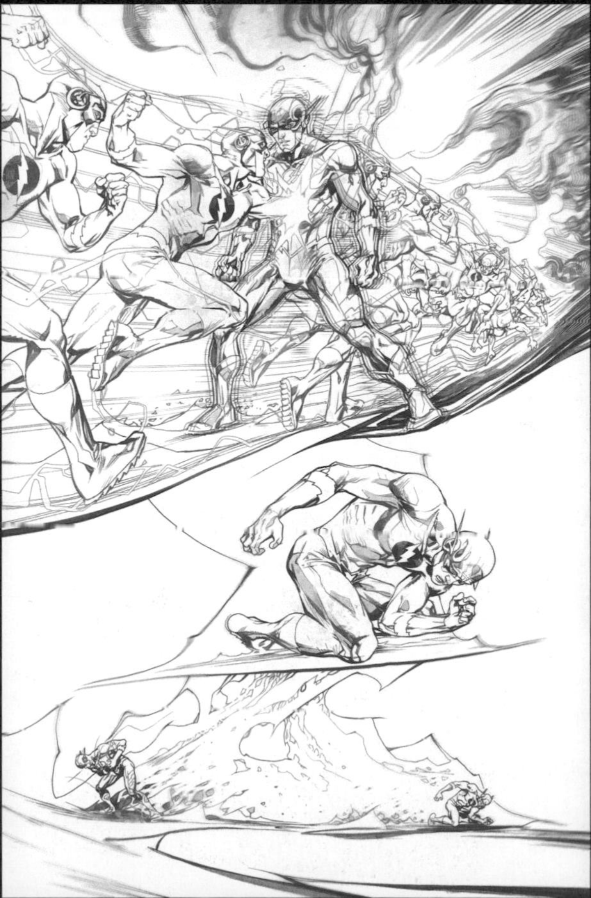

***The Flash* #762** page 8,
Pencils and Inks by
Howard Porter

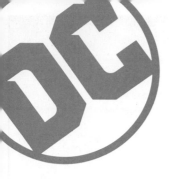

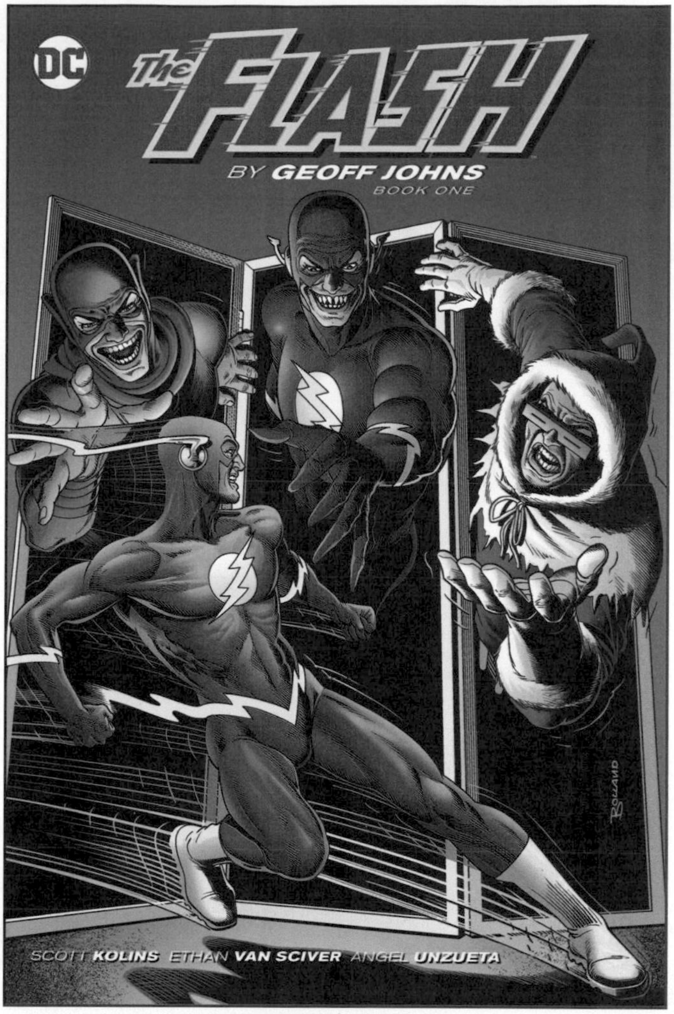
The FLASH
BY GEOFF JOHNS
BOOK ONE
SCOTT KOLINS ETHAN VAN SCIVER ANGEL UNZUETA

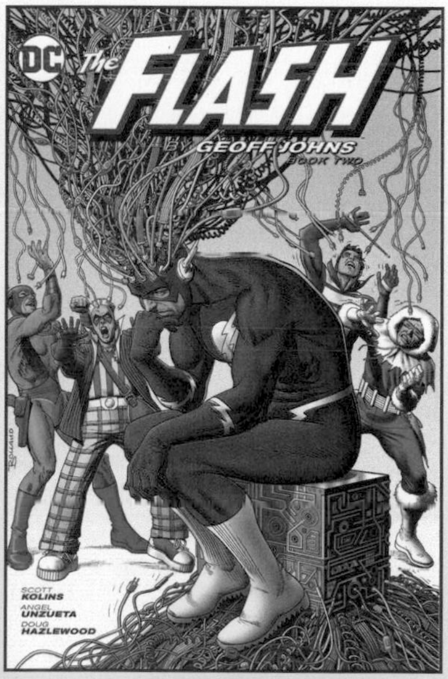
The FLASH
BY GEOFF JOHNS
BOOK TWO
SCOTT KOLINS
ANGEL UNZUETA
DOUG HAZLEWOOD

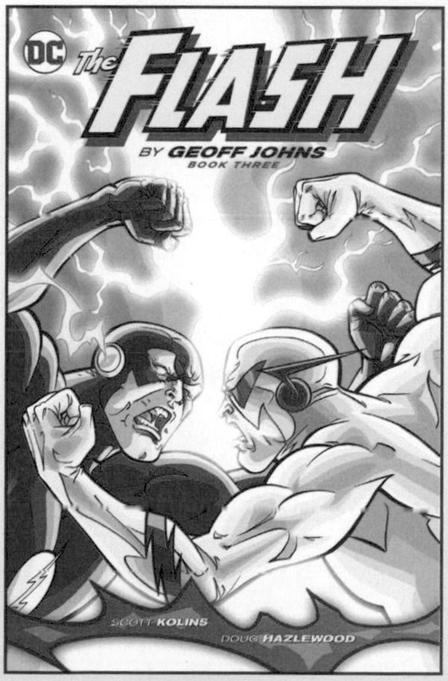
The FLASH
BY GEOFF JOHNS
BOOK THREE
SCOTT KOLINS
DOUG HAZLEWOOD

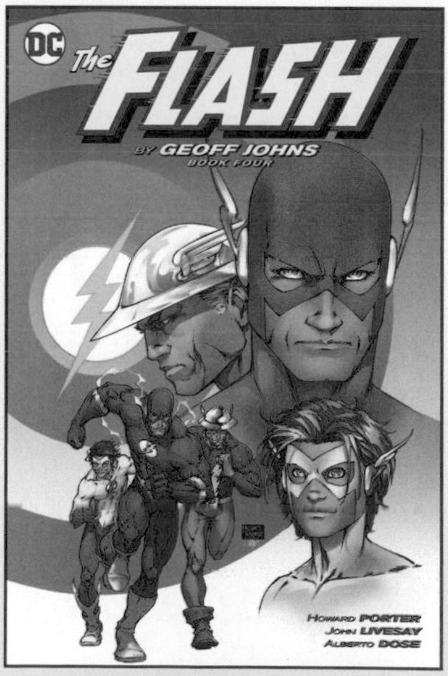
The FLASH
BY GEOFF JOHNS
BOOK FOUR
HOWARD PORTER
JOHN LIVESAY
ALBERTO DOSE